STEAK HOUSE

THE PEOPLE, THE PLACES, THE RECIPES

ERIC WAREHEIM
WITH GABE ULLA

PHOTOGRAPHY BY MARCUS NILSSON
ADDITIONAL IMAGES BY ERIC WAREHEIM

TEN SPEED PRESS
California | New York

CONTENTS

Introduction	8
A Brief History of the Steak House	15

THE JOURNEY, PART I: THE SOUTH — 16

Charlotte
BEEF 'N BOTTLE — 21

Atlanta
LITTLE ALLEY STEAK — 30

Tampa
BERN'S — 37

RECIPES: BREADS & CRUDITÉS

Popovers	46
Garlic Bread	48
Port Cheddar Dip	48
Parker House Rolls	49
Relish Tray with Creamy Dip	50

THE JOURNEY, PART II: NEW YORK CITY — 52

KEENS	56
PETER LUGER	62
DONOHUE'S	68
THE GRILL	72

Jersey Interlude
THE PUB — 78

RECIPES: APPETIZERS

Chips & Truffle-Ranch Dip	86
Shrimp Cocktail	88
Shrimp de Jonghe	89
Steak Bites	91
Fried Calamari	93
Steak Crudo	94

THE JOURNEY, PART III: CHICAGO — 96

GENE & GEORGETTI	100
BAVETTE'S	104

RECIPES: SALADS

The Mighty Wedge	112
Classic Wedge	112
Mariani Wedge	115
Korean Wedge	115
Classic Caesar	116
Tomatoes & Onions	119
Garbage Salad	119
Tomato & Stone Fruit Salad	120
Bacon Roasted Tomato	121

The Good Steak:
A Visit to Cream Co. Meats — 124

RECIPES: STEAKS

Rib Eye with Roasted Garlic	130
New York Strip with Chimichurri	132
T-Bone au Chipotle	133
Churrasco con Papas	135
Chopped Steak au Poivre	136
Steak Diane	138
Surf 'N Turf	139
Classic Prime Rib	140
Eye of Delmonico with Truffle Aioli	140
Smoked Tomahawk	143

THE JOURNEY, PART IV: TEXAS — 144

San Antonio
LITTLE RED BARN — 148

Houston
PAPPAS BROS. — 155
TASTE OF TEXAS — 164

Dallas–Fort Worth
FOGO DE CHÃO — 170
CATTLEMEN'S — 172

RECIPES: OTHER MEATY DELIGHTS

Pollo Asado	178
A Fine Pork Chop	180
Chicken-Fried Ibérico Pork Steak	181
Beef Wellington	182
The Crown of Pork	185
Steak House Juicy Lucy	186

THE JOURNEY, PART V: NORTH BY NORTHWEST — 188

Portland
RINGSIDE	192
ACROPOLIS	200
SAYLER'S OLD COUNTRY KITCHEN	206

Bay Area
HOUSE OF PRIME RIB	211
"SECRET SONOMA STEAK HOUSE"	216

RECIPES: SIDES

Hash Browns	222
Chopped Hash Ode to Keens	225
Creamed Spinach	226
Honey-Glazed Carrots	226
Thin Onion Rings	228
Thick Onion Rings	228
Mashed Potatoes & Three Sauces	230
Lobster Mac & Cheese	233
Sweet Potato Casserole	234

THE JOURNEY, PART VI: LOS ANGELES — 236

THE MUSSO & FRANK GRILL	240
MAJORDOMO	243
BEEFSTEAK	244
A Night at Taylor's with Bob, Tim, and John	248
CLEARMAN'S STEAK 'N STEIN INN	257

RECIPES: DESSERTS

Cheesecake with Strawberry Sauce	262
The Major Donut	265
Espresso Martini Baked Alaska	266
Ice Cream Sundae	267
Apple Strudel mit Schlag	268

THE JOURNEY, PART VII: LAS VEGAS — 270

Las Vegas
GOLDEN STEER	275
THE STEAK HOUSE AT CIRCUS CIRCUS	281

Henderson Interlude
BOROS STRAVA	282

THE JOURNEY, PART VIII: MEXICO — 288

RECIPE: THE MARTINI

Aziz's Martini: Simple Perfection	298

WINE

Steak House Wine: For Your Health	304
Acknowledgments	314
About the Contributors	315
Index	316

INTRODUCTION

I love a big ol' bone-in rib eye, nicely marbled and grilled to perfection. I love how I can never really have more than a few bites of it because I always go too hard on the sides. I love telling the server that the cheesecake is for the table and then scarfing down the whole glorious thing by myself—and *then* ordering a second slice to take home "for tomorrow." (Only for it to disappear from the fridge before midnight.)

This book is about the place that offers these and many more delights: the steak house.

It's a kinder dimension, a universe where the portions are always generous—and sometimes friggin' huge—the chairs are the type you can sink into for hours, and the volume on everything worldly that might be worrying you has a way of magically getting muted.

There's no better rush than settling into a dimly lit dining room, nibbling on some garlic bread, and hearing the rumble of the Caesar salad cart coming your way. Everyone at the table becomes fully alert. *Could that be for us? I think so . . . Wait, it's moving left. But didn't we order before them? Oh, now he's coming. Here we go . . . SHOWTIME.*

The star performer this evening may not be famous the world over, but their skills are unmatched. Witness how the grand gestures come naturally. Notice how they can time a joke perfectly while in the middle of lighting a gigantic slab of hanging meat on fire. Get ready to celebrate.

You can also hide in the steak house's darkness, alone but never lonely. Unwinding without talking to a soul, focusing your senses on just how nice it feels to sit atop a leather stool at the bar while you nurse a martini and decide whether it'll be the petit filet or the lamb chops with mint jelly this evening. Don't feel bad about skipping dessert so you can get home at a somewhat reasonable hour. You can swing by for a sundae tomorrow. It won't be out of place there. A back-to-back visit just means you're one step closer to becoming a regular—and being able to call yourself a regular is, to me, one of the best things in this life.

Pretty soon, the bartender will greet you with a smile and start stirring your martini the second you walk through the door. The kitchen will be more than happy to do half portions for you. They showed you that move when you were there with your niece last year. Even after her mom explained to her that it would be too much food, the servers could tell that she wanted the onion rings really bad. So they surprised the both of you with a mini-pile instead of the full tower.

Those onion ring moments reflect the kind of care you can't really teach or put your finger on. But you can always tell when it's there and when it's not. In my experience, the first sign is receiving a real hug—not one of those quick, half-hearted embraces from an ex you see at a party—I mean the profound variety of hug. The wizardry of a good steak house is that you get that hug without even having anyone's arms wrapped around you. It's a vibe-hug and it's intoxicating.

That's what originally sparked the idea for this book: I wanted an excuse to settle into a handsomely upholstered red banquette, chomp on a wedge, go head-to-head

The 24-ounce, 28-day dry-aged porterhouse at Little Alley Steak in Atlanta.

with that mid-rare rib eye . . . and be able to tell people it was a professional obligation. I wanted to have a good time every night. For a year. I pictured many glasses of properly aged red wine and the jolt of joy every time someone told me there was a baked Alaska waiting in the wings.

At the same time, I knew deep down that pure pleasure was not what all this obsession was about. I went looking for books on the steak house to find some clues. There was loads of stuff on the good, the bad, and the ugly of the beef industry in the United States. There were enough cookbooks on grilling meat to keep you sweating in front of the coals for the rest of your time on this earth. But what about books that are fully dedicated to exploring a culinary style that's represented in almost every city of this weird, frustrating, and wonderful nation?

I kept digging. I talked to chefs and scholars. They were very patient with me. They enlightened me. They confirmed that this is a tradition as uniquely American as jazz, baseball, and keeping the AC on during a blizzard. One very smart person, Professor Joshua Specht, told me that in a lot of ways the history of the American steak house is the history of what it has meant to be an American in the twentieth-century: a quote-unquote Golden Age, followed by a period of decline, followed by an existential conversation about who we are and who we should be in the future. That sure is a lot to tackle. Especially because I am not a historian. But maybe, I figured, I could go deep on the subject in my own way. The way I know how. Living it and documenting it with insane devotion. It was enough to convince my publisher to let me go on an adventure.

And so, welcome to our *Steak House*. Jerome will be taking care of you this evening.

JEROME WILLIAMS & THE JOURNEY

I remember the exact moment when I realized that the steak house might be my favorite place on earth. It was 2021 and my partner-in-comedy Tim Heidecker and I were in Charlotte, North Carolina. We were exhausted after a long day of shooting a commercial and in need of some sustenance and perhaps a beverage or two. On the road, where time is valuable, colleagues don't always share the same likes and dislikes, and it can be hard to avoid culinary disappointment, you come to rely on the steak house. This night was no different. Our producer messaged me, "The Capital Grille is a four-minute walk from the hotel. Should I book?" To which I replied, "Good evening, Bernard. Would you mind doing me a favor? Jump out of your window. I'm in the middle of downloading the entire internet to figure out a proper dinner plan. Give me precisely three minutes."

After a bit of research, I had a good feeling about Beef 'N Bottle, a mom-and-pop on the side of the highway. Looked like a barn. Only one location. A few key items represented on the menu; dishes that are good even when they are bad. Proper lighting, twinkly and warm. The issue was that we'd have to drive an hour to get there. That's nothing for me personally. Over the past ten years, what started as an intense interest in food has turned into the most important pursuit in my life. Tim, however, is not quite as fanatical, although he knows something special when he sees it. I managed to convince him to go. I knew that if I failed, if the place was a stinker, I would be hearing about it for many years to come. That's the Philly in us. We're born ball-breakers.

Luis Fernando, master carver at House of Prime Rib in San Francisco.

Little Richard was piping from the porch speakers when we pulled into the parking lot. We opened the door, crossed the threshold, and—from one second to the next—found ourselves swept to a table inside a Southern Comfort–style remake of the Tropicana scene from *Goodfellas*. It was a carpeted cabin with a pile of saltines on every table. It felt so good in there. A man approached us. He was sporting a black dress shirt tucked into a pair of black jeans, with an immaculately groomed beard and a big golden crucifix hanging around his neck.

"How you doing, y'all? I'm Jerome. I'm your bartender *and* your server, and tonight we're gonna have some fun. What kind of martini y'all want?"

Those simple words sent goose bumps through my body. Tim gave the approving nod. I didn't know it just yet, but when Jerome left to fix our drinks at the bar—a tiny corridor between the two dining rooms—and I felt that invisible vibe-hug I was talking about earlier, it was the first step into the journey that culminated in this book.

The original plan I mapped out for my editor had me visiting a solid ten legendary steak houses across America. The idea was to document the hell out of each one: to "artistically" capture every inch of the place, record all the stories the staff would tell us, and shoot as many portraits as possible.

We did exactly that—me, writer-producer Gabe Ulla, and photographer Marcus Nilsson. The captain, the skipper, and the Swede. The only thing that wound up changing about the book was its scope. By the end of 2023, exactly twelve months after we'd started, we had visited more than sixty steak houses. Sixty! We even squeezed in a trip to Mexico. In the end, we couldn't fit it all into one book. Painful. But also amazing.

People tend to say that the reason everybody likes a steak house is that they know what they're going to get. They're all the same. This is true. It's also not true at all. A steak house can have everything from gruff lifers to clumsy robots working the floor. It can even be a strip club. You've got massive steak houses and small steak houses, struggling steak houses and cover factories that must make millions in a week. There are places that have served the same ten things for more than a hundred years, and spots where bold chefs are cooking some of the most exciting, soulful food in the world.

That's America. The lady's got range.

I've always been partial to the old places. The classics. I remember tearing up a little after reading a line in a classic Ruth Reichl piece about steak houses in New York City: "It's hard to understand how anyone could prefer the new places with their polite blandness to the old ones where history is dancing in the dust." Ruth gets it.

I love giving into nostalgia so much that I didn't expect this adventure to show me that there's a whole lot of greatness to experience right this very second.

At all the establishments we experienced, we wound up talking to more staff members than I dreamed would be possible. I got to spend time with the people that keep me chasing after the steak house high. Scores of steak houses later, I'm still not satiated. But I think we made a dent.

Now let's get to it, pardner.

Morgan Smith of Sayler's in Portland, Oregon, presenting the 72-ounce steak challenge. You'll meet her again on page 206.

A BRIEF HISTORY OF THE STEAK HOUSE

"Steak is fast, mobile, improvised, casual, egalitarian, reliable, raw, bloody, and violent . . . it represents both freedom and independence, and the camaraderie of campfires. It's the closest we can get to yoking the raw and the cooked, the savage and the civilized. . . . It goes with beer or wine, bourbon or tequila, and (God help us) Coke or iced tea."
—Betty Fussell, *Raising Steaks*

Even though I am but a humble student of the steak house, we should cover a few of the basics. The first is something you've probably noticed, which is that there's something about cows that has hit deep with humans ever since they started painting them on rocks thousands of years ago. In America in the late nineteenth century, that manifested itself in people wanting fresh, clean, and *cheap* beef. They didn't care to ask too many questions about how it was produced, as long as it was on their plate.

Meat became a cultural object in which people could assert their prosperity, both as individuals and as a society. For the poor, eating beef symbolized progress. For immigrants, it was a way of reclaiming the abundance that had been taken from many of them back home.

And for the middle class and elites who started to socialize more frequently outside their homes, especially in New York, eating beef in the most rarefied way you could access was a flex. This mood struck just as these places called "restaurants" started popping up around town. Spots like Delmonico's, which introduced America to French styles of cooking and dining-room theater.

In the late 1880s, middle-class man William S. Miller got sick of all the fanciness and invited a dozen of his dude friends to his bar on the Lower East Side to talk politics, drink beer, and eat steak with their hands: the first beefsteak. It set the stage for the steak house to flourish as a place mainly for male social bonding.

Then, in the 1970s, the steak house became something of a relic, as we (very, very, very slowly) began to get new ideas of what it meant to "be a man" as well as assert your prosperity through food. Nowadays, it's a different economy, an even more different world. But most Americans still eat meat. I'm writing this during the same week that the *New York Times* declared red meat is making a giant comeback for people of all political persuasions.

I honestly thought this book was going to be about a disappearing icon, but we've found ourselves in the middle of a steak house boom. If this institution is sticking around, what can it be? Quite a few of the places in this book have interesting answers. They all create communal life for their guests, each in their own special way, which I at least find moving.

The amazing Inessa, preparing House of Prime Rib's signature salad with secret dressing. You'll meet her again on page 211.

JOURNEY, PART I

THE S

TWENTY YEARS AGO, WHEN I VISITED THE AMERICAN SOUTH FOR THE VERY FIRST TIME, I STOPPED INTO A DONUT SHOP IN BIRMINGHAM.

The woman behind the counter called me "honey buns." Now, being from Philadelphia, I thought she was making fun of me. I put my guard up. Then I realized it was just kindness. I would end up spending a lot of time in the region—in Apalachicola, Florida, during my college days, Atlanta when I was working with Adult Swim, and everywhere else while touring with Tim. The energy at our shows was top-notch. We formed a forever bond with the region.

It felt like the right place to ease into the steak house mission with my newly formed team, but that didn't mean the pressure wasn't on. I knew the first stop needed to be a good one. So I decided to bring them down to Charlotte to experience Beef 'N Bottle, the birthplace of my steak house journey. I was excited to eat there, of course, but I wanted to speak to the icons on the team whom I'd met only briefly on my first visit. We also managed to squeeze in next-level barbecue with my friends at Jon G's, which included a smoked tomahawk that almost made us miss a flight we could not miss.

Atlanta wasn't part of the original plan, but deep down I think I knew we'd at least be passing through. How could I not go see my guy T-Pain, the top-notch musician, producer, podcast host, and king of the ATL? He has shown me some of the most wonderful times of my life. In many ways, he's the reason the South might be my favorite part of the country—a hunch that was only bolstered when Pain introduced me to the steak house where he's a regular.

I got butterflies in my stomach whenever I remembered that we'd be wrapping up this leg of our trip in sticky Tampa with two long nights at Bern's. It's a historic steak house and the Disney World of wine. When fans try to explain Bern's Steak House to people who've never been, it sounds like they're making the whole thing up. What you will soon read here follows in that tradition. But it happened.

There were also some lovely "steak-adjacent" establishments, and I want to mention one of them. After landing in Charlotte, we headed straight to Dixie Grill & Grocery for some post-flight sustenance. This tiny shack by the side of Dixie River Road serves wings that are lovingly battered and fried by professionals who clearly want to make sure the wings don't get soggy after being slathered in all that sauce. There are eight sauces to choose from! I was happy to be back below the Mason-Dixon.

Lunch at Dixie Grill & Grocery.

CHARLOTTE

BEEF 'N BOTTLE

Back to where the idea for this book began, crew in tow. I told them about my revelatory visit, but I needed them to feel it. I needed to set the tone.

BY THE NUMBERS

Opening year: 1958
Founder: George Fine
Address: 4538 South Boulevard, Charlotte, North Carolina 28209
House special: Surf 'n turf, garnished with an onion ring

I invited Garren and Kelly Kirkman to join us. They own the nearby barbecue destination Jon G's. Bringing guests became a tradition everywhere we went.

The Beef 'N Bottle dining room is heavenly. Sconces adorn the dark-walnut-colored booths, casting dim light. The paint is chipped on the edges of the walls that get bumped the most during a busy service. Walnut paint is used to fix the wear and tear, but it more so adds a patina to the place, making it feel loved and lived in and charmingly imperfect.

The staff are obviously all fond of each other. "Oh, you are with Jerome? He's the darn best!" Everyone has each other's back there, and that communal energy sends loving shock waves through the restaurant and into every single diner's heart. Jerome reminded us that he is the server *and* the bartender. Then he proceeded to ask us what kind of martinis we wanted. No cocktail menu to look at. No drink specials. For a martini guy like myself, this was a sign of greatness to come. Just the good stuff. Relax. Take a load off. You are family. Jerome's got you.

. . . And should you decide to ask for a second martini, no one will make a big deal of it. You'll get the refill discreetly.

First out of the kitchen was a basket of saltines and a pewter saucer of port cheese dip. Then an arctic shrimp cocktail, all the steak house standards, and a few of Beef 'N Bottle's signatures, like chopped steak with sautéed onions. I keep thinking about the pork belly bites—never had a chicharrón at a casa de steak like that!

The line between front and back of house at Beef 'N Bottle is blurred on purpose. Bernice Jenkins is one of the few team members we met who likes to stay in the kitchen. She has a gift for making all kinds of sauces and dips. She started working for George Fine, the late owner, in the 1960s, both at his restaurant House of Steak and as a go-go dancer at his club, the Amber House. She was sixteen, and now she is sixty-eight. She is shy, but when she speaks, you pay attention: "I learned to cook on the job. It ain't tough. It's easy. I love to do frog's legs and crab legs. Those are my favorite. People come in that door and they make sure that nobody else makes those frog's legs but me." Once in a while, as long as you are one of the people she likes, she'll head into the dining room and do what she calls the "boogie, boogie, boogie."

My friend Jerome Williams, captured here fixing the first drinks of another memorable night at Beef 'N Bottle.

Lisa Massis Guerra—The Powerhouse

Lisa is a Beef 'N Bottle veteran. Now that the restaurant is busier than ever, she keeps things in order. She's got her stories about George Fine, too.

"I started at Beef 'N Bottle in 1992. This restaurant is like one of my children. When I came here to interview, I asked the old owner, George Fine, if I could get an application. He said, 'We don't do applications here, but you get five stars because you got a skirt on, three because you have blond hair,' and stuff like that. I felt so creepy when I left. I was like, 'No way am I going back.' He followed me with his eyes all the way to my car. No sooner did I get home than he was asking if I could come in that same night: 'You're going to train for thirty minutes and then you will be on the floor.'

When I started, we only did about fifty people a night. Now we do over two hundred. I was just a server until one of the managers quit and George thought I would be a good fit, so I could come in and close his books at night. Right now, I manage Monday, Tuesday, Wednesday, and sometimes on the weekend. Then I serve the rest of the time. On Tuesdays and Wednesdays, I wait tables the first half of the night and then manage the second half.

The front of house does a lot here. We don't really have assigned tasks. We all just kick in and do all the work together. All the servers have to know how to bartend: As fast as we can make it, your table will get it. We also do the back-of-house work that prep cooks would usually do. We make our own salads, our own desserts. We run glasses. We clean up. And at the end of the night, we have side work. It's a lot to do on top of waiting on tables.

But they let you shine in your personality here. My style is making people feel welcome. I like to be funny, too. I'll tease the men and tell them they are little hotties. I make sure to tell groups of ladies that they look beautiful. I also love that we really feed you. Your order comes with all the sides. My favorite item is the black-and-blue rib eye with a loaded baked potato. That steak is the one with the Cajun rub and blue cheese crumble."

That's Lisa, who moved to Charlotte in 1989 after the coal industry in her native West Virginia faded.

ATLANTA

LITTLE ALLEY STEAK

BY THE NUMBERS

Opening year: 2018
Founders: *Hicham Azhari and Fikret Kovac*
Address: *3500 Lenox Road NE, Suite 100, Atlanta, Georgia 30326*
House specials: *Roasted bone marrow canoes; Progression of New York strip*

"No shit? A book about steak houses?! There's one here that changed my life. Not even joking with you, man. Of course you can bring your friends. Bring your entire fucking family if you want. Gives us an excuse to order more food."

Like I mentioned, Atlanta was not printed on the original itinerary. Now that *Tim and Eric Awesome Show, Great Job!* is off the air, I sadly don't travel to Atlanta as often. I didn't feel like I had gathered strong enough intel on the primo steak experiences in the city. Then T-Pain found out I was in his neck of the woods.

I incorrectly assumed that in Buckhead, Georgia, you're only going to find the megachains. But that all changed thanks to Pain and Little Alley Steak, which was the first modern steak house we encountered. His favorite steak house. His spot. There are 250 seats, and cleavers scattered around the space for decor. The menu is a monster. You can get wet-aged steaks and dry-aged steaks of all sizes and provenances; they sous vide them all to medium-rare and finish them on the grill. There are more than eight sauces and compound butters to choose from, plus cheese and charcuterie boards, Moroccan-style shrimp, and roasted bone marrow canoes.

We ate upstairs in a quiet room with Pain and his wife, Amber, with the sound of the action downstairs in the background. Nothing primes you for fun like the roar of people having a good time. We saw Pain holding court at the middle of the table, and suddenly we weren't at a restaurant anymore. We were in my friend's home. Every once in a while I'd hear somebody on the staff pass by and yell something like, "How's it going, Pain?" One of the few things in this life that might be better than being a regular is going to dinner with one.

I always learn something when I'm with him. Not only was Little Alley one of the most solid contemporary steak houses we visited, but I also got schooled in the ways of Pain's "Tequila-Only Diet." It's impressive. Like Pain himself. I gifted him a magnum of 2013 Domaine Fourrier Gevrey-Chambertin Premier Cru "Clos Saint-Jacques Vieille Vigne." It is one of the finest bottles we had on the entire journey.

Pain sipped, and he enjoyed, and then he swiftly returned to tequila . . . because it's time to finish the night at Magic City!

Crispy Maine lobster tail with yuzu-herb beurre blanc.

T-Pain—The Mayor

"Little Alley was the place that taught me how to eat steak. For most of my life, I was your typical Black-guy steak-eater. I'd get it very well-done, slice it up, drown it in A.1. sauce, and fucking go to town. That's how I was.

I showed up at Little Alley for the first time and ordered my usual, and they gently said, 'Sir, we think you would like this steak much more if it were medium. Please, trust us.' I got the steak, and with my limited knowledge at the time, I thought the red-colored liquid was straight-up blood. *Man, I can't eat this!*

They explained everything to me. I was like, 'Okay, cool! Now where's the steak sauce?' They respectfully encouraged me to try it without sauce. *All right, fine.* Now, man, I couldn't tell you if A.1. even exists anymore.

My wife and I save an experience like Little Alley for super-special moments. Maybe we have friends in town. Maybe we're about to go on a diet the next day. What a dumb concept. We'll show up to Little Alley, load up the table with like forty items, and fucking chow down. 'Let me get the forty-ounce porterhouse real quick.' On more normal nights, I'll get the fourteen-ounce bone-in filet mignon, lobster mac and cheese, creamed corn, and three shots of reposado.

Yep! Reposado. I like eating steak because it allows me to enjoy more tequila, my preferred drink. My wife, my friends: We time the three shots to show up before, during, and after the meal. If we're gonna pack our stomachs up, we should throw some tequila on top of that so that later on in the night, we can 'evacuate.' Boom! The combination of steak and tequila is like a time-release capsule for a 'movement.'

But seriously, a steak house is such a great place to host people, which is something I care about. I try to do all the fun things first and then make time to relax. Everyone who comes on my podcast says it's the best because the typical interview elsewhere is absolutely terrible. Why would I invite you here to do the shit that I hate myself?

Everybody loves a steak house, and in Atlanta it's probably even more special. Everyone gets treated like a celebrity, because you never know if someone you're dealing with actually is—kind of like in Dubai. They might be royalty. Folks who are not famous experience it and are like, 'Holy shit! This place is friendly as fuck.' The fanciness of a steak house combined with the Southern hospitality of Atlanta? That's a winning formula."

T-Pain is also the mayor of my heart and soul.

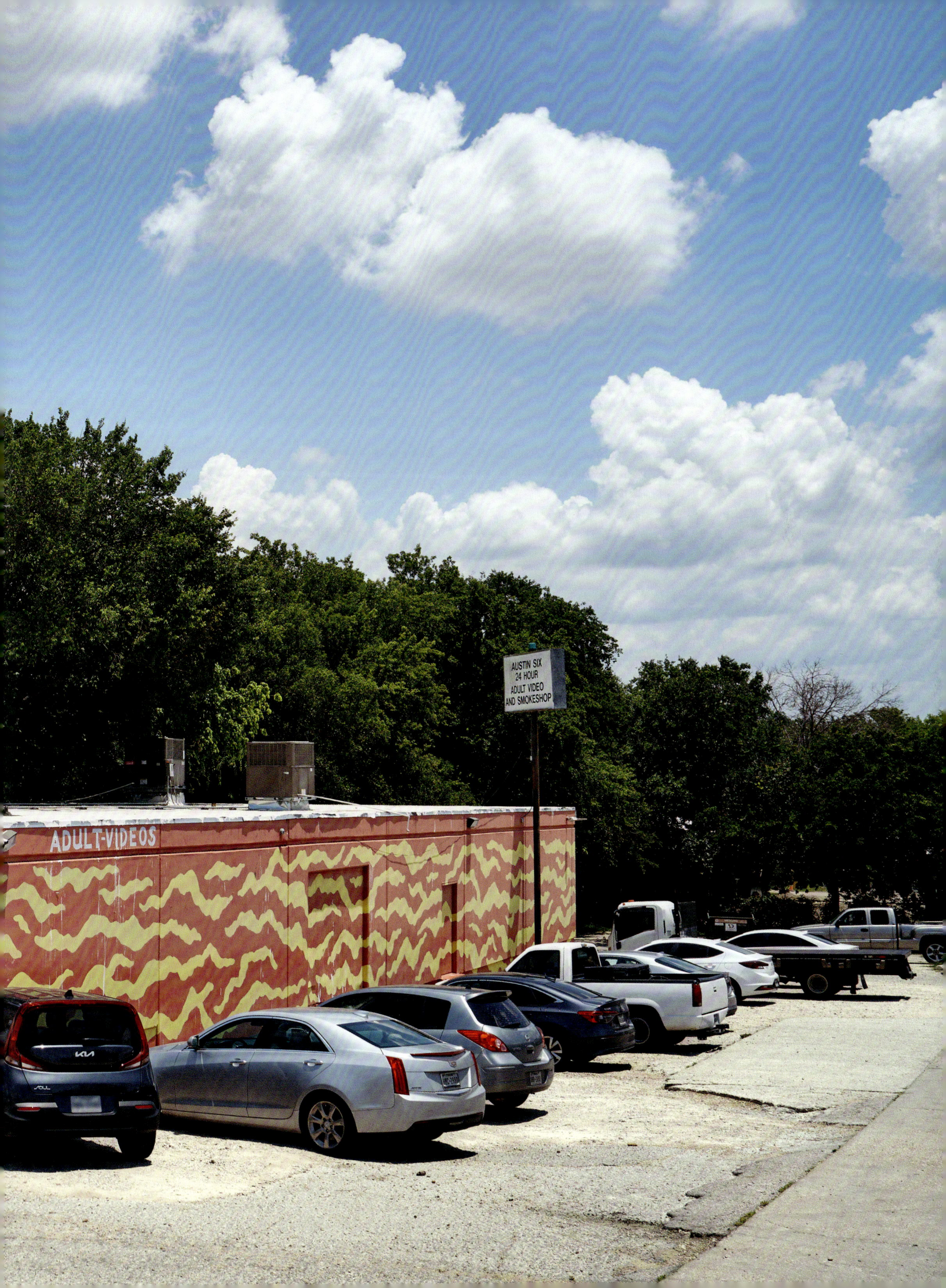
AUSTIN SIX
24 HOUR
ADULT VIDEO
AND SMOKESHOP
ADULT-VIDEOS

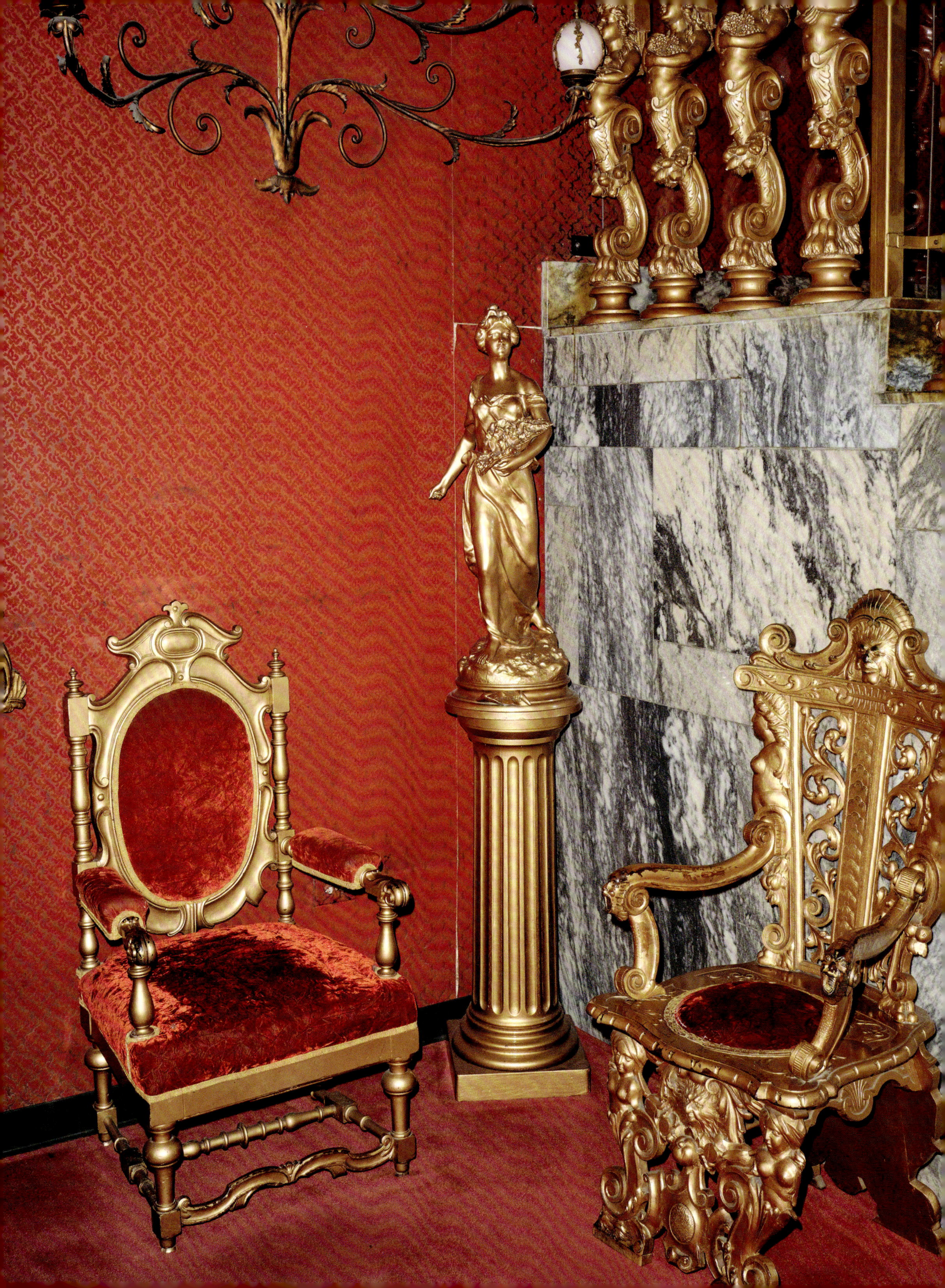

TAMPA

BERN'S

The person who put everything together for us, sommelier Eric Renaud, met us out front. He pulled a set of keys from his slacks, twisted open the lock of the janky door to the warehouse on Howard Avenue, and led us into the catacombs for a welcome beverage. The Tampa air was thick with anticipation.

BY THE NUMBERS

Opening year: 1956
Founder: Bern Laxer
Address: 1208 South Howard Avenue, Tampa, Florida 33606
House specials: Chateaubriand; Onion rings

Some people go to Orlando to explore a world created by an American dreamer named Walter. My friends and I go to Tampa to live in the steak-and-wine universe Bern Laxer and his wife, Gert, built from scratch nearly seven decades ago. There is nothing like it today, and there was NOTHING like it back then.

Everything about Bern's Steak House is wild, and none of it might have happened if it hadn't been for the fact that an ad guy and his NYU sweetheart moved to Tampa because of his asthma. What started as a humble juice bar became a 350-seat campus with a test kitchen, a garden dedicated to farming organic vegetables, a trainee program offering hospitality education, a full-time biochemist, and an in-house coffee roaster. The ice cream was (and still is) homemade. The onion rings were (and still are) as thin as the strings on an angel's harp.

For years I walked the earth without knowing that Bern's existed. But once I dove into wine, it seemed it was all anyone was chatting about. *Have you been? No? Oh, you MUST go.* I would hear this over and over, but I needed guidance!

My buds provided it. They invited little Eric in. *Come. We'll set everything up.* That's the kind of love that's found in my wine community. It's special.

They introduced me to Eric Renaud. He doesn't chase the spotlight. Keeps his head down by nature. He grew up dirt poor in Rhode Island and worked as a mechanic in the military, fixing F-16s at bases around the country. He wound up getting stationed in Tampa. To make some extra bucks, he got a gig at Bern's as a part-time cellar rat. He'd carry boxes, sweep the floor, watch the wine team. Take notes. Thirty years later, he still has only one restaurant on his résumé.

"I don't know how much longer I'm going to be at Bern's," Eric told me. This news had already been passed through the grapevine, but getting the information straight from the source stung. Things had been changing at Bern's. The restaurant had been sold to a management company. Eric had to do things like inventory now.

"I don't like talking to people—the boss knows this—but I do like spending eight or nine hours in the cellar, because by the end, I'll find thirty bottles I didn't know we had. One time, it was three cases of '61 Haut-Brion. They were in heavily stapled cardboard and not wood. Go figure!"

It was time to go to dinner across the street. Entering the foyer of Bern's is an experience unto itself. Red velvet wallpaper runs all the way up the twenty-foot ceilings. There's a grand gilded staircase and wrought iron chandelier, about a dozen antique busts, just as many portraits of aristocrats who may or may not have ever existed, and a goddang throne. A dozen people fit behind the comically large host stand. They need that many people on the welcoming committee because Bern's has seven dining rooms, a piano lounge, and an entire floor dedicated to letting guests linger for hours after their meal.

Detail of the grand foyer at Bern's.

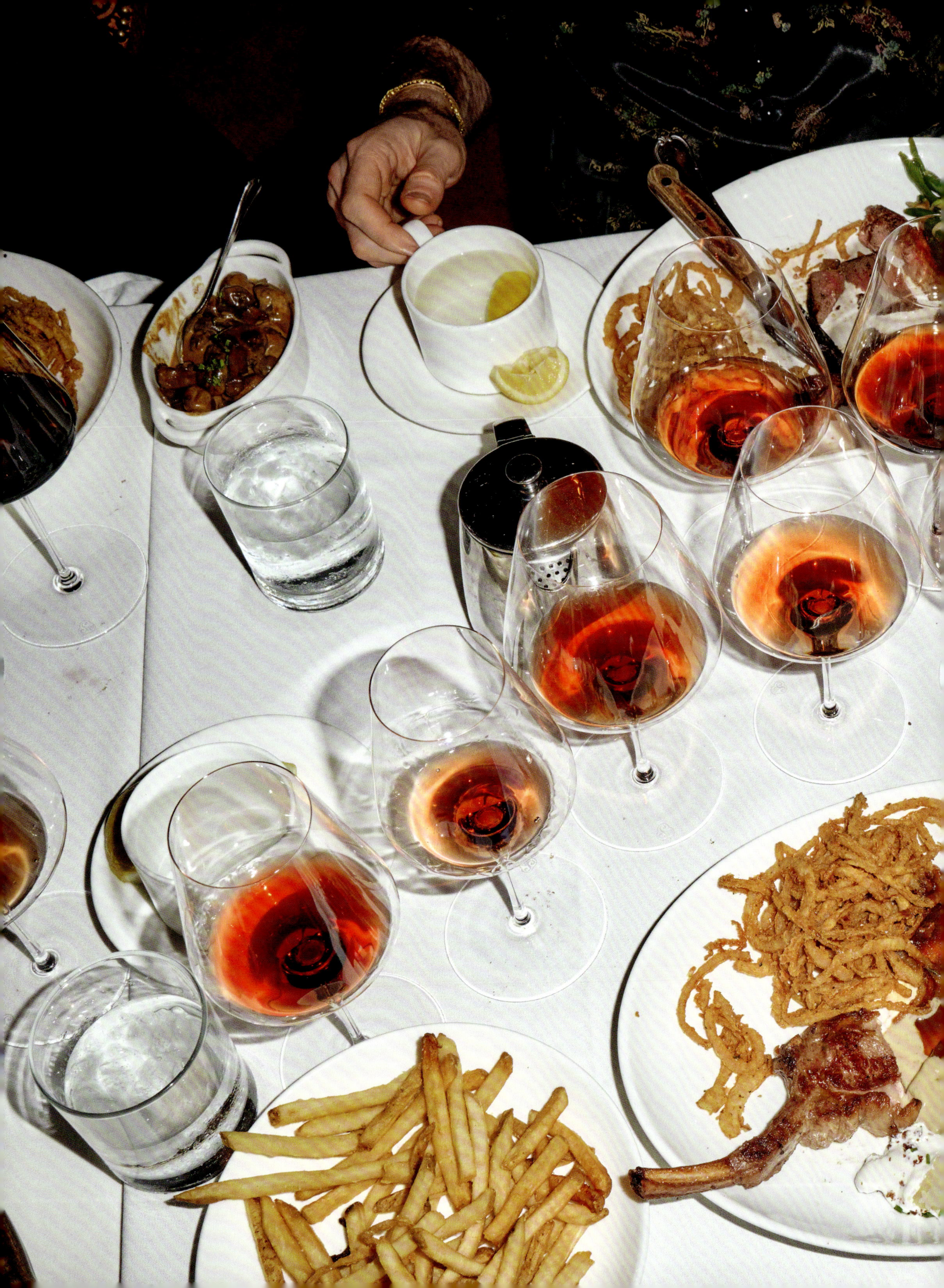

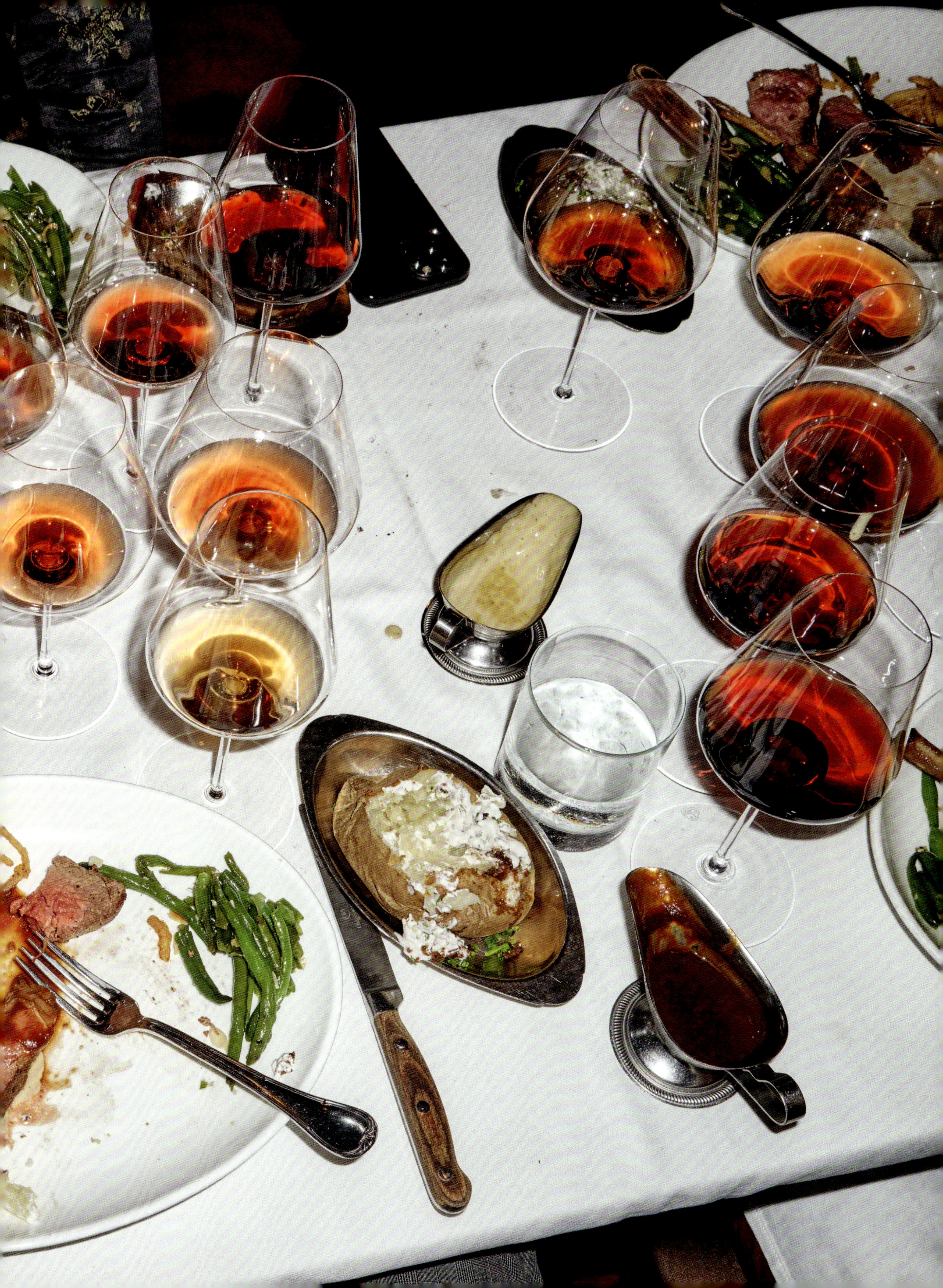

"Guys, go ahead and take as many pictures as you want, but don't post any of the bottles on social media. I don't want to get into trouble," Eric Renaud told us. Like the other lead sommeliers at Bern's, Eric kept his own special stash of unicorn wines to pull out for special occasions—birth-year bottles for friends, things of that nature. Stuff that big spenders would pay a fortune to try. But Eric doesn't work that way.

"I have to teach a lot of the newer guys who just want to sell the big, expensive stuff that it's not about that. First, find out who truly appreciates it, and hold on to those people. I don't know, I guess I'd rather have three nickels to a dime."

Nicholas Sieben—The Sweeper

It was two in the morning by the time we wrapped up night one at Bern's. All the other guests had gone home, and we were welcomed to snap some photos of the empty rooms. That's when we saw Nicholas sweeping the floor with palpable focus. This young man, we soon discovered, was part of the infamous Bern's trainee program.

"I joined right after COVID. I didn't know too much about what I was going to do aside from the fact that it was going to be quite a process. To get into the program, they make you stage a couple of times. If they think you have the right attitude and work ethic, the game begins. And it's a long game.

It's been a little over a year and a half so far. Historically, how quickly it proceeds is all kind of based on the demand for servers. The trainees have a ranking system. When you are at the bottom and fresh, you are doing the most thankless work—the trash, broken toilets, any disaster from a guest. You'll work every position, pretty much.

The worst is the onion-cutting station. That guy is cutting onions for seven, eight hours straight on a deli slicer. That is about as close to hell as I can think of. But you get used to it. I joke with all the tours that most people cry for the first ten minutes at work anyway, so it's not all that different.

Honestly, 85 percent of the days you'll think you are going crazy. But I guess that's the mentality of restaurants. And I've found that I really do love people and hospitality. I used to be a hotel manager. When people have good experiences, it fuels me.

Now it's worth stressing that I am still not there. But talking to the older servers definitely keeps me on track. They have families. They're able to live contented and solid existences while also interacting with customers from all walks of life and the best in the hospitality world. They taught me that it's possible."

Nicholas, whom we met just two months before he graduated from the trainee program.

STEAK HOUSE

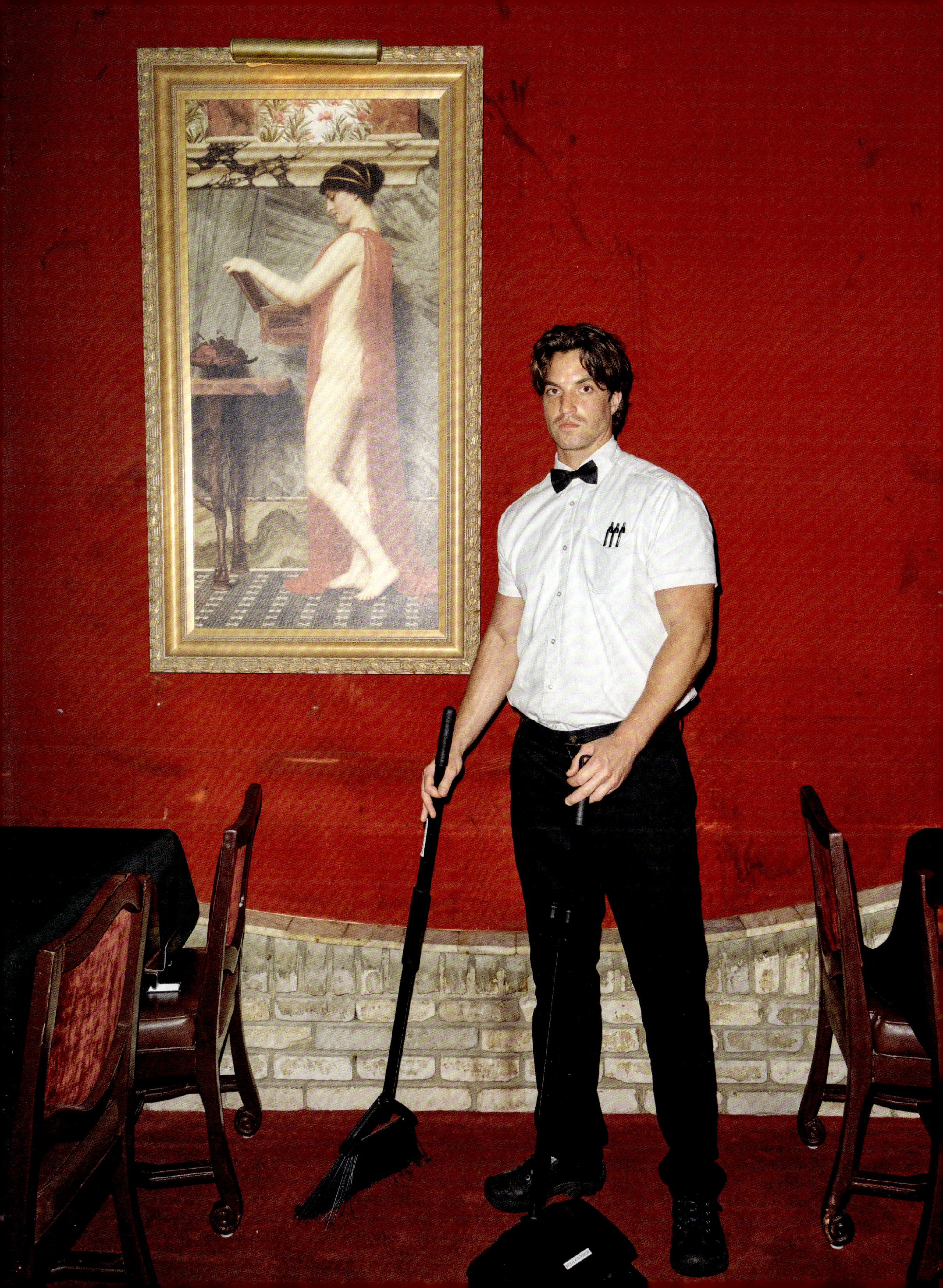

BEYCHEVELLE
1953
POMMARD
1959
POMMARD
CUVAISON
Gamay Vivace
1982
Côte-Rôtie
1979
CABERNET SAUVIGNON
DEHLINGER WINERY
2015
LE MUSIGNY
GRAND CRU
LOUIS JADOT

CHATEAU
TALBOT
MEDOC
1926
KRUG
CHAMPAGNE
KRUG
ROMANÉE
1952
Morey-Saint-Denis
Pommard
BARBERA D'ALBA
LA ROMANÉE

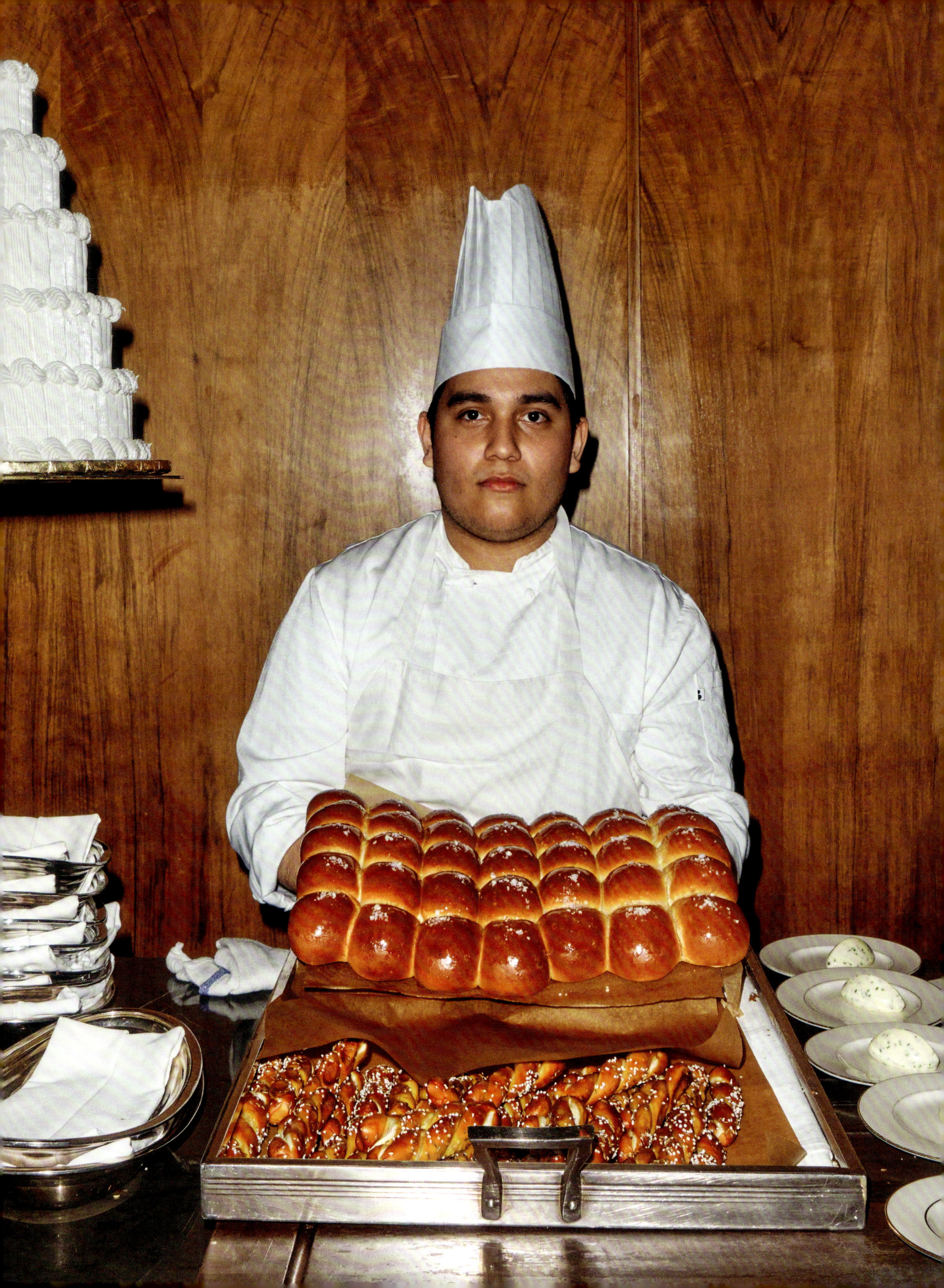

RECIPES

BREADS & CRUDITÉS

POPOVERS

Makes 6 hefty popovers

10 eggs

2 cups plus 1 tablespoon whole milk

¾ cup rendered grass-fed beef tallow

2¼ teaspoons Diamond Crystal kosher salt

1½ teaspoons freshly cracked black pepper

2⅔ cups all-purpose flour

A warm basket of pillowy popovers is a grand way to begin a meal of legendary excess. The English have known this for centuries. Over there, egg batter that inflates and literally "pops over" the muffin tin as it bakes is referred to as Yorkshire pudding. No matter what you decide to call these, you can expect to hear a heck load of *oohs* **and** *aahs* **from your guests—just like I witnessed at JEFFREY'S in Austin, Texas. Beef tallow, aka rendered fat, is the stuff McDonald's used to cook their fries in up until the '90s. It gives the popovers that savory something-something. You can order beef tallow online or even get it delivered, but try to buy it from your local butcher. Make friends with the butcher. Then pop it up!**

In a large bowl, use an immersion blender to combine the eggs, milk, 6 tablespoons of the tallow, the salt, and pepper. With the blender running, add in the flour gradually until fully mixed and no dry flour remains. Alternatively, combine the ingredients in a blender and blend until fully mixed. Pass the batter through a medium-mesh strainer into a clean bowl to remove lumps. Let it rest, covered, at room temperature for 1 hour.

Preheat the oven to 425°F.

Five minutes before you are ready to bake, in a popover pan or 6-cup muffin pan, add 1 tablespoon of tallow to each mold. Put the pan in the oven for 5 minutes, until it is ripping hot and a little pool of liquid has formed around the bits of tallow. Working quickly, remove the pan from the oven and add ⅓ cup of batter to each mold. Bake until deep golden brown, 25 to 30 minutes. Turn the popovers out of the molds onto a platter and serve immediately.

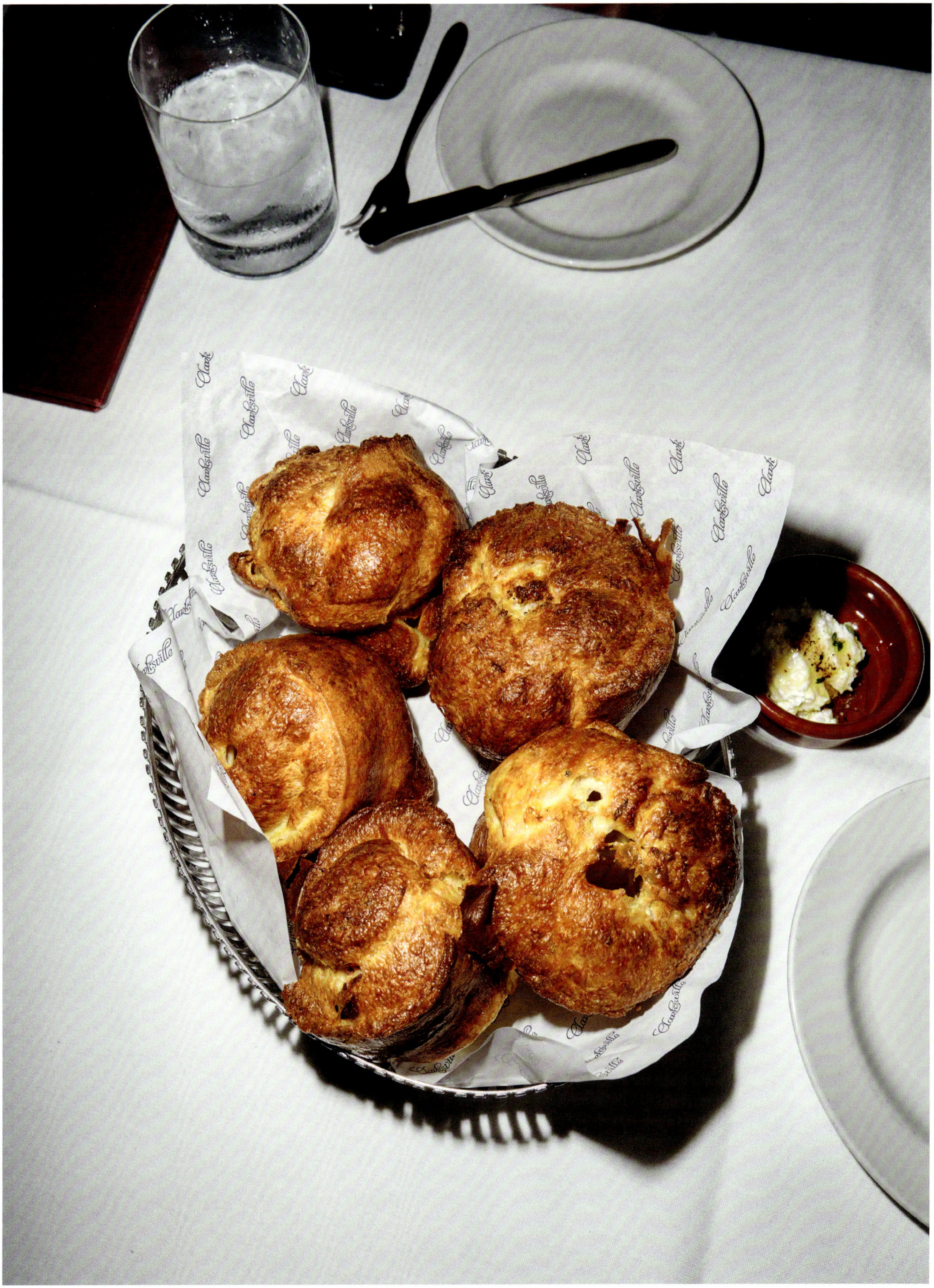
Clarksville

Serves 4

½ cup (1 stick) salted butter, at room temperature

3 small garlic cloves, grated

¼ cup freshly grated Parmesan cheese

1½ teaspoons garlic powder

½ teaspoon Diamond Crystal kosher salt

1 medium loaf white Italian bread, cut into 1-inch-thick slices

Fresh flat-leaf parsley, roughly chopped, for garnish

GARLIC BREAD

At CLEARMAN'S STEAK 'N STEIN INN (page 257), that first hit of garlic-herb ecstasy after unwrapping the tinfoil that envelops their garlic cheese bread is like Christmas morning with much better mood lighting. Your bread buddies instantly reach for a piece and recoil—"That's hot!" For the longest time, I thought it made no sense to jail such a properly charred slice of white bread. But after visiting sixty-five steak houses, I now look at it differently. For the people of Pico Rivera, California, who count on Clearman's, that chewiness better always be there. You have to understand that this is THEIR garlic bread and you're lucky to be let in on the tradition, not least because it comes free with any entrée.

I don't call for the foil swaddle in this recipe. I'm only saying that it's important to know that you can and must do whatever will lead you to YOUR garlic bread. Here's mine.

In a medium bowl, mix the butter, garlic, Parmesan, garlic powder, and salt until combined.

Place a large cast-iron pan over medium-high heat. Spread a thin layer of the garlic butter on one side of each slice of bread. Working in batches to prevent overcrowding, put the bread, butter-side down, in the pan in a single layer and toast until golden, 1 to 2 minutes. Transfer to a serving plate and toast the remaining slices. Sprinkle with parsley and serve immediately.

Serves 4

2 cups shredded extra-sharp orange Cheddar cheese

¼ cup (½ stick) unsalted butter, at room temperature

2 tablespoons port wine

Kosher salt

Crackers or bread for serving

PORT CHEDDAR DIP

I decided to write a book about steak houses in the moments between Jerome Williams at BEEF 'N BOTTLE (page 21) dropping this dipper's dream on my table and the storm of saltines that followed. It hit me on a deep level. Growing up, my mom took tremendous pride in cooking from scratch, but whenever she would have the neighbors over, she knew that nobody could resist the store-bought port cheddar dip she'd pick up at Genuardi's. Least of all her tall son. That creamy sphere would get attacked. I'd put HUGE scoops of it onto Ritz crackers and run off to my bedroom to enjoy the golden spread all by my lonesome.

Now that I'm a big boy, I can make it for myself. From scratch. Sometimes I'll top it with butter-roasted walnuts. I recommend getting this simple approach under your belt first. Then play around. It's a very forgiving recipe.

In a food processor, add the cheese, butter, and wine and blitz until a smooth paste forms, 2 to 3 minutes, stopping if necessary to scrape down the sides. Taste and season with salt as needed. Refrigerate in an airtight container until ready to use. (The dip can be made up to 1 week in advance.) To serve, let the dip return to room temperature and transfer to a serving bowl. Serve with bread or crackers.

PARKER HOUSE ROLLS

Makes 16 rolls

Allow me to present you with another exquisite baby bun to add to your collection, a sweeter, more buttery alternative to the popover. The Parker House rolls at Sean Brock's THE CONTINENTAL in Nashville inspired me to include black pepper in the dough and the topping of a version I could actually pull off, just like he used to before the restaurant tragically closed. May the glorious tradition live on in your kitchen.

Make the dough: In a small saucepan over low heat or in a heatproof bowl in the microwave, warm the milk and honey to between 100° and 110°F. Remove the pan from the heat. Transfer to a clean heatproof bowl and stir in the yeast; allow to activate and foam, about 10 minutes.

Meanwhile, in the bowl of a stand mixer fitted with the hook attachment, add both flours, the fine salt, and pepper; stir on low speed just for a few seconds to combine. Add the milk mixture, butter, and egg and mix on low speed until fully incorporated (the dough should form into a rough ball), about 5 minutes.

Remove the dough from the bowl and shape into a smooth ball. Oil a large bowl and add the dough, cover with a kitchen towel, and let the dough rest until it has doubled in size, about 1½ hours.

After the dough has risen, grease a 9 by 13-inch ceramic or metal baking dish with butter and set aside. Scrape the dough out onto a lightly floured surface and gently knead it into a ball just to deflate it. Divide the dough into four equal pieces, then cut each into four equal pieces (for a total of 16 rolls). Gently knead one piece to shape it and develop the gluten, 10 seconds, then shape it into a ball by pulling in the sides and tucking them into the center. Flip the ball over so it's seam-side down, cup your hand around the ball, and gently roll the ball in a small circle using the heel of your hand to help seal the bottom and create surface tension. Place the ball seam-side down in the baking dish, then repeat with the remaining dough, making sure to space the balls evenly. Cover with a kitchen towel and let rest at room temperature for 1 hour, or until the rolls have doubled in size and feel pillowy.

About 20 minutes before the rolls are done rising, preheat the oven to 375°F. Uncover the rolls and brush the tops with the beaten egg. In a small bowl, mix together the melted butter and honey.

Bake the rolls for 20 minutes. Carefully remove the dish from the oven, brush the tops of the rolls with the honey-butter mixture, and sprinkle to taste with pepper and flaky salt. Return the dish to the oven and bake until golden brown and an instant-read thermometer inserted in the center of the rolls reads at least 200°F, another 10 to 12 minutes. Serve warm with more butter. Always more butter.

Dough
1 cup whole milk
3 tablespoons honey
3½ teaspoons active dry yeast
3¼ cups bread flour
¼ cup all-purpose flour, plus more for dusting
2 teaspoons fine sea salt
½ teaspoon freshly cracked black pepper
¼ cup (½ stick) unsalted butter, diced and softened, plus more for greasing
1 egg
Neutral oil for the bowl

Topping
1 egg, lightly beaten
1 tablespoon unsalted butter, melted, plus more for serving
1 teaspoon honey
Freshly cracked black pepper
Flaky sea salt, preferably Maldon

RELISH TRAY WITH CREAMY DIP

Serves 4

½ cup sour cream

½ cup mayonnaise

2 tablespoons buttermilk

1½ teaspoons garlic powder

¾ teaspoon Diamond Crystal kosher salt

¼ teaspoon freshly cracked black pepper

½ cup crumbled blue cheese

2 tablespoons chopped fresh chives

1½ teaspoons finely chopped fresh flat-leaf parsley

Crushed ice for serving

Carrot sticks, celery sticks, dill pickle spears, and pitted green or Kalamata olives for serving

At steak houses, a very cold plate of crudités—aka a relish tray—is oftentimes offered to the table as a welcome gift and a message: "Eat your greens now, because we're about to go OFF." But once you clock what's in the cool, creamy dipper doodle—usually, it's a blue cheese–forward meditation on dairy—you smile. The situation has *already* gotten naughty.

I like to keep half my veggies and dip for the main event so that I can enjoy something fresh and briny between bites of porterhouse and garlic mash. Make sure to serve it all on ice, just like they do at KEENS (page 56)!

In a medium bowl, whisk together the sour cream, mayonnaise, buttermilk, garlic powder, salt, and pepper. Fold in the blue cheese, chives, and parsley. Chill in the fridge in an airtight container until ready to serve. (The dip can be made up to 3 days in advance.)

Arrange a layer of crushed ice on a serving platter. Transfer the dip to a serving bowl. To serve, top the ice with the carrot sticks, celery sticks, pickle spears, olives, and chilled dip.

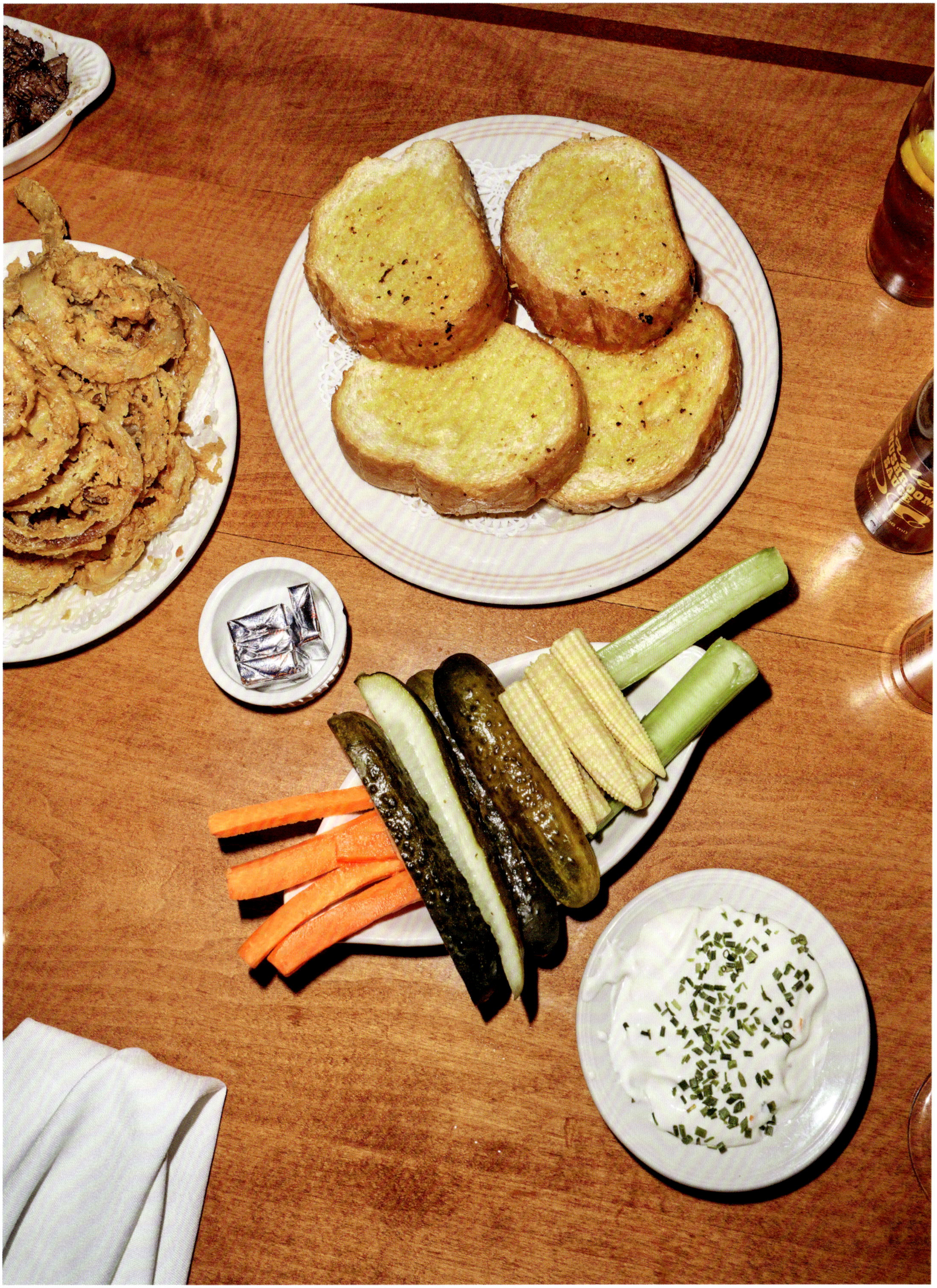

THE JOURNEY, PART II

NEW
C I

YORK
T
Y

NEW YORK CITY IS WHERE I FEEL MOST LIKE MYSELF.

This town is where the American steak house exploded into the national consciousness nearly two centuries ago. People were just starting to regularly eat outside their homes at these places called "restaurants." It was a new thing, and the folks with money took a liking to it. They enjoyed going to Delmonico's, where they could put their pinkies up while watching a server carve a big bird or light a dish on fire in front of them—theatrical European service fit for royalty. *See, we can be fancy, too.* Down the line, when it became more of a steak house, Delmonico's would also (supposedly) be the first place to put chilly iceberg lettuce and creamy dressing onto a plate and call it a wedge salad.

All the beef from Chicago found a very enthusiastic audience in New York, which became the center for meatpacking in this nation. Downtown, south of Chelsea, a city within a city dedicated to beef came into being. The oldest running steak house in the country, Old Homestead, opened in the Meatpacking District in 1868. When they started out, a five-course meal cost nineteen cents. In 1885, a bit farther north by what is now Madison Square Garden, Keens started welcoming guests and hanging pipes from the ceiling. Two years later, across the Williamsburg Bridge, Peter Luger arrived on the scene with the thunk of a golden chocolate coin hitting a thick wooden table.

All three of these steak houses are still around. In this chapter we will highlight two of them, Keens and Luger. It kills me that there wasn't enough space to feature Old Homestead Steakhouse or the special spots that are not yet considered historic, like the first Korean barbecue restaurant to earn a Michelin star. With marinated galbi, top-quality flat irons, and choice red wines, COTE is one hell of a steak house. I'm happy we went to Queens to experience El Gauchito, which opened in 1979, on a cozy Sunday night in the middle of winter. It's one of the first establishments to introduce this city to the Argentinean style of meat-eating, which is impossible not to love. It also introduced me to provoleta, a flying saucer of crispy provolone! You eat it with chimi and bread, and it's an outstanding bite. Someone told our server it was my birthday, and that person may have been me. They paraded a cake with a big old sparkler through the dining room. My new friend Raul clapped for me.

Ladies and gentlemen: New York City.

Monkey Bar was one of many, many places I wish I could have given the full treatment. Turns out 320 pages is nowhere near enough. But I'm glad to honor its majestic sunken dining room here.

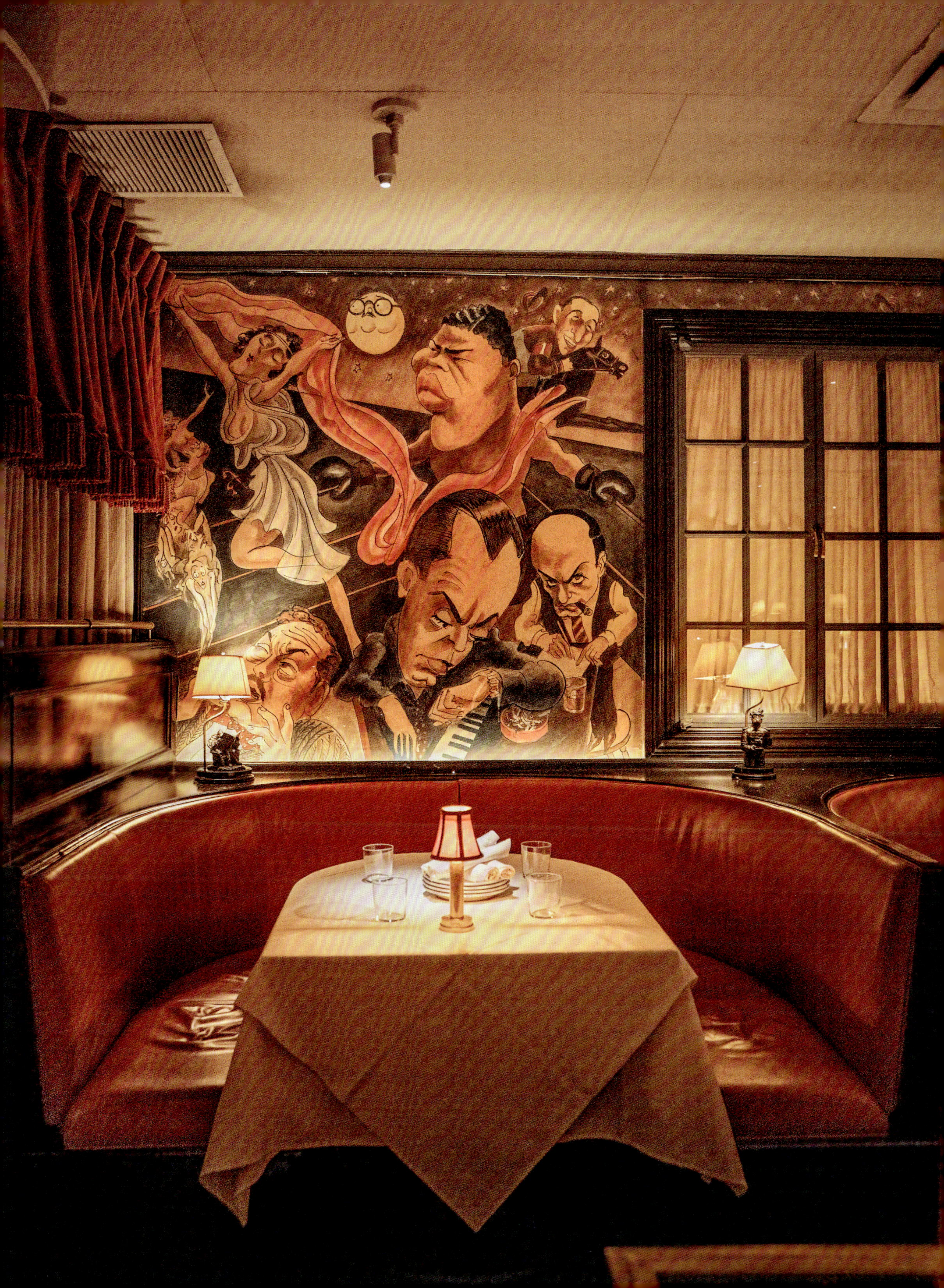

KEENS

BY THE NUMBERS

Opening year: 1885
Founder: Albert Keen
Address: 72 West Thirty-Sixth Street, New York, New York 10018
House specials: Mutton chop; Hash browns

I have spent many birthdays sitting in the dimly lit rooms at Keens, gazing up at those churchwarden pipes, thinking about how cool it must have been to store your delicate "clay" here back in the day . . . and reminding myself to duck on my way from the table to the washrooms. I still daydream about what it would be like to have the chance to host a beefsteak dinner there, like we do in Los Angeles and like Keens used to do, big time, over a century ago (see page 244).

I own a few pipes that Tim and I bought from the establishment back in our Adult Swim days, in fact. For some reason, we were pipe crazy at our office. We even wrote an episode of our first series, *Tom Goes to the Mayor*, called "Pipe Camp."

You can imagine my surprise when we stepped into Keens recently for lunch and a full tour, and the great Bonnie Jenkins—manager, keeper of a flame that was first lit back in 1885—showed us up that creaky zigzag of mahogany staircases that connects three townhouses that make up the restaurant, past that majestic oil painting of the tiger, to present me with a pipe of my very own. With that gesture, Bonnie was putting me—or at least my pipe—in the company of Babe Ruth *and* Dr. Ruth. It now lives on the ceiling . . . somewhere. If any of you manage to find it among the other 89,999 pipes, the mutton is on me.

But just so you know, the mutton isn't mutton. That's not a bad thing, I promise. Part of the reason people love the Keens "mutton chop" so much is because it's lamb, which is nowhere near as funky as sheep.

Keens used to serve real, proper mutton like it was going out of style. Then World War II happened, and it went out of style. People were sick of it. They wanted beef. The good stuff. But some lamb would do. So the team at Keens swapped out the old signature for a cut of lamb that looked just like it.

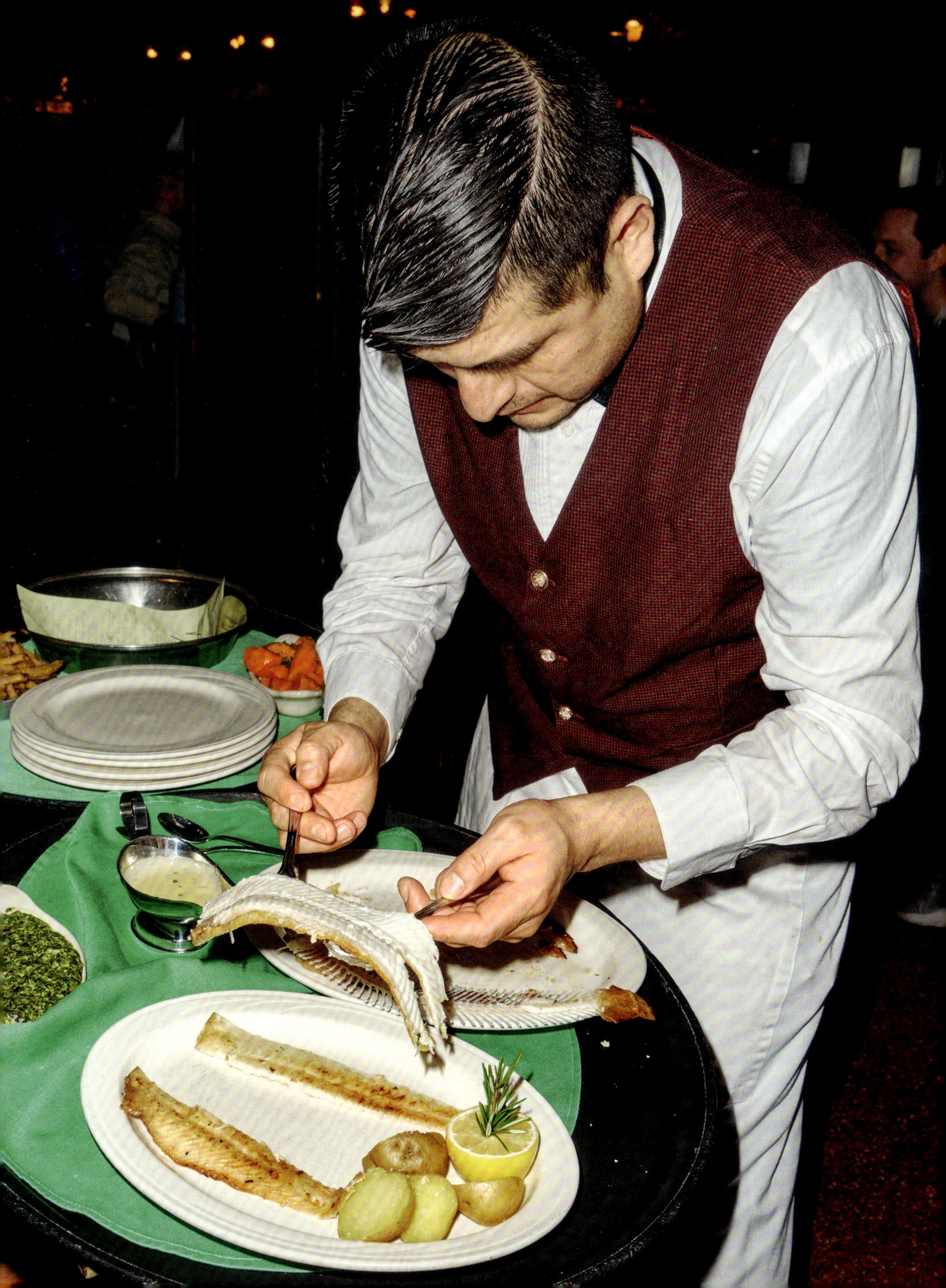

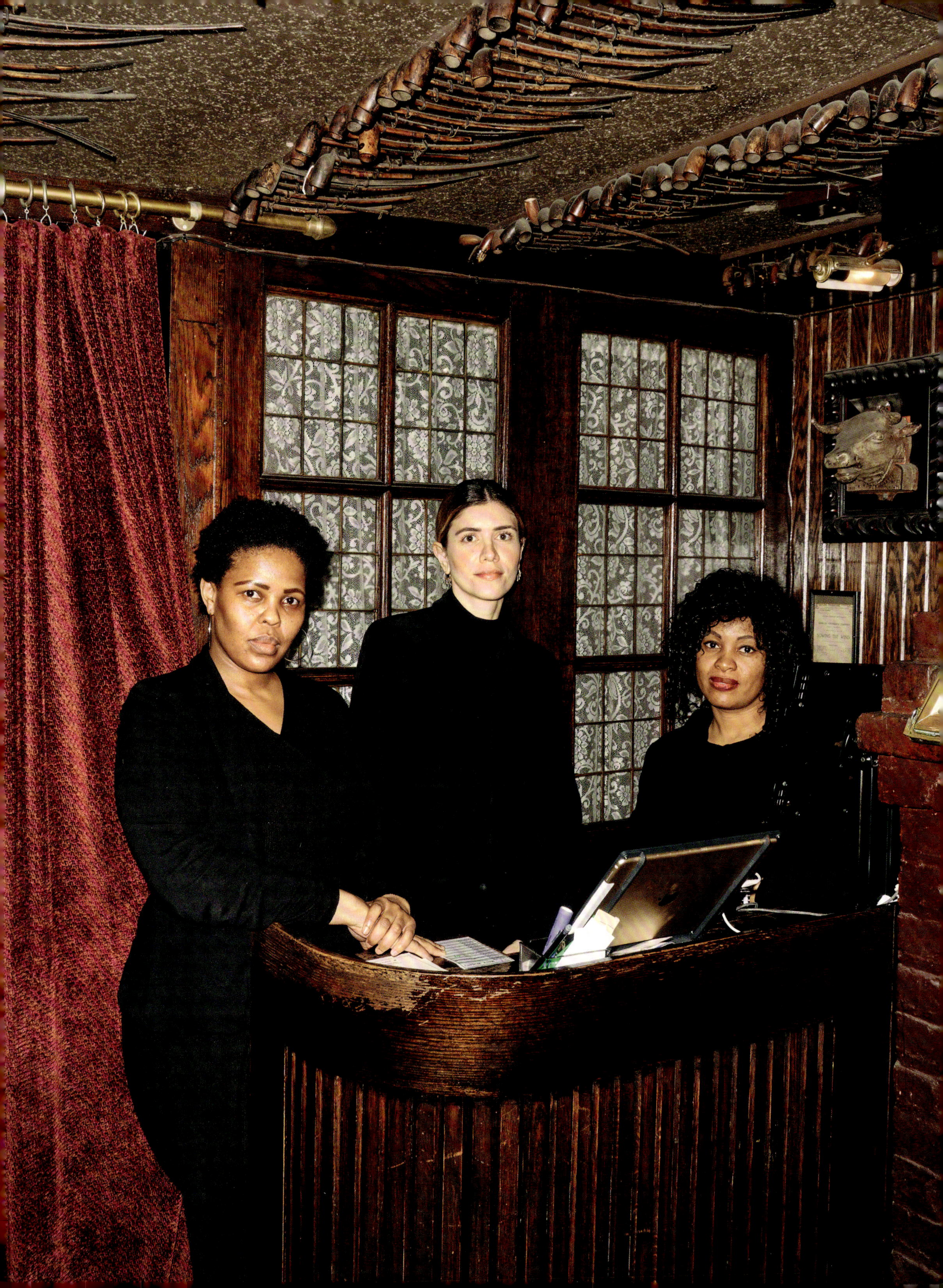

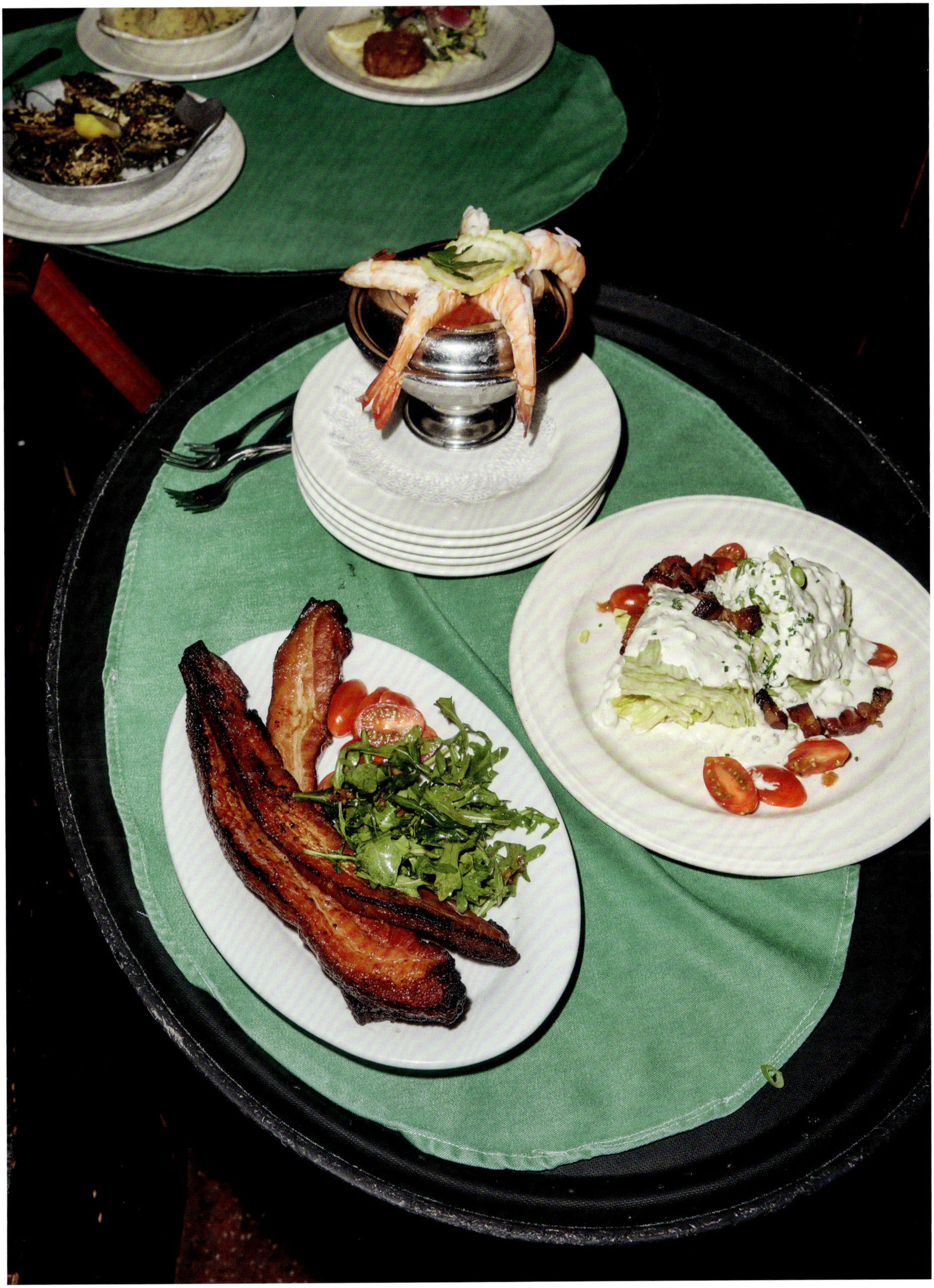

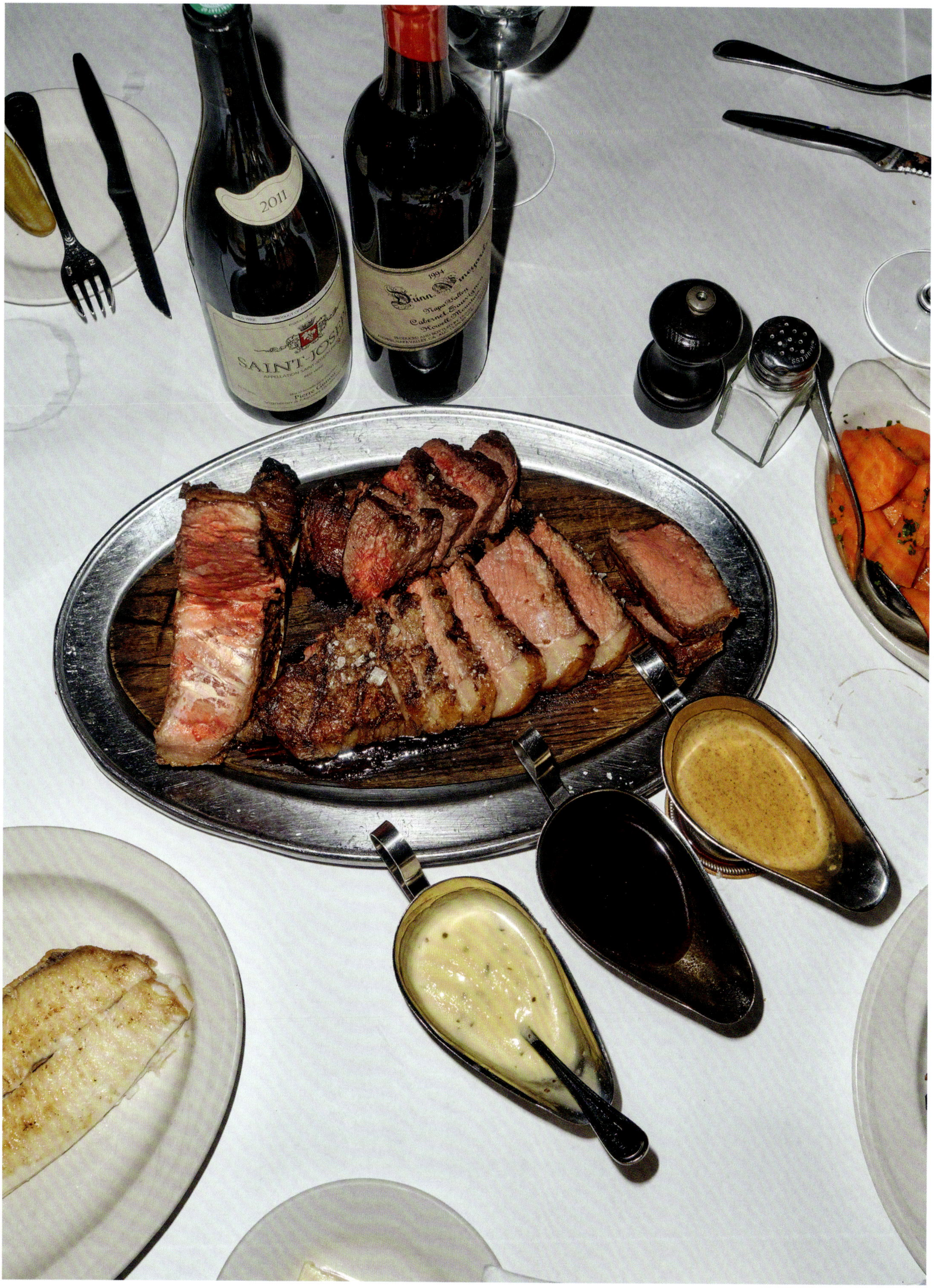
2011
1994

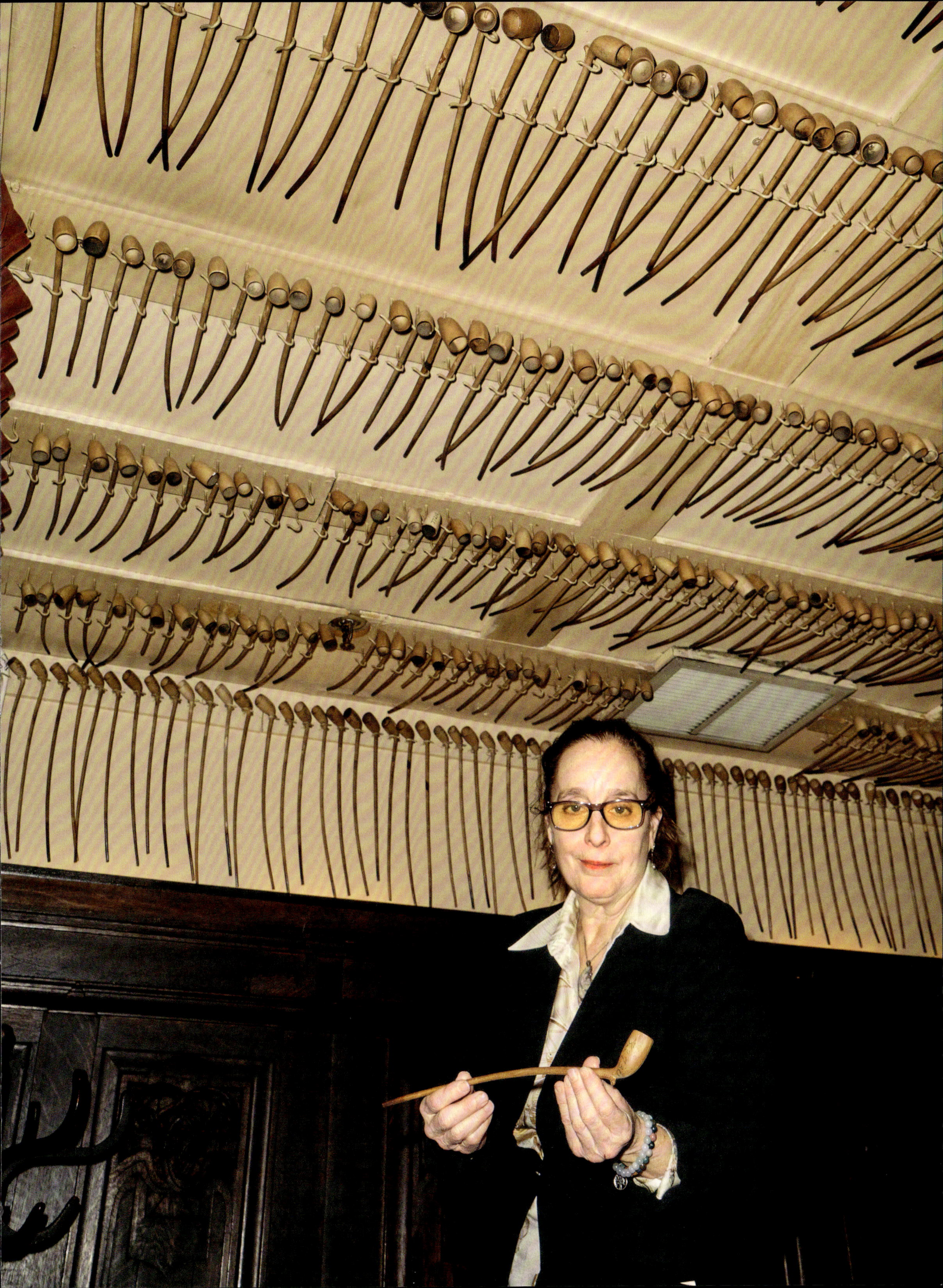

NEW YORK CITY

PETER LUGER

BY THE NUMBERS

Opening year: 1887
Founder: Peter Luger
Address: 178 Broadway, Brooklyn, New York 11211
House specials: Steak for two to four; Apple strudel

A lot of people would say that Peter Luger doesn't cook their steaks properly. To prepare the porterhouse, they hit both sides with kosher salt, sear it in a giant broiler, and then—this is the controversial part—the chef will take out the steak, cut the filet and strip into slices, and arrange the meat and bone on a white platter onto which he's just ladled some warm clarified butter. Back into the broiler it goes. Once the steak is a minute out, the kitchen pages everyone in the dining room to make sure the porterhouse makes it to the table hot and sizzling. The less time it rests, the better. It's a beautiful dance, the servers making way for the bubbling platters coming out of the kitchen.

Our server gives each diner a few slices, tilting the platter so he can spoon the myoglobin and butter that's pooled at the bottom end onto each plate. "You need your vitamins," says a mustachioed man named Aloisius. It's one of many Luger-isms, along with asking a guest who is considering the salmon, "Do you go to Hawaii to ski?"

David Berson is one of the four family members who run things at Luger these days. The other three are his grandmother Amy and his cousins Jody and Daniel. The restaurant has still never played music in the dining room or accepted credit cards. When David first started working there in the '00s, reservations were written out by hand in a giant book that would never leave the host stand. They started accepting online reservations a couple of years back, but that host stand, a cubicle flanked by two panes of glass, still looks like the check-in counter at the DMV.

The Bersons keep each other in check. Each one uses their own personalized stamp at the market when hand-selecting meat for the restaurant. David's great-grandmother Marsha started this practice. He grew up hearing stories of relatives getting shamed for making bad meat calls at the market.

Today, David's not-so-secret mission is to find a way to keep things the same while making them better—or at least better than Pete Wells thought they were when he dropped the hammer on Peter Luger in 2019. The review heard 'round the world. David didn't talk about the takedown, but the tell came when we were touring the kitchen. We took a portrait of the fry cook, or who we *thought* was the fry cook. When we spoke to him a few months later, we learned that a more accurate title for Taylor Adams might be "Mr. Fix-It." He gave up cooking in trendy restaurants to accept the mission. The challenge?

Consistency. Making sure the onions are caramelized the same way every time. Making the croutons instead of buying them. Doing our own stocks. Not that many pieces at Luger, but we have to make sure we nail them, and that can be difficult when you caramelize 150 pounds of onions in a single day.

The Luger steak for four. Behold the vitamins.

Very interesting, but that wasn't what brought me to tears.

STEAK HOUSE

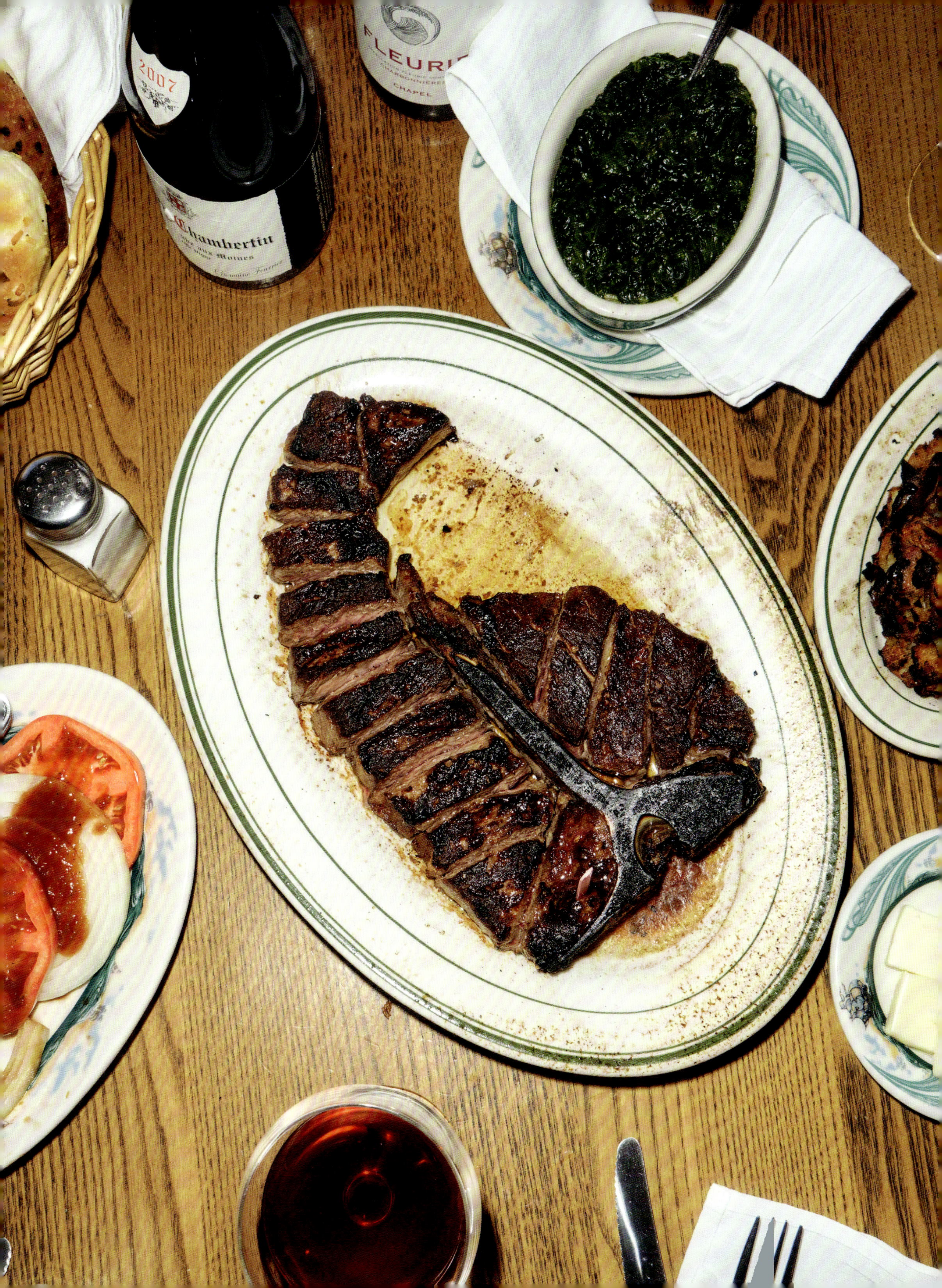
2007
Chambertin
CHAPEL

The thing I didn't really know about Peter Luger is that it is one of the few restaurants where the American dream is still alive. People don't leave, for starters. A first-generation American or immigrant can come here without a college education and support a family . . . in New York City. This is the only place I've worked where waiters can retire. Most of our kitchen staff is ESL. Servers, too. They are able to work this job and provide for their family in a way that most restaurants don't. And yeah, until I worked here, I had no fucking idea.

Aloisius Grunauer—The Lifer

Of the veterans at Luger, Aloisius is considered the friendliest. I still wouldn't want to get on his bad side.

"In my opinion, the owners should not make any fucking changes whatsoever here. If they put mushrooms instead of onion rings or add a crab cake, nobody gives a shit.

Listen, if you go back through the years, we have never had a good review from the *New York Times*. Ruth Reichl said the steak is good, but everything else is bad. She was not wrong. But the potatoes are good, I think. Anyway, you don't go to Peter Luger for a fillet of sole. You are an idiot if you do. But you won't find a better piece of meat anywhere. Listen, the Pete Wells review is still advertising at the end of the day. Of course, if I was the owner, I would be bothered tremendously—but it didn't do any harm to our business.

I am one of the two last German-speaking guys to be hired at Luger. Carl is the other one and is still here. Now we are the United Nations here. I am originally from Austria. I have been in New York since 1977. I came here on my graduation trip and I stayed. Straight from Vienna. I don't miss the schnitzel. I can make my own.

The key to making it here is doing your damn job. In Peter Luger, if you do your job, nobody will bother you. You also gotta gauge your customers. You have to see how much you can mess with them. With the bacon, I can't make this joke anymore: 'Do you prefer a long, skinny one or a short, fat one?' With the steak, I still say, 'This is the best cholesterol that money can buy.' And the one that is truly my line is rolling the r's when I say, 'Crrrispy, crrrrunchy, German-frrrried potatoes.'

I believe you have to be nice to the customer. Some of my colleagues don't. I am not one of the grumpy old men. I love my customers, no matter where they come from. We have everybody and their grandmother coming here. I was selected to take care of Eminem because his mom speaks German. I texted my wife, 'Listen, I have to take care of M&M tonight.' She told me I was an idiot."

Aloisius started his career at his parents' restaurant in Austria: "I was cleaning ashtrays when I was five."

STEAK HOUSE

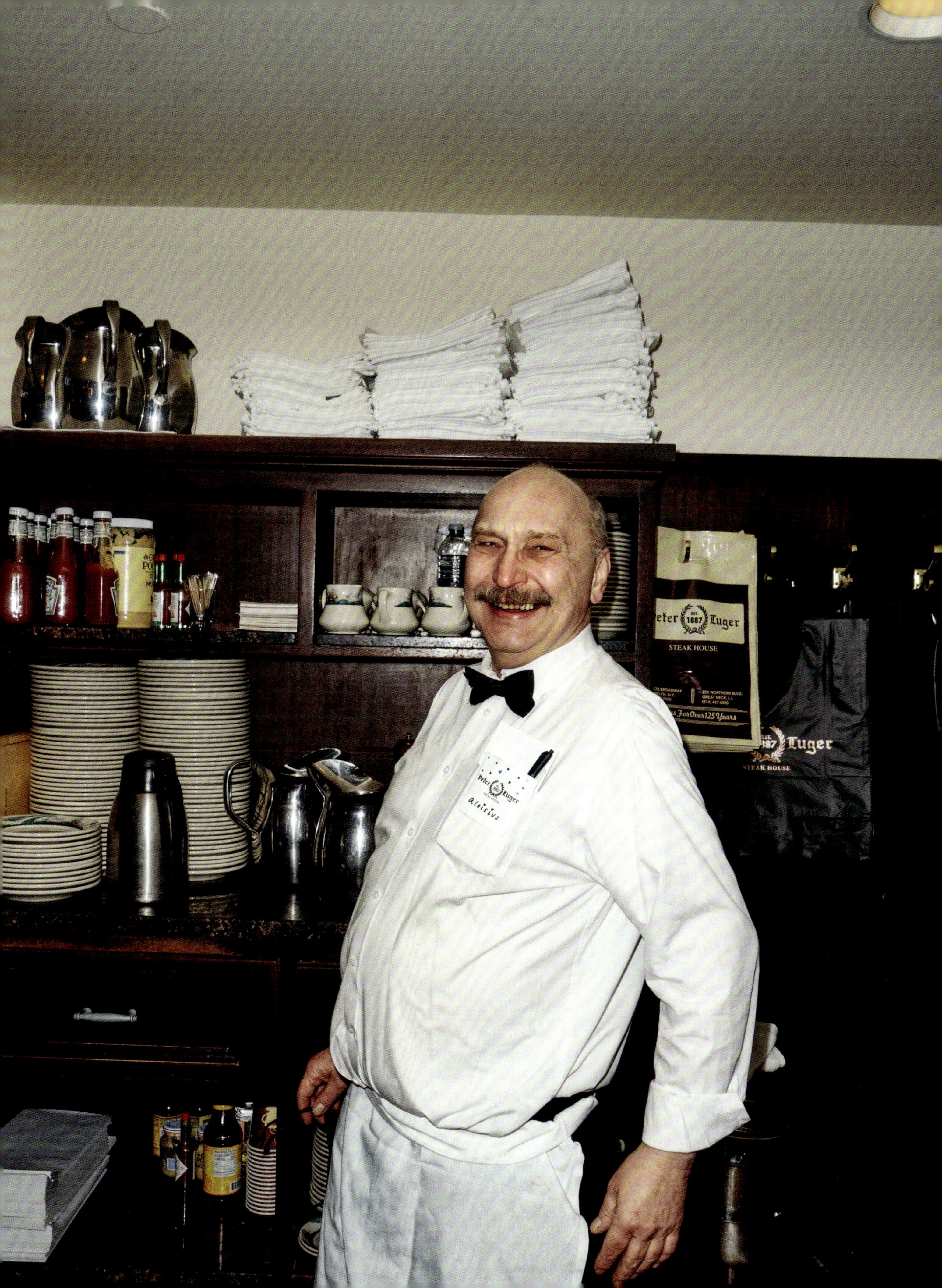
1887 Luger
STEAK HOUSE
1887 Luger
STEAK HOUSE

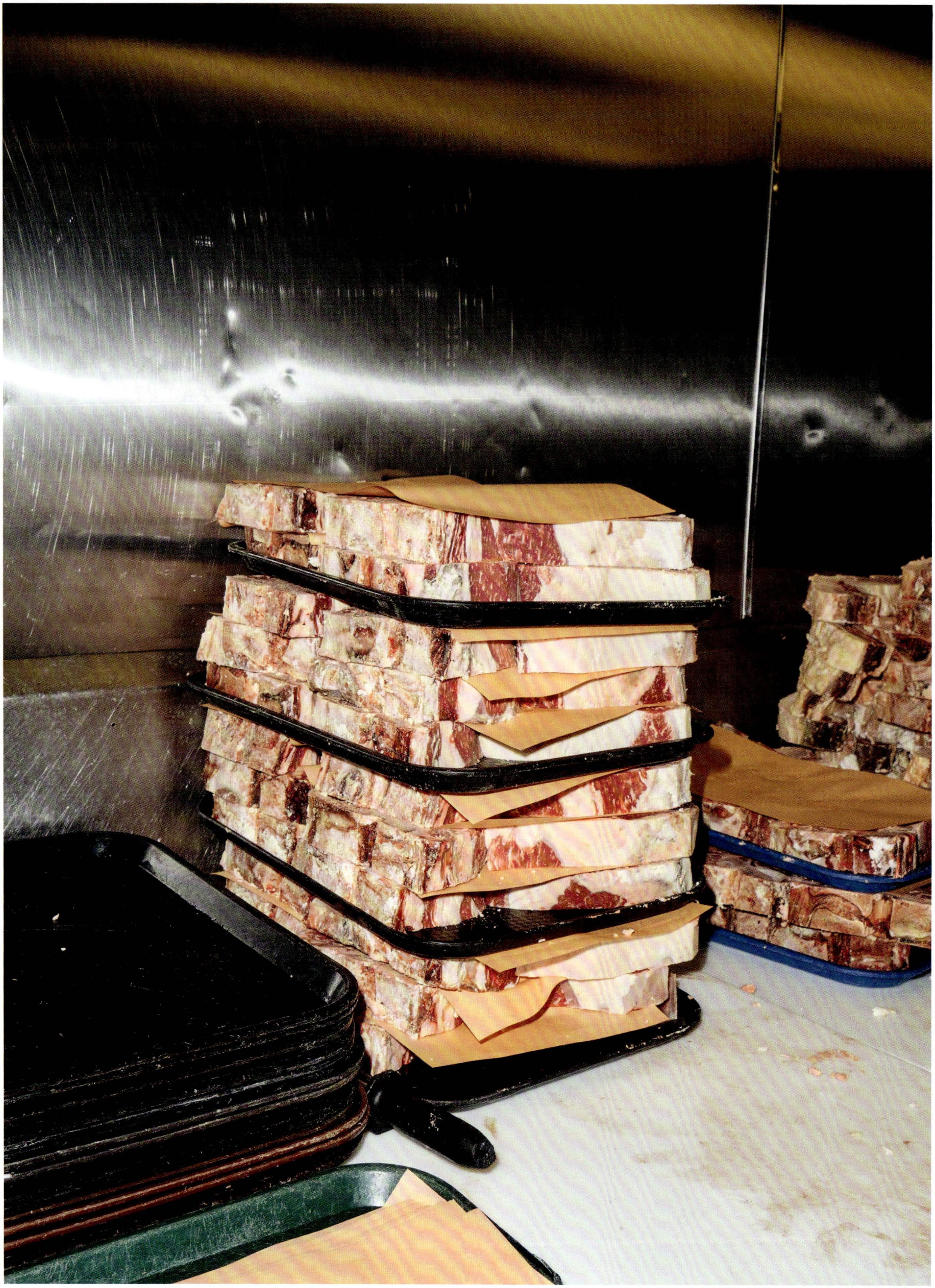

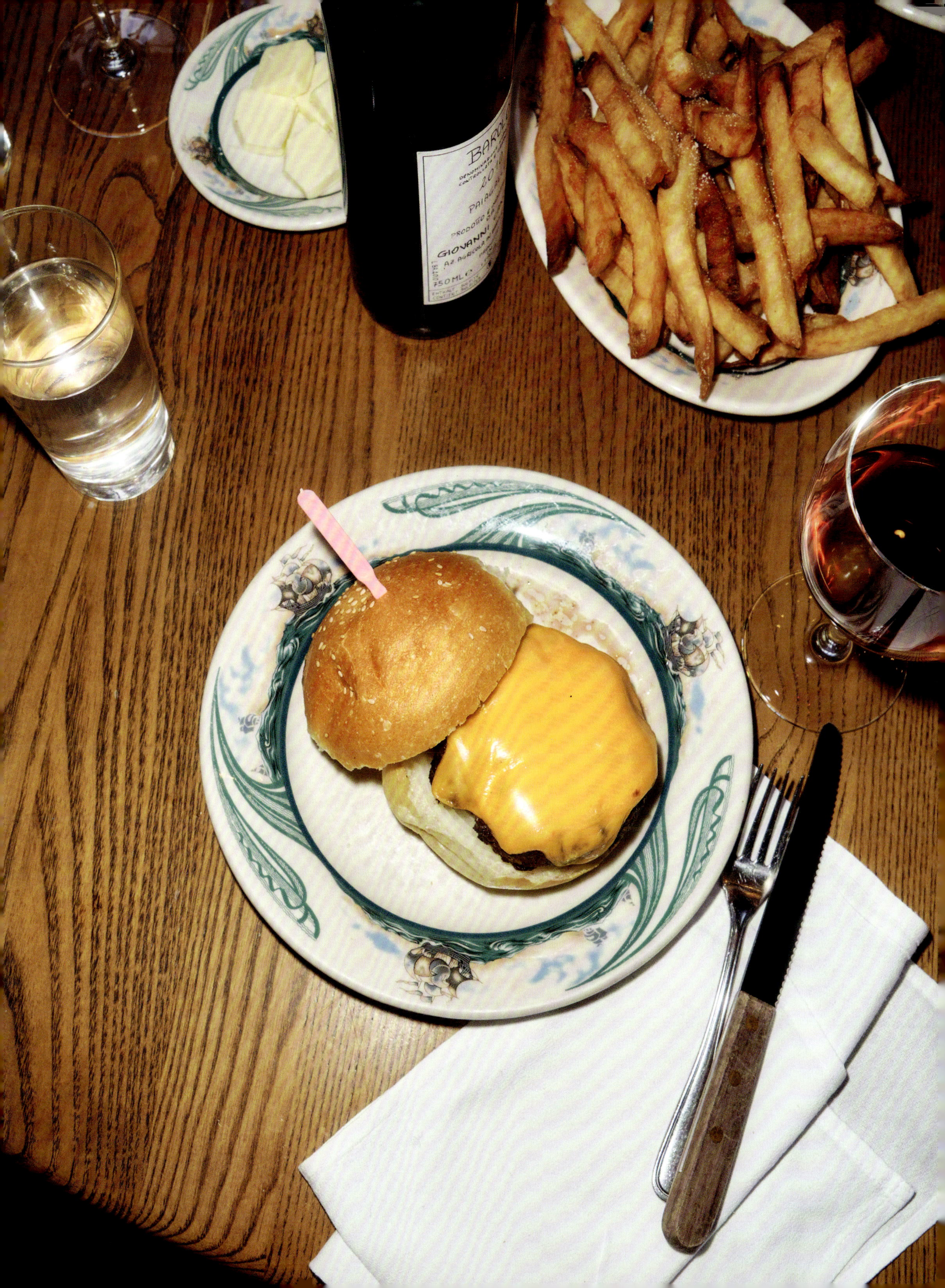
GIOVANNI
750 ML

DONOHUE'S

BY THE NUMBERS

Opening year: 1950
Founder: Martin Donohue
Address: 845 Lexington Avenue, New York, New York 10065
House specials: Yankee pot roast; Maryland turkey with cranberry sauce

Even though you're dining a few blocks away from Daniel on the Upper East Side, how much you make or who your parents are stops mattering the second you walk through the door at Donohue's.

The only clue might be the Patagonia fleece with the name of a bank on it that one *Succession*-looking fella is wearing. But he's too busy digging into the potpie to talk business. A few kids from one of the prep schools nearby shimmy behind his stool to take their seats in the dining room. They order a round of burgers for the table.

It's the middle of December, but I bet that in here it's always like Christmas, or at least like Thanksgiving because the turkey plate is available year-round. The third-generation owner, Maureen Donohue-Peters, makes sure to preserve the atmosphere. Sometimes it means jumping through hoops to keep the veteran bartender from retiring. He works the bar by himself. It's one, but not the only, reason why he sticks to the classics.

Johnny Kelly—The Irishman

"I was born in a place called Donegal. I left high school and became a computer programmer for the IRS in Dublin. They said to us at the IRS, 'You can take up to five years off, and as long as you come back before the five years are up, you will still have a job.' I decided to spend a year in New York.

The city was crazy. It was bad. But it was exciting. My first job was at a bar called Higgy's on Thirty-Third between Sixth and Seventh. I walked in and said I'd take anything. 'I only have four days to offer you,' the owner told me. Those four days happened to be the Big East [NCAA Conference]. I ended up staying exactly four days and four years.

Been at Donohue's for about ten years now. It's the right kind of legendary. If you know it, lucky you. It's not advertised. It's unpretentious. But you notice little changes. Used to be, you'd have twelve people at the bar and you would have conversations the whole night. Learn something new. Now it's people on their cellphones. Even at Donohue's. But I still enjoy it.

I don't really do any signature drinks. We sell mostly martinis and Manhattans and red and white wine. A good still old-fashioned. Mr. Bond has a lot to answer for when it comes to the martini. Has to be stirred, always. What's changing is that the martinis are getting dryer and dryer. Less and less vermouth. I'm fine with that because I can drink a martini or two.

I like making people feel welcome. Like in an Irish public house. Like you're coming into my home. Do I get tired of it? Between us, right now after forty years, I can see Florida and the sunset, the next phase of my life. But it's been good fun."

Flip to page 71 to see Johnny's portrait. One of my favorites from the journey.

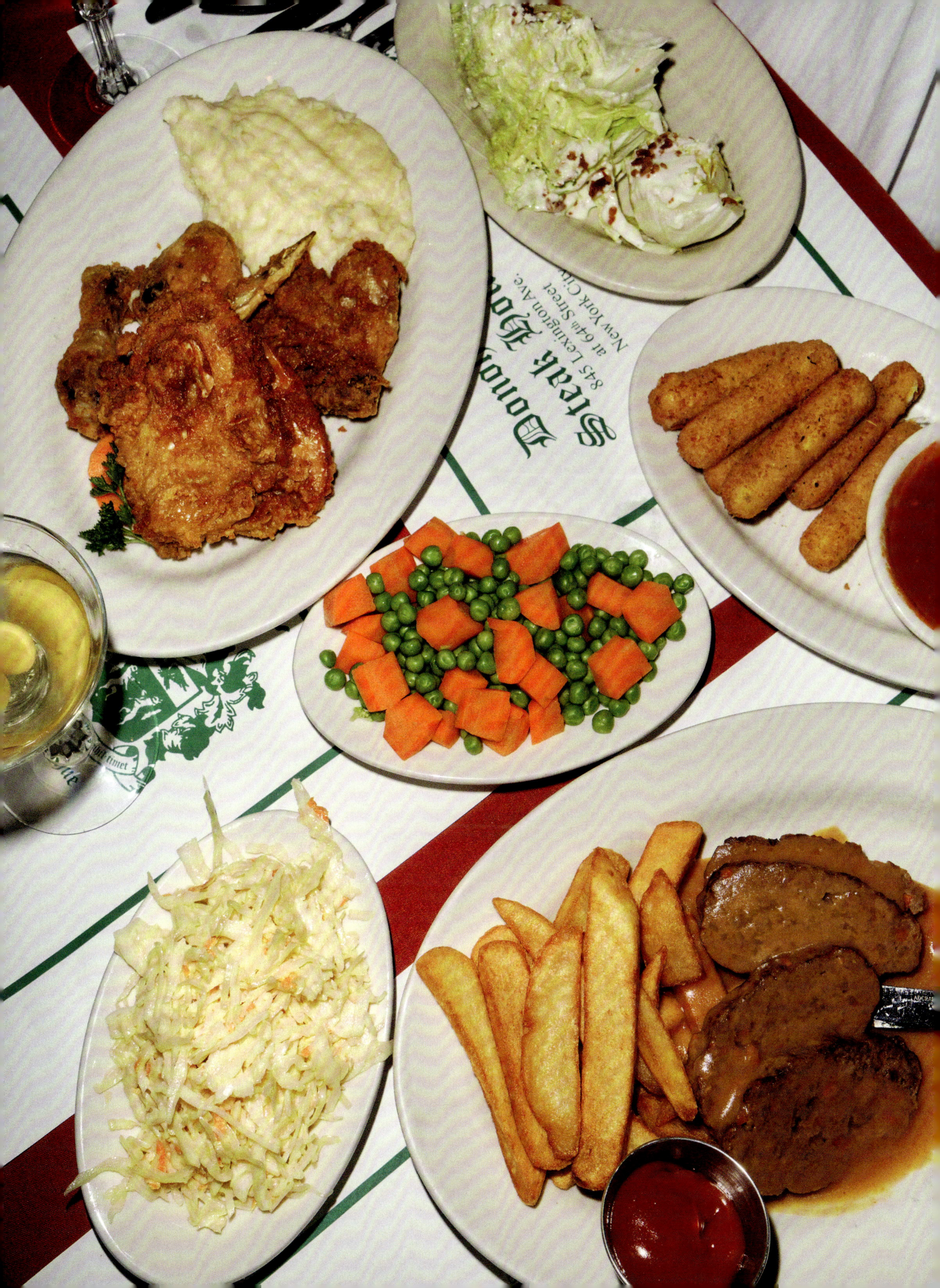
845 Lexington Ave.
at 64th Street
New York City

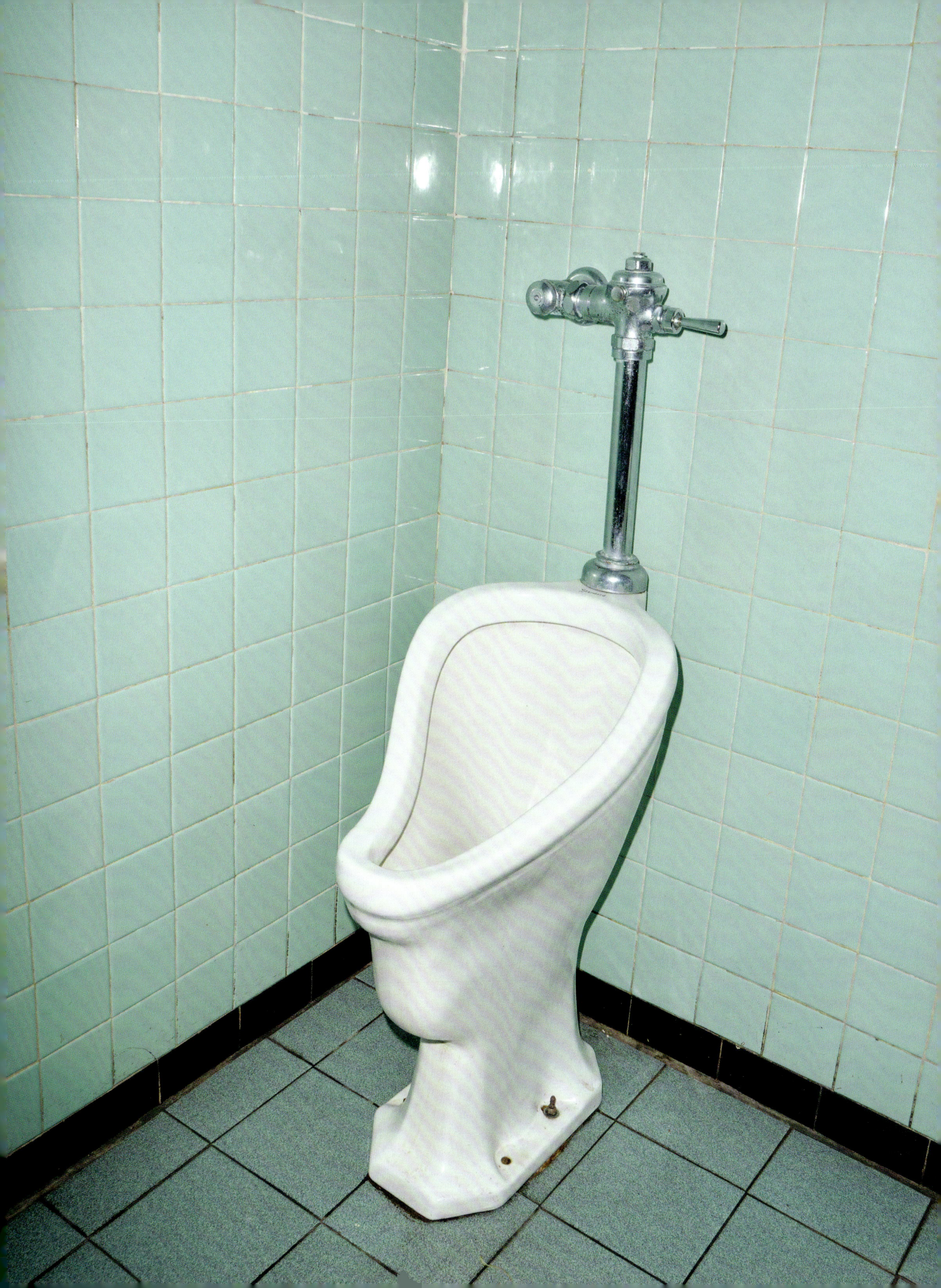

KNOB CREEK
KNOB CREEK RYE WHISKEY
Hennessy
Thompson
100 PIPERS
Donohue's Steak House

NEW YORK CITY

BY THE NUMBERS

Opening year: 2017
Founders: Mario Carbone,
Rich Torrisi, and Jeff Zalaznick
Address: 99 East Fifty-Second Street,
New York, New York 10022
House specials: Vegetable crudités;
Pasta a la presse; Prime rib

THE GRILL

The power lunch was born at the Four Seasons on Park Avenue. That kind of daytime debauchery isn't as popular as it used to be. But after having been to The Grill, which replaced the Four Seasons in 2020, many, many times now, I can tell you that the power dinner is alive and well. I like to save my three martinis for the evening anyway.

I always arrive at the Seagram Building a little early to admire the slender perfection and hushed bronze glow of this architectural masterpiece. The offices are closed and the streets are quiet. I can take in the sound of the fountain. The porter opens the doors to the reception area and the portrait of Gorbachev smiles at me. He's probably thinking to himself, *Does this tall dork really think he has the self-control to not order the birth-year Chateau d'Yquem? Survey says nyet!*

Up the stairs, Julian Black awaits. He's the general manager and my friend. My party takes our seats and right away I order the grandest of crudités for the table. I think we should proceed with crab cake under a translucent layer of potato coins. Almost forgot about the pasta à la presse. Gotta do that: somebody brings an old duck press over and winds it like a music box until the most concentrated broth flows from the buffed silver onto your plate.

Not everybody thought that the young team behind Carbone would be able to take the most iconic dining room in the history of the United States and return it to its former splendor. Those Knoll chairs? They had 'em completely reupholstered in Italy so that they would look and feel just like the one Henry Kissinger first sat in fifty years ago. They use the same linens from the Four Seasons. The plates? They are the ones JFK and Jackie O. had designed for the White House but never got to use. "If every inch of this place doesn't look great, then we've failed in the eyes of Jeff, Mario, and Rich, the new custodians," Julian tells me. There's a person on the nightly maintenance team whose sole job is to clean the iconic shimmering curtains. She starts in The Pool and makes her way over to The Grill. Then she starts all over again. The process takes a full calendar year.

The new owners have made it more of a steak house with a SEAL Team 6 of tuxedoed captains who know how to read some of the most distinguished diners in New York, and a presentation box filled with the best beef money can buy, including a $700 dry-aged rib eye from Snake River Farms. But they'll make you whatever you want. "One time," Julian says, "a woman came in and said she could only eat boiled chicken, boiled eggs, olive oil, and lemon. We figured it out."

Look up: the iconic Richard Lippold sculpture hanging from the ceiling matches the natural pattern of the French walnut walls.

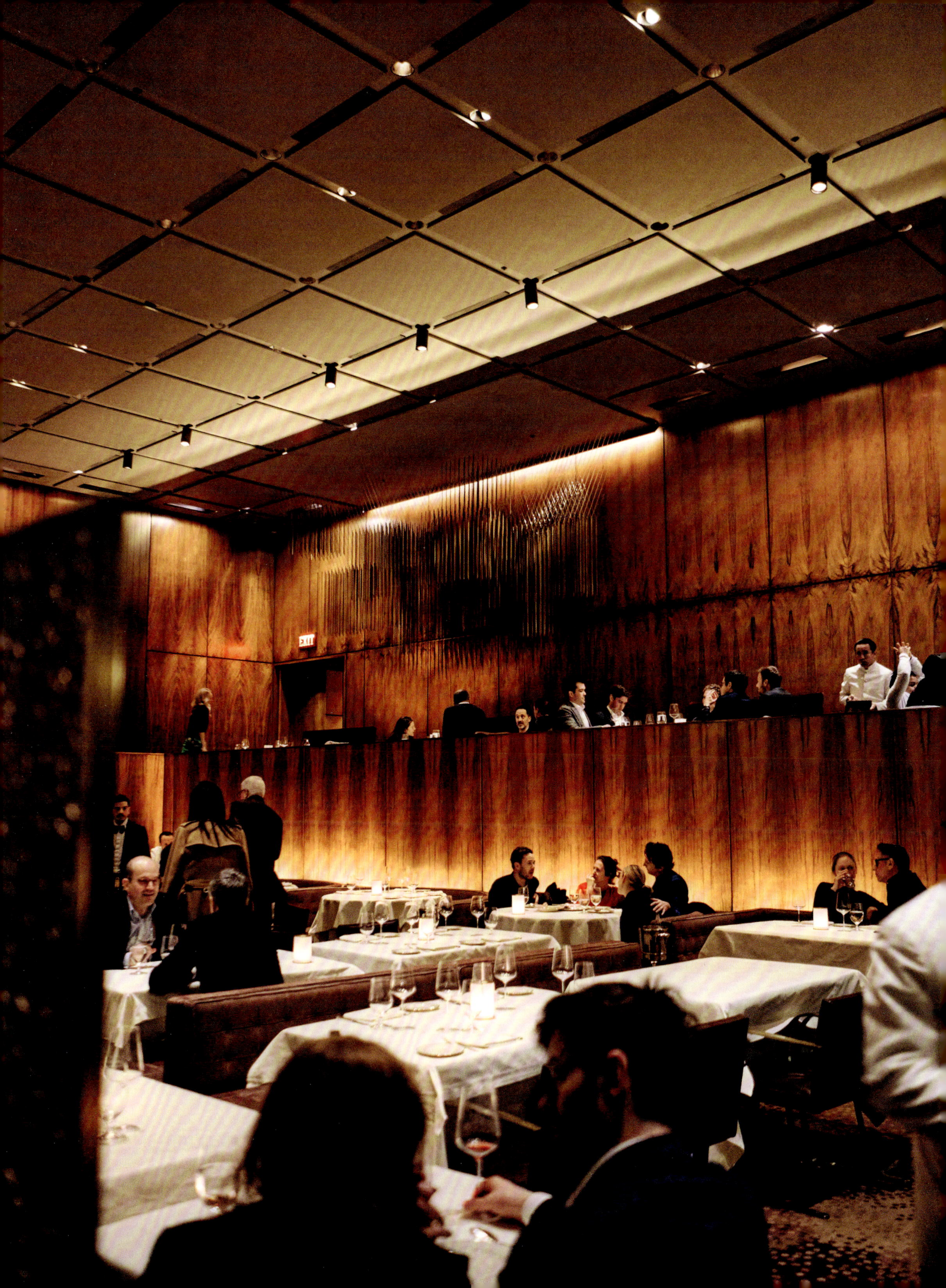
EXIT

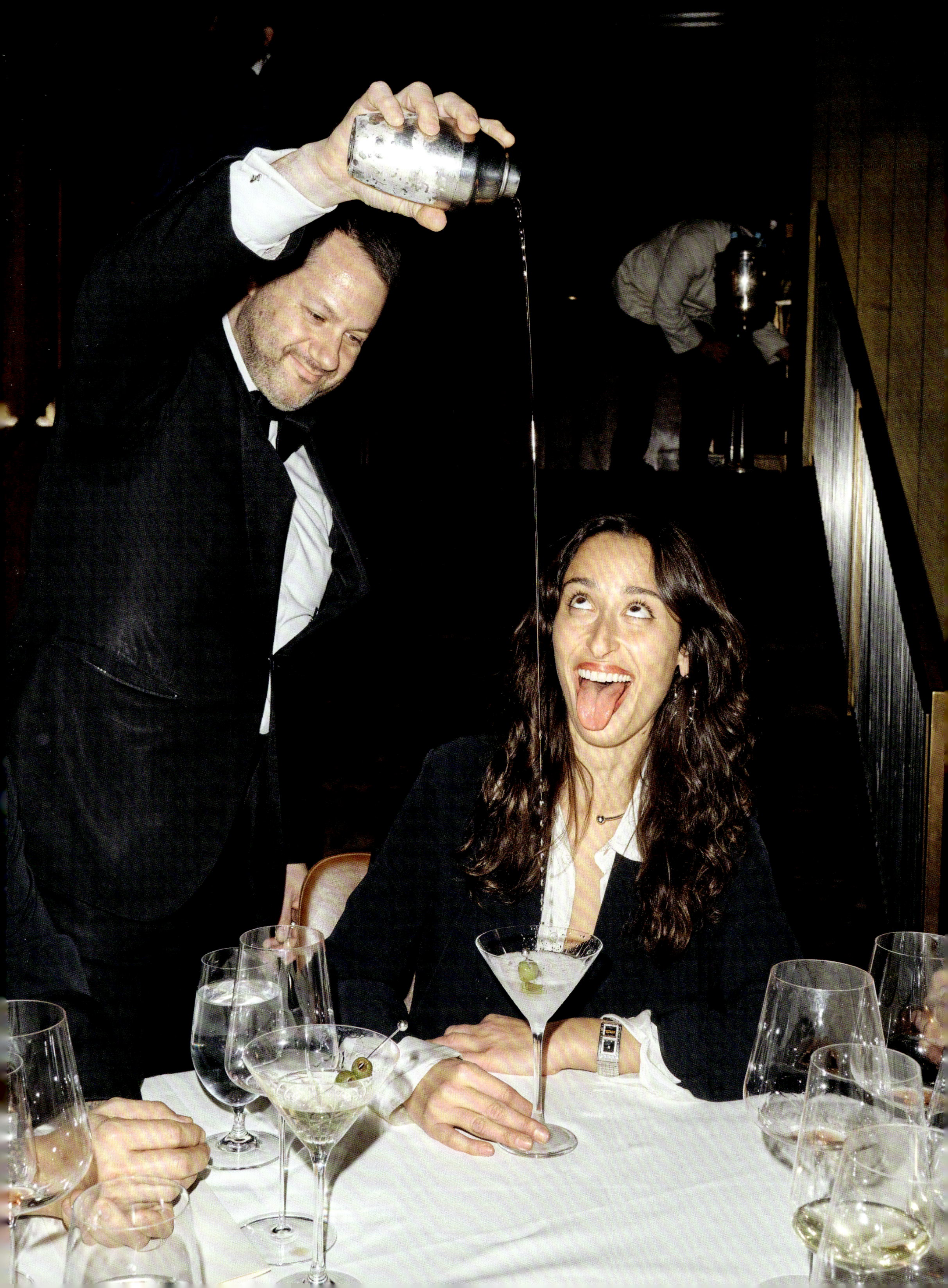

WAGYU STRIP
Heartwood, Texas

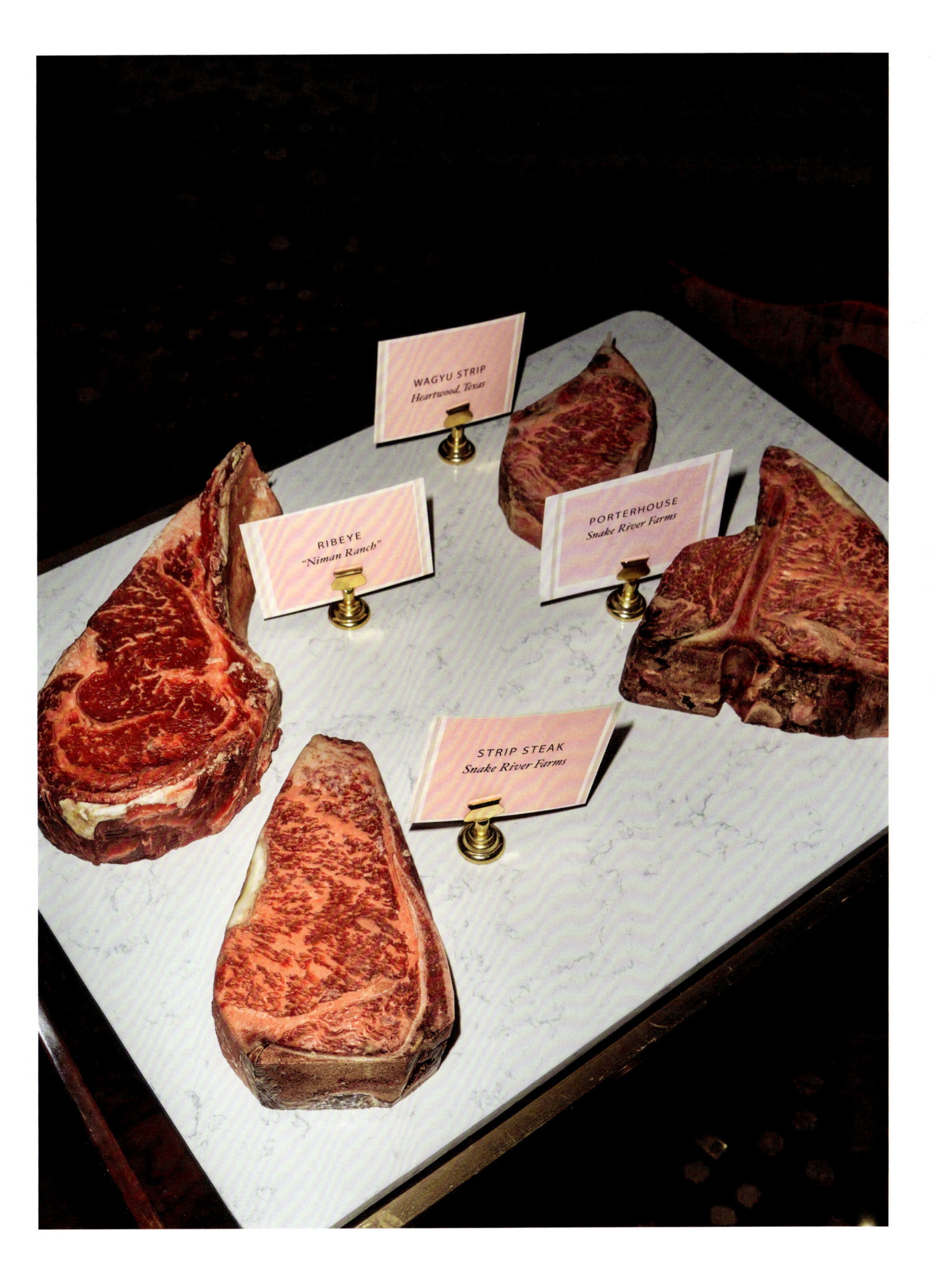

RIBEYE
"Niman Ranch"

PORTERHOUSE
Snake River Farms

STRIP STEAK
Snake River Farms

THE GRILL

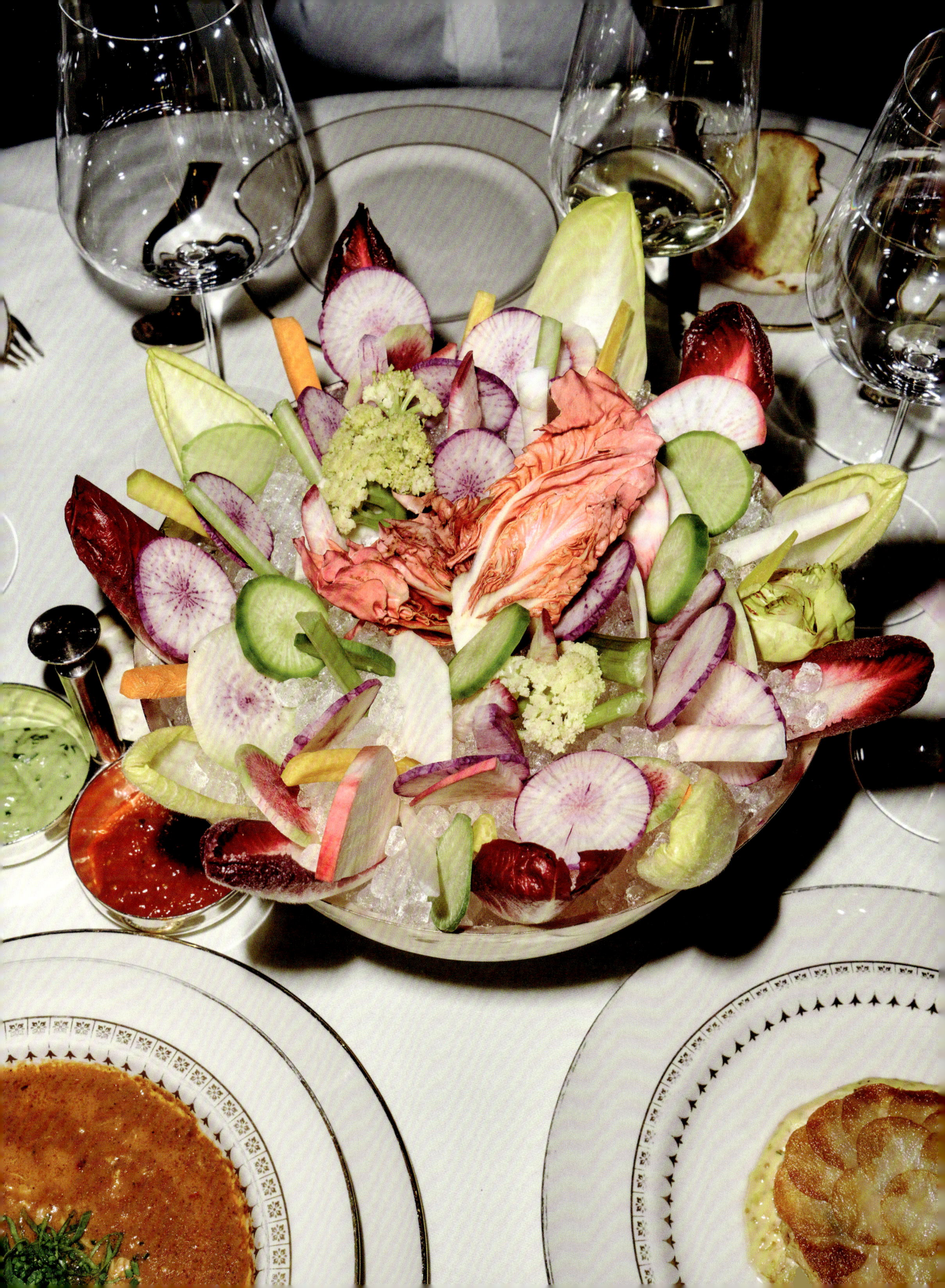

JERSEY INTERLUDE

THE PUB

BY THE NUMBERS

Opening year: 1953
Founders: George Wolfman, William Mirsky, and Morris "Duffy" Shover
Address: 7600 Kaighn Avenue, Pennsauken, New Jersey 08109
House specials: "Burgundy Street" sirloin marinated in red wine and spices; Filet mignon

I'd just wrapped up the principal photography for my New York adventure and went to Philadelphia to see my friends and family and nurse my steak-y wounds. My mom was worried about my health. My friends were more concerned that I had not documented The Pub in South Jersey, right over the bridge. They were offended!

I packed up my camera, and one of my oldest and dearest friends, Mike Parsell, drove me and his daughter Mila to The Pub for a royal feast. Mila forced us to listen to Taylor Swift as loud as the radio could go. I tried singing along but she was not having it. She also told us that we should not even try to get her to share her rib eye with us.

Upon pulling into The Pub's parking lot and witnessing the mass of American flags and the castle that houses the restaurant, Mike and I took a second to collect ourselves. At twenty-four thousand square-feet, The Pub is the only steak house I have ever seen described as "Tolkien-esque" in more than one article, and that is not just because it has two salad bars.

I walked into the dining room and almost fell to my knees at the sight of hundreds of people enjoying all the bounties of the house. It looked like a member of King Arthur's court was marrying somebody from Jersey. I reacquainted myself with the space, which I hadn't visited in years. The brick-walled phalanx of hickory-smoked charcoal ovens spanning the front of the dining room: still there. The carafes of wine: still listed as "flagons" on the menu. Every inch of the place: still carpeted.

It takes about fifteen minutes to walk from your table to the salad bar and back. It's quite an enjoyable journey, as all the memories of growing up in that area always flood back to me. Glad I took the camera so I can show you.

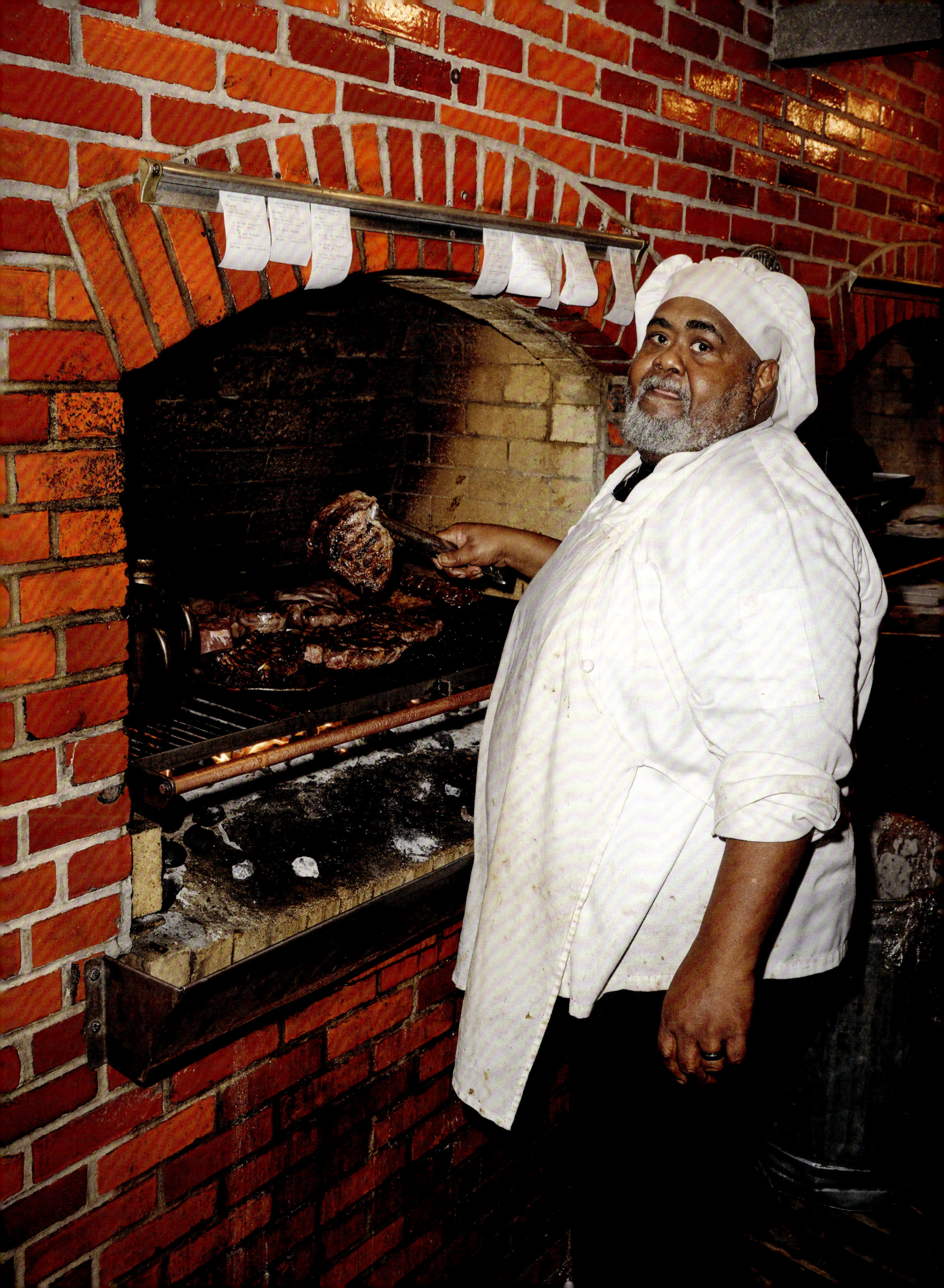

CAESAR
SALAD

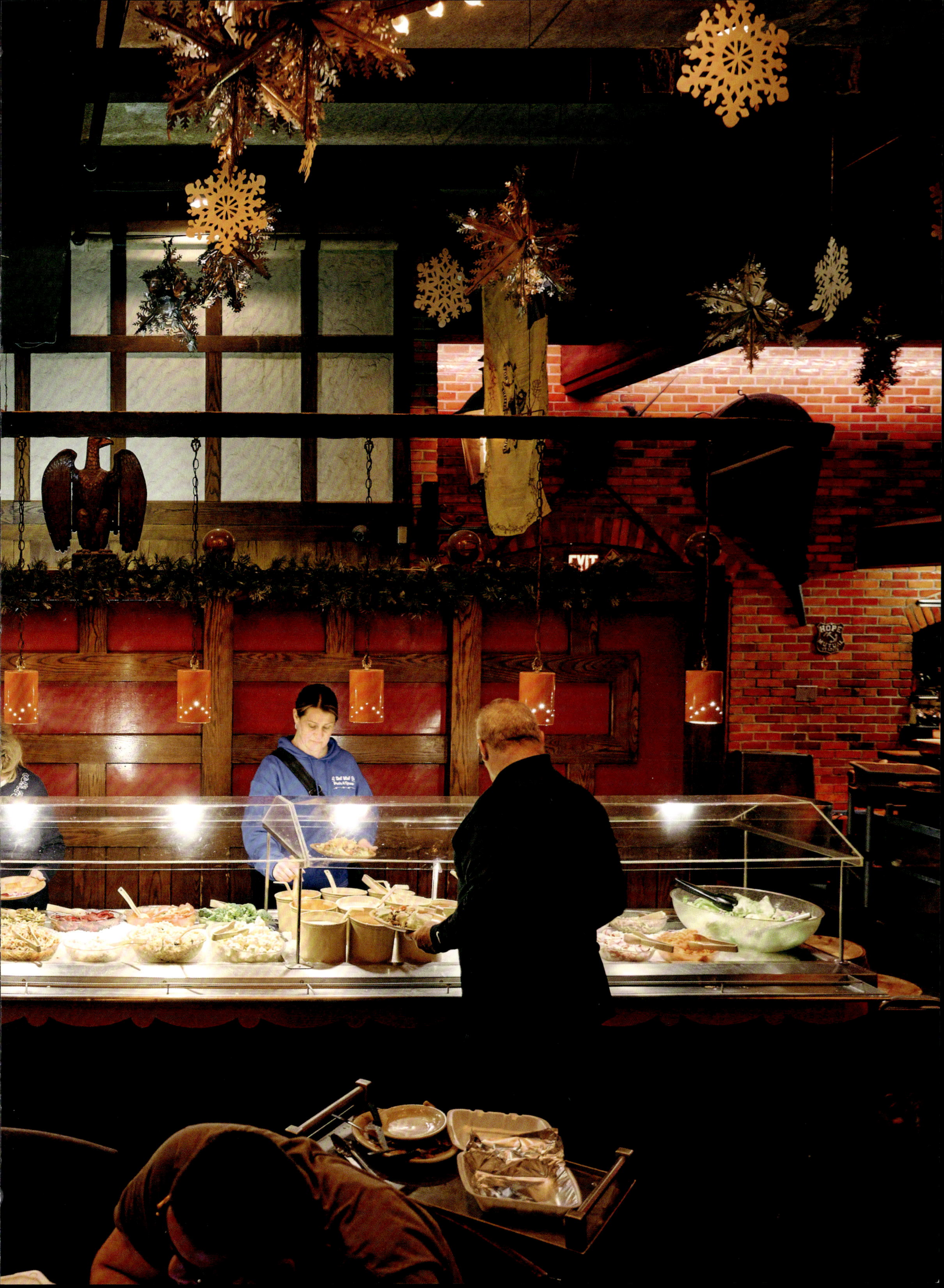
EXIT
HOPE

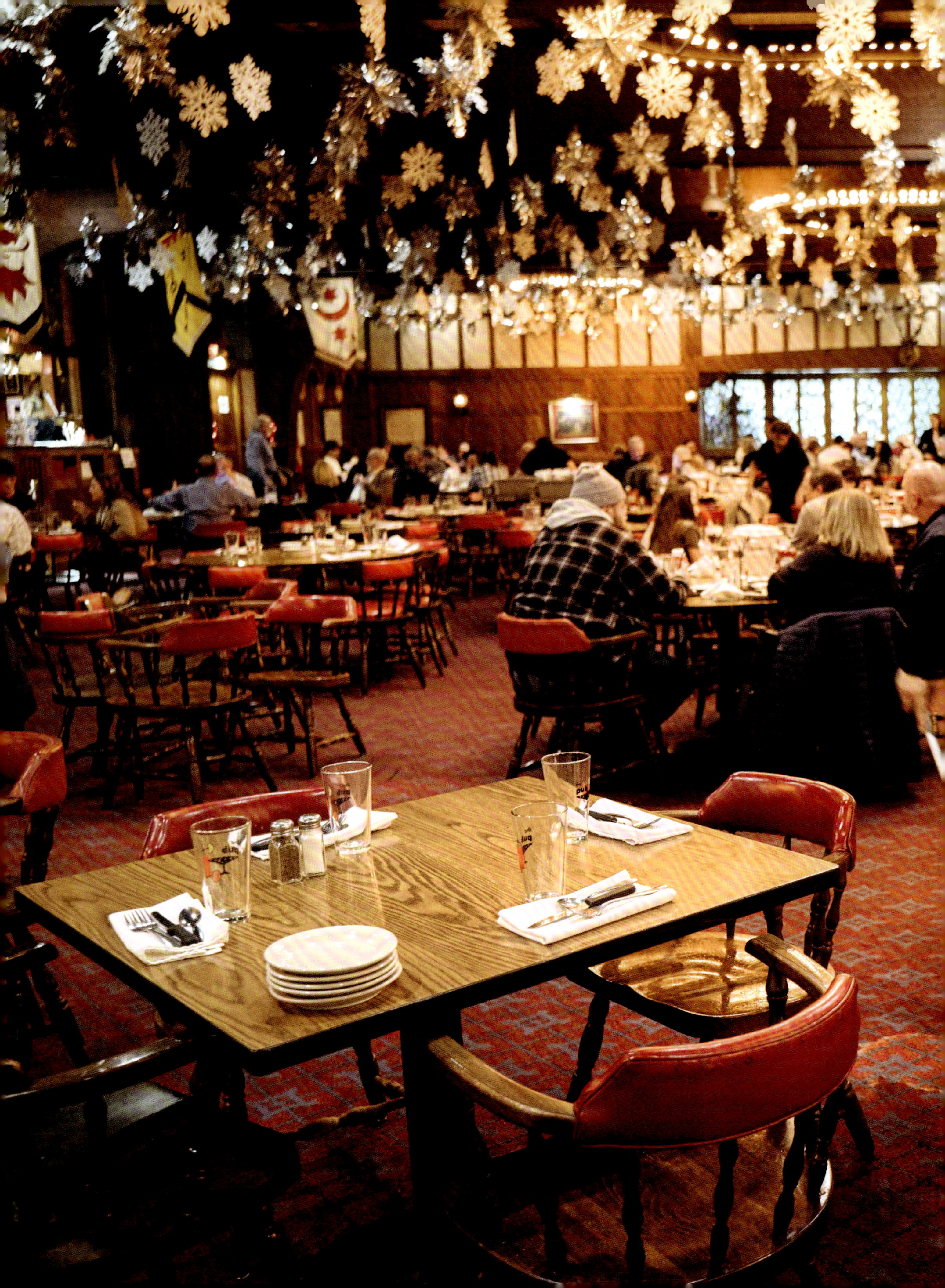

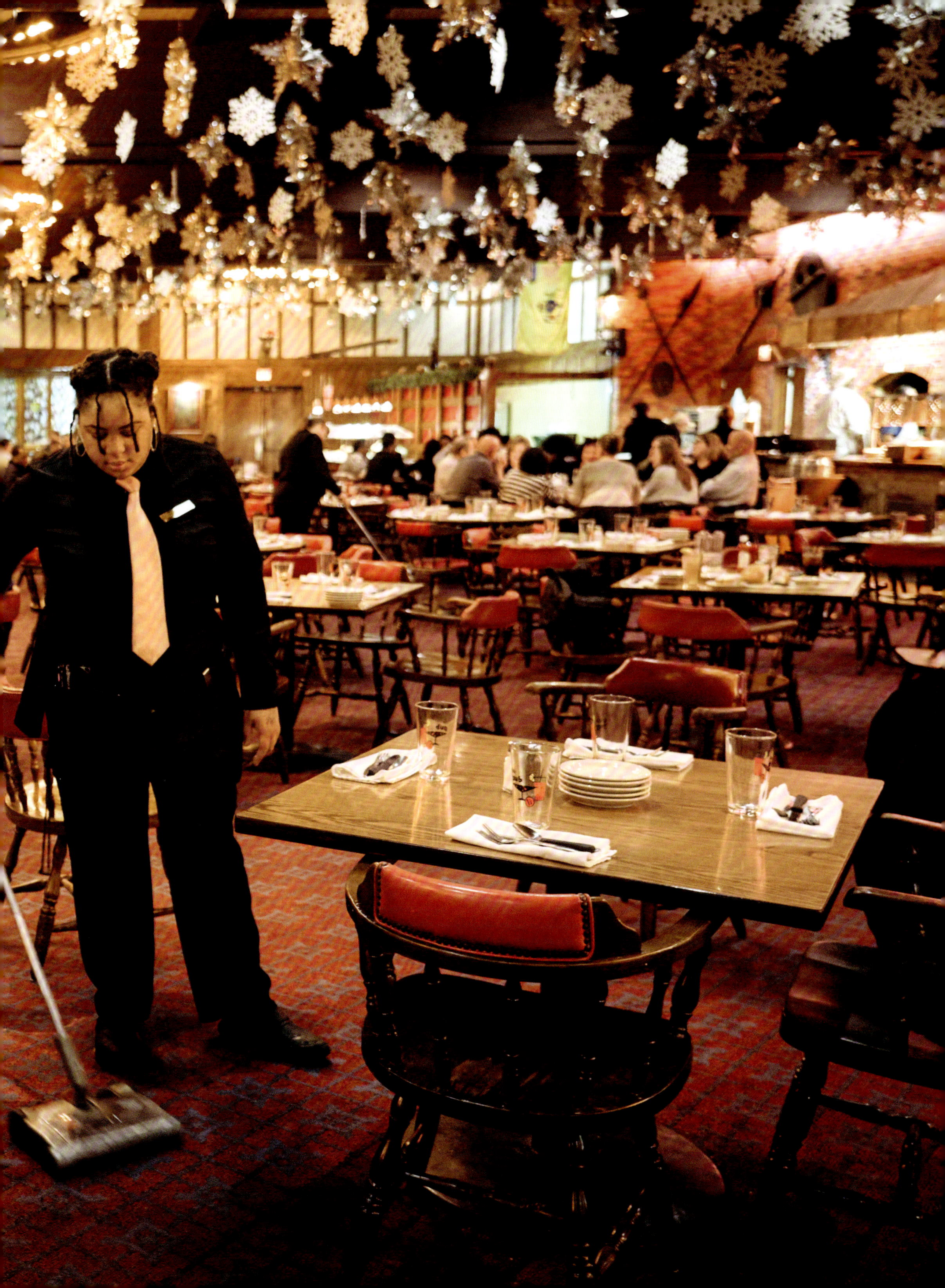

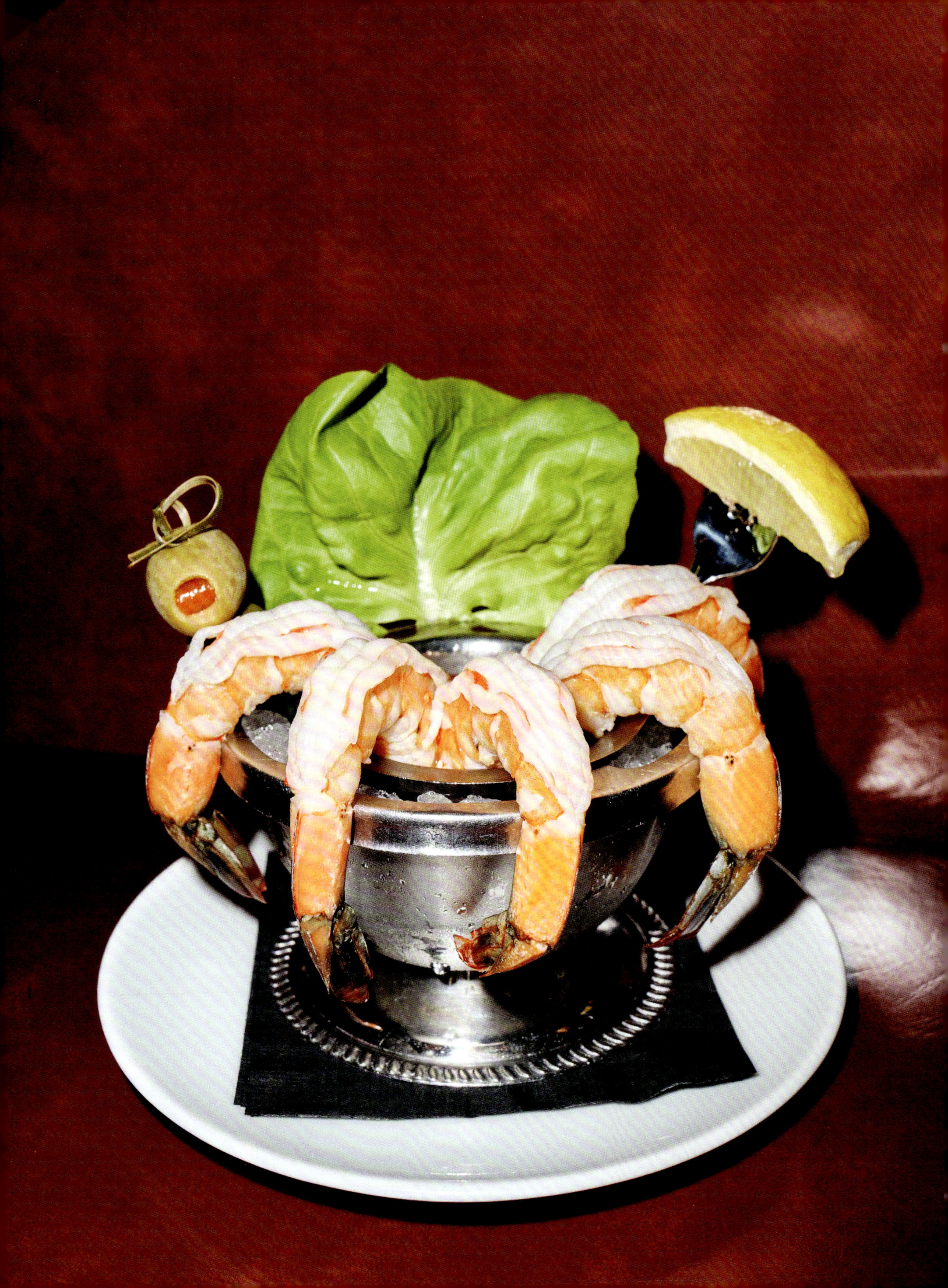

RECIPES

APPETIZERS

CHIPS & TRUFFLE-RANCH DIP

Serves 6

Chips

1 quart distilled white vinegar

½ cup Diamond Crystal kosher salt, plus more for seasoning

2 pounds Kennebec or russet potatoes, scrubbed

Neutral oil for frying

Freshly cracked black pepper

Dip

1¼ cups crème fraîche, preferably Kendall Farms

½ cup sour cream

¼ cup mayonnaise

1½ tablespoons black truffle oil, preferably Truff

1 tablespoon white truffle oil, preferably Truff

1 tablespoon minced black truffles

½ teaspoon garlic powder

½ teaspoon onion powder

½ teaspoon truffle salt, preferably Truff

Zest of ½ lemon

2 tablespoons roughly chopped fresh chives

1 tablespoon roughly chopped fresh flat-leaf parsley

A ridged potato chip and a creamy ranch dipper is a match made in store-bought heaven, but sometimes you feel like dressing up for the occasion. This homemade version, which came into my life at BERN'S (page 37), will take you from basic bitch to BOOM SHAKA LAKA. It's the kind of dip that will show you that truffle oil has its proper place, the kind of dip that I'm confident will finally make my dad, Poppa Heimy, cry out, "Good lord, son, I congratulate you on your success in life, and I'm proud of you for all of your accomplishments."

Prepare the chips: In a large bowl or gallon-size container, combine 1 quart water, the vinegar, and salt. Mix to dissolve the salt. Using a mandoline, slice the potatoes into ⅟₁₆-inch-thick slices and place immediately in the vinegar solution. Let the potatoes soak for 2 hours.

Meanwhile, make the dip: In a medium bowl, whisk together the crème fraîche, sour cream, mayonnaise, black truffle oil, white truffle oil, black truffles, garlic powder, onion powder, truffle salt, and lemon zest until smooth. Fold in the chives and parsley and refrigerate in an airtight container until ready to use. (The dip can be made up to 3 days in advance.)

Pour enough neutral oil into a large pot to reach a depth of 2 inches and place over medium heat until the temperature reaches 350°F. Meanwhile, use a strainer to drain the potatoes. Arrange them in an even layer on paper towels to absorb excess water; pat them completely dry with more paper towels and keep covered until the oil is ready.

Line a sheet pan with more paper towels and place a wire rack on top.

Working in batches to prevent overcrowding, carefully place a handful of potatoes into the oil. Cook until golden brown and crisp, stirring occasionally to encourage even browning, about 5 minutes. Remove the chips from the oil and drain on the rack. Immediately season to taste with salt and pepper while hot. Repeat with the remaining potatoes. Serve the chips warm with the chilled dip.

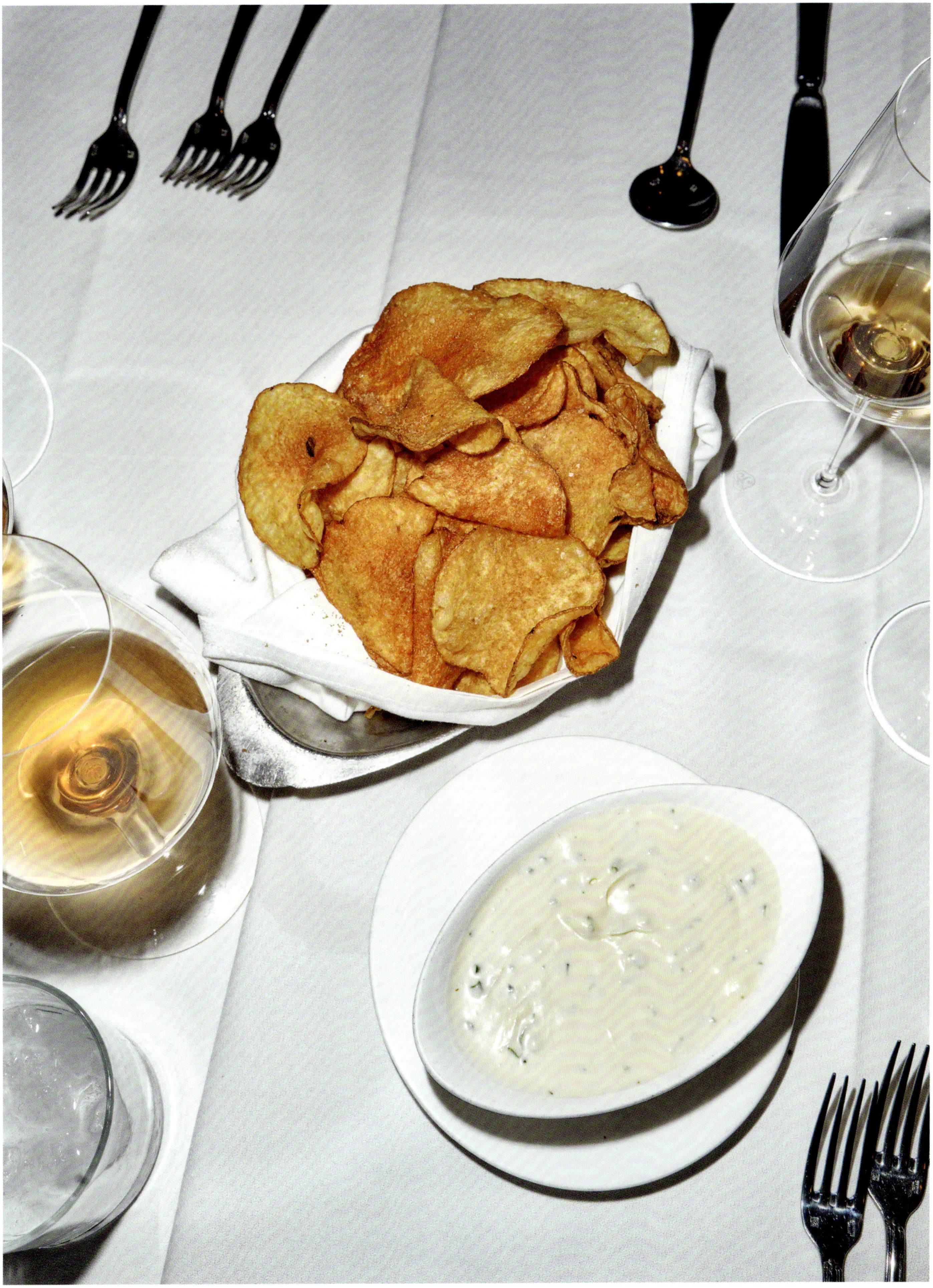

SHRIMP COCKTAIL

Serves 4

Cocktail Sauce
1 cup ketchup
1½ tablespoons prepared grated horseradish
2 teaspoons Frank's hot sauce
2 teaspoons Worcestershire sauce
½ teaspoon Old Bay seasoning

Shrimp
1 lemon
2 bay leaves
8 whole black peppercorns
2 teaspoons Old Bay seasoning
2 teaspoons Diamond Crystal kosher salt
1 pound large shrimp, peeled and deveined

Lemon wedges for serving

Shrimp cocktail is the quintessential steak house starter. I had no idea about this when I was a kid, but for some reason I would order it everywhere I saw it on the menu. The Seafood Shanty in Ocean City, Maryland, was one such place. We would eat there precisely once a year when visiting my grandparents. Those plump shrimp were always the best part of my summers. Once, I had a stupid sinus infection, and no amount of Momma's Afrin would clear the passages to let lil' Eric fully savor the primo sea meats on offer. It was a nightmare.

Perhaps that explains why I hold the shrimp cocktail in such high esteem. Or maybe it's the elegance of the shrimp's crescent shape; a scoop invented by mother nature. Whether plated simply with some curly parsley or dangled sensuously from the rim of a shiny metal bowl, as at RINGSIDE in Portland (page 192), the ShrimpCock (that's what I like to call it in front of new friends) is a welcome addition to every table.

Make the cocktail sauce: In a small bowl, whisk together the ketchup, horseradish, hot sauce, Worcestershire, and Old Bay. Cover and refrigerate until ready to serve. (The cocktail sauce can be made up to 3 days in advance.)

Prepare the shrimp: Use a vegetable peeler to remove the peel from the lemon in strips; save the peeled lemon for another use. Place the lemon peels, bay leaves, peppercorns, Old Bay, and salt in a large pot with 2 quarts water; bring to a boil over medium-high heat.

Fill a large bowl with ice water and set aside. Once the water starts boiling, add the shrimp and cook until just opaque, 2 to 3 minutes. Remove the shrimp from the pot with a slotted spoon and immediately transfer to the ice bath. Once cooled, about 3 minutes, drain the shrimp and chill on a plate in the fridge, covered, until ready to serve, at least 1 hour and up to 2 days. Serve the chilled shrimp on a platter with the lemon wedges and cocktail sauce.

SHRIMP DE JONGHE

Serves 2 to 4

In Chicago at the turn of the nineteenth century, a couple originally from Belgium decided to make a compound butter with what I can only imagine was every single thing in their pantry, pair it with some sizzling shraaaaamp, and name it after themselves. We encountered much de Jonghe along our travels, but I have to say, the one they serve at GOLDEN STEER (page 275) left the most lasting impression out of all the entries in what turned out to be a very competitive field of de Jonghe. Plus, I won fifteen dollars at video poker the moment after I popped a drippy shrimp down the ole hatch.

Make the butter: In a large bowl, use a spatula to fold together the butter, parsley, tarragon, wine, shallot, garlic, mustard, lemon juice, nutmeg, Worcestershire, paprika, and cayenne until thoroughly combined. Spoon the butter onto a sheet of plastic wrap, use the plastic to mold the butter into a 1-inch-thick log, twist the ends of the wrap, and place in the fridge to harden, about 3 hours (or until ready to serve).

Cook the shrimp: Preheat the oven to 400°F. Meanwhile, slice the butter log into ⅓-inch-thick pats. Place the shrimp in a small oven-safe casserole or skillet. Place the butter pats on and around the shrimp and sprinkle the breadcrumbs on top. Bake until the shrimp is completely cooked through and opaque, 8 to 10 minutes. Toast the baguette slices on a sheet pan in the oven, about 7 minutes. Squeeze lemon juice over the shrimp and serve in the casserole with the bread on the side for dipping.

De Jonghe Butter

1 cup (2 sticks) salted butter, at room temperature

½ bunch fresh flat-leaf parsley, stems removed and leaves finely chopped

10 to 12 fresh tarragon leaves, finely chopped

2 ounces dry white wine

1 small shallot, minced

2 garlic cloves, minced

1 tablespoon Dijon mustard

1 tablespoon freshly squeezed lemon juice

½ teaspoon freshly grated nutmeg

2 dashes Worcestershire sauce

Pinch of sweet paprika

Pinch of cayenne pepper

Shrimp

4 large shrimp (about 8 ounces), peeled and deveined

¼ cup breadcrumbs

4 slices French baguette

½ lemon

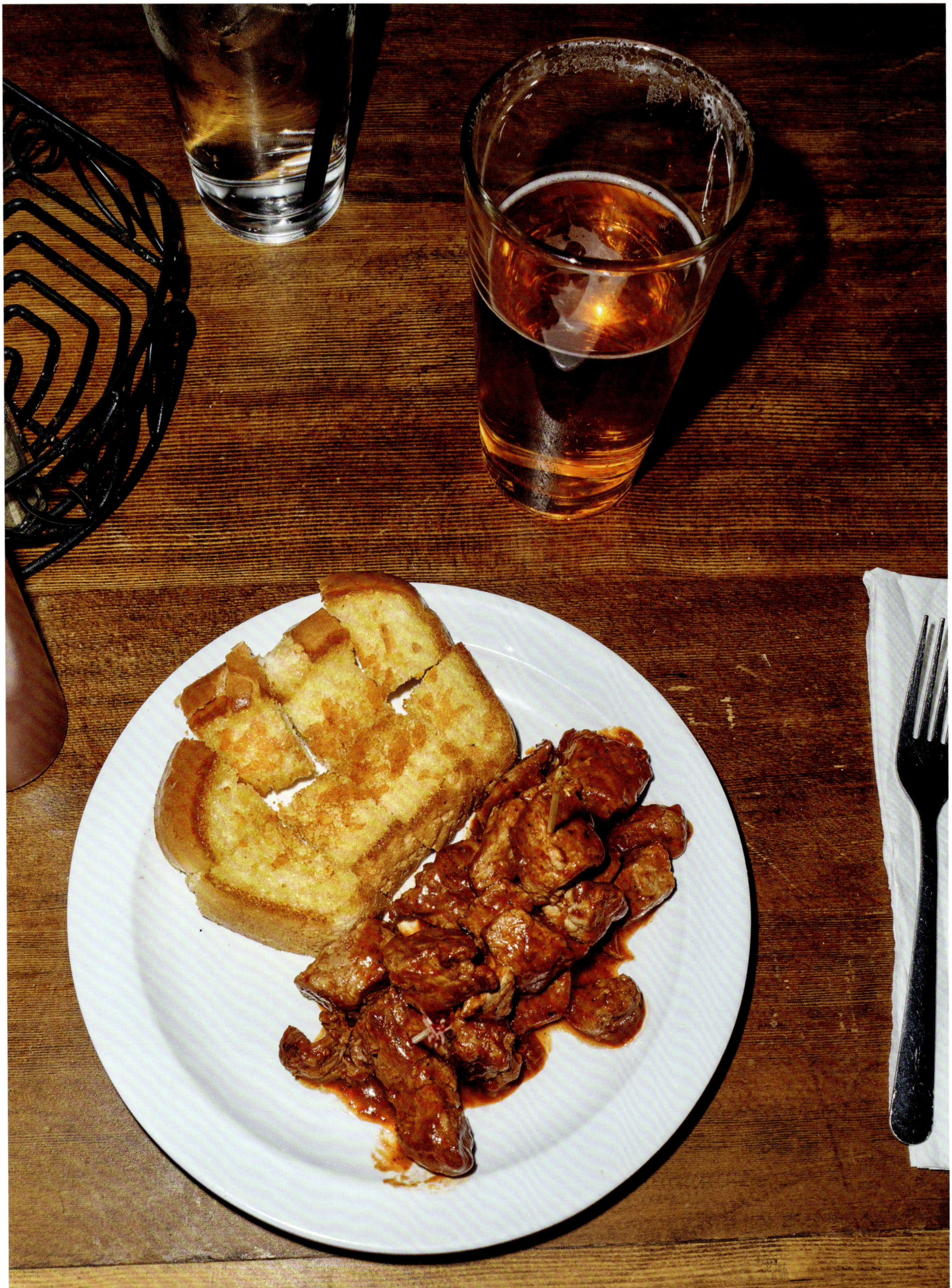

STEAK BITES

Serves 4

An ice-cold draft beer, some Cannibal Corpse on the jukebox, a performance by Portland's most gifted entertainers, and a plate of saucy, sweet, tangy Steak Bites: it's the best sensorial combo money can buy—and, at **ACROPOLIS** (page 200), it doesn't cost much money at all. What a place.

    This homage to their secret Steak Bites is a great belated use of those filets mignons Grandma gifted you from Omaha Steaks nine months ago. The only thing that matters here, really, is cutting the beef into cubes of the correct size, keeping in mind that you should be able to pop them into your mouth with a toothpick. The real star is the sauce.

One 8-ounce filet mignon, cut into ½-inch pieces

Kosher salt

½ cup Steak Bites Sauce (recipe follows)

Garlic Bread (page 48) for serving

Pat the filet mignon pieces dry and season with a few pinches of salt. Place a large sauté or cast-iron pan over medium-high heat. When the pan is hot, sear the steak pieces for 1 minute on each side, until deeply browned. Remove the pan from the heat and pour in the sauce. Toss to coat the steak pieces and serve immediately with garlic bread.

STEAK BITES SAUCE

Makes a generous ¾ cup

In a small bowl, whisk the potato starch with 1 teaspoon of the tamarind juice to make a slurry. Set aside.

1 teaspoon potato starch

6 tablespoons tamarind juice

¼ cup ketchup

In a small saucepan, combine the remaining tamarind juice, the ketchup, vinegar, molasses, red pepper flakes, ginger, cayenne, and soy sauce. Bring to a boil over medium heat while whisking, then lower the heat to medium-low. Simmer, continuing to whisk occasionally, until reduced slightly to the consistency of a thin gravy, about 3 minutes.

¼ cup white wine vinegar

2 teaspoons unsulfured molasses

¼ teaspoon crushed red pepper flakes

¼ teaspoon ground ginger

¼ teaspoon cayenne pepper

¼ teaspoon soy sauce

Whisk in the potato-tamarind slurry and let it simmer for 30 seconds. Remove from the heat and let the sauce cool and thicken, 15 to 20 minutes. Once cooled, whisk again until smooth. If not serving immediately, store in an airtight container in the fridge for up to 1 week.

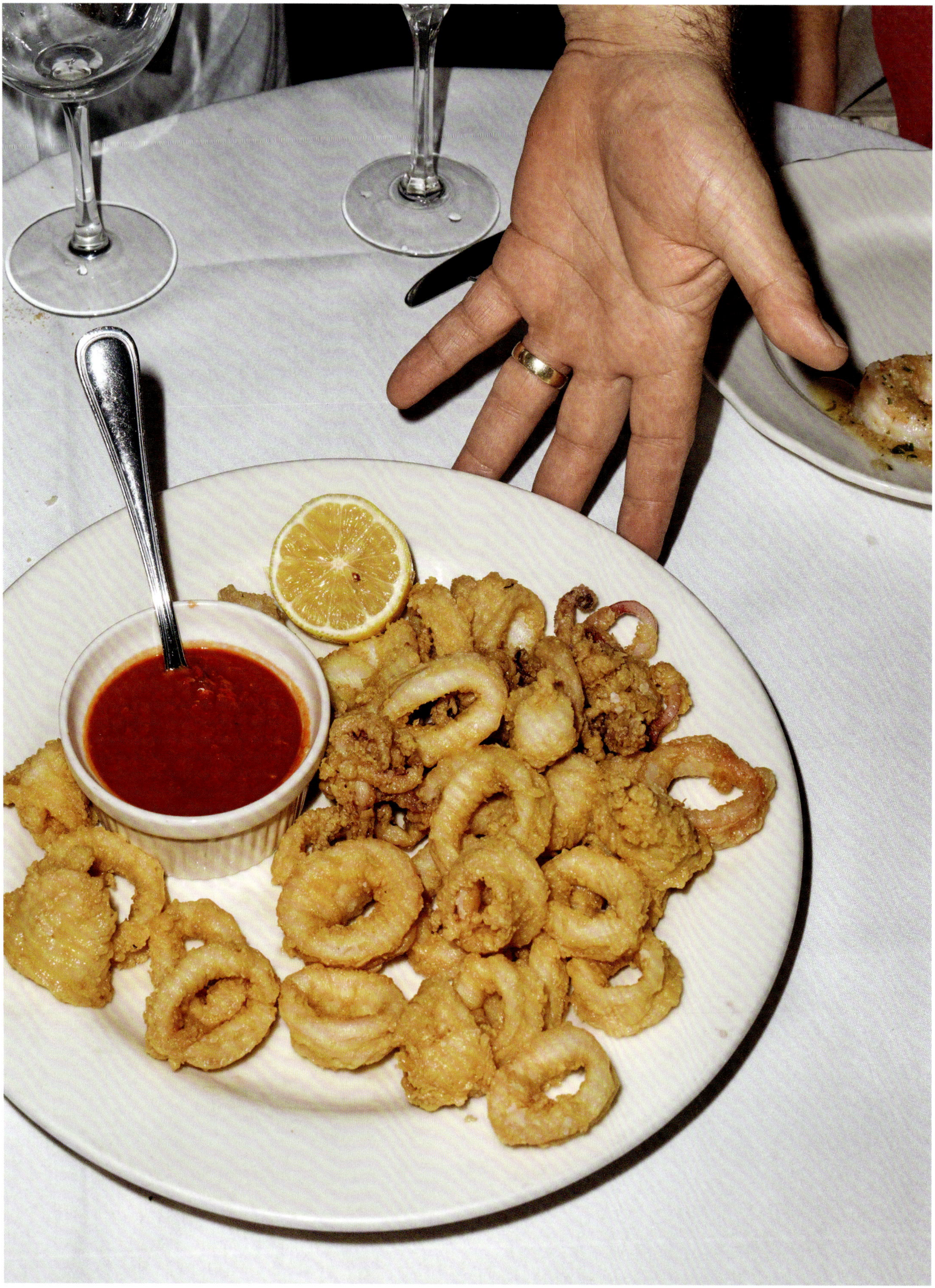

FRIED CALAMARI

Serves 4

I call it *galamar.* Living in South Philly for a good stretch of time gives you license to say it that way without somebody having to do something unpleasant to your kneecap. Anyway! What started as a rebranding exercise to get Americans to eat squid in the '70s turned into one of the most beloved dishes of the red sauce tradition. And when you get a chance to experience those lil' rings at *the* red-sauce steak house, **GENE & GEORGETTI** (page 100)? It's time to party like it's Sunday supper at Bobby Bacala's!

Make the marinara: In a small saucepan over medium heat, warm the olive oil. Add the onion and garlic and cook, stirring often, until fragrant and softened, about 5 minutes. Add the crushed tomatoes and red pepper flakes and season to taste with kosher salt. Bring to a simmer, turn the heat down to low, and simmer for 10 to 15 minutes, stirring occasionally and adding a little water if it begins to thicken too much. Remove the marinara sauce from the heat. (For a smoother marinara, blitz the marinara in a food processor until you reach your desired texture.) Tear the basil leaves and stir them into the warm sauce. Taste and adjust with salt as needed. Set aside and cover to keep warm while you prepare the calamari.

Make the calamari: In a large bowl, whisk together the flour, cornstarch, garlic powder, kosher salt, and black pepper.

Pour enough neutral oil into a medium pot to reach a depth of 2 inches and place over medium heat until the temperature reaches 375°F. Line a plate with paper towels.

Pat the calamari dry and toss in the flour mixture to coat. Working in batches to prevent overcrowding, place the calamari in a strainer and sift the excess flour over the bowl. Place the calamari in the hot oil and fry until golden brown, 1 to 2 minutes, moving them around in the oil to ensure they cook evenly. Remove the calamari from the oil with a slotted spoon or spider and transfer to the paper towel–lined plate to drain. Sprinkle some flaky salt on top and serve hot with the marinara sauce and lemon wedges on the side.

Marinara

2 tablespoons extra-virgin olive oil

⅓ cup finely diced yellow onion (about ½ small onion)

2 garlic cloves, crushed

One 15-ounce can crushed tomatoes

½ teaspoon crushed red pepper flakes

Kosher salt

2 fresh basil leaves

Calamari

1 cup all-purpose flour

¼ cup cornstarch

½ teaspoon garlic powder

½ teaspoon Diamond Crystal kosher salt

¼ teaspoon freshly cracked black pepper

Neutral oil for frying

1 pound calamari, cleaned and sliced into ½-inch rings

Flaky sea salt, preferably Maldon, for garnish

Lemon wedges for serving

STEAK CRUDO

Serves 4

Crudo Sauce
1 tablespoon ponzu sauce
1 tablespoon rice vinegar
1 tablespoon finely diced red onion
2 teaspoons sake
1½ teaspoons soy sauce
1 teaspoon toasted sesame oil
½ teaspoon extra-virgin olive oil

Steak Crudo
One 14-ounce New York strip steak
1 cup neutral oil for frying
4 garlic cloves, thinly sliced
Kosher salt
1 teaspoon toasted sesame oil
¼ teaspoon black sesame seeds
¼ cup arugula
½ avocado, pitted and peeled

When this stupendous creation hit the table at LA NACIONAL on our mission to Monterrey (see page 290), I was speechless. Part of the credit goes to the mezcal, but not all. In Mexico, at this bustling steak house with some of the most talented servers I'd ever met, I could enjoy Japanese tataki, Mexican aguachile, and Italian carpaccio on a single plate. Served at room temp, this recipe allows you to savor the char and chew of the thinly sliced steak and the bright sesame-soy-ponzu sensation that is the sauce.

Make the crudo sauce: In a small bowl, whisk together the ponzu sauce, rice vinegar, onion, sake, soy sauce, sesame oil, and olive oil. Set aside.

Make the steak crudo: Let the steak sit for about 45 minutes to come to room temperature.

In a small pot, heat the neutral oil over medium heat until the temperature reaches 350°F. Line a plate with paper towels.

Fry the garlic until it turns golden, stirring to help encourage even browning, about 45 seconds, then use a spider or a slotted spoon to transfer the slices to the paper towel–lined plate. (It's okay if they are not all golden; they will continue to cook as they cool.) Reserve the garlic oil for another use; it can keep in a lidded jar or airtight container in the fridge for up to 1 week.

Place a large cast-iron pan over high heat. Pat the steak dry with paper towels and season both sides to taste with salt. Fill a medium bowl with ice water and set aside. Line a plate with paper towels.

When the pan is hot, use tongs to sear the steak's fat cap without moving it, until golden brown and the fat has rendered, about 2 minutes. Sear the rest of the steak for 3 minutes total, flipping every 30 seconds, until nicely browned. Plunge the steak into the ice bath and chill for 1 minute. Thoroughly dry the steak and let it rest for 5 minutes on the paper towel–lined plate.

Slice the steak into ¼-inch pieces and arrange in a circle on a serving plate. Set aside 1 tablespoon of the crudo sauce and drizzle the remaining sauce and all the sesame oil over the steak slices. Sprinkle the black sesame seeds and fried garlic over the steak. Place the arugula in the center of the circle. Place the avocado over the arugula and spoon the reserved crudo sauce into the center of the avocado.

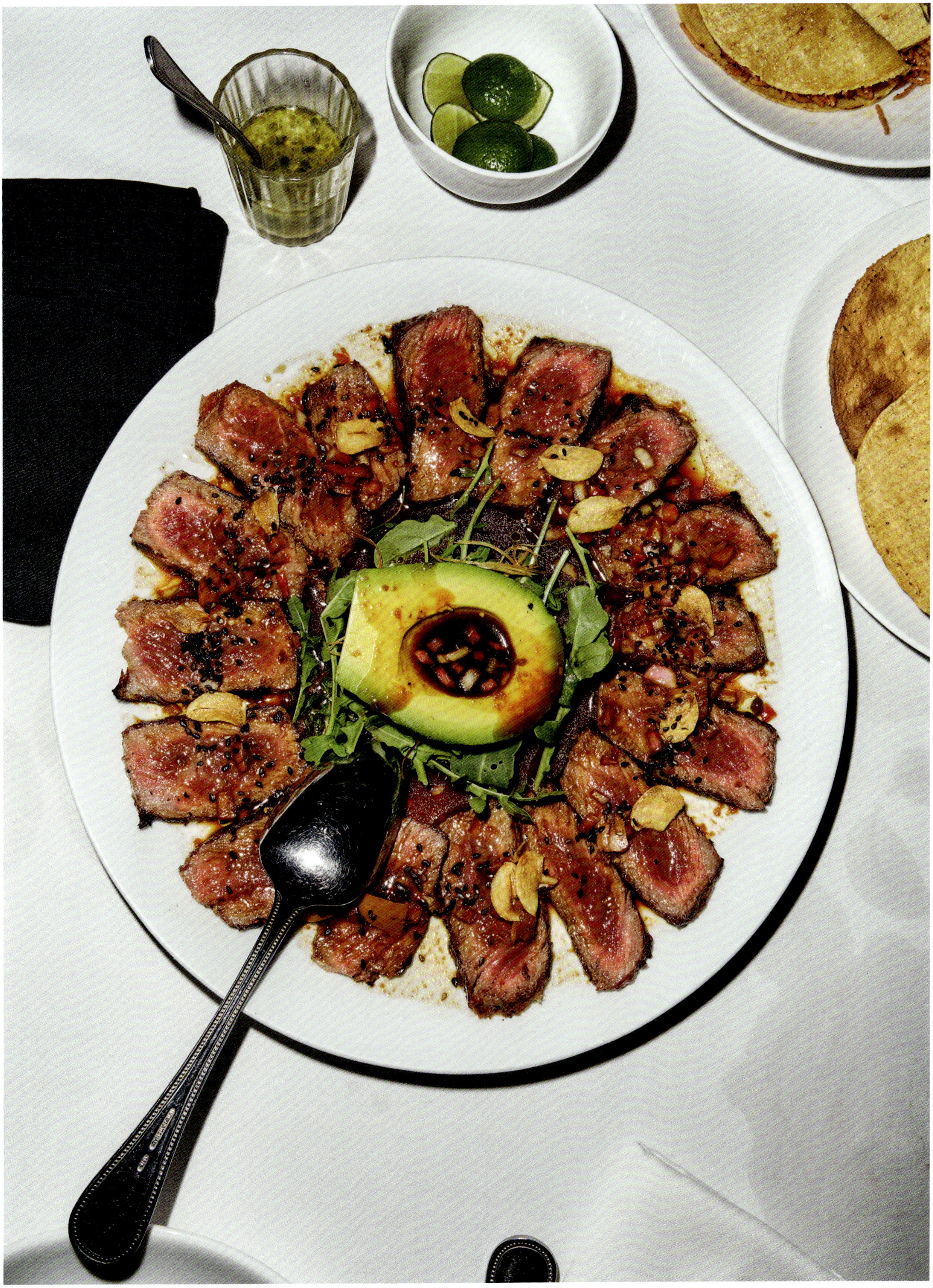

THE JOURNEY, PART III
CHIC

CAGO

CHICAGO AND I CLICKED THE MOMENT WE MET.

It felt like the Philly of the heartland, a real food mecca with hot dogs that go snap on every corner, deep-dish *and* tavern-style pizza, and unpretentious people. It's also a city where imaginative chefs can truly do their thing. The first time I went to Grant Achatz's three-Michelin-starred Alinea, it honestly changed everything for me.

Chicago is a town built on beef. A hundred years back, meatpacking in this city helped make it the industrial capital of America. Forty-thousand people worked at the Union Stock Yards on the South Side in 1920, when Chicago processed more meat than any other place on the planet. The stockyards were once called one of the wonders of the world. All that's left of them is a gate.

Years ago, Tim and I ate at a meat mansion called Bavette's with Dr. Steve Brule, aka John C. Reilly, while we were on tour, doing our best to entertain America with spoofs and goofs one city at a time. Chicago is John's hometown and, by that point, had become my second home. On our day off, he generously chartered a beautiful old wooden boat for the entire crew. We spent the ride down the Chicago River looking up, taking in the finest collection of architecture in the country.

There's nothing like experiencing Chicago from the river. That's how we started things off when I went back with the steak crew to document Gene & Georgetti, where some people say red sauce was born, and good old Bavette's.

The house-made meatballs at Gene & Georgetti.

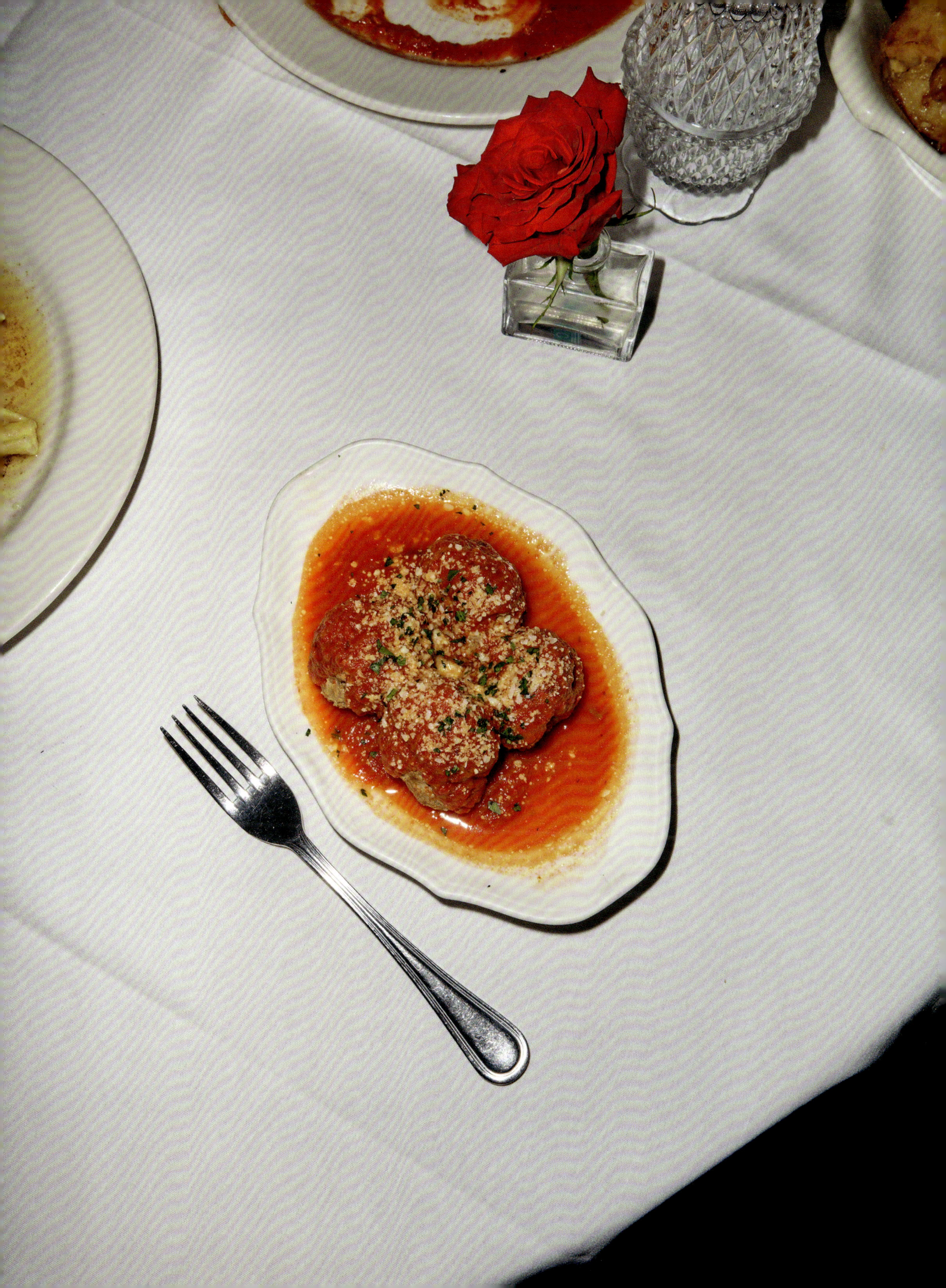

CHICAGO

GENE & GEORGETTI

BY THE NUMBERS

Opening year: 1941
Founders: Gene Michelotti
and Alfredo Federighi
Address: 500 North Franklin Street,
Chicago, Illinois 60654
House specials: Garbage salad;
Bistecca fiorentina

How is this for hospitality: Gene & Georgetti may not have a somm working the floor, but if you smoke Parliaments, like a certain someone in our group, there's a valet who will save you a trip to the tobacco shop by walking back over to his car and miraculously pulling out a fresh pack. Louis, you left for the night before we could properly thank you. You're the best!

Gene & Georgetti is a red sauce joint with a heavy emphasis on red meat. That wasn't the case at the beginning, in the '40s, when the owners did everything possible to hide any traces of their Italian heritage on the menu. Back then, bias dictated that Italian food was as inferior as the newly arrived immigrants who prepared and consumed it. Across the country. In Chicago, the seat of the nation's beef industry, serving steak was the safer bet.

Shifting gears, are you familiar with the Garbage Salad? It's a chopped salad and shrimp cocktail in one that you will find on many menus in Chicago. Gene & Georgetti invented it, so we went there to eat it. Meatballs and gravy, too. A little sausage and peppers. Sides of Bolognese. Baked clams and big reds from Italy and California, with most bottles on the reserve list printed without their vintages. I feel sorry for anyone who sits in that room and spends any time wondering whether the Gaja is from 1963 or 2023. Just have a martini. Maybe, if you are nice, the third-generation owner, Michelle Durpetti, will pull up a chair. She doesn't really do small talk:

> I have a love-hate relationship with this place. My grandfather Gene died at seventy-three due to stress from the restaurant. My dad now lives with Parkinson's, lung disease, and congestive heart failure, much of which was due to stress. The restaurant industry takes from you. It really takes.

But if it weren't for Michelle, a major event planner by trade, nobody would be eating at Gene & Georgetti tonight. In October 2019, she flew home from a wedding she'd organized in Puglia, Italy. Later that night, at four in the morning, she got a call from one of the servers. The restaurant was on fire. She says she remembers standing on the second floor, talking with the fire chief, and seeing the L train pass by through a hole the fire had burned into the wall. She was hit by this gut feeling—something that told her it could all go away from one day to the next. So she took the reins.

> Every time I walk in and see the wood paneling everywhere, I say to myself, *I mean, not exactly my vibe,* but you try to respect what is here, why it is here, and drive it forward.

There is no nightly pre-shift meeting at G&G. Everybody knows the routine by now.

STEAK HOUSE

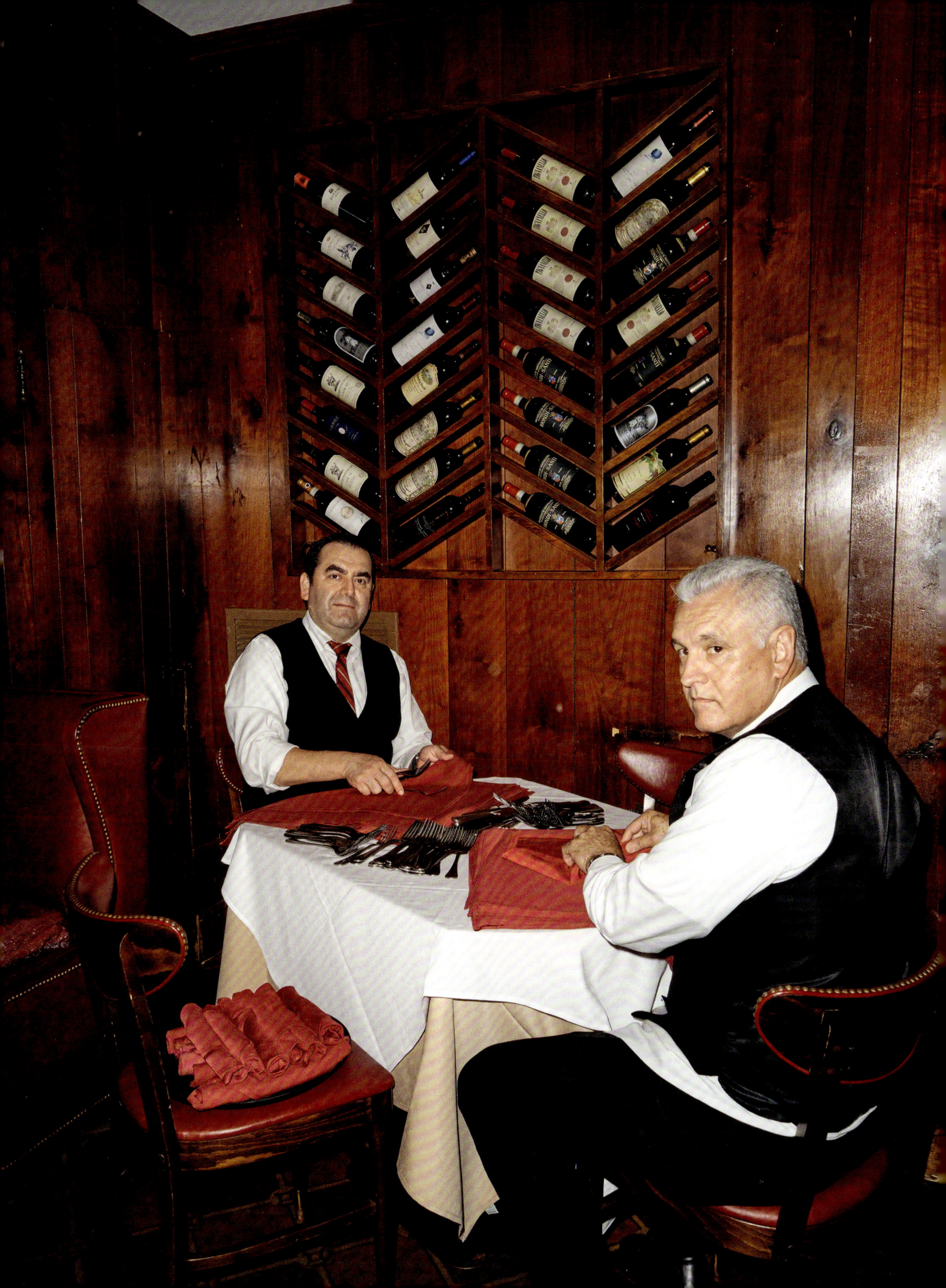

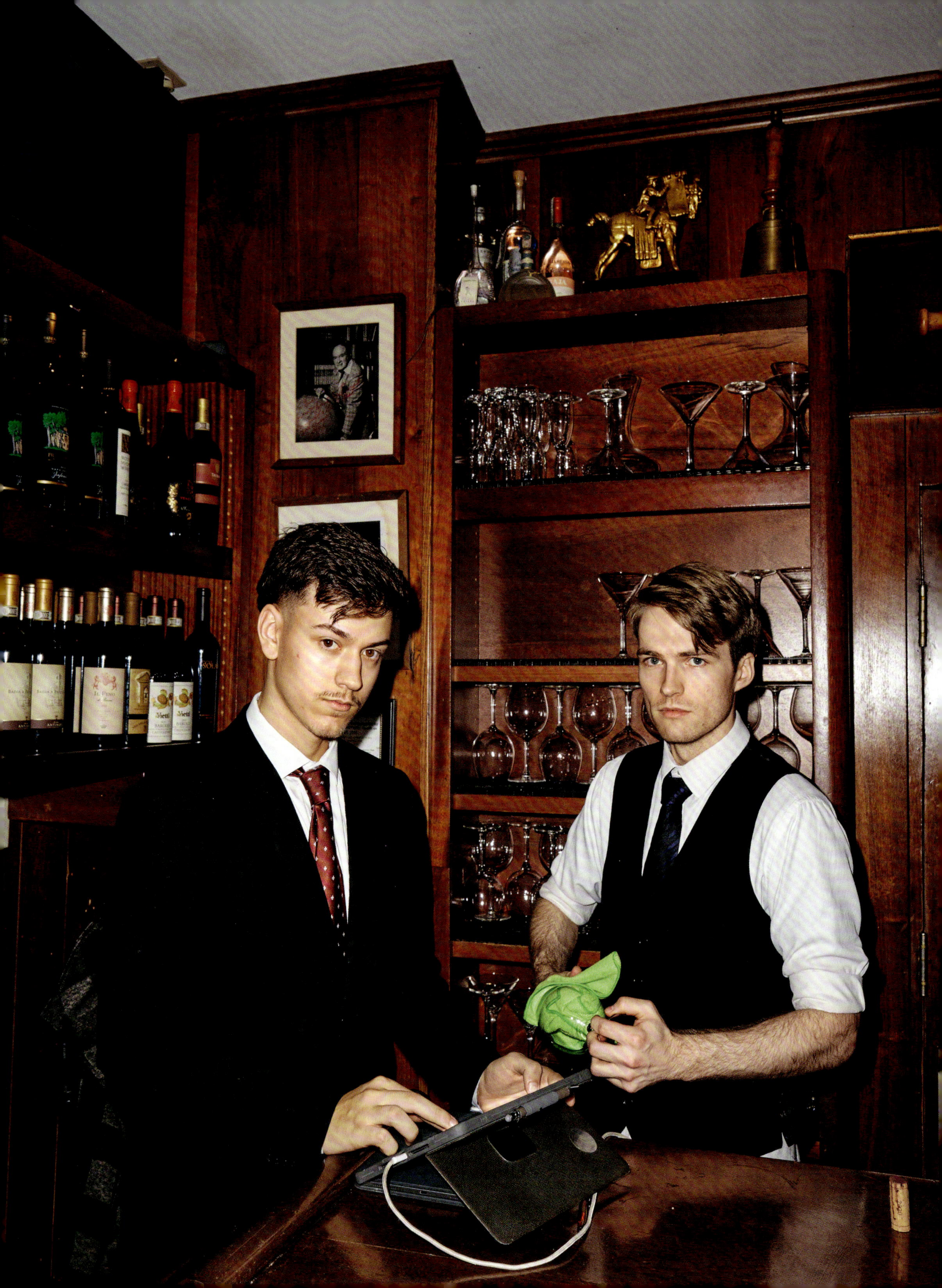

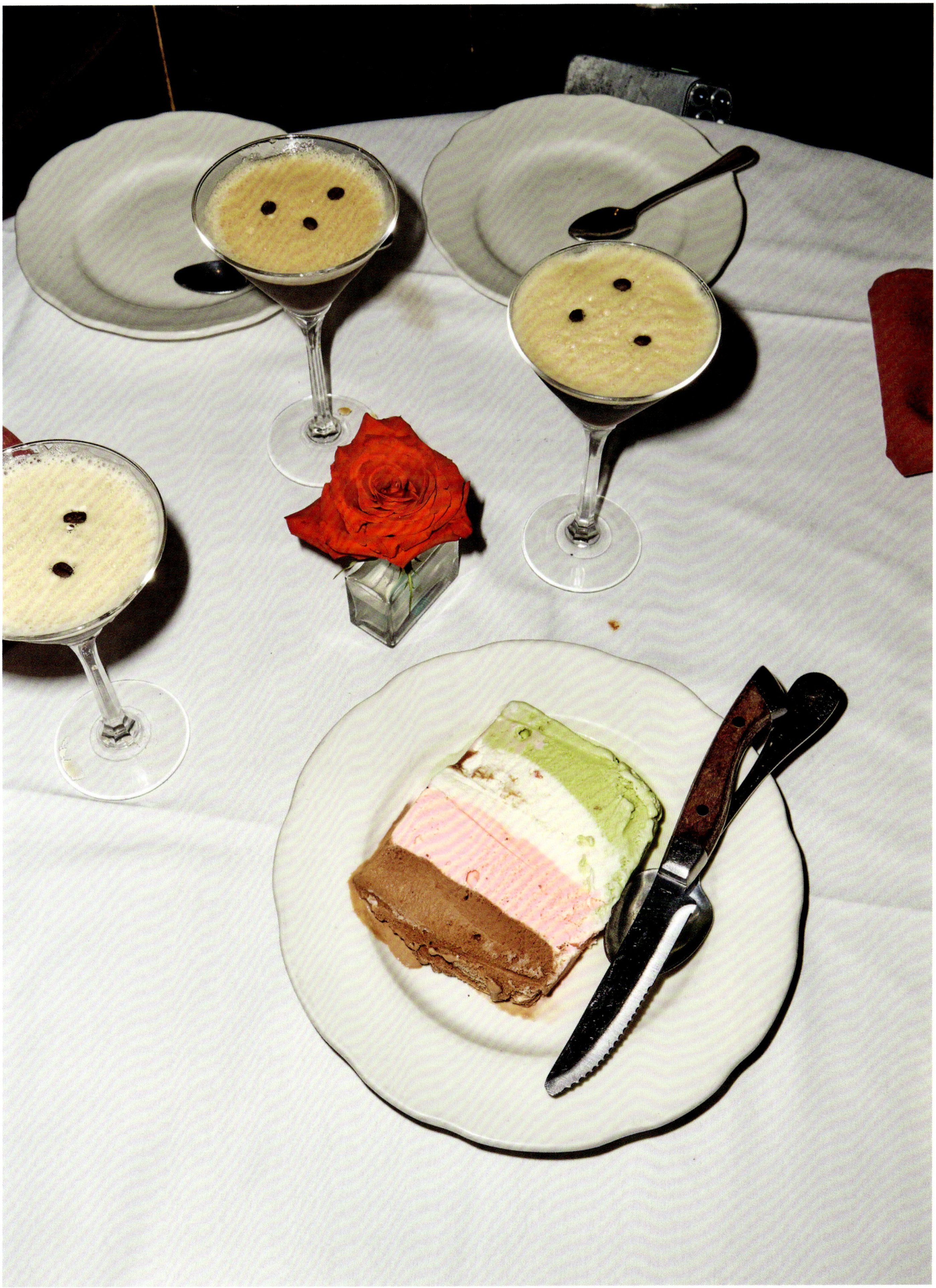

CHICAGO

BAVETTE'S

BY THE NUMBERS

Opening year: 2012
Founder: Brendan Sodikoff
Address: 218 West Kinzie Street, Chicago, Illinois 60654
House special: The whole dang menu!

We booked a late-afternoon reservation at Bavette's Bar & Boeuf so we could rest later on in the evening. It was nice and breezy and still light outside on a Sunday in Chicago, but we already understood that even a simple meal can get out of hand. These are some thoughts inspired by what transpired between when we walked in at 3:30 p.m. on the dot and the time our check was printed at 9:23 p.m.

I love a good neon sign. Bavette's doesn't have one. You could walk up and down Kinzie Street a million times without the slightest clue that six hundred people are in there, going hog wild on ultra-premium bites and sips. The owners don't do much press; we had to beg them to let us take photos. No chef or founder is listed on the menu. Not even on the website! They're legit and they know it.

Service captains like Erik Hampe are trained to lead with the work. Erik understands that there's a difference between asking someone in a group if they'd like another round and inquiring if they can *refresh that for you*. Erik knows what you want, even if you're like us and THINK you know everything, and he gets you to let him take the wheel without a single ounce of macho steak house gruffness. He knows how to make you remember something as unsexy as the saltwater brine that brings the shrimp cocktail to new heights: "The raw product is of such great quality that we'd be idiots to mess with it. We just put some lip gloss on and get the eyebrows done." As the Heritage Duroc pork chop hit the table, he told us, "We're shooting for the best ever with that one. But that doesn't require a fancy sauce—not full contour, just a little zhuzh." The velvety bone-in filet, a cut we didn't encounter at many other places, was outstanding. Erik, to no one's surprise, explains it best: "A dry-aged rib eye is like a Napa cab. This is a plush red Burgundy."

Don't overlook Bavette's stroganoff with its lovely demi-glace. Just the right amount of horseradish cream. Sweetness and depth. Like receiving a deep, dankadent hug. A vibe-hug. We were also embraced by the crab claws, the wedge, the rib eye, the fries, and many more delights.

After all that, you'll just want to have a quick spoonful of something sweet to reset and a digestif in consideration of the tummy. But of course, the desserts at Bavette's are HUGE! None of it feels like a stunt, though. There's a line between "This is bananas" and "That was stupid," and Bavette's toes it with a kind and light-hearted confidence.

Erik says that he still looks forward to the moment when he checks in on a table ten or so minutes after dropping off the lemon meringue pie (which looks like a freeze-frame of a tsunami) and gets to say, "Hmm. Looks like you did find some room."

Rib eye steak frites, beárnaise, hand-cut fries, and fresh flat-leaf parsley.

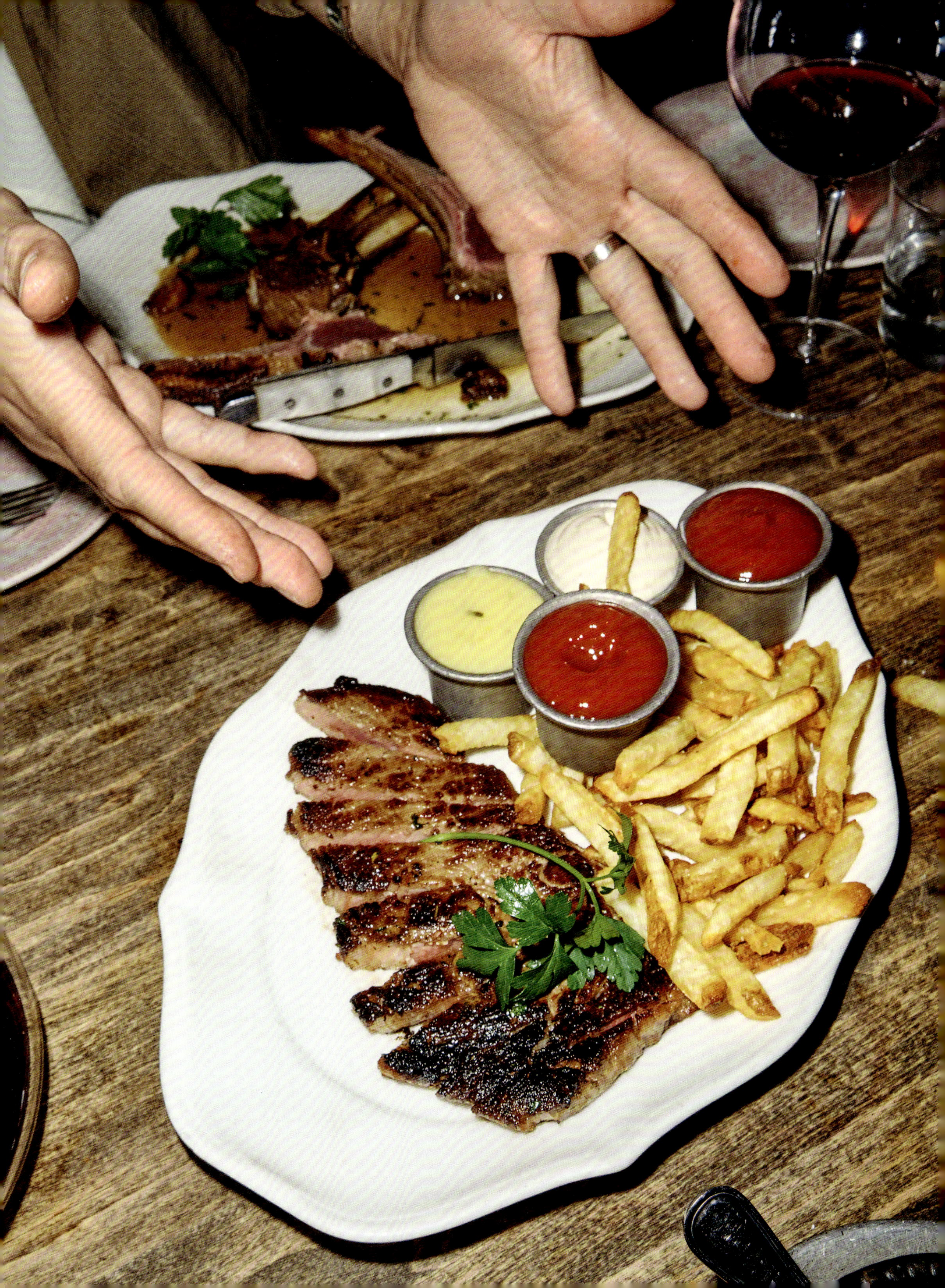

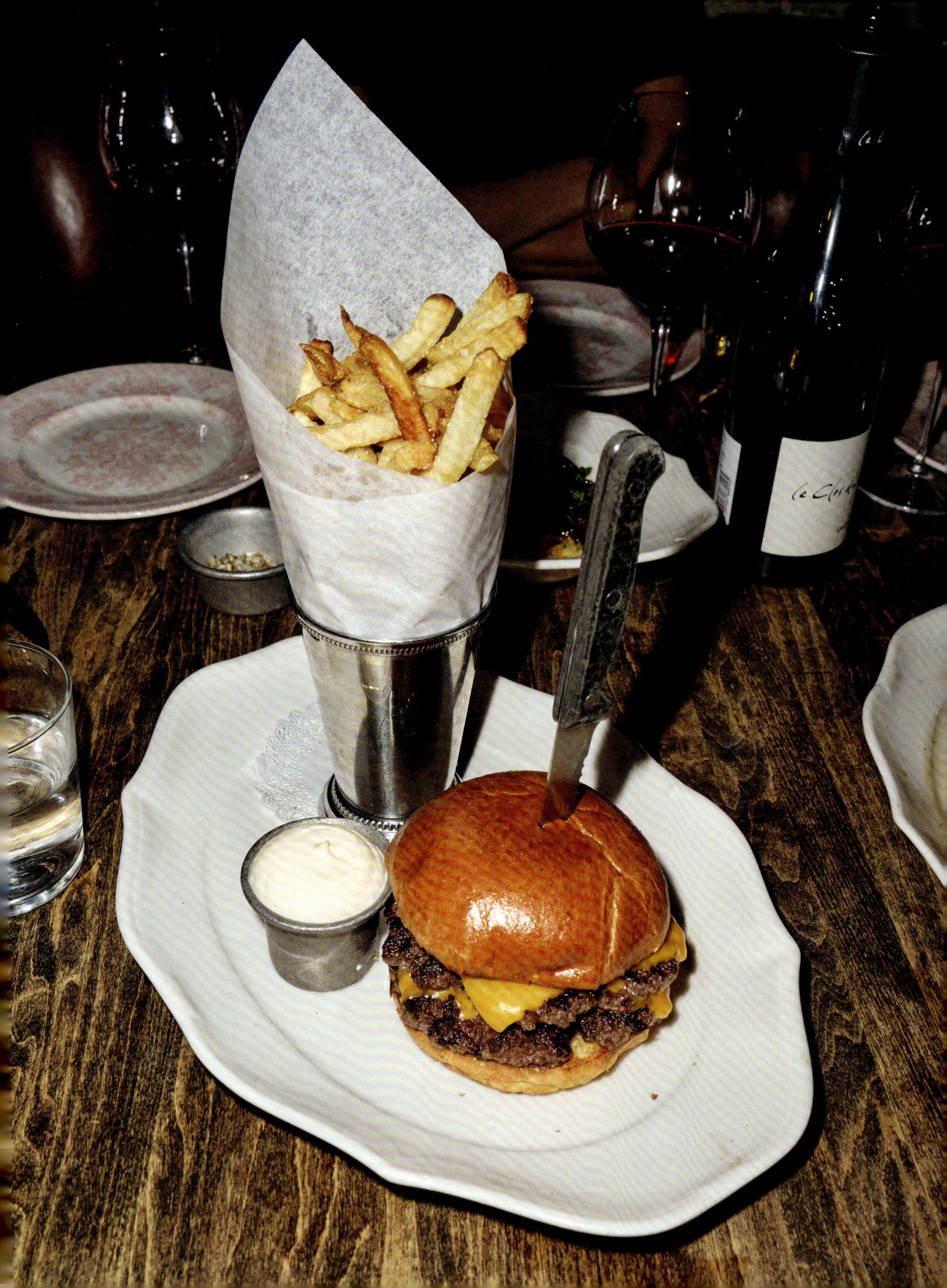

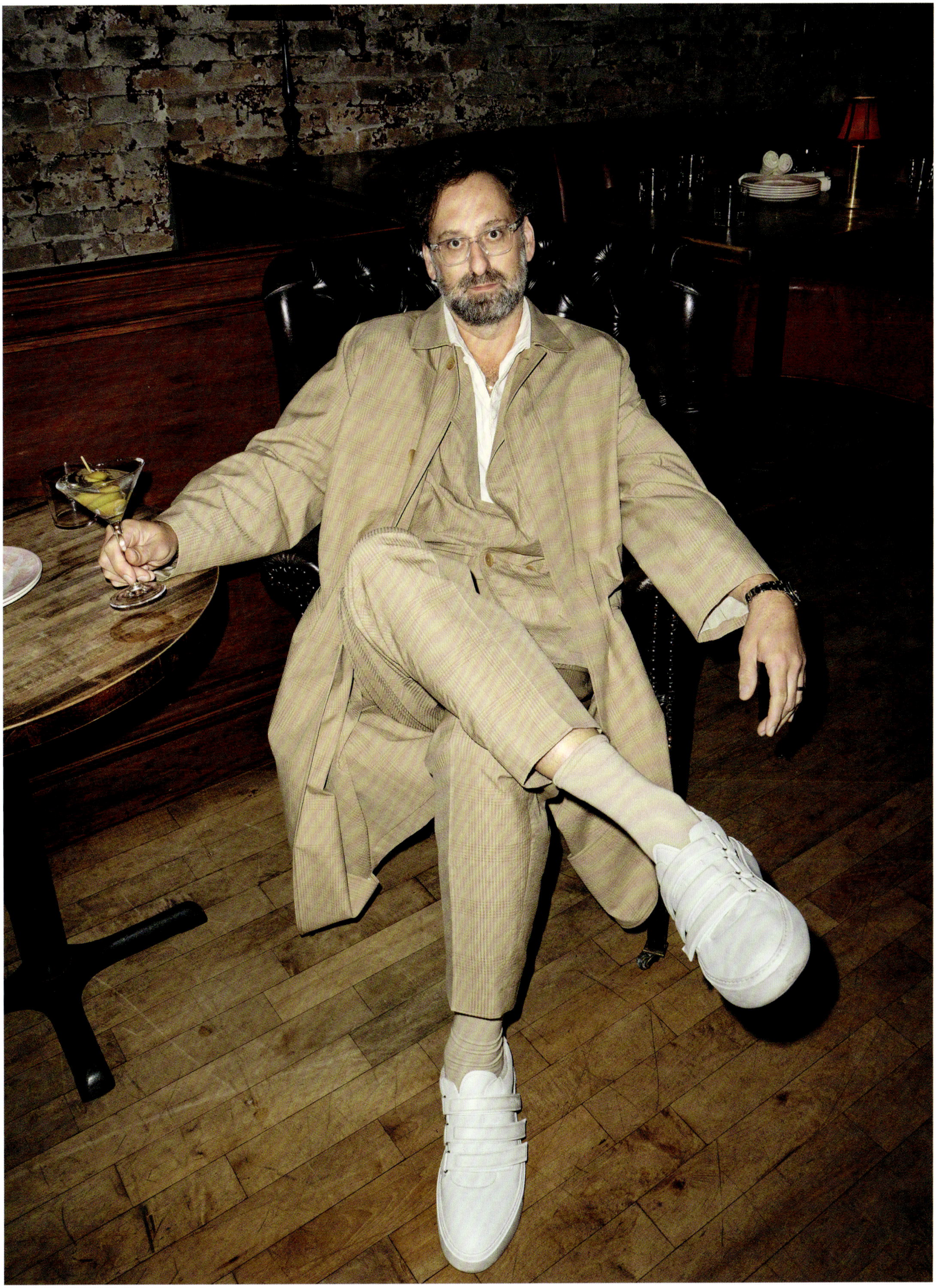

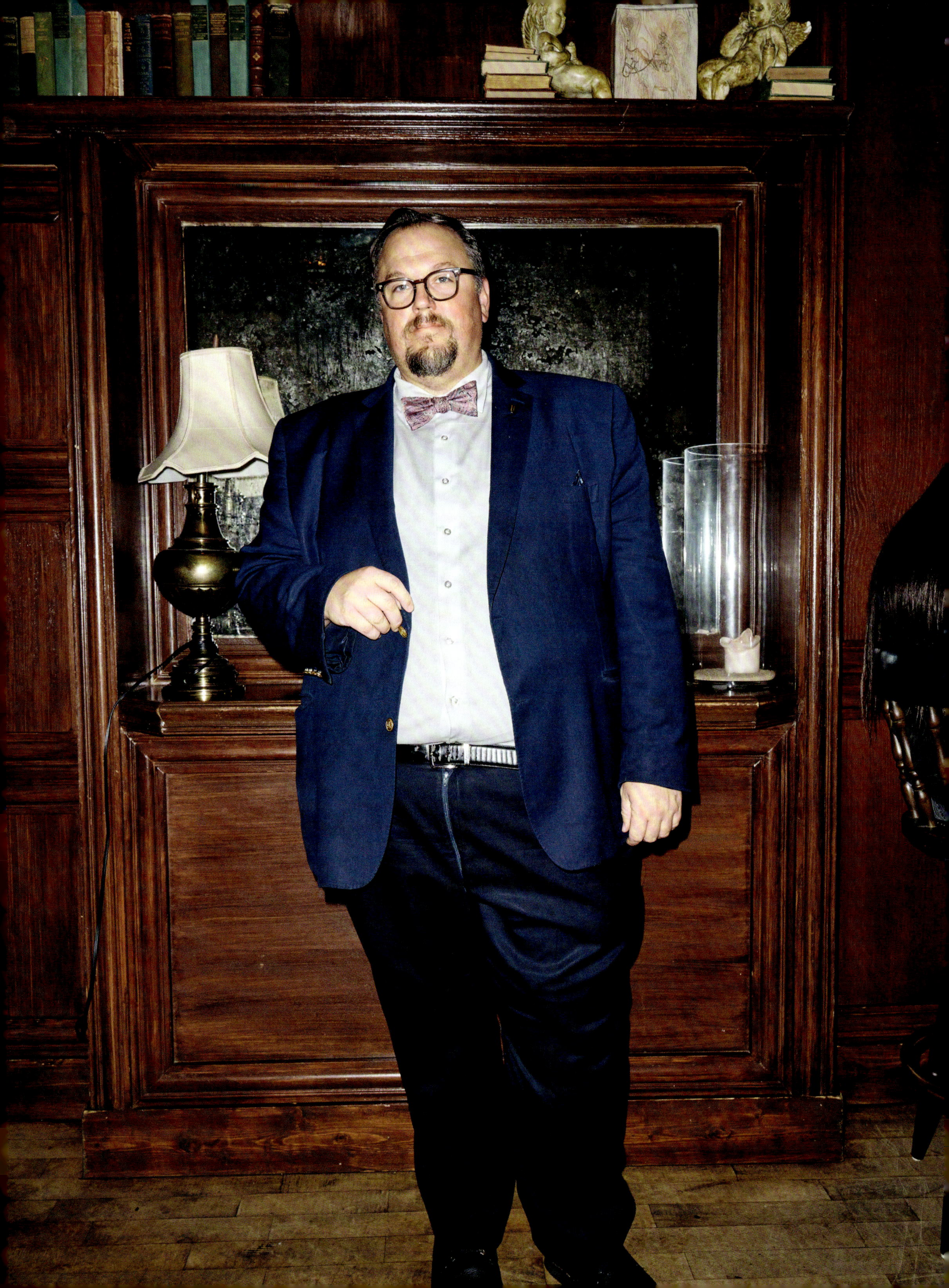

Erik Hampe—The Captain

"When you step into Bavette's, it's like a movie. Every time. Because it's the preservation of food and wine culture. Brendan [Sodikoff, the founder] trained under Alain Ducasse, who has preserved quite a few historic spots in Paris. In a lot of ways, that's what Brendan aspires to do at all his restaurants.

Consistency is the other important piece. Every day before service, we have the chefs prepare a random dish and then we walk through it together. Is the sauce broken? Is the salt slightly off? Whether it's steak houses or chef-driven places, I am not sure the majority of restaurants welcome too much feedback from servers. Here, it is strongly encouraged. Even the food runners are encouraged to say something whenever they see it: 'Hmm, looking a little weird today.'

We also obsess about food allergies. We aren't too cool to brush that off because we don't want people dying. It's great when people don't die.

By now, I know that the food is almost always going to be good. Really good. So I want the guest to walk away talking about how the experience with me took it to another level. It's important, especially in this dumpster-fire moment in history, to be able to step into a space where you are taken care of.

What really keeps me inspired, though, is dealing with the guest who feels like they didn't get their way. The other day we had someone who had dined at our location in Vegas. From the jump, they said flat-out that they didn't have a very good experience there and weren't expecting much greatness here, either. On the way out, they said, and I quote: 'Holy fuck, that was amazing.'

Sure, the days are long. But if you love what you do, that's what it takes. When I'm training new hires, I tell them, 'This is not the restaurant where you come to work tired and hungover after a bender. If that's your vibe, sweet, but this is probably not going to be a fit, honey.'

The routine might seem repetitive, but when you have a different mix of 550 personalities every night, each with their own varying degrees of shit going on, it couldn't be more exciting."

Erik has been working in restaurants for twenty-five years, ever since he moved to Chicago in 2000 to attend design school.

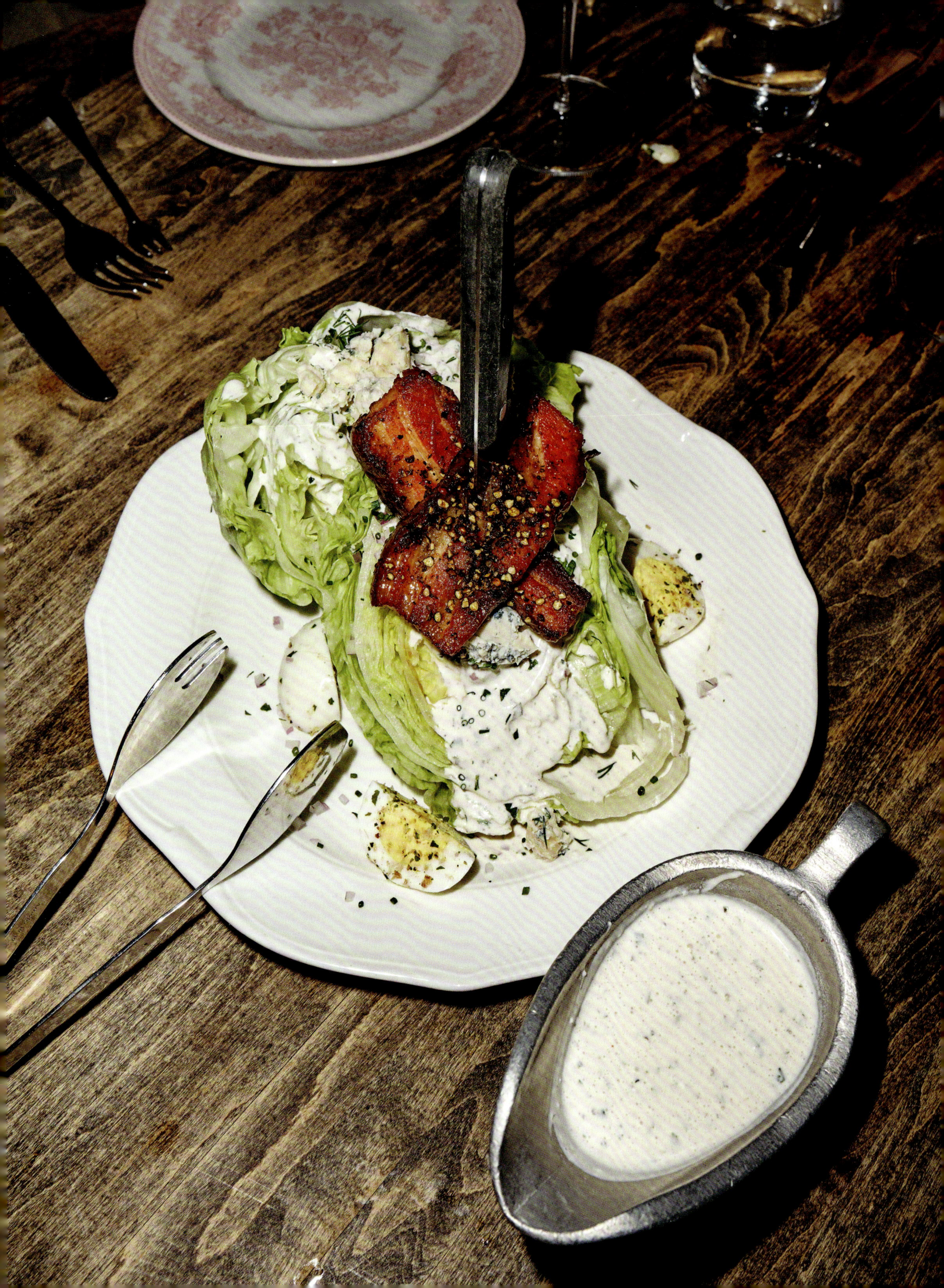

RECIPES

SALADS

THE MIGHTY WEDGE

They should make the wedge salad a mandatory still-life subject in every Painting 101 course—a study of shape and color, crunch and cream that lends itself to an endless number of expressions. I am including three different wedges from three different schools. You can decide what you are feeling this evening. Maybe you'll be moved enough to sketch what you make and send it to me so I can add it to my collection of salad art? I would like that.

    The Classic Wedge, inspired by the one served at RINGSIDE (page 192), features our spin on their secret Russian-style house dressing (which is also amazing with onion rings). The Mariani Wedge is pure sunshine, the kind of wedge you'd make if you lived on a stretch of Sonoma that is more pleasant than paradise (which Scribe Winery co-owner Kelly Mariani does). And the Korean Wedge is Seoul by way of Manhattan—it's everything I love about living in, and eating around, this country.

Serves 4

Tangy Dressing
⅔ cup ketchup
6 tablespoons distilled white vinegar
¼ cup sugar
3 tablespoons mayonnaise
1 teaspoon onion powder
¾ teaspoon Diamond Crystal kosher salt
6 tablespoons extra-virgin olive oil

1 head iceberg lettuce, cut into 4 wedges
1 cup crumbled cooked bacon bits
1 cup crumbled blue cheese
1 cup cherry tomatoes, sliced
2 hard-boiled eggs, chopped
2 cups sourdough croutons, such as the ones on page 116
Fresh chives, roughly chopped, for garnish

CLASSIC WEDGE

Prepare the dressing: In a medium bowl, whisk together the ketchup, vinegar, sugar, mayonnaise, onion powder, and salt. Once combined, slowly drizzle in the olive oil and whisk until emulsified. Refrigerate until ready to use. (The dressing can be made up to 2 days in advance.)

Assemble the salad: Place the iceberg wedges on a serving platter. Drizzle the dressing over each wedge. Top with equal portions of the bacon, blue cheese, cherry tomatoes, eggs, and croutons. Garnish with chives.

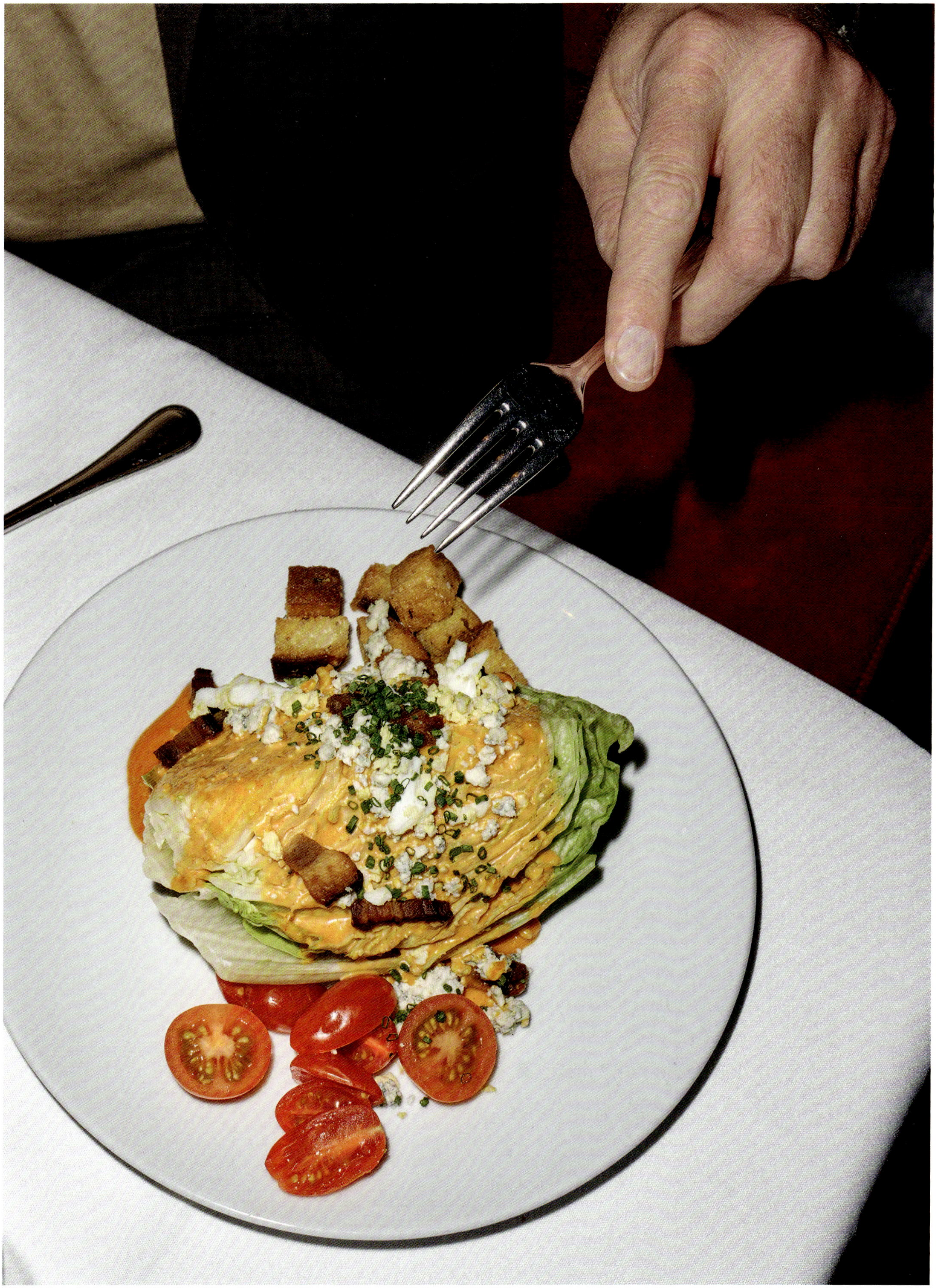

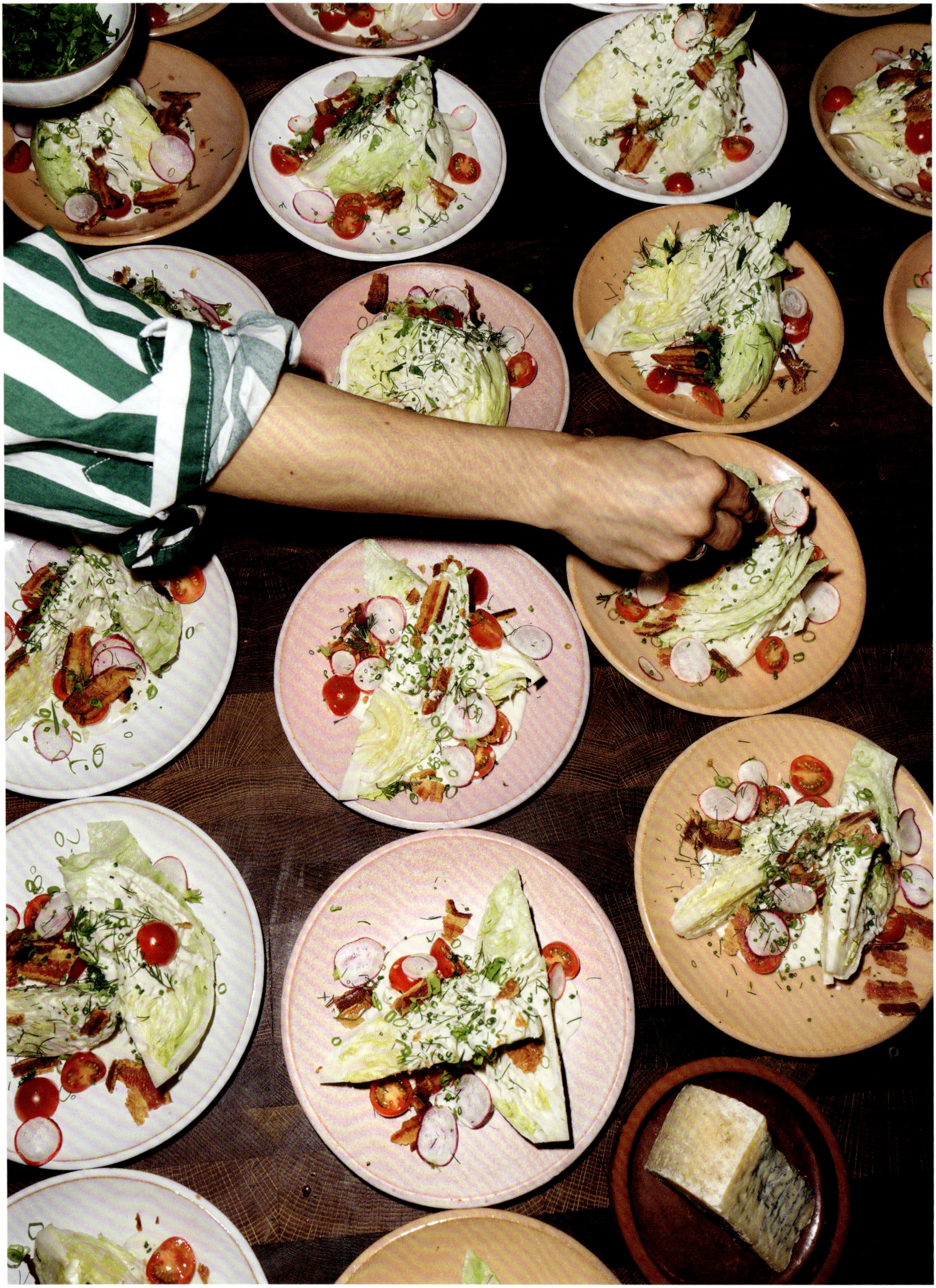

MARIANI WEDGE

Prepare the dressing: In a medium bowl, whisk together the crème fraîche, olive oil, vinegar, chives, garlic, salt, and pepper. Once combined, mix in the blue cheese to taste. Refrigerate until ready to use. (The dressing can be made up to 3 days in advance. If it thickens in the fridge, add a splash of water and stir to loosen the consistency.)

Assemble the salad: Place the iceberg wedges on a serving platter. Drizzle the dressing over each wedge. Top with equal portions of the tomatoes, radishes, bacon, and blue cheese. Garnish with the parsley and dill and finish with the pepper to taste.

Serves 4

Blue Cheese Dressing
1 cup crème fraîche
¼ cup extra-virgin olive oil
2 tablespoons red wine vinegar
2 tablespoons roughly chopped fresh chives
1 garlic clove, grated
½ teaspoon Diamond Crystal kosher salt
½ teaspoon freshly cracked black pepper
3 ounces blue cheese, crumbled

1 head iceberg lettuce, cut into 4 wedges
1 cup cherry tomatoes, sliced
1 small bunch radishes, trimmed and thinly sliced
8 slices thick-cut bacon (about 1 pound), cooked and chopped
Blue cheese crumbles
Fresh flat-leaf parsley, roughly chopped, for garnish
Fresh dill, roughly chopped, for garnish
Freshly cracked black pepper

KOREAN WEDGE

Prepare the dressing: In a food processor, add the tofu, sesame oil, vinegar, miso, soy sauce, garlic, sugar, salt, and gochugaru and blitz until thoroughly combined and smooth. Refrigerate until ready to use. (The dressing can be made up to 5 days in advance.)

Assemble the salad: Place the iceberg wedges on a serving platter. Drizzle the dressing over each wedge. Top with equal portions of the bacon, cherry tomatoes, and crispy fried onions. Garnish with chives.

Serves 4

Tofu Sesame Dressing
1 cup silken tofu
6 tablespoons toasted sesame oil
¼ cup rice vinegar
3 tablespoons white miso paste
2 tablespoons soy sauce
5 garlic cloves, grated
2 teaspoons sugar
¾ teaspoon Diamond Crystal kosher salt
½ teaspoon gochugaru

1 head iceberg lettuce, cut into 4 wedges
8 slices triple-thick butcher-cut bacon (about 1 pound), preferably Neuske's, diced and cooked
2 cups cherry tomatoes, sliced
1 cup crispy fried onions, preferably French's
Fresh chives, chopped, for garnish

SALADS

CLASSIC CAESAR

Serves 4

Sourdough Croutons
Neutral oil for frying
4 cups cubed day-old sourdough bread (about ½ round loaf), crusts removed
Kosher salt

Dressing
1 tablespoon Dijon mustard
1 egg yolk
2 garlic cloves, minced
3 or 4 oil-packed anchovies, smashed into a paste
5¼ teaspoons neutral oil
¾ teaspoon extra-virgin olive oil
1 teaspoon Worcestershire sauce
2 dashes Tabasco sauce
1 dash red wine vinegar
Juice of ½ lemon
1 tablespoon freshly grated Parmesan cheese

1 head romaine lettuce, torn into pieces
Freshly cracked black pepper

For the longest time, the idea of making a Caesar dressing intimidated me. I mean, just think about the showmanship required to pull off the incredible tableside version at **GOLDEN STEER** (page 275) in Vegas. I am here to tell you that you can do it. These days, the Caesar is a staple of the Sunday Red-Sauce Suppers I host at my house in Los Angeles. Sometimes when it's just me and the cats, I put on my tux, roll a cart into the living room, and do a routine show for them. They don't really say much, but I toss them an anchovy, and I think they love the experience.

Make the croutons: Pour enough neutral oil into a heavy Dutch oven or deep stockpot to reach a depth of 3 inches and place over medium-low heat until the temperature reaches 350°F. Have a spider or a slotted spoon handy and line a sheet pan with paper towels. Working in batches to prevent overcrowding and to keep the oil temperature consistent, add the bread cubes to the hot oil and fry until golden brown, about 2 minutes. Use the spider or slotted spoon to transfer the croutons to the paper towel–lined sheet pan and season to taste with salt immediately.

Make the dressing: In a large bowl, whisk together the mustard, egg yolk, garlic, and anchovies. Slowly whisk in the oils until emulsified and the desired thickness is reached. Add the Worcestershire, Tabasco, vinegar, lemon juice, and Parmesan and whisk until combined.

In a large salad bowl, toss the romaine and croutons with the dressing, using your hands to coat it well. Give the salad a few cracks of black pepper to taste.

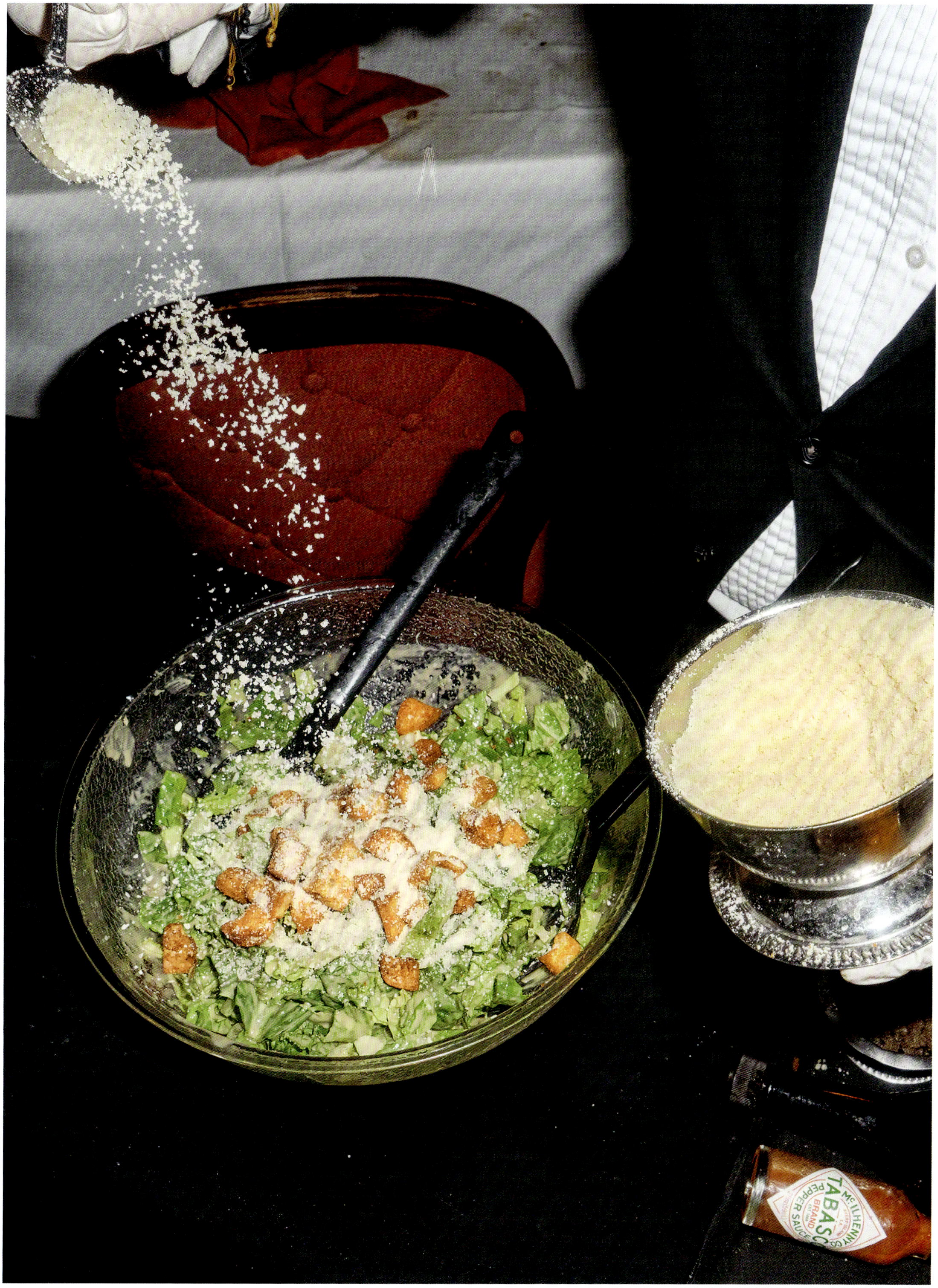
McILHENNY CO
TABASCO
BRAND
PEPPER SAUCE

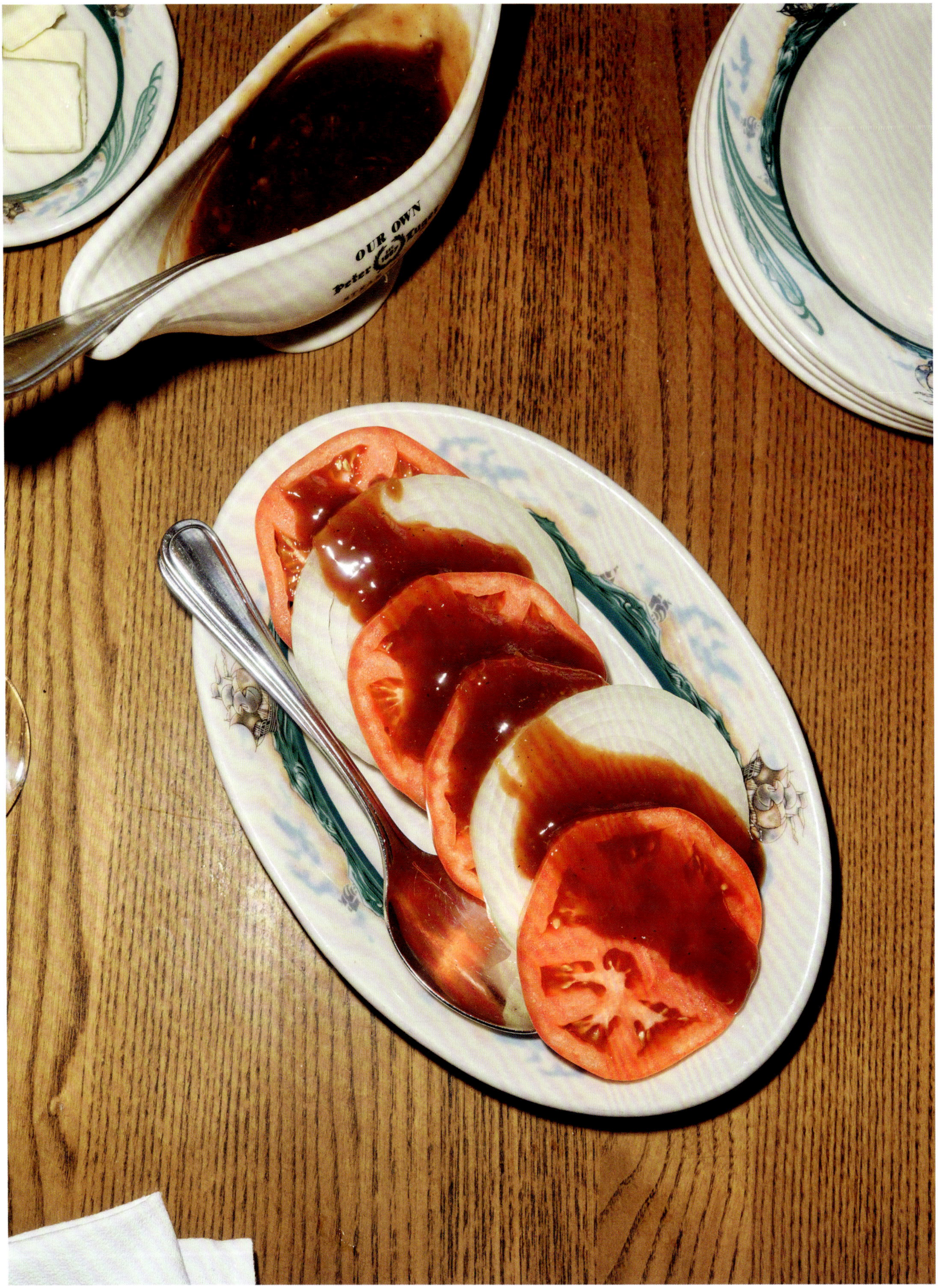
OUR OWN

TOMATOES & ONIONS

Serves 2

This absolute classic from PETER LUGER (page 62) will obviously taste incredible if you use a juice-bomb summer heirloom tomato from the local farmers' market. But you know what? A firm biggin from the deli might be even better. The regulars at Luger like to get a side of thick-cut bacon, chop up the onion and tomato, and mix it all up with the iconic Luger sauce—which we have re-created here for your pleasure as well.

The night before serving, prepare the onions: Place the onions and salt in a large bowl and cover with water. Stir to dissolve the salt and refrigerate, covered, overnight.

Make the sauce: In a small saucepan over medium heat, warm the olive oil. Add the garlic and shallot and cook, stirring often, until translucent, 3 to 5 minutes. Add the brown sugar and stir continuously until the sugar begins to caramelize and bubble in the oil, 1 to 2 minutes. Add the tomato sauce, both vinegars, the Worcestershire, salt, and pepper. Stir to combine. Let the sauce come to a simmer, then turn the heat down to low. Cook, stirring often to prevent it from burning, until reduced slightly and darkened in color, 10 to 15 minutes. Remove from the heat and let the sauce cool to room temperature. Taste and adjust with salt as needed. Transfer to an airtight container and refrigerate until chilled, 2 hours or up to overnight.

When ready to serve, drain the onions and pat dry. Layer the tomatoes and onions on a plate and spoon the chilled sauce over the salad.

Salad
1 large sweet onion, such as Vidalia, cut crosswise into ¼-inch-thick slices

½ teaspoon Diamond Crystal kosher salt

1 firm beefsteak tomato, cored and cut crosswise into ¼-inch-thick slices

Luger-Style Sauce
2 tablespoons extra-virgin olive oil

2 garlic cloves, minced

1 small shallot, minced

3 tablespoons brown sugar

½ cup canned tomato sauce

3 tablespoons apple cider vinegar

2 tablespoons distilled white vinegar

1 tablespoon Worcestershire sauce

1½ teaspoons Diamond Crystal kosher salt, plus more for seasoning

⅛ teaspoon freshly cracked black pepper

GARBAGE SALAD

Serves 4

The Garbage Salad is anything but. What we have here is one of the most infamous members of the throw-it-all-in-the-bowl salad tradition, and the pride and joy of GENE & GEORGETTI (page 100) in Chicago. If there ever was a recipe you could adapt, it's this one.

In a large bowl, combine the lettuce, salami, mozzarella, pimiento, onion, radishes, celery, and Parmesan.

In a small bowl, add the garlic and a pinch of salt and black pepper and use a fork to mash them together. Whisk in the vinegar until combined, then whisk constantly while slowly pouring in the olive oil until just emulsified. Taste and adjust with salt and pepper as needed.

Pour the dressing over the salad and toss until well coated. Divide the salad among four plates and top each with a shrimp.

¼ head iceberg lettuce, roughly chopped

3 ounces Toscano salami, sliced into ¼-inch-wide strips

3 ounces mozzarella or provolone, sliced into ¼-inch-wide strips

2 ounces (1 whole) pimiento pepper, sliced into long strips

¼ small red onion, thinly sliced

4 radishes, trimmed and thinly sliced

½ stalk celery, chopped

2 tablespoons freshly grated Parmesan cheese

1 garlic clove, minced

Kosher salt and freshly cracked black pepper

2 tablespoons red wine vinegar

6 tablespoons extra-virgin olive oil

4 jumbo shrimp, peeled, deveined, cooked, and chilled

TOMATO & STONE FRUIT SALAD

Serves 4

½ cup neutral oil

⅓ cup sherry vinegar

2 tablespoons sugar

1 tablespoon toasted sesame oil

1½ teaspoons soy sauce

1 pound heirloom tomatoes, cut into bite-size wedges

1 pound assorted stone fruit, such as peaches, plums, and apricots, pitted and cut into bite-size wedges

Fresh flat-leaf parsley for garnish

Torn fresh basil leaves for garnish

Toasted sesame seeds for garnish

Right here is my desert-island salad. I wake up every day craving it. Not kidding. Luckily, I live five minutes from MAJORDOMO (page 243) and can order it every night of peach and plum season if I want. It reminds me of the salad my mom makes from her garden that is similarly juicy and balanced. For both, I will pick up my bowl and drink the fruit juice dressing. Remember that tomatoes are a fruit, too, dude.

In a large bowl, whisk together the neutral oil, vinegar, sugar, sesame oil, and soy sauce until the sugar dissolves. Add the tomatoes and stone fruit and toss to combine; let stand for at least 10 minutes or up to 30 minutes.

Transfer the salad to a serving bowl and garnish with parsley and basil. Sprinkle with sesame seeds before serving.

BACON ROASTED TOMATO

Serves 4

Under the peppery watercress and thick-cut bacon in this salad, you will discover a cooked tomato that is just waiting to share its piping hot essence with you. This is a BLT as I've never experienced before, and it's inspired by the one that keeps me coming back to BAVETTE'S (page 104) time and again.

2 slices thick-cut bacon

1 tablespoon maple syrup

¼ teaspoon freshly cracked black pepper, plus more for seasoning

½ teaspoon dried oregano

½ teaspoon fine sea salt, plus more for seasoning

1 large beefsteak tomato, cut into ½-inch-thick slices

4 ounces watercress

Juice of ½ lemon

2 teaspoons extra-virgin olive oil

Kosher salt

Preheat the broiler to high. Fit a sheet pan with a wire rack.

Place a medium skillet over medium heat. When the skillet is hot, add the bacon and cook until the fat has rendered and the bacon looks just partially cooked, 3 minutes on each side. Turn the heat down to low. Carefully drizzle the maple syrup over the bacon. Continue to flip and cook until sticky, glazed, and crisp, an additional 2 to 3 minutes. Transfer the bacon to the wire rack and season each side with the pepper. Set aside.

In a small dish, combine the oregano and sea salt. Arrange the tomato slices in a single layer on another sheet pan or broiler-safe platter. Sprinkle the oregano-salt mixture over the tomatoes. Broil the tomatoes on one side until slightly wilted (but not browned), 5 minutes.

In a medium bowl, toss the watercress with the lemon juice and olive oil. Season to taste with kosher salt and pepper. Serve the tomatoes in a single layer on a platter with the watercress piled on top and the bacon nestled into the watercress.

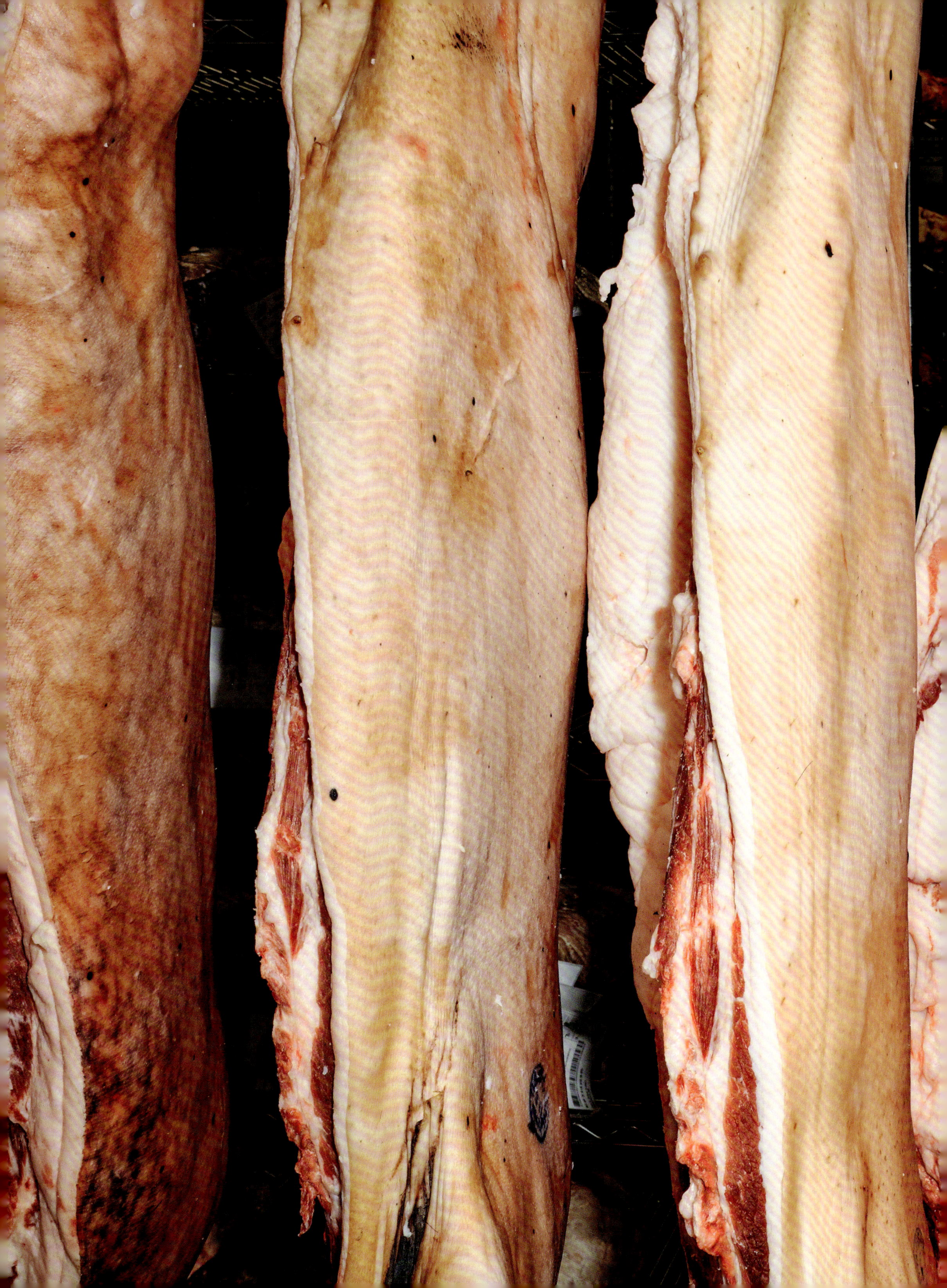

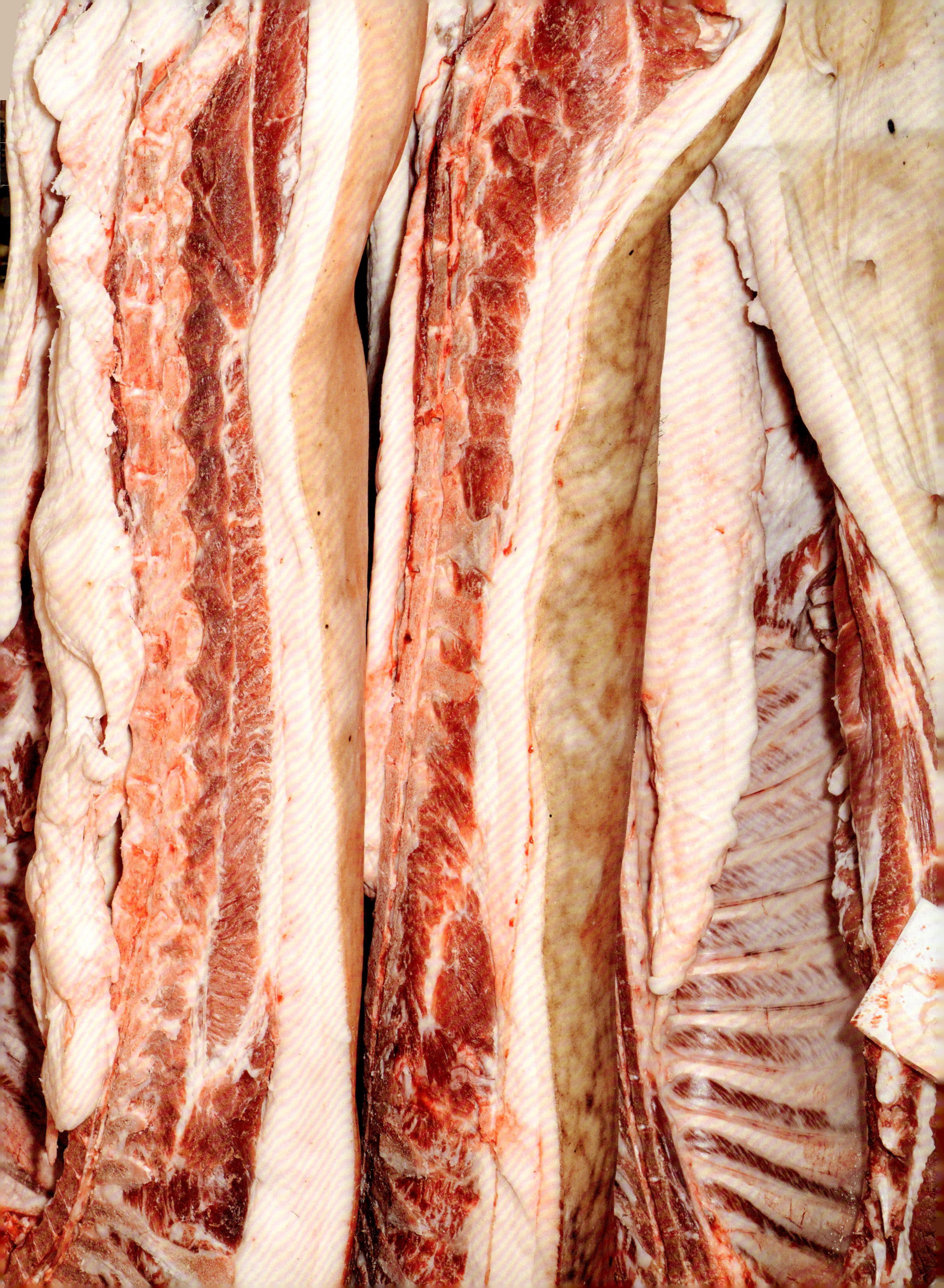

THE GOOD STEAK: A VISIT TO CREAM CO. MEATS

"Ninety-nine percent of the beef in America is the product of an industrialized system that is homogenized, cruel to animals by design, a disaster for our environment, and just generally pretty fucked."

When Cliff Pollard opened the meat distribution enterprise Cream Co. Meats a decade ago, he signed up for a David and Goliath–league battle. Except this time there were four giants: Tyson, Cargill, JBS, and National Beef. "Big Ag is primarily focused on developing and weaponizing different shapes of meat," Cliff explained on a tour of his headquarters in Oakland, California. "They scale and scale and scale, knowing it will always look and taste the same."

Picture a fourteen-hundred-pound Aberdeen Angus steer at a conventional operation. For its entire life, it has been forced to eat the same diet as practically every other member of its breed, as part of a one-size-fits-all approach that leads to the steer having the same physical characteristics as every other member of its breed. Eventually, it ends up at a huge slaughterhouse to be processed in the same way as every other member of its breed, and it winds up tasting . . . the same as every other member of its breed.

Now picture a second Aberdeen Angus steer raised and finished on pasture in the Sierra Foothills. It feeds on grass, native perennials, silage, hay, and maybe some locally milled grain during the winter. It's not confined to a concrete pad or made to eat mono-cropped cereals of soy and corn that will fatten it up faster. Free to forage and explore, the steer picks up the characteristics of the land, grazing on ryegrass one season, bluegrass the next. The same breed, raised in two radically different ways. One working against nature, and the other working with it. Once harvested, their meat winds up delivering two noticeably different expressions of flavor and texture.

This alternative Cliff champions is both better for the planet and our pleasure. "Genetics, age both on and off the hoof, diet, and context lead to nuance," said Cliff. "There is a direct correlation between how well raised an animal is and how good it tastes. I have witnessed it throughout my entire career."

That belief is the driving force behind Cream Co.'s mission to develop a system that can scale the quality and flavor you get from animals raised on independent farms. Cliff uses three terms to describe it: (1) "an aggregation model," (2) "a microregional decentralized supply chain," and (3) "a lot of words." Basically, Cream Co. has built a network of many small purveyors who practice good husbandry but who alone wouldn't be able to meet the demand required to compete for the big contracts. But by representing the combined force of many small farms, Cream Co. can. Cliff and his team don't just buy meat from these independent breeders. They

As of this writing (early 2025), Cliff's company directly invests in over twenty sustainable, regenerative, and family-owned farms.

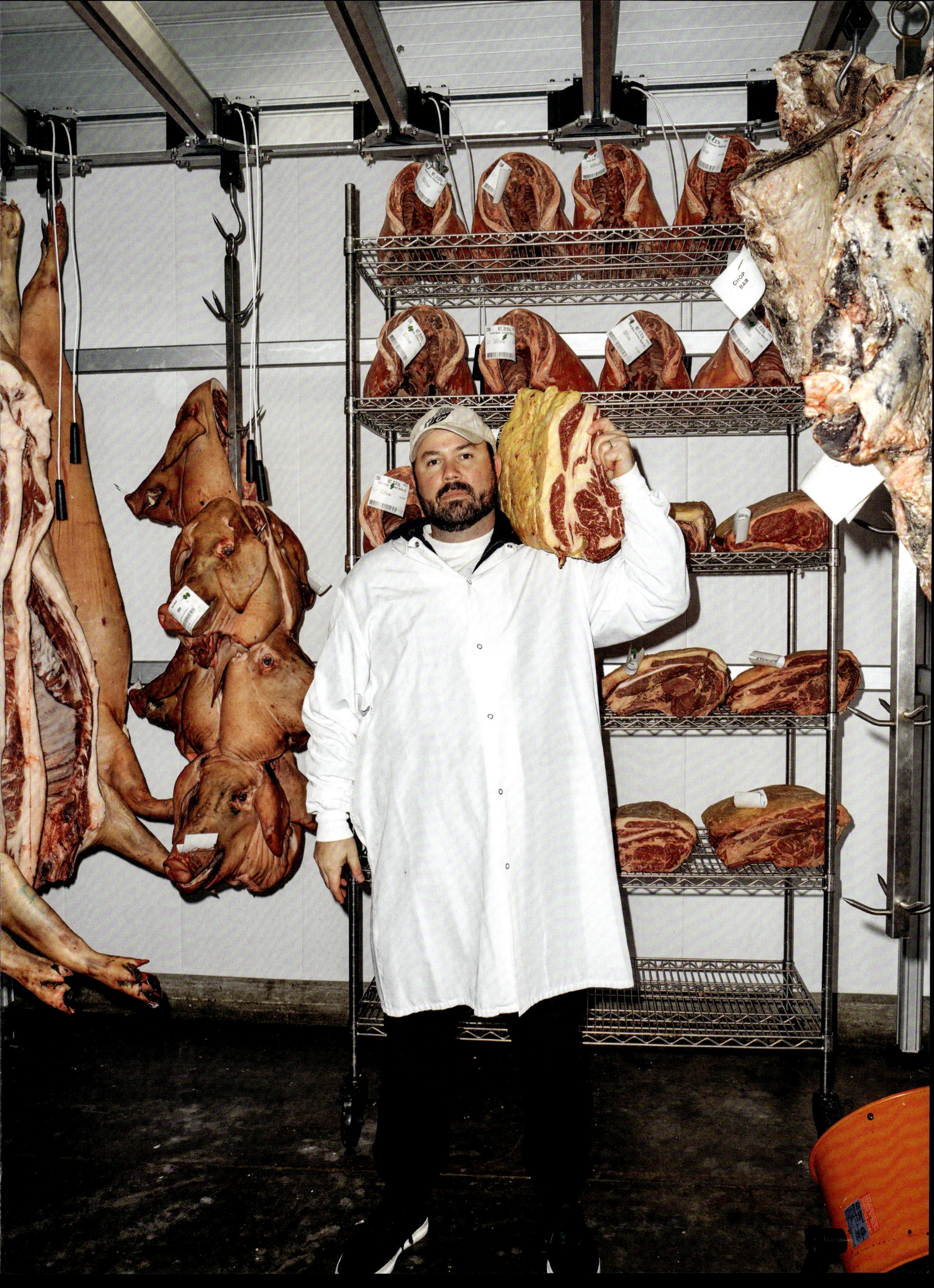
CHOP BAR

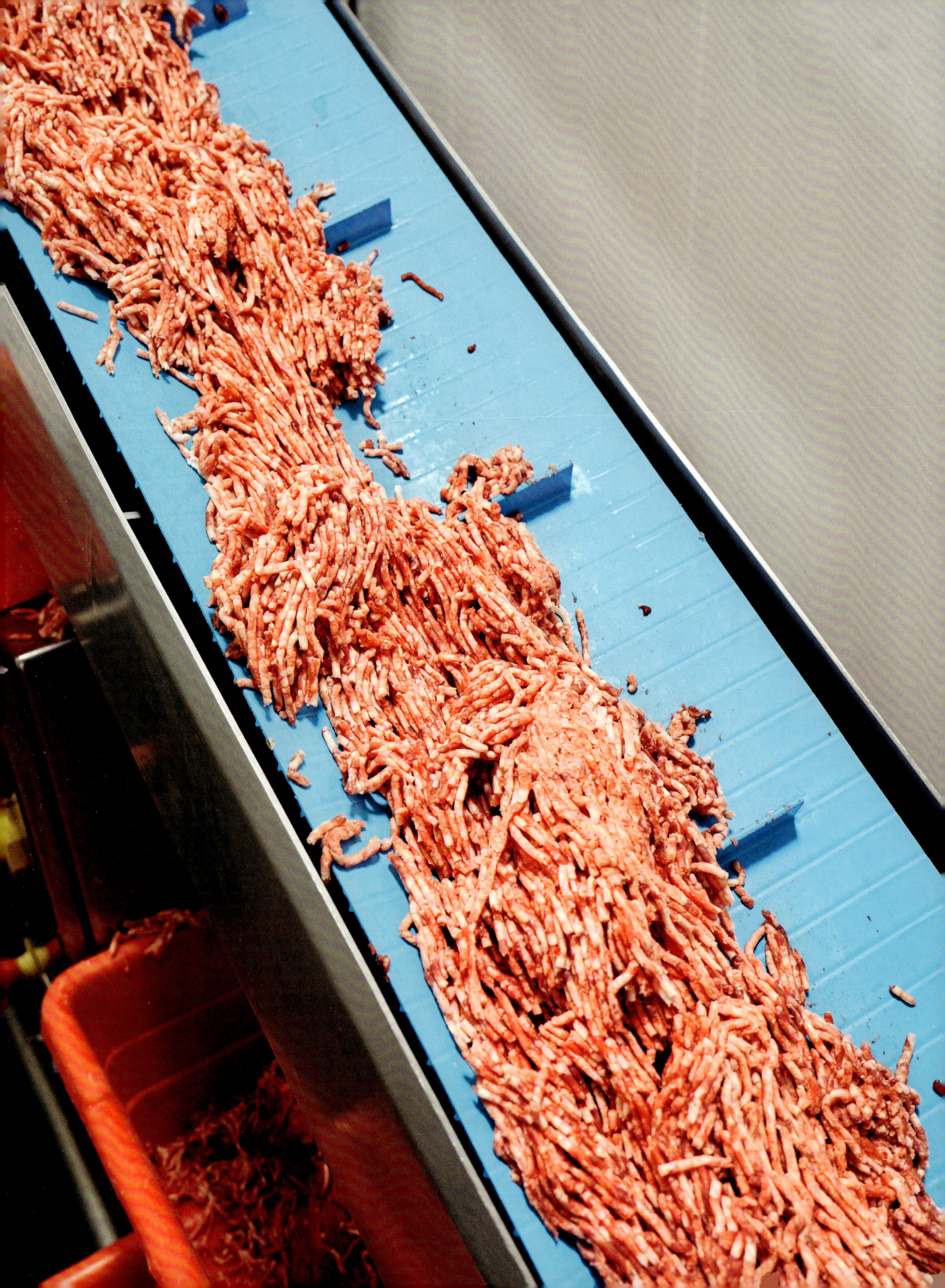

work with each farm to help maximize their potential, build up their supply chains to be more resilient, and partner with them to navigate the complicated "missing middle" of regional food distribution.

The farms raise the cows, pigs, and chickens. After the harvest, Cliff and his team handle everything else: transportation, processing, butchering, aging, sales, and distribution. They want to be able to stand behind the finished product. They also like to get in whole animals whenever possible. Less goes to waste, for one thing, because they find a home for the tougher sells like innards and ears. But the part that really blew us away, given that we were well into our steak journey, was hearing Cliff say this: "We don't see a lot of properly aged beef in this country anymore."

Then how do you explain all those cold rooms lined with stacks of beef that we saw almost everywhere we went? That is dry-aging on the *primal* level, for each cut of meat.

Cliff broke it down: "When you age a whole carcass, which used to be the standard, you see an enzymatic breakdown across the entire animal. Those enzymes break down the connective tissues in the meat, resulting in increased tenderness and intensified flavor. There is also a significant water reduction, up to fifteen percent in the first twenty-one days. Water leaving the muscle creates a bolder flavor profile." That concentration of flavor prized for the middle meats highlighted throughout this book can be applied to every muscle of the animal.

So please, when the craving for beef hits, first ask yourself if you need it. If the answer is yes, then it's time to find the good steak.

In 2018, Shake Shack opened in the San Francisco Bay Area and became the first global restaurant chain to serve a regenerative burger, but Cream Co. still provides the blend for the Golden State Double.

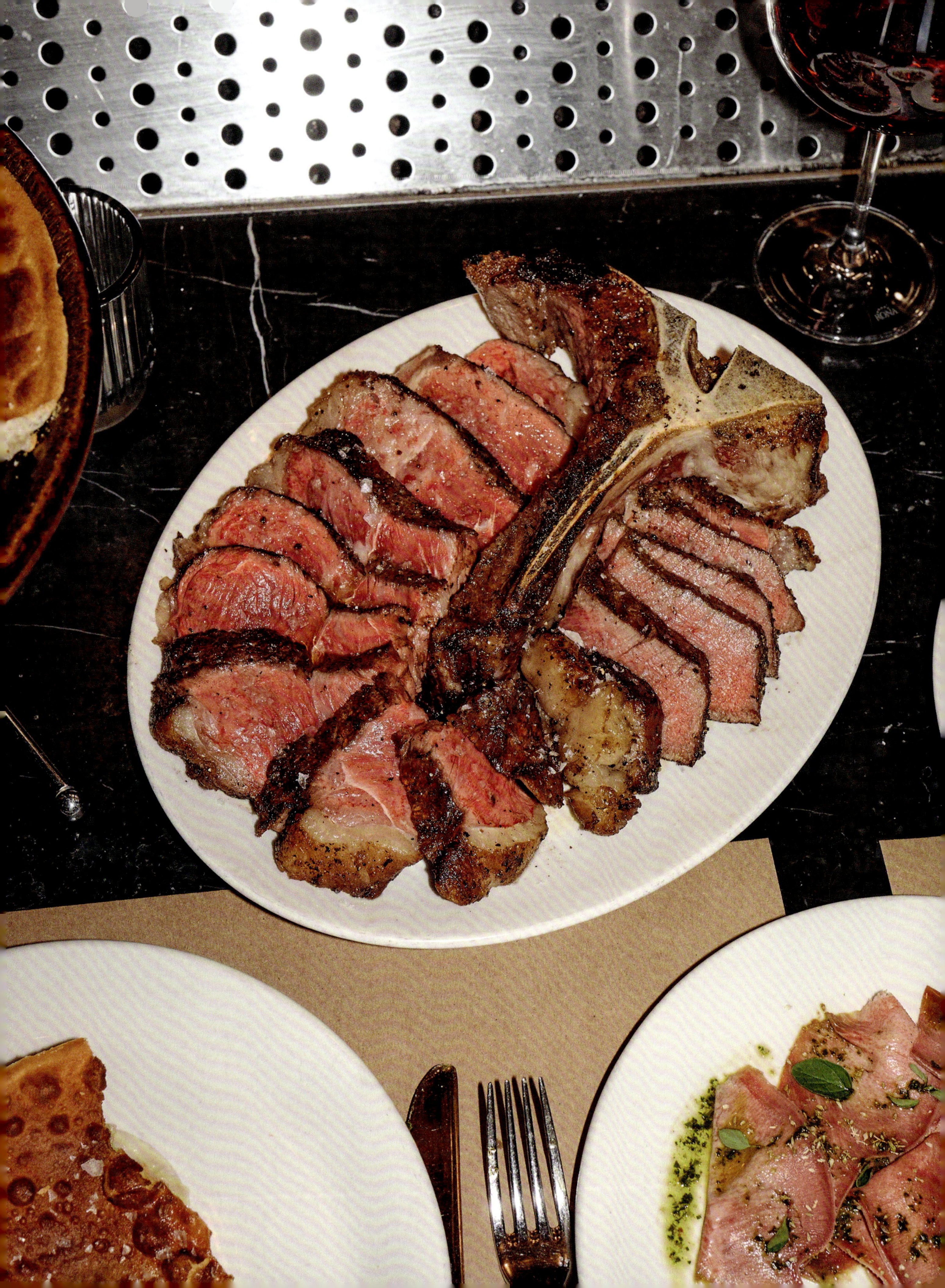

RECIPES

STEAKS

Serves 2

Steak
One 16-ounce rib eye steak

1½ teaspoons Diamond Crystal kosher salt (see Note)

Freshly cracked black pepper

Roasted Garlic
2½ teaspoons extra-virgin olive oil

1 garlic head, top trimmed to expose the cloves

Kosher salt and freshly cracked black pepper

4 large shallots, peeled and halved lengthwise

2 tablespoons (¼ stick) unsalted butter

2 rosemary sprigs

Flaky sea salt, preferably Maldon, for garnish

RIB EYE WITH ROASTED GARLIC

"That's what I want," I remember saying when the rib eye landed on the table at JEFFREY'S in Austin. With the right ratio of fat (that is, lots of it) and so much flavor, that distinguished cut hits me so.

At home, you should always cook it medium-rare with a nice char. Basting with herbs, butter, garlic, and shallots adds an entirely new dimension. Start with a bit of steak by its lonesome. Then scoop up some of that soft, sensuous garlic and spread it over the char. I'm getting all worked up writing this. I'm sweating . . .

Preheat the oven to 425°F.

Prepare the steak: Season the steak with the salt and pepper. Let the steak sit for about 45 minutes to come to room temperature.

While the steak rests, roast the garlic: Drizzle ½ teaspoon of the olive oil over the cut side of the garlic and season with a pinch of salt and pepper. Wrap the garlic in foil and roast in the oven until the cloves have softened and are slightly golden, about 30 minutes. Remove the garlic from the foil and set aside. Leave the oven on at 425°F.

In a large cast-iron pan over medium-high heat, warm the remaining 2 teaspoons olive oil. When ripping hot, place the shallots cut-side down around the edges of the pan, and place the steak in the center. Using tongs, sear the steak's fat cap without moving it, until crisp and some of the fat has rendered, 1 to 2 minutes. (This will equal more flavor!)

Lay the steak flat and sear one side until deeply, beautifully golden brown, 2 to 3 minutes. Check the shallots, flip them over once nicely charred, and season with a pinch of salt. Add the butter and one of the rosemary sprigs. Flip the steak to sear on the other side and spoon some of the melted butter over the steak as it cooks for another 2 to 3 minutes. Place the whole garlic head cut-side down in the pan. Put the pan in the oven and cook until the internal temperature of the steak reaches 130° to 135°F on an instant-read thermometer for medium-rare, about 5 minutes.

Remove the steak, shallots, and garlic from the pan and let the steak rest for 5 minutes on a cutting board. Slice the steak against the grain into ½-inch-thick slices and plate with the roasted garlic and shallots. Pour over any meat drippings from the pan and cutting board. Finish with flaky salt and garnish with the other sprig of rosemary.

Note: A rule to live by is to use about a teaspoon of kosher salt per pound of meat when seasoning your steak. While we would never do *less*, sometimes we like to get a little saucy and add more. It's your steak, your life.

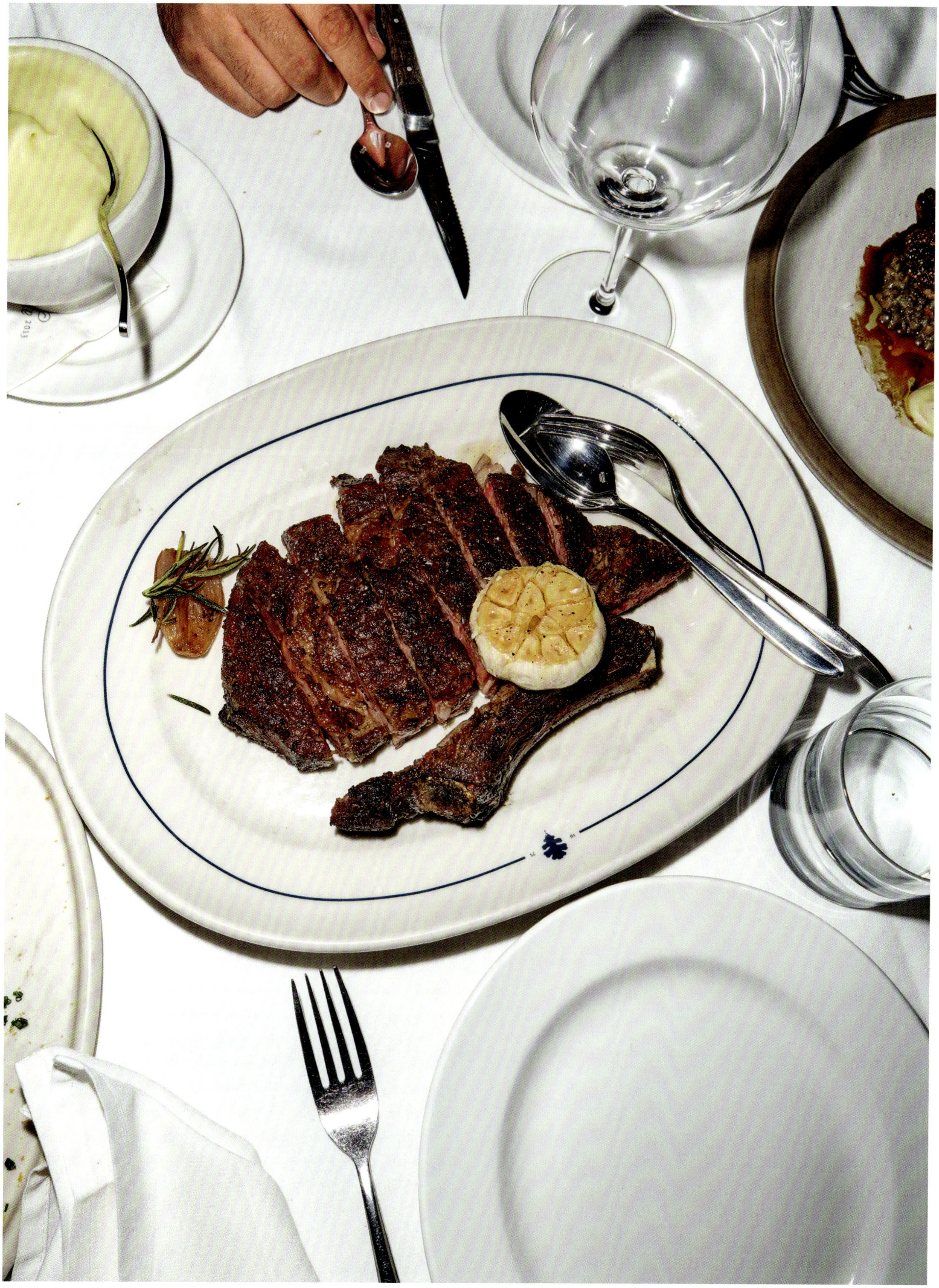

NEW YORK STRIP WITH CHIMICHURRI

Serves 6

Steaks

Four 12-ounce dry-aged New York strip steaks

2½ teaspoons Diamond Crystal kosher salt

1 tablespoon freshly cracked black pepper

Flaky sea salt, preferably Maldon, for garnish

Chimichurri

¼ cup freshly squeezed lime juice (about 2 limes)

5 garlic cloves, minced

1 tablespoon plus 1 teaspoon Diamond Crystal kosher salt

1 teaspoon freshly cracked black pepper

1 teaspoon crushed red pepper flakes

¾ cup extra-virgin olive oil

½ cup roughly chopped fresh cilantro (about ½ bunch)

½ cup roughly chopped fresh flat-leaf parsley (about ½ bunch)

Flaky sea salt, preferably Maldon, for garnish

Here's a fresh and fun take on the classic strip, a master class from Brooklyn culinary kings Frank Castronovo and Frank Falcinelli in what a difference Japanese binchotan, the long-burning hardwood charcoal prized by chefs around the world, can make. Many of us are familiar with the pride of Argentina, chimichurri. I bet you eat it at home every weekend, you herb freak. It's a fine example of how herbs, oil, lime, salt, and spice can bring both richness and balance to a savory steak. I'm always trying to introduce those sensations into my cooking.

Prepare the steaks: Season the steaks with the kosher salt and black pepper. Let the steaks sit for about 45 minutes to come to room temperature.

Prepare a charcoal grill for direct high-heat grilling. Light your binchotan (see Note) using a chimney until red and glowing. Preheat a grill rack over the coals.

While the binchotan is heating, prepare the chimichurri: In a small bowl, stir together the lime juice, garlic, kosher salt, and black pepper. Let it sit for 2 minutes to mellow the garlic. Add the red pepper flakes, then whisk in the olive oil until combined. Stir in the chopped herbs and set aside.

Place your steak on the preheated grill rack and sear on one side until deeply, beautifully golden brown, without moving it, letting the fat drip and ignite the coals, about 2 minutes. (Keep a spray bottle with water handy in case the flames become too aggressive, spritzing the flames to tame the fire as needed.)

Once a nice sear has formed on one side, flip to sear the other side, another 2 minutes. Then use tongs to sear the steak's fat cap without moving it, until some of the fat has rendered, about 2 minutes.

When the steak reaches an internal temperature of 125°F on an instant-read thermometer for rare, remove it from the grill and let it rest on a cutting board for 5 minutes. To serve, slice against the grain, sprinkle with flaky salt, and serve with the chimichurri spooned on top.

Note: If you can't find binchotan, regular charcoal can be substituted, but the binchotan is highly recommended.

T-BONE AU CHIPOTLE

Serves 2 to 4

Chef Fermín Nuñez happens to serve one of the finest steaks in the country at ESTE, his Mexican *seafood* restaurant in Austin, Texas. There is no brandy or cognac in his au poivre. To bring a jolt to the cream without overpowering it with spice, he uses chipotle chiles and mezcal. Yes, MEZCAL! That and a beef stock made with cow's heads that you don't need to prepare to be able to appreciate this masterpiece. But visit Fermín, and maybe he'll show you.

Serve with with Chef Nuñez's hash browns (see page 222) on the side.

Preheat the oven to 400°F.

Prepare the steak: Season the steak with the salt and pepper. Let the steak sit for about 45 minutes to come to room temperature. Fit a sheet pan with a roasting rack.

Place a large cast-iron pan over medium-high heat. When the pan is hot, add the steak and sear until deeply, beautifully golden brown, 2 to 3 minutes, then flip to sear on the other side, 2 to 3 minutes more. Reserving the cast-iron pan, set the steak on the roasting rack and place in the oven. Cook until the internal temperature of the steak reaches 130° to 135°F on an instant-read thermometer for medium-rare, 10 to 15 minutes. Remove from the oven and let the steak rest on a cutting board for about 10 minutes.

While the steak is in the oven, make the au poivre sauce: Place the reserved pan, without cleaning it, over low heat. Add the onion and cook, stirring occasionally, until soft and slightly caramelized, about 5 minutes. Add the pepper and chiles and cook, stirring occasionally, until fragrant, 1 to 2 minutes. Carefully add the mezcal and cook for 20 seconds, then add the vinegar and stir, scraping the bottom of the pan with a wooden spoon and allowing the liquid to reduce until the pan is almost dry, about 2 minutes. Pour in the stock, increase the heat to medium, and stir to combine, then simmer until the sauce is reduced by half, about 5 minutes. Add the cream and cook until the liquid is reduced by half, about 5 minutes. Add the butter, stir until melted and combined, and taste for seasoning. Set the sauce aside and cover to keep warm.

To serve, cut the steak against the grain into ½-inch-thick slices. Spoon the warm sauce onto the bottom of a serving plate, then rearrange the slices of steak with the bone on top.

Note: For a less spicy sauce, leave the chipotle chiles whole and remove them from the sauce before serving.

Steak

One large (about 24-ounce) T-bone steak

2 teaspoons Diamond Crystal kosher salt

1 teaspoon freshly cracked black pepper

Au Poivre Sauce

⅓ cup finely diced red onion (about ½ small onion)

2 tablespoons plus 2 teaspoons freshly cracked black pepper

2 chipotle chiles, roughly chopped (see Note)

¼ cup mezcal

¼ cup sherry vinegar

1 cup beef stock

1½ cups heavy cream

¼ cup (½ stick) unsalted butter

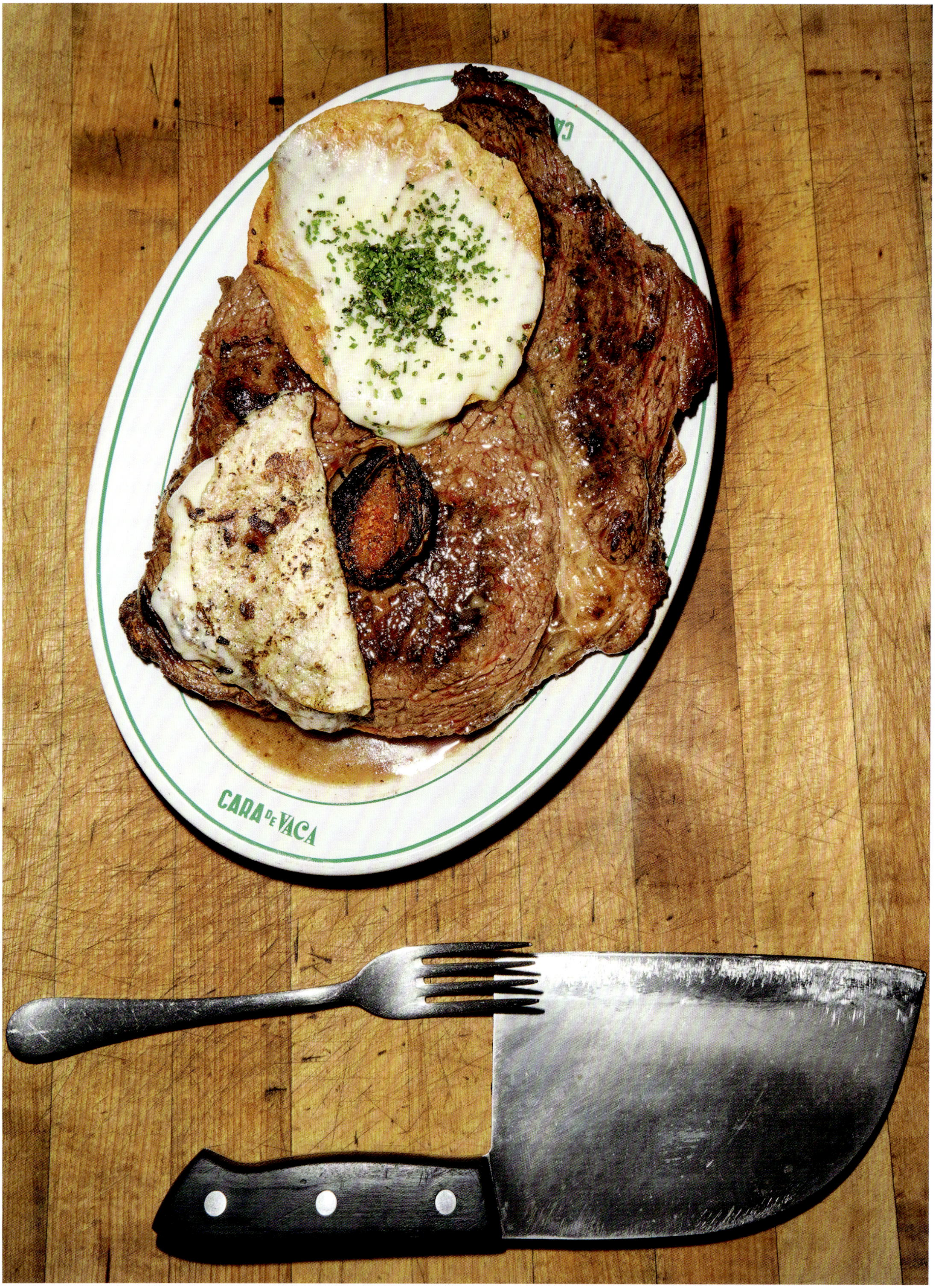
CARA DE VACA

CHURRASCO CON PAPAS

Serves 2 to 4

Churrasco con papas is a full steak house meal on a single plate. Wood-fired top sirloin with fat homemade fries swimming in a deep, drippy jus. And then they put a quesadilla on top? GOODNIGHT, WORLD. In the weeks leading up to our trip to Monterrey, I obsessed over a photo of this dish on my phone from chef Chuy Villarreal's CARA DE VACA. I was ensorcelled, and when I finally saw this behemoth in front of me, I was emotional. I vowed to bring it to the States.

1 pound russet potatoes

One 2-inch-thick top sirloin steak (about 40 ounces; see Note)

1 tablespoon plus 1 teaspoon Diamond Crystal kosher salt, plus more for seasoning

2 tablespoons (¼ stick) unsalted butter

2 cups good-quality beef stock

Neutral oil for frying

Line a sheet pan with a single layer of paper towels or a wire rack. Halve the potatoes lengthwise, then turn skin-side up and slice lengthwise into fries between ¼ and ½ inch thick. Add to a large saucepan and cover generously with cold water. Place over high heat and bring to a boil. Cook the potatoes until still firm but pierceable with a knife or fork, 5 to 10 minutes. Drain well and dry on the paper towels.

Season the steak all over with the salt. Let the steak sit for about 45 minutes to come to room temperature.

Prepare a charcoal grill for direct high-heat grilling, preferably using wood or wood charcoal. Grill the steak for about 15 minutes on each side, or until the internal temperature reaches 135°F on an instant-read thermometer for medium-rare. Remove the steak from the grill and let it rest for 10 minutes.

Place a large cast-iron pan over high heat. When the pan is hot, add the grilled steak and sear briefly until deeply, beautifully dark brown, about 1 minute per side. Add the butter, quickly turn the steak to coat all over, then transfer the steak to a cutting board and let it rest for 10 to 15 minutes. Cut against the grain into ½-inch-thick slices.

While the steak rests, line a plate with paper towels. In a small saucepan over medium heat, warm the beef stock.

Pour enough oil into a large pot to reach a depth of 3 inches and place over medium-high heat until the temperature reaches 375°F. Working in batches to prevent overcrowding, add the potatoes and cook, stirring to encourage even browning, until deep golden brown, 5 to 7 minutes. Remove from the oil, drain on the paper towel–lined plate, and sprinkle with salt while hot.

Spread the hot fries on a serving platter and top with the sliced steak. Just before serving, ladle just enough beef stock over the steak to moisten the steak and the fries and pour over any drippings from the cutting board. Serve immediately.

Note: Make sure you get a steak with an even thickness. Avoid the sirloin tip (the top of the top sirloin), which is rounder and will take much longer to cook, and the center-cut base sirloin, which is chewier and sometimes sold as top sirloin.

Serves 2

Steak

One 16-ounce New York strip steak

Kosher salt and freshly cracked black pepper (see Note, page 130)

2 teaspoons neutral oil

Sauce

1 tablespoon unsalted butter

1 small shallot, minced

1½ tablespoons cognac

6 tablespoons veal demi-glace (homemade or store-bought)

¾ cup crème fraîche

2 tablespoons freshly cracked black pepper

¼ teaspoon Diamond Crystal kosher salt

CHOPPED STEAK AU POIVRE

Emile Haynie, a great friend, prolific music producer, bread tosser, and fellow steak house admirer, turned me on to the chopped steak at THE MUSSO & FRANK GRILL (page 240). It is by far my favorite Musso signature. Jon Shook and Vinny Dotolo used to do a chopped steak at their dearly departed restaurant, Animal, that ramped up all things Yum Town. I miss that place so much. It means the world that they went into the vault and prepared the exact recipe for old times' sake. Try making homemade veal stock for the demi-glace.

Prepare the steak: Remove any sinew from the steak, but keep the fat on the whole steak. Cut into ¼-inch-thick slices in any direction, lay the slices flat, julienne each slice lengthwise, then cut into small dice horizontally. Run your knife through the diced meat and fat a few times to mix them evenly.

Season the minced steak lightly with a pinch of salt. Split the meat into two patty portions, about 8 ounces per patty. Store in the fridge until ready to cook. (No need to cover the patties, but only prep up to a few hours before using; otherwise the beef will oxidize.)

When ready to cook, generously season each patty with salt and pepper on both sides. Place a large cast-iron pan or other heavy skillet over high heat. When very hot, add the oil and swirl to evenly coat the bottom of the pan. Add the patties and sear for 1 minute, until a deeply, beautifully golden brown crust forms on the bottom, then flip to sear on the other side, 1 minute more, for a rare patty. Remove from the heat and let the patties rest on a plate or cutting board.

Make the sauce: In a medium saucepan over medium-high heat, melt the butter then add the shallots. Cook, stirring often, until they begin to sweat and are translucent, 2 to 3 minutes. Add the cognac, then carefully ignite with a long lighter to cook off the alcohol. Stir to deglaze the pan and cook until the liquid has almost entirely cooked off, 1 to 2 more minutes. Add the veal demi-glace, stir, and bring to a boil. Then lower the heat to medium-low to let simmer, stir in the crème fraîche, and remove from the heat (do not let the crème fraîche boil). Season with the pepper and salt.

To serve, put a few spoonfuls of sauce on each plate, then place a steak patty on top.

STEAK HOUSE

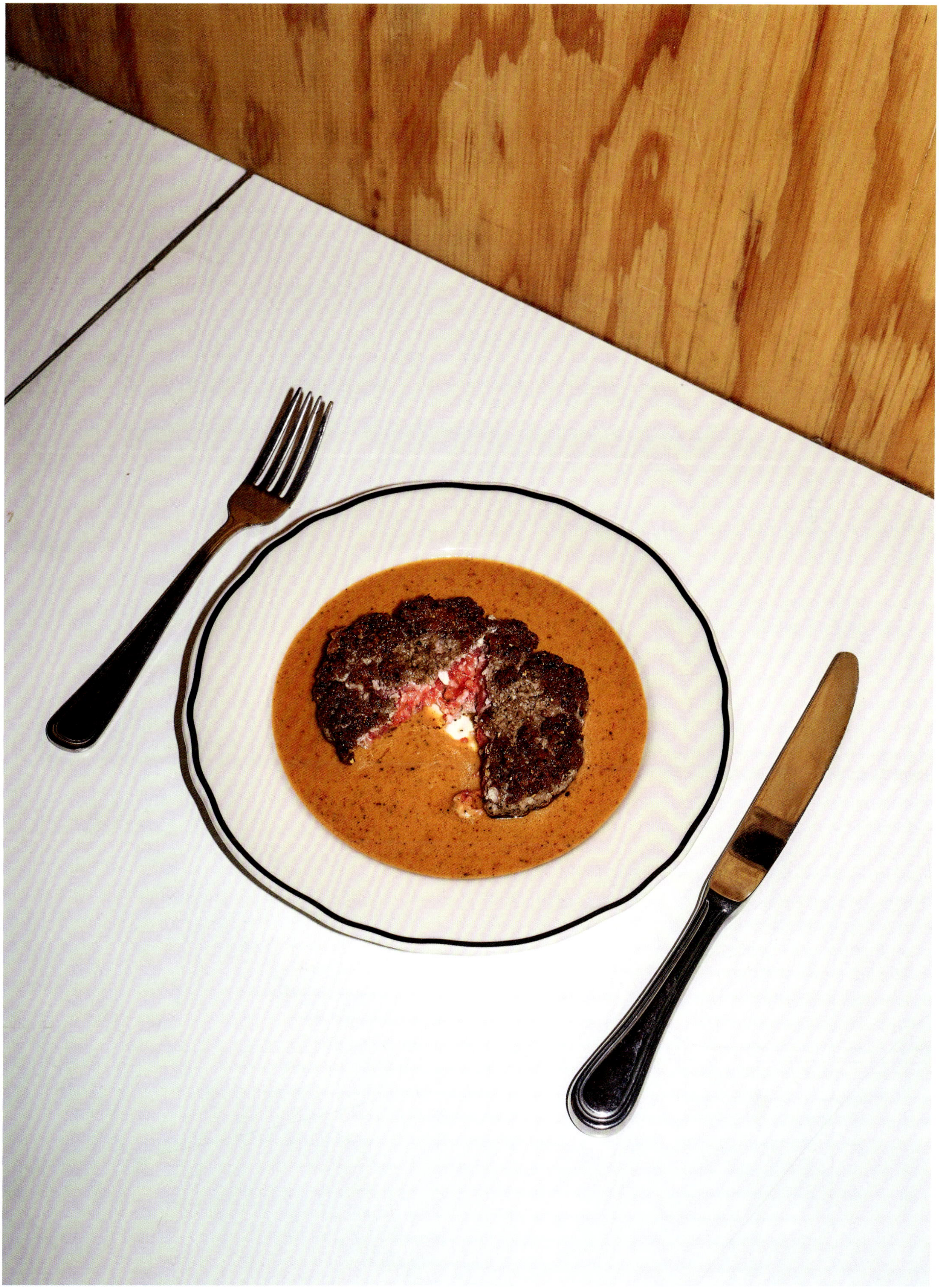

STEAK DIANE

Serves 4 to 6

Steaks
Four 8-ounce Wagyu zabuton (Denver) steaks
1 cup shio koji

Diane Sauce
½ cup (1 stick) unsalted butter
¼ cup thinly sliced garlic (about 12 cloves)
½ cup thinly sliced shallots (about 1 large shallot)
¾ cup Shaoxing wine
2 cups beef stock
1 cup heavy cream
Freshly cracked black pepper
½ cup Worcestershire sauce
2 tablespoons Dijon mustard

Steak Diane is named after Diana, the ancient Roman goddess of the hunt, and it's very worthy of the mythical association. I'd like to take a moment and worship thee, Diana, for bestowing such a succulent offering to humankind. You see, I'm a pan sauce guy. Not so much for wild animals, but for things like a nice crispy chicken thigh or a Wagyu rib eye like Jude Parra-Sickels does at MAJORDOMO (page 243). His Diane sauce is brown butter, shallot, mustard, and a little Shaoxing wine—pure Domo style. He marinates the meat in shio koji, which is a thick, savory-sweet elixir made with fermented rice, salt, and water that you can easily find online or at markets like Whole Foods.

Prepare the steaks: Set the steaks on a large plate or rimmed sheet pan and rub all over with the shio koji. Cover the plate in plastic wrap and refrigerate the steaks for at least 8 hours or up to overnight. Before cooking, let the steaks sit for about 45 minutes to come to room temperature.

Make the sauce: In a medium saucepan over medium heat, melt the butter. Continue cooking, swirling the pan often, until it is just beginning to brown. Add the garlic and shallots and cook, stirring often, until golden brown and soft, 5 to 7 minutes. Pour in the Shaoxing wine and beef stock then bring the sauce to a simmer; cook until reduced by one-quarter, 10 minutes.

Add the cream, season to taste with pepper, and return the sauce to a simmer, stirring often to ensure it doesn't boil over. Reduce the sauce until it reaches a thick consistency that begins to coat the back of a spoon, 2 to 3 minutes. Add the Worcestershire and mustard and stir to combine. Continue simmering until the sauce reduces to a heavy cream–like consistency and coats the back of a spoon smoothly, about 2 minutes. Turn the heat down to low and cover to keep warm while you cook the steaks.

Prepare a charcoal grill for direct high-heat grilling or preheat a gas grill to high. Add the steaks and cook, turning and flipping every 2 to 3 minutes to ensure an evenly, deeply, beautifully golden brown exterior and until the internal temperature reaches 130°F on an instant-read thermometer for medium-rare. Remove the steaks from the grill and let them rest on a cutting board for 10 minutes. Serve with the sauce on the side.

SURF 'N TURF

Serves 4

Surf 'n Turf, called Reef 'n Beef in Australia (sounds like I made it up but it's true), offers the best of both worlds because the steak house is a place where two pleasures are always better than one. We had our first S 'n T at another X 'n X: BEEF 'N BOTTLE (page 21). I emulated their version with a Snake River Farms gold-grade filet mignon, and it forever changed the way I think about that cut.

Make the compound butter: In a small food processor, add the butter, paprika, honey, lemon zest, and garlic and blitz until combined. (Alternatively, fold everything together with a spoon.) Mix in the herbs. Reserve half of the compound butter at room temperature for cooking. Spoon the remaining half onto a sheet of plastic wrap, use the plastic to mold the butter into a 1½-inch-thick log, twist the ends of the wrap, and refrigerate until firm, about 1 hour. (The compound butter can be made up to 1 week in advance.)

Prepare the surf and turf: Season the steaks with ½ teaspoon salt each and the pepper to taste. Let the steaks sit for about 45 minutes to come to room temperature.

Meanwhile, prep the lobster tails. Place a lobster tail, soft-underside down, on a cutting board. Use kitchen shears to cut down the center of the top shell, stopping right before the tail fan. Turn the lobster over and break the bottom shell by pushing your thumbs into the center, cracking the shell from top to bottom. Turn the lobster slit-side up and carefully work the meat away from the shell with your hands and pull it out, then rest it back on top of the shell. (The meat should still be connected to the tail fan.) Repeat for each lobster tail. Refrigerate the lobster until ready to cook.

Preheat the oven to 425°F. Place a large cast-iron pan over medium-high heat. When the pan is hot, add the oil and the steaks. (If the pan isn't large enough, cook two steaks at a time and use 1 tablespoon of oil for each batch.) Sear the steaks until deeply, beautifully golden brown, 2 to 3 minutes on each side. Brush the steaks generously with some of the reserved room-temperature compound butter, then place the steaks in the oven for 10 minutes, until the internal temperature reaches 130°F on an instant-read thermometer for medium-rare. Remove from the oven and let the steaks rest on a cutting board while you cook the lobster tails.

Preheat the broiler to high. Place the prepared lobster tails on a sheet pan shell-down and season with the remaining ½ teaspoon salt and pepper. Brush the lobster meat with some of the room-temperature compound butter and broil until the internal temperature reaches 140°F on an instant-read thermometer, 5 to 7 minutes. Remove the tails from the oven and brush with more of the room-temperature compound butter.

Slice the chilled compound butter into four ½-inch-thick pats. Top each steak with a pat of compound butter and serve with the lobster tails and lemon wedges on the side.

Compound Butter

1 cup (2 sticks) unsalted butter, at room temperature

1 tablespoon smoked paprika

1 teaspoon honey

Finely grated zest of 2 lemons

4 garlic cloves, grated

2 tablespoons chopped fresh flat-leaf parsley

2 teaspoons chopped fresh thyme

Surf & Turf

Four 8-ounce filets mignons, each about 2 inches thick

2½ teaspoons Diamond Crystal kosher salt

Freshly cracked black pepper

Four 5-ounce lobster tails

2 tablespoons neutral oil

Lemon wedges for serving

CLASSIC PRIME RIB

Serves 8 to 10

1 whole bone-in prime beef rib eye (4 to 5 pounds), tied up

6 tablespoons fresh thyme leaves

3 tablespoons plus 2 teaspoons fennel pollen

2 tablespoons plus 2 teaspoons crushed red pepper flakes

¼ cup Diamond Crystal kosher salt, plus more for seasoning

¼ cup freshly cracked black pepper, plus more for seasoning

Neal Fraser's prime rib, which he prepares for five hundred hungry people at our annual BEEFSTEAK bacchanalia (page 244), makes my eyes roll back inside my head. His recipe calls for a whole rib eye to feed a small army.

Season the rib eye with the thyme, fennel pollen, and red pepper flakes. Add the salt and pepper to evenly coat the outside, adding more if necessary to completely cover the roast. Place on a sheet pan, cover, and let sit at room temperature for 2 hours.

Preheat the oven to 450°F. Fit a sheet pan with a roasting rack. Transfer the rested rib eye to the roasting rack and cook, rotating the roasting rack occasionally, until the outside of the rib eye is golden brown. After 45 minutes, check on the color and doneness to make sure the internal temperature reads no more than 100°F.

Lower the oven temperature to 250°F and continue cooking to the desired temperature: 1 hour 20 minutes for rare (120°F); 1 hour 45 minutes for medium-rare (125°F); 2 hours for medium (130°F). Remove from the oven, tent with foil, and let the rib eye rest on the rack for 20 minutes before slicing.

Slice between the bones, but you can also remove the bones and cut thinner rib eyes as well. Spoon any extra jus from the pan onto each slice to serve.

EYE OF DELMONICO WITH TRUFFLE AIOLI

Serves 2 to 4

Truffle Aioli

2 garlic cloves, grated

1 tablespoon black truffle oil, preferably Truff

1 tablespoon freshly squeezed lemon juice

½ teaspoon Diamond Crystal kosher salt

½ teaspoon freshly cracked black pepper

1 cup mayonnaise

Steaks

Two 12- to 16-ounce chuck eye (Delmonico) steaks

Kosher salt and freshly cracked black pepper

2 tablespoons (¼ stick) unsalted butter

Just as our journey was finally winding down, the legendary DELMONICO'S, founded in 1827 in New York City, miraculously reopened after a long dormant stretch. I had the chuck eye, which is now commonly referred to as the Delmonico at butcher shops across the nation. The Delmonico at Delmonico's. Now I make it at mine.

Make the aioli: In a small bowl, mix together the garlic, truffle oil, lemon juice, salt, and pepper. Stir in the mayonnaise until smooth. Cover and refrigerate until ready to serve.

Prepare the steaks: Season the steaks generously with salt and pepper. Let the steaks sit for about 45 minutes to come to room temperature. Preheat the oven to 400°F.

Place a large cast-iron pan over medium-high heat. When the pan is hot, add the butter then the steaks. Sear the steaks until deeply, beautifully golden brown, 2 to 3 minutes on each side. Spoon some of the melted butter over the steaks, then place the steaks in the oven until the internal temperature reaches 130°F on an instant-read thermometer for medium-rare, 6 to 10 minutes. Remove from the oven and let the steaks rest on a cutting board for 10 minutes. Slice against the grain into ¼-inch-thick slices and serve with the truffle aioli on the side.

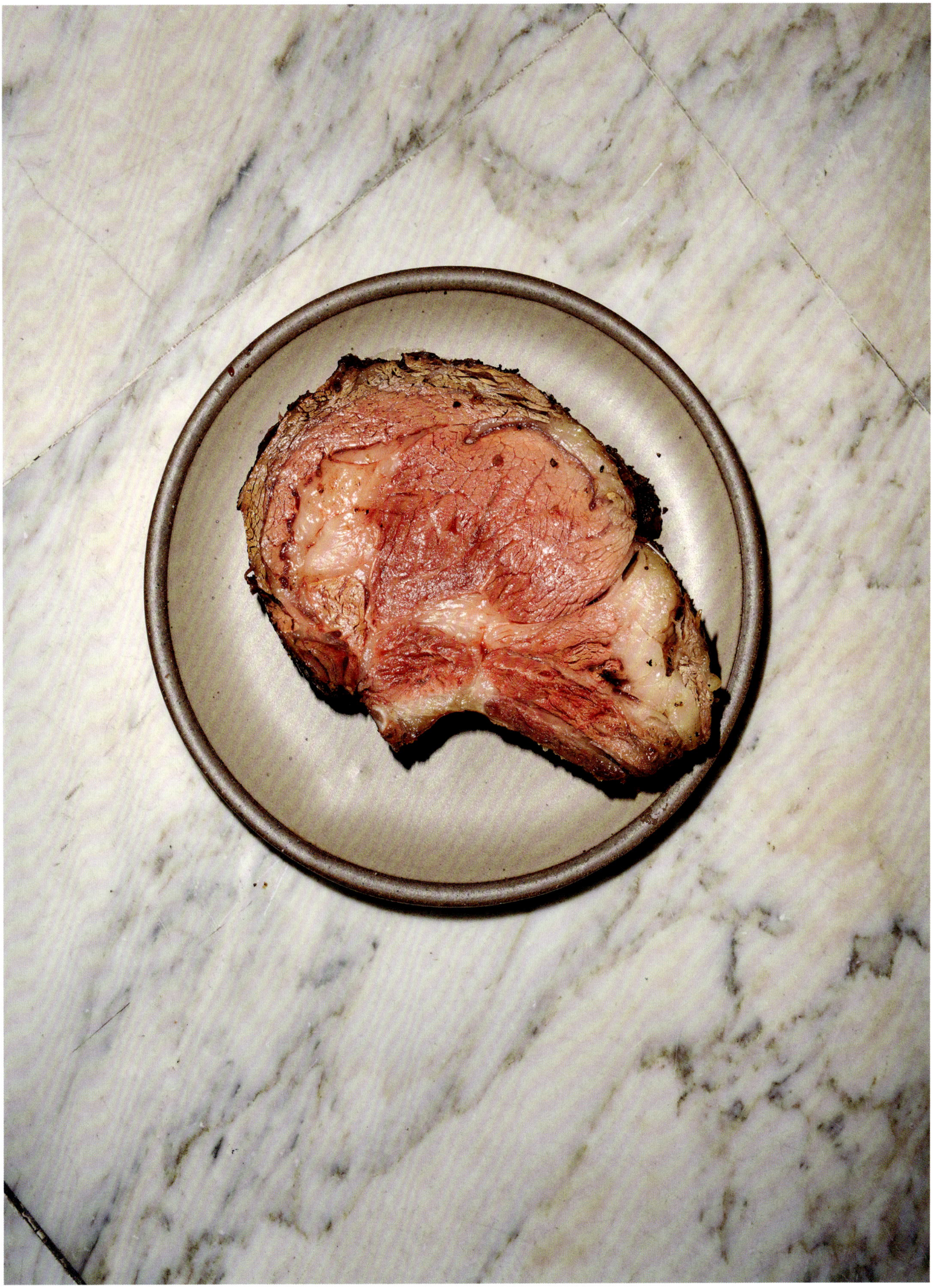

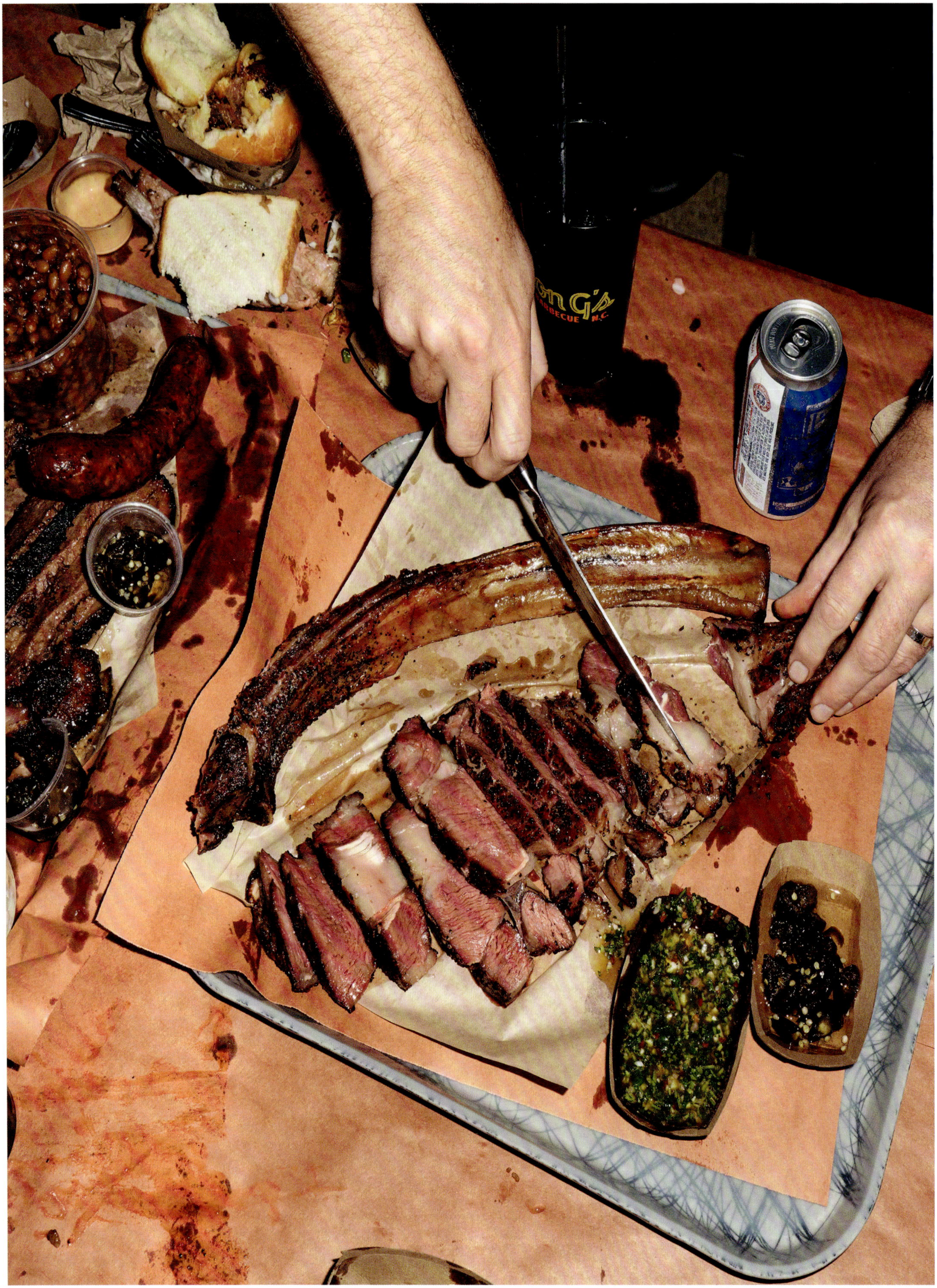

SMOKED TOMAHAWK

Serves 6

We missed our flight out of Charlotte because we drove over to JON G'S BARBECUE to try a steak that pitmaster Garren Kirkman was working on in one of the monster smokers out back. Ever since that day, I've had this recurring dream: There's this big bad boy flying through the air while I jump to try and take a bite, but it's always just a bit too far away to reach. I guess it was worth it.

One 46-ounce tomahawk steak

1 tablespoon plus 1 teaspoon Diamond Crystal kosher salt

2 tablespoons freshly cracked black pepper

1 tablespoon unsalted butter, cut into 2 pats

Flaky sea salt, preferably Maldon, for garnish

Chimichurri (page 132) for serving

Preheat a smoker to between 225° and 250°F for indirect cooking, using well-seasoned white oak. The wood should be burning in the flame, not smoldering. Let the steaks sit for about 45 minutes to come to room temperature.

Season the steak with the kosher salt and pepper on both sides, rubbing it evenly into the meat. Place the steak over the cool side of the grill and smoke the steak for 2½ to 3 hours, flipping it halfway through, until the temperature reaches 120°F on an instant-read thermometer. Remove the steak from the smoker and let it rest on a carving board until cooled to 105°F.

While the steak is cooling, prepare a charcoal grill for direct high-heat grilling.

Once cooled to temperature, place the steak on the grill grate with the flame nearly touching the meat. Flip the steak often, every 1 to 2 minutes, until deeply, beautifully golden brown all over and the internal temperature reaches 125°F on an instant-read thermometer for rare.

Transfer the steak to the carving board, place the butter pats on the steak, and tent with foil for about 5 minutes. Uncover, slice the steak against the grain into ¼-inch-thick pieces, and sprinkle with flaky salt. Serve with chimichurri on the side.

THE JOURNEY, PART IV

T E X

X A S

AND NOW, WE HEAD TO THE LAND OF THE LONGHORN, THE BREED OF CATTLE THAT THE SPANISH BROUGHT WITH THEM WHEN THEY FIRST SETTLED IN THE EASTERN PART OF THE STATE.

People didn't care for the meat at first. But by the middle of the nineteenth century, tastes had changed. Ranches were everywhere. The cows started to multiply. And their numbers kept multiplying during the Civil War, when cattle couldn't be traded beyond the Mississippi. Once the war was over, folks in big cities across the country were hungry for red meat. The cowboys and cattlemen of the Lone Star State were ready to give it to them.

Today Texas produces five billion pounds of beef a year, and it holds the titles for most farmland, cattle, and meat-eaters in America.

I've always loved it here. My family recently discovered some blood relatives deep in Texas. They are taller than me. Finally, I found my people. The Big Boys! On top of all the obvious reasons, I wanted to go to Texas as part of this journey because the people in each major city are proud to have THEIR way of doing things. On every visit, I try to appreciate those differences and absorb all the cool things they give rise to. I was in Houston and I asked a local if they had any tips for Dallas, my next stop. He told me, "Wish I could help, but we don't go to that place." He was kidding, but he wasn't.

In Austin, which isn't much of a steak house town, we hit up a seafood restaurant named Este for steak au poivre, as well as the historic Jeffrey's. In Houston, we experienced the Platonic ideal of a steak house at Pappas Bros. (and snuck in a meal at Viet-Cajun miracle Crawfish & Noodles). In San Antonio, we stopped into Little Red Barn for some chicken-fried steak (and had an amazing breakfast at Garcia's Mexican Food). Then we made our way to bling city, Dallas, to visit the original US location of the only chain restaurant featured in this book.

At the Fort Worth Stockyards, where you can buy all hats but no cattle.

HAT SIZE	INCHES
6	18 ¾
6 ⅛	19 ⅛
6 ¼	19 ½
6 ⅜	19 ⅞
6 ½	20
6 ⅝	20 ¾
6 ¾	21 ⅛
6 ⅞	21 ½
7	21 ⅞
7 ⅛	22 ¼
7 ¼	22 ⅝
7 ⅜	23
7 ½	23 ½
7 ⅝	23 ⅞
7 ¾	24 ¼
7 ⅞	24 ⅝
8	

SAN ANTONIO

LITTLE RED BARN

BY THE NUMBERS

Opening year: 1963
Founder: Ralph Hernandez
Address: 1836 South Hackberry Street, San Antonio, Texas 78210
House special: Country fried steak

Sixty years ago, a Mexican American butcher named Ralph Hernandez thought it was weird that he could dedicate his life to mastering meat but still couldn't find a steak house in town where he could enjoy it with his wife, Lili, and feel welcome.

So they built eight picnic tables and turned their meat market in the shadow of the highway into a place for steak. Affordable, thoughtfully prepared, quickly served. Large chalkboard menus. Staff wearing blue-and-white Dale Evans fringe with holsters in their skirts, who place a salad on the table before anybody has taken their seats.

Little Red Barn outgrew its opening seating plan and today attracts hundreds of diners a day. It's a sensation. The chicken-fried steak probably has something to do with it. As did Lili's idea of having the baked potatoes wrapped in gold and not aluminum foil.

Ralph died in 2011 and Lili in 2020. Their children and grandchildren run the place now. It's getting harder for them to offer solid steaks, cooked on the flat-top grill, at affordable prices. But seeing as the dining room was once the founders' home as the couple started raising a family, the consensus is that it's worth the trouble.

I got to meet the whole Hernandez clan that day at Little Red Barn, including granddaughter Marissita. She juggles marketing for the family business while attending business school. We met Jewel Arriaga, too. She explained how dining at LRB has become a San Antonio tradition. Now I gotta go back for rodeo and a Dos-A-Rita!

Jewel Arriaga—The Rodeo Queen

"I've been working here at Little Red Barn a good three years. Before I got the job, I was a stay-at-home mom, and then some things happened, and I got a job at Bill Miller's. I was there for three weeks and it wasn't for me. I live just down the street. I was like, 'I'll check Little Red Barn out; it's not that far.' And then I became a host, which I did for a good four months. And then I asked, 'Hey, you think I could turn into a server?' They trained me, and then I started serving around this month, around the rodeo and stuff like that.

I love rodeo; people come in, they're great, they are very generous. They love to tell us about everything that's going on, but the only thing is, it kind of smells like manure. The cows. But other than that, it's great. Some people come in and are trying to eat and get out. It can be 'quick-quick-quick' because some people want to go to a concert that's happening or an event that's happening. Sometimes it's even the workers that come.

It's nice because you see the same people year after year. One year, I saw the same people come in and the kids that come in; they're the ones that are raising the animals and stuff like that. And then you see them another year and you're like, 'Oh, look, he's here again.' It's real nice to see them growing up."

Another thing Jewel likes about the gig: the hours. Yet another: the margaritas.

H&P ANGUS
BOERNE, TX
Sheriff
Glen
Sachflaben
Constable
Don
Sachflaben
Bee County
EST.
1857
Pascual Becerra
Snuff Ridge
RANCH
Cleveland
TX

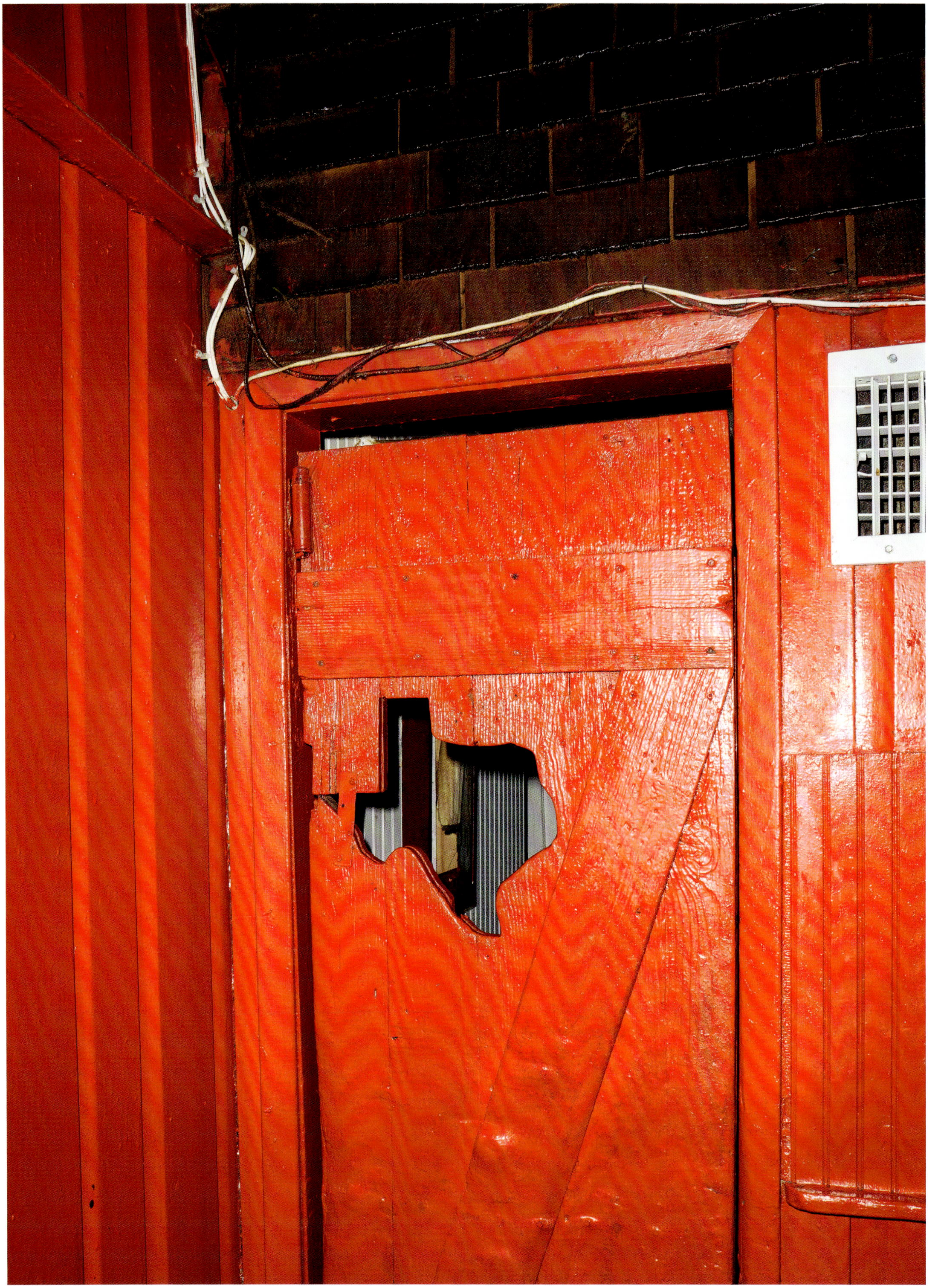

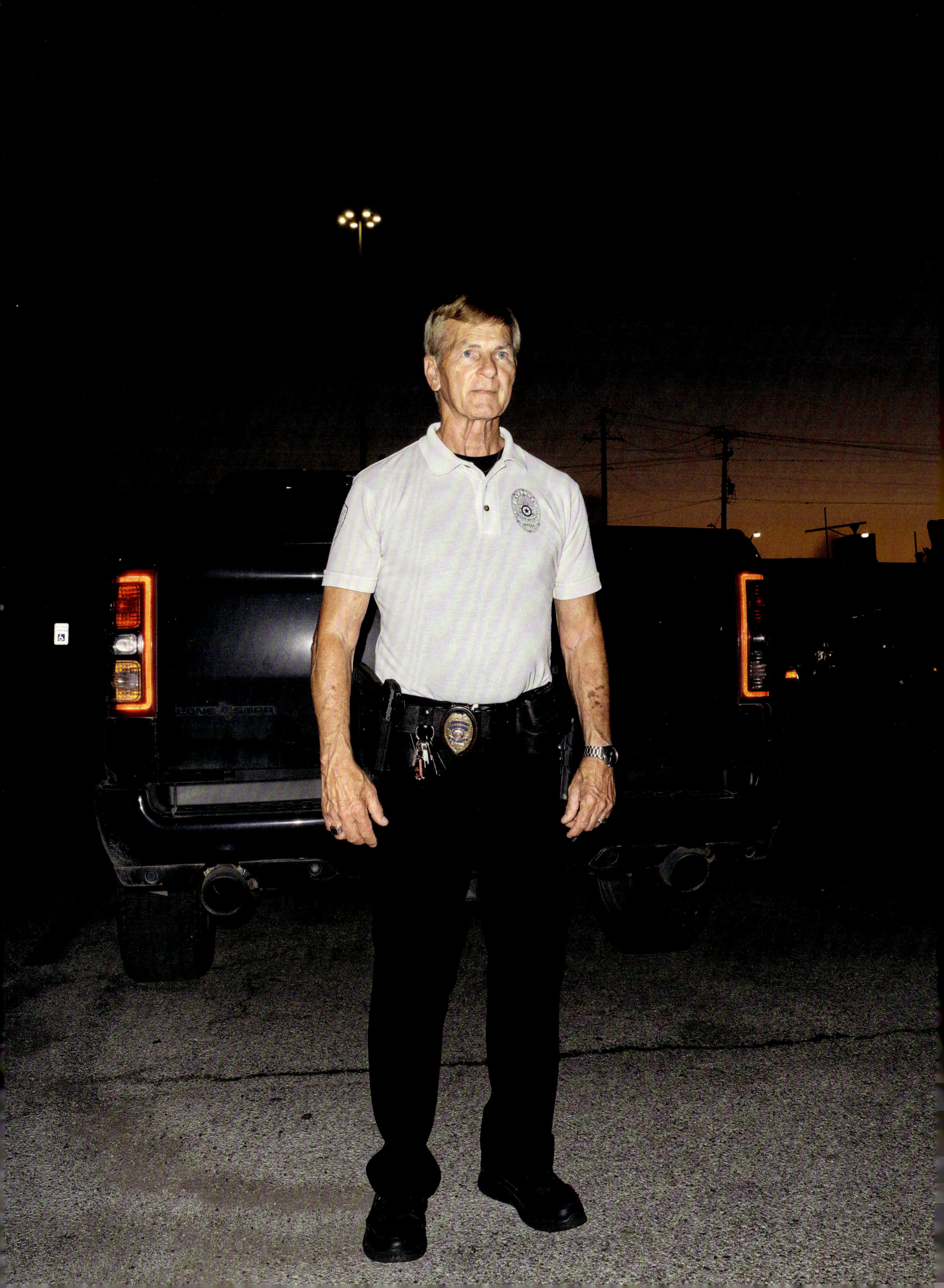
LONE STAR

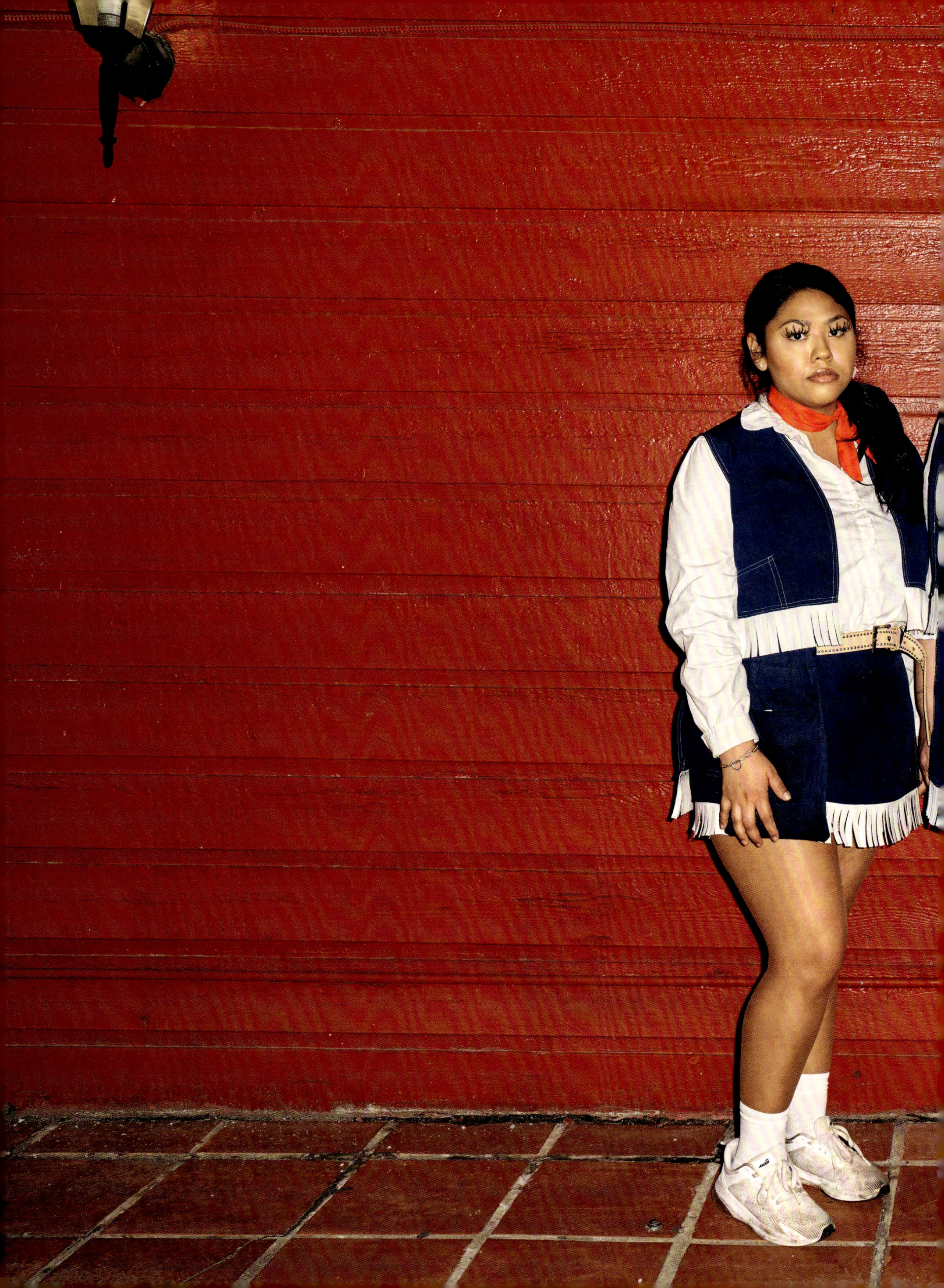

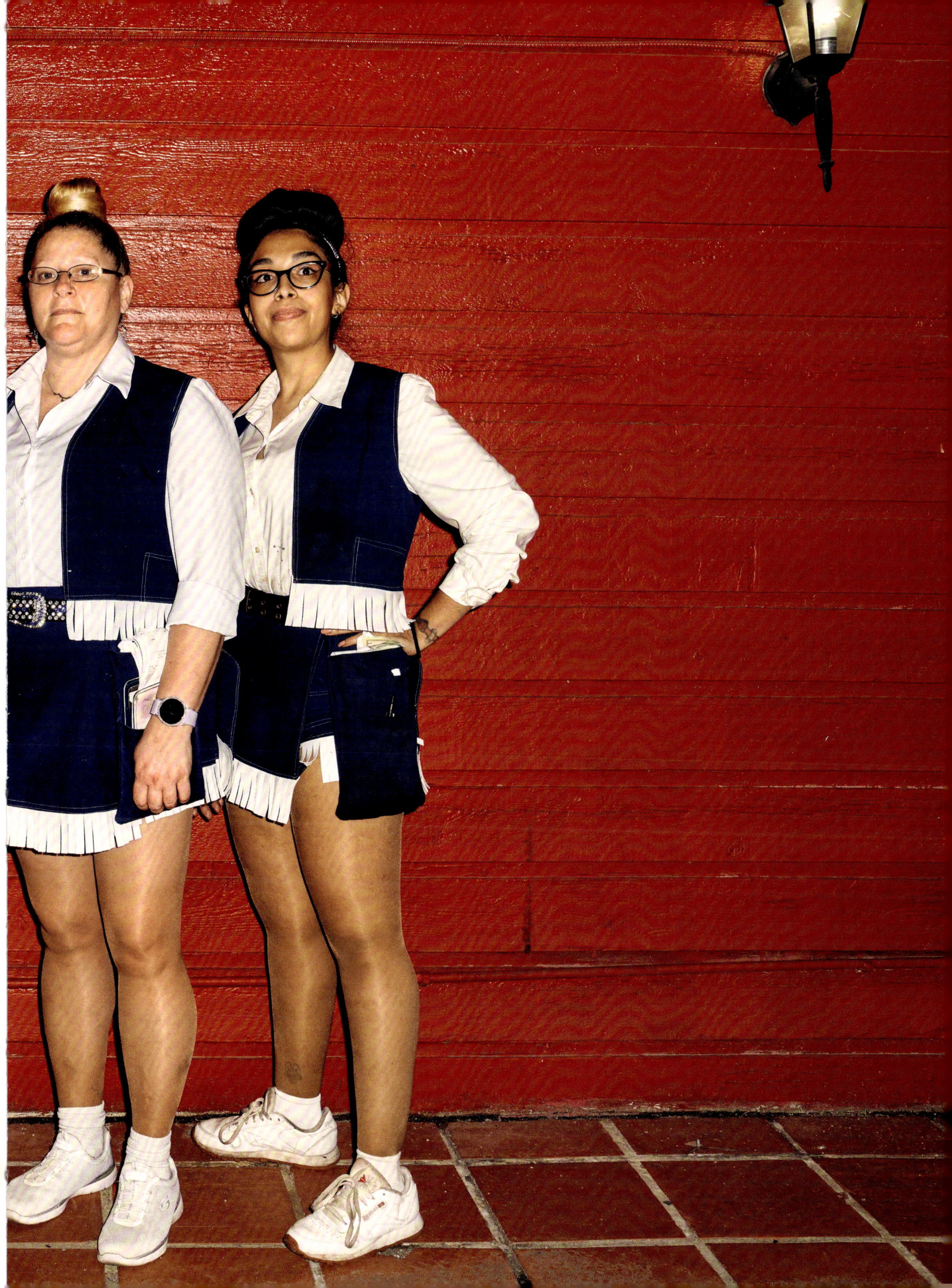

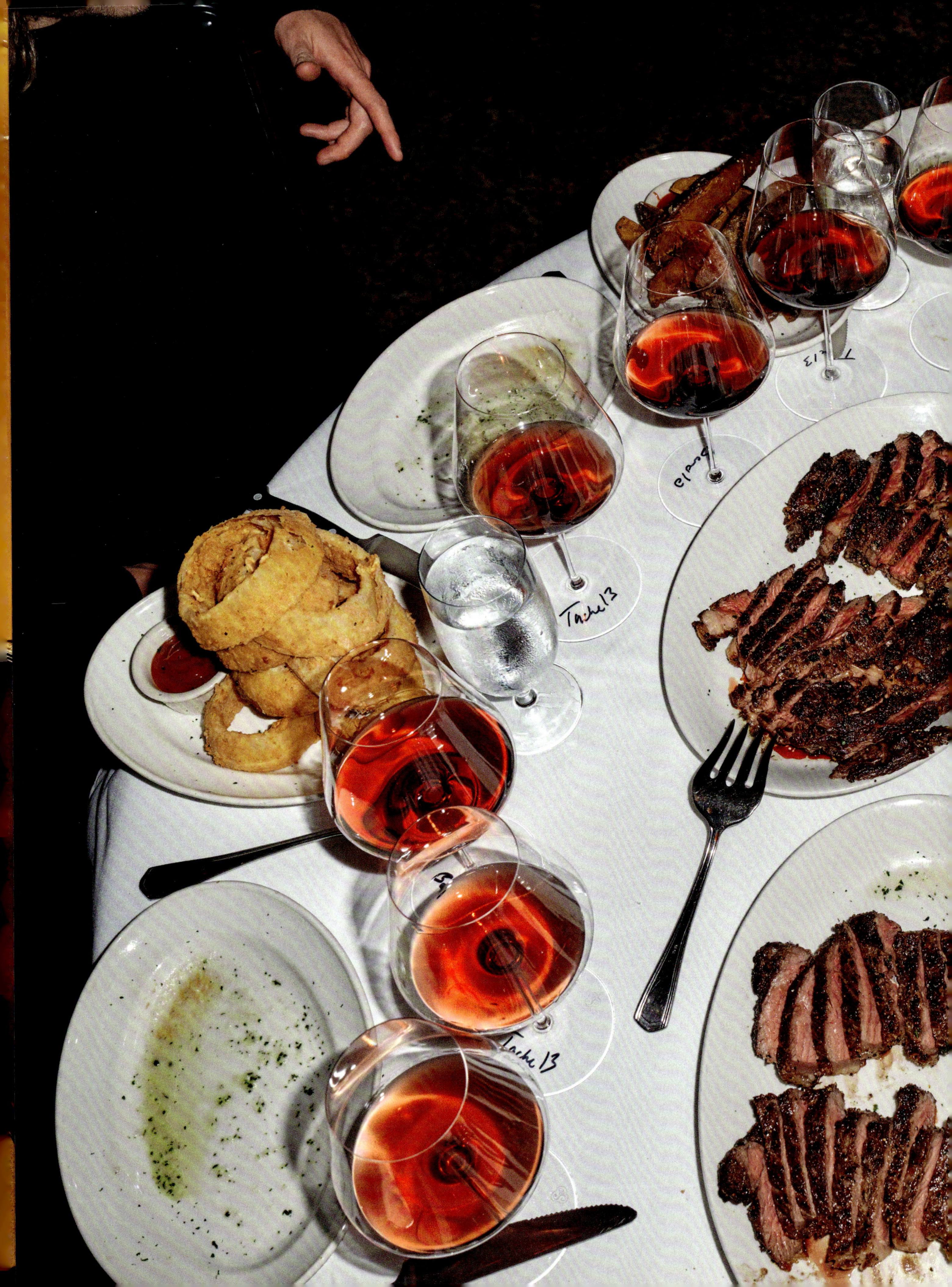
Tache 13
Tache 13

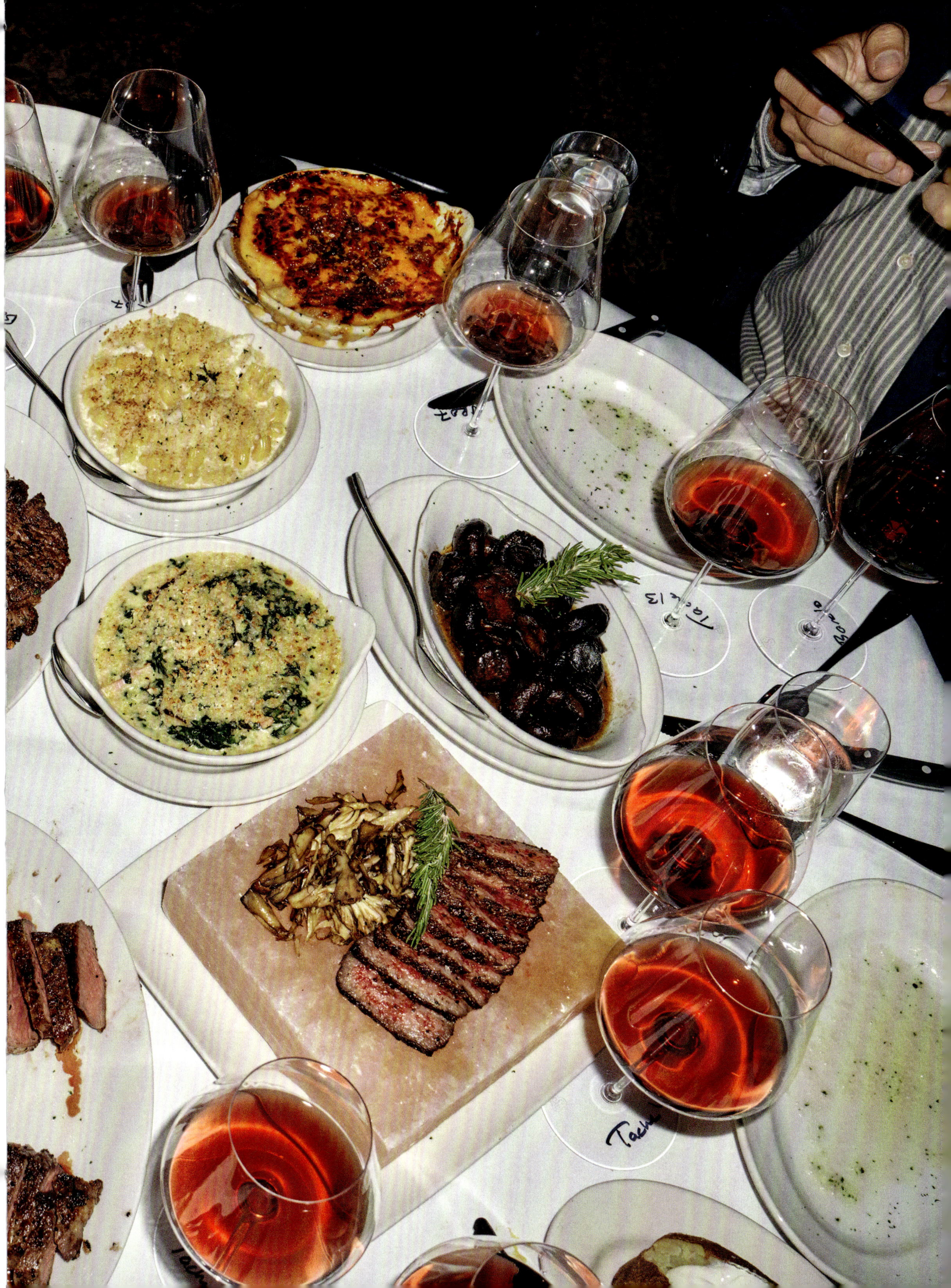

Johnny Hernandez Villaverde—The Grill Master

"I've been working in steak houses for almost twenty years, ever since I left Puebla, Mexico. From the beginning, the goal was always to work the grill. It was very hard, but practice, practice, practice and it gets better. The last eight years, I have been at Pappas. It was different from the other places. They dry-age for a month or so, and it is a gas grill, not wood. That was new for me. The training is not easy because the standard is high. Things are more precise. On Father's Day, we cooked nine hundred steaks on our three grills. You have a responsibility to cook each one right.

The ticket comes in, you season with salt and pepper, and it goes straight to the grill. The less you touch it, the better. Get it seared and don't flip it over and over. You also must be very careful not to open the grill too much and have the temperature go down. We have thermometers to check doneness, but there are some of us who can tell by instinct. We've been doing it a long time. You can look at the clock, press against the meat with the tongs, and just know. Then you let it rest. I think that is the correct way."

Chris Shepherd—The Regular

Another person who was born to explain just how well they undersell and overdeliver at Pappas is Houston-based chef, humanitarian, and bon vivant Chris Shepherd. He was our guest of honor.

"I would say that for the most part, restaurants do not get better with age—but the best steak houses get better with age. Think about why: you're making mac and cheese and creamed spinach. It's a matter of technique and execution. If you do it over and over and over again, what happens? It gets better.

You can achieve that consistency quite frankly because, as a steak house, you usually have a bigger bottom line. You can pay the people in those positions more than they'd get elsewhere. And what that grill guy's job entails is walking in, cooking steaks, and then leaving. He doesn't have to clean up at the end of the night, set up before service, or do anything else. That person is gonna be there forever. Same thing with the cheesecake person.

At Pappas the wine program is so deep that you can find anything at any budget that you want, which I think is pretty cool. They cut the steaks tableside. They give you the show. It's gonna be expensive. But they give you all the things that make it worth it."

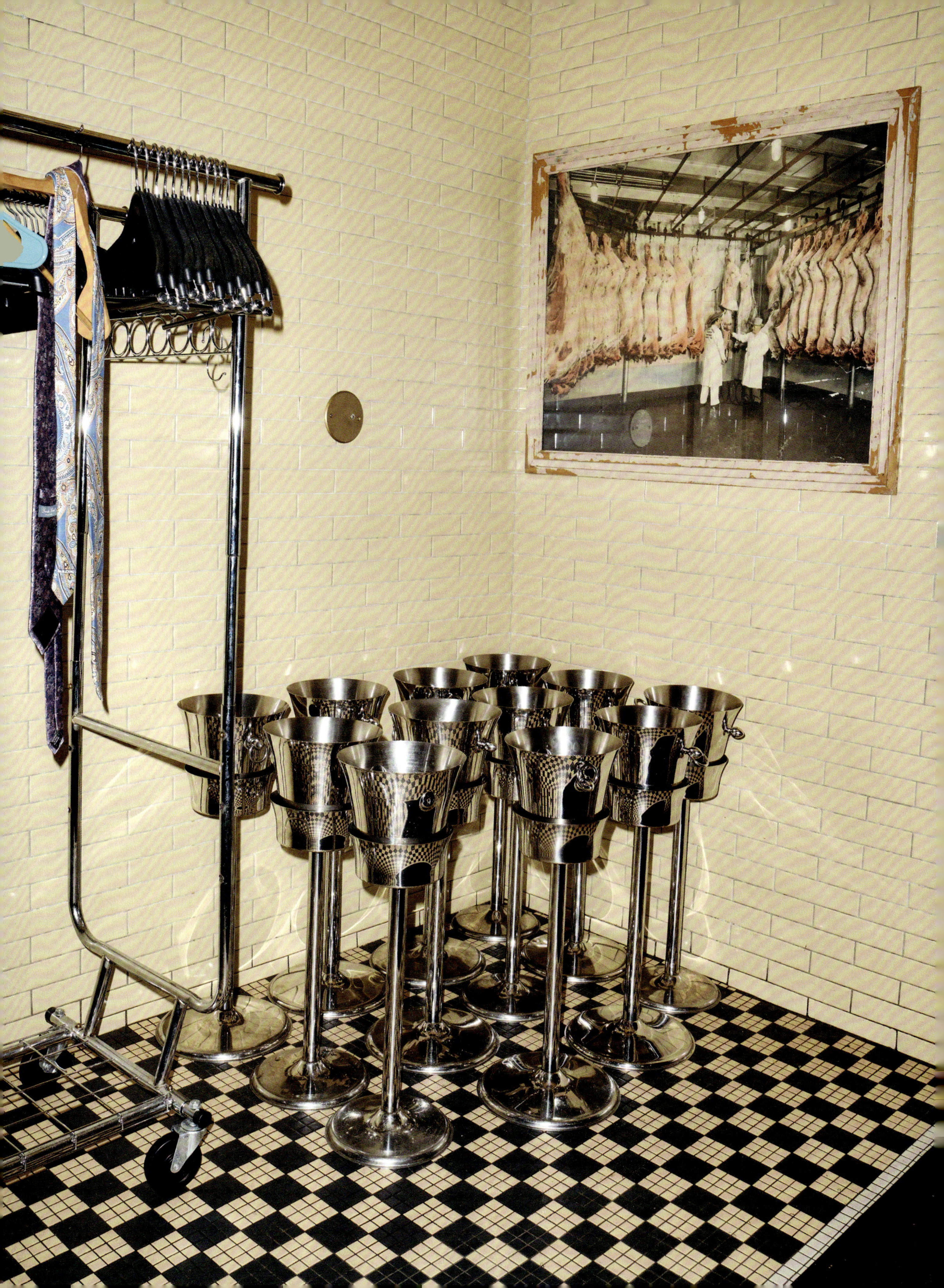

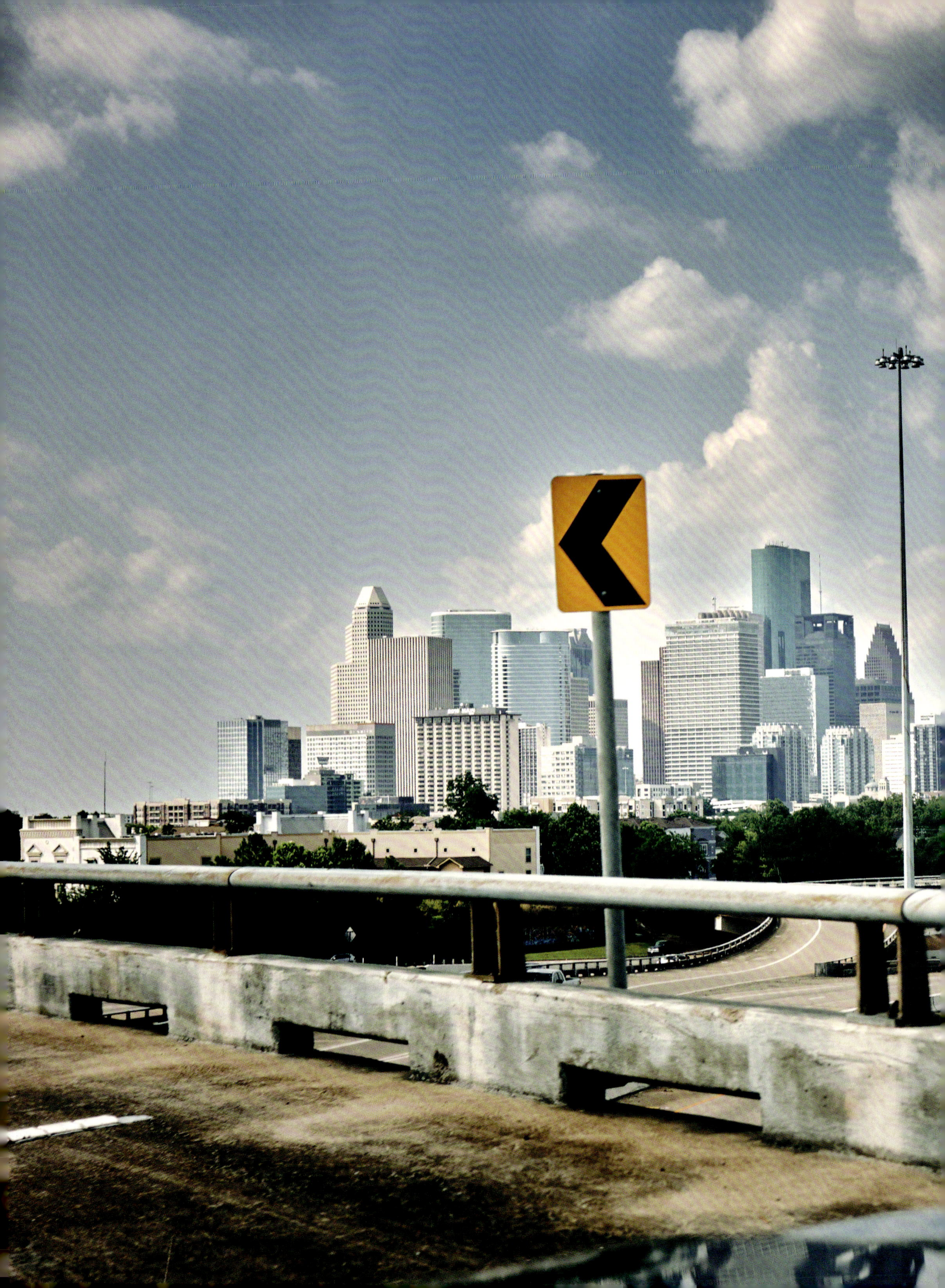

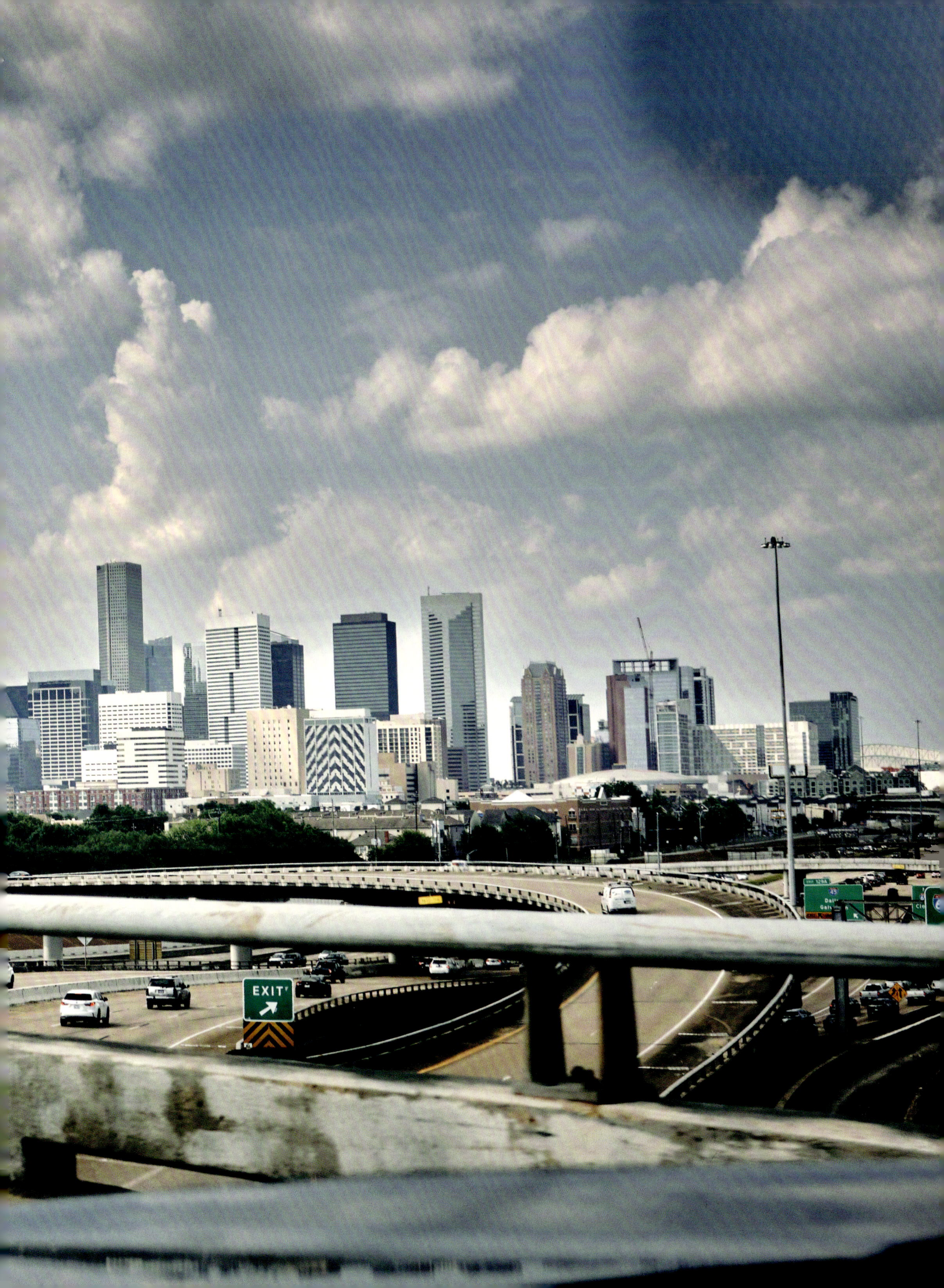
EXIT

HOUSTON

TASTE OF TEXAS

BY THE NUMBERS

Opening year: 1977
Founders: Nina and Edd Hendee
Address: 10505 Katy Freeway, Houston, Texas 77024
House specials: Texas quail bites; Tomahawk rib eye

Whoever came up with the phrase "Everything's bigger in Texas" probably did it while they were standing in line at the salad bar at Taste of Texas. We walked into the highest-grossing independent restaurant in the entire state just before lunch service and instantly got separated like distracted toddlers at Epcot.

I roamed around. Staffers in the restaurant's signature uniform—brown vest over black dress shirt—gathered for pre-shift. Christian rock played from the speakers. We didn't get to meet the owners, Nina and Edd Hendee, who founded Taste of Texas in 1977. The Hendees are passionate about politics, religion, and their salad bar. They met while working at Steak and Ale, the place that some say invented the salad bar. In the beginning, they served chili. Then they became the first steak house in Texas to serve Angus beef. Now they feed at least five hundred people a day, all while operating a museum next door dedicated to the history of Texas. In the foyer, they've got the interior doors of the Alamo hanging behind a pane of glass.

"Can I help you find your table, sir?" A fellow tall person named Austin Henry saw that I was deep in thought, standing in the middle of the restaurant. Or maybe that I was just lost. He helped me find our table. At the time, I knew him only as "Austin H." That's what was printed on the name tag. It made it easier to track him down months later when I wanted to see if he could answer some of the questions I didn't get to ask him during the meal.

Austin Henry, who will tell you all about Taste of Texas on page 169.

STEAK HOUSE

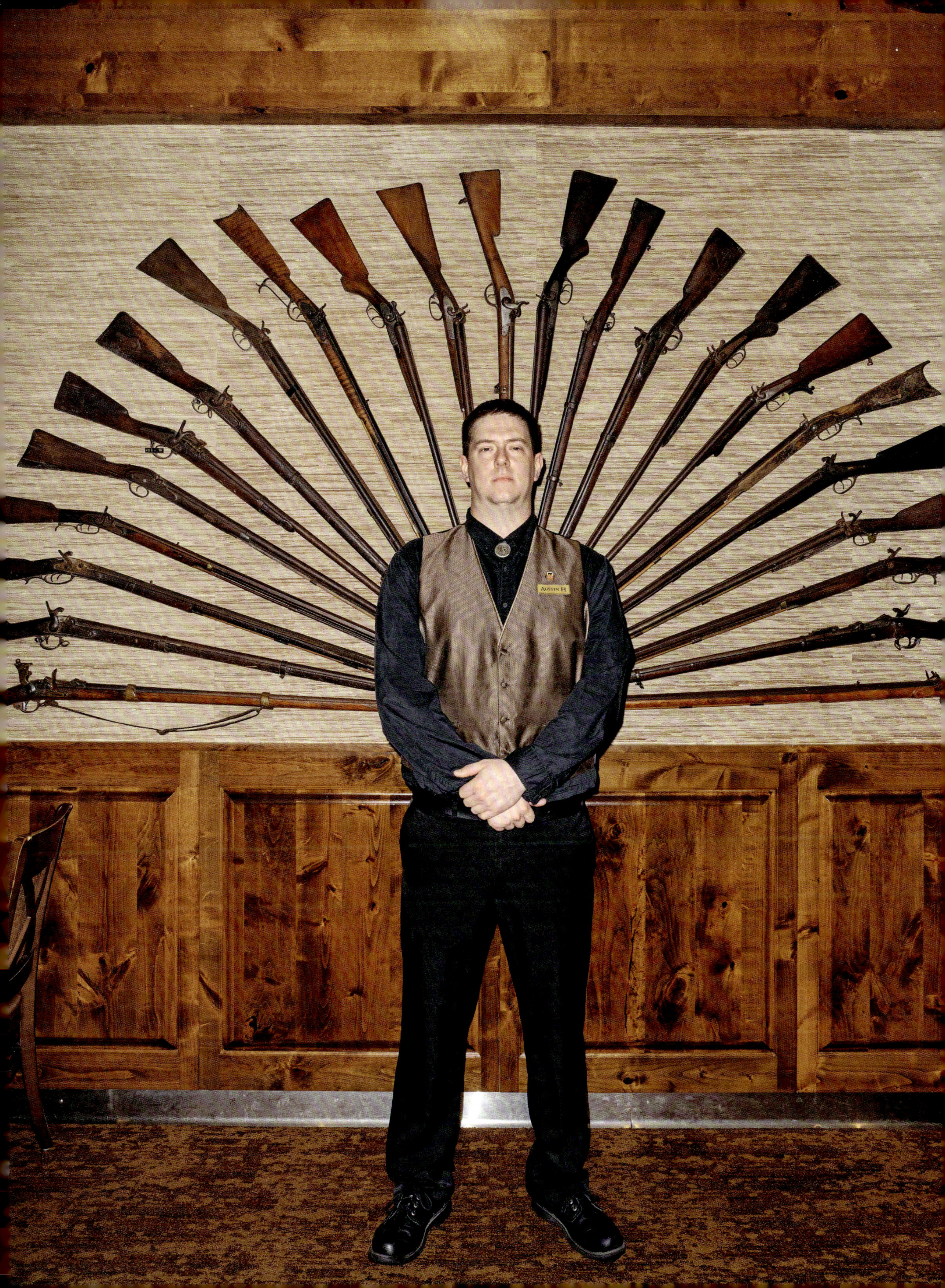
AUSTIN H

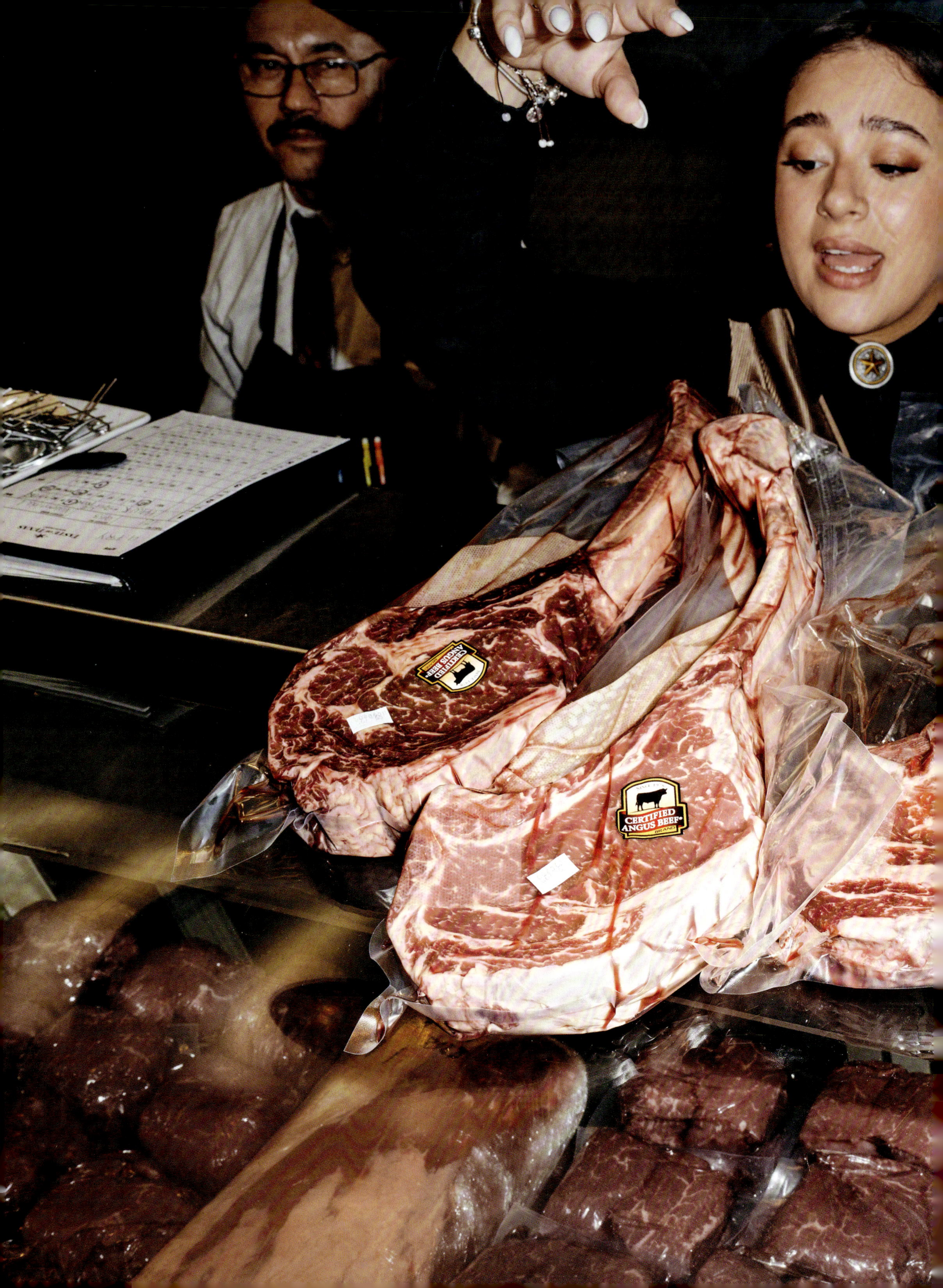
CERTIFIED ANGUS BEEF
CERTIFIED ANGUS BEEF

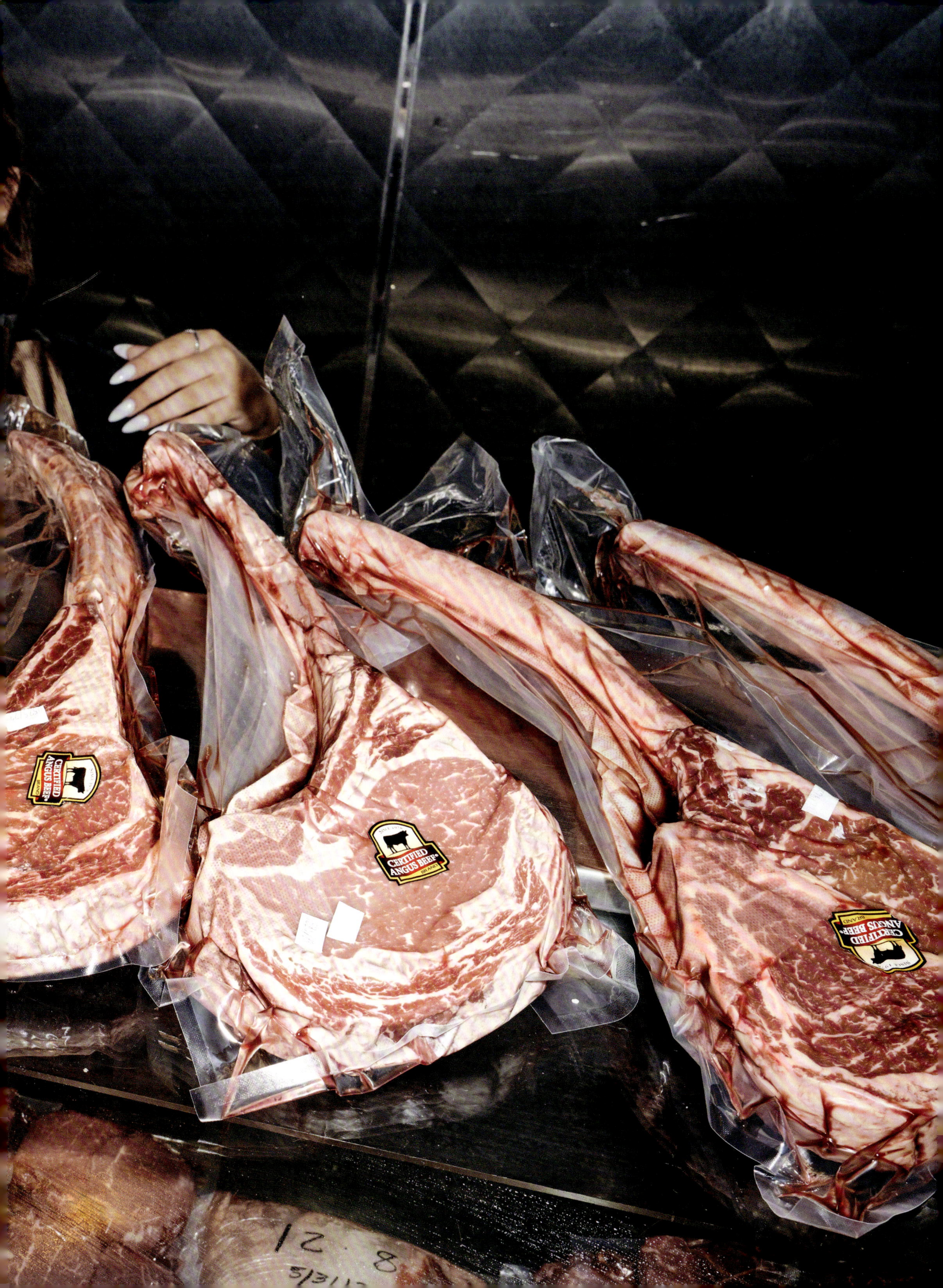
CERTIFIED ANGUS BEEF®
CERTIFIED ANGUS BEEF®
CERTIFIED ANGUS BEEF®

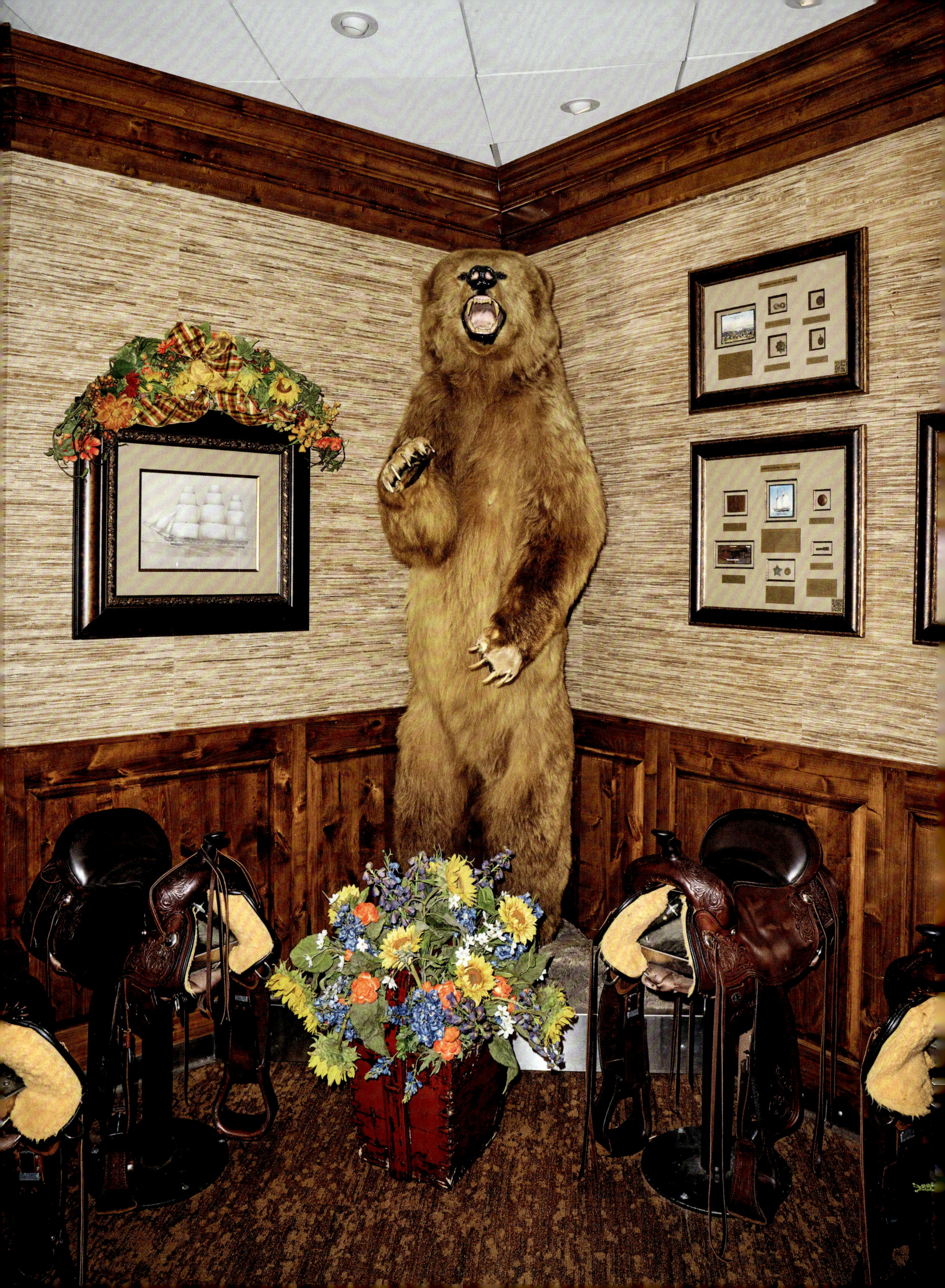

Austin Henry—The Gentle Giant

"Before I started working at Taste of Texas, my first couple of experiences here were date nights with the now-wife. It was overwhelming being presented with 450 different bottles of wine on an iPad. You can get lost in the building. You go to the salad bar and make a mental note of where you are sitting, but after picking 25 ingredients and breads and butters and cheeses, you forget.

If you call Taste of Texas at the moment, you will get a voicemail that says that the only way to get a table is by using the online system. You cannot speak to a person because there is no way we could keep up. Next year, we are thinking of not taking walk-ins at all during the holidays because reservations dominate so hard.

There's an extensive training process. They can't expect you to know all of it right away, but they are not handing anything out to anybody. For the training side of it, you need to know a lot more than the shorthand, the abbreviations, and the table numbers. You need to know the ingredients, the sides that come with particular entrées, the type of add-ons and toppings that are available, whether it be the Oscar topping or maybe the fried shrimp on the side to complement the big tomahawk.

There's eighteen feet worth of grill back in the kitchen. You have three six-foot grills side by side, and you have eight to ten guys working the line on the inside of the kitchen. Down on the fryer, you have another guy, then another two guys doing sides, pecan-crusted chickens, and appetizers. That is not counting everybody else. Staff in the building is up to 225 people, 90 or so of whom are servers.

Faith is definitely a core part of this establishment—the owners lead through God. I didn't really grow up religious, but since I have been here, whenever they do have prayer or ask us to keep someone in our prayers, I definitely stick around. It is not an easy life for everybody out there. Everybody has something or other going on and could use a little help.

People might be surprised to learn that in many, many cases our guests are from out of the country. We have our menu available in like 15 different languages. We treat our international guests to a bandana and cowboy hat for photos and let them keep the bandana as a gift."

DALLAS–FORT WORTH

FOGO DE CHÃO

BY THE NUMBERS

Opening year: 1997
(in the United States)
Founders: Arri and Jair Coser
Address: 2619 McKinney Avenue, Suite 150, Dallas, Texas 75204
House specials: Picanha; Fraldinha

The traffic on the way to Dallas was beyond brutal, but in the end we made it to dinner at the place that introduced America to the mesmerizing dance of the spear-wielding gaucho—the first outpost of Fogo de Chão to open in the United States.

Being famished allowed me to better understand how the Fogo phenomenon spread with the power of a flaming wall of skewers in the late '90s. I started eating the minute I sat down and I didn't have to say a single word. All I had to do was flip the card at my place setting to red and dart over to the glistening buffet to awaken my palate with its icy-fresh bounty. I helped myself to a nurturing bowl of bean stew, too. Then I thought about just how dang cool it was that my first taste of Dallas's steak house culture was going to be a bowl of feijoada at a chain restaurant in the suburbs.

When Fogo opened in 1997, the locals didn't really understand what was going on. They'd come to peek at the menu, but there was no menu. They had stumbled upon a steak house from South America with no entrées and an interesting name. *Fogo de Chão* means "fire on the ground," a reference to the concept's humble southern Brazilian origins, where the art of celebrating over barbecue is called the churrasco. Fogo specializes in a specific style called rodízio, in which gauchos pull giant skewers of meat from blazing wall-to-wall grills in the kitchen and parade them around the dining room, their eyes trained toward red cards on tables like bulls charging the crimson side of a matador's cape.

Instead of going into all that, a woman named Selma Oliveira would tell curious passersby, "Please allow us to share what we do with you and let me know what you think." Sometimes she'd take them by the arm when showing them into the dining room. Selma had moved to America from Brazil in 1986. She worked at the Marriott in Addison, Texas, for twelve years. That's how she met the owners of the Fogo de Chão in São Paulo, which she loved. It was a very big deal down there. Pretty soon, Selma was teaching her countrymen English and working with an immigration lawyer to move a dozen gauchos from Brazil to Texas. To this day, all new Fogo hires must train for three months before they can work their first shift in the dining room. They learn to butcher, grill, slice, and serve with panache.

I had a bit of everything. When one gaucho stood before me with a skewer of bife do vazio, I asked what the name would be in English. *Oh! Flank steak.* Turns out that Fogo helped turn Americans on to that cut. Same with picanha. I was already familiar with that one.

PS: *Gaucho* is the Portuguese word for "cowboy." I love that.

The gauchos arrive. And they keep arriving. All night long. Until you surrender.

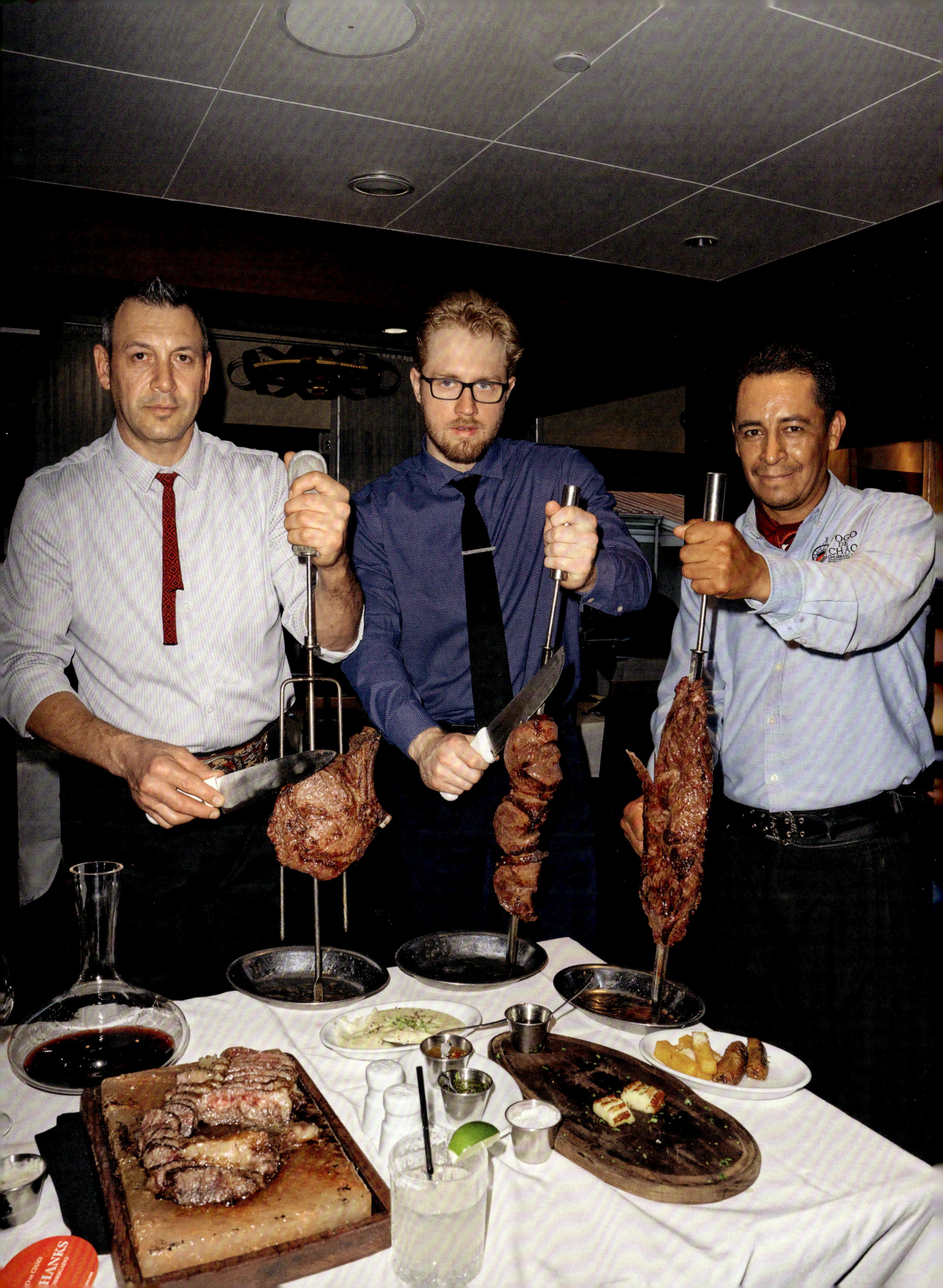

OGO
DE
CHÃO
HANKS

DALLAS–FORT WORTH

CATTLEMEN'S

BY THE NUMBERS

Opening year: 1947
Founders: Jesse and Mozelle Roach
Address: 2458 North Main Street, Fort Worth, Texas 76164
House special: Heart O' Texas rib eye

"That the cattle business is a form of show business was apparent from the start."

In a very amazing book called *Raising Steaks: The Life and Times of American Beef,* Betty Fussell writes that "American cowboy competitions [like the rodeo and cattle drive] were used to promote something—the ranch, the cattle business, the town, the nation." Things like guts. American reinvention. Just not the Mexican *vaqueros* the cowboys modeled themselves after.

We went to the Fort Worth Stockyards to witness the longest continuing cattle drive in America. Blink, and the show's over. But you could certainly spend days trying on boots and Stetsons in this 100-acre historic district that was once the largest site of livestock trading in the region. From what I can gather, it boomed from the 1880s to the 1950s.

That day, I got to accomplish my mission: having a bite at the oldest steak house in the Stockyards, which is aptly named Cattlemen's, just before the restaurant and its Big Saloon Energy finally faded away for good. At least that's what I thought was about to happen. There'd been rumors floating around that the business never recovered from the pandemic—but when we stopped by, there was all sorts of construction going on.

Turns out that Cattlemen's was getting a remodel from none other than the showrunner of *Yellowstone*. He and his team donated two million bucks to refresh the space, install a smoker, and keep the prices low. Reportedly, all ninety staff members stuck around and were paid full salaries while they fixed up the place. I hope the cows in Cowtown are happy about that.

Here's a photo of the longhorns, in case you were wondering why they're called that.

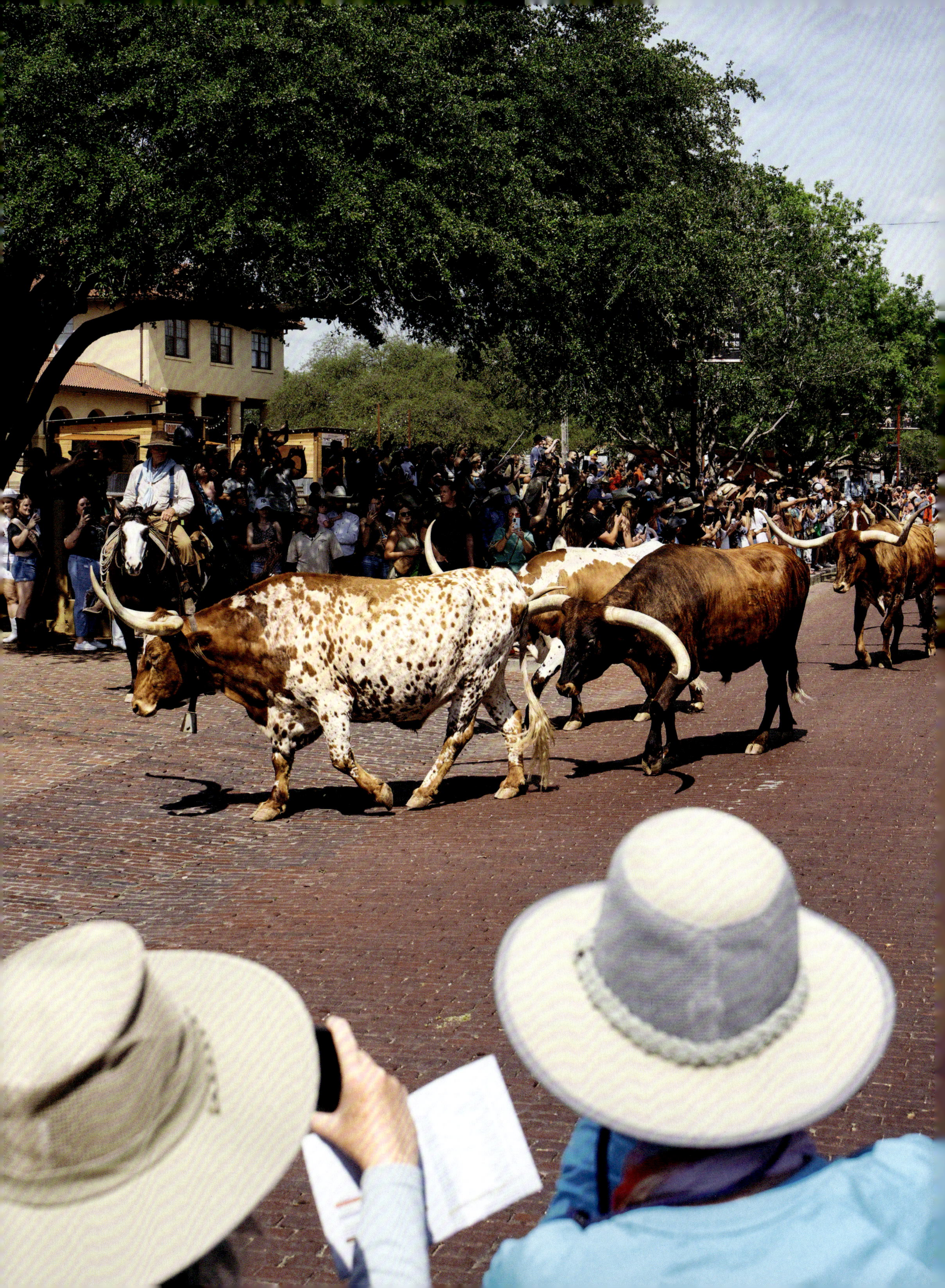

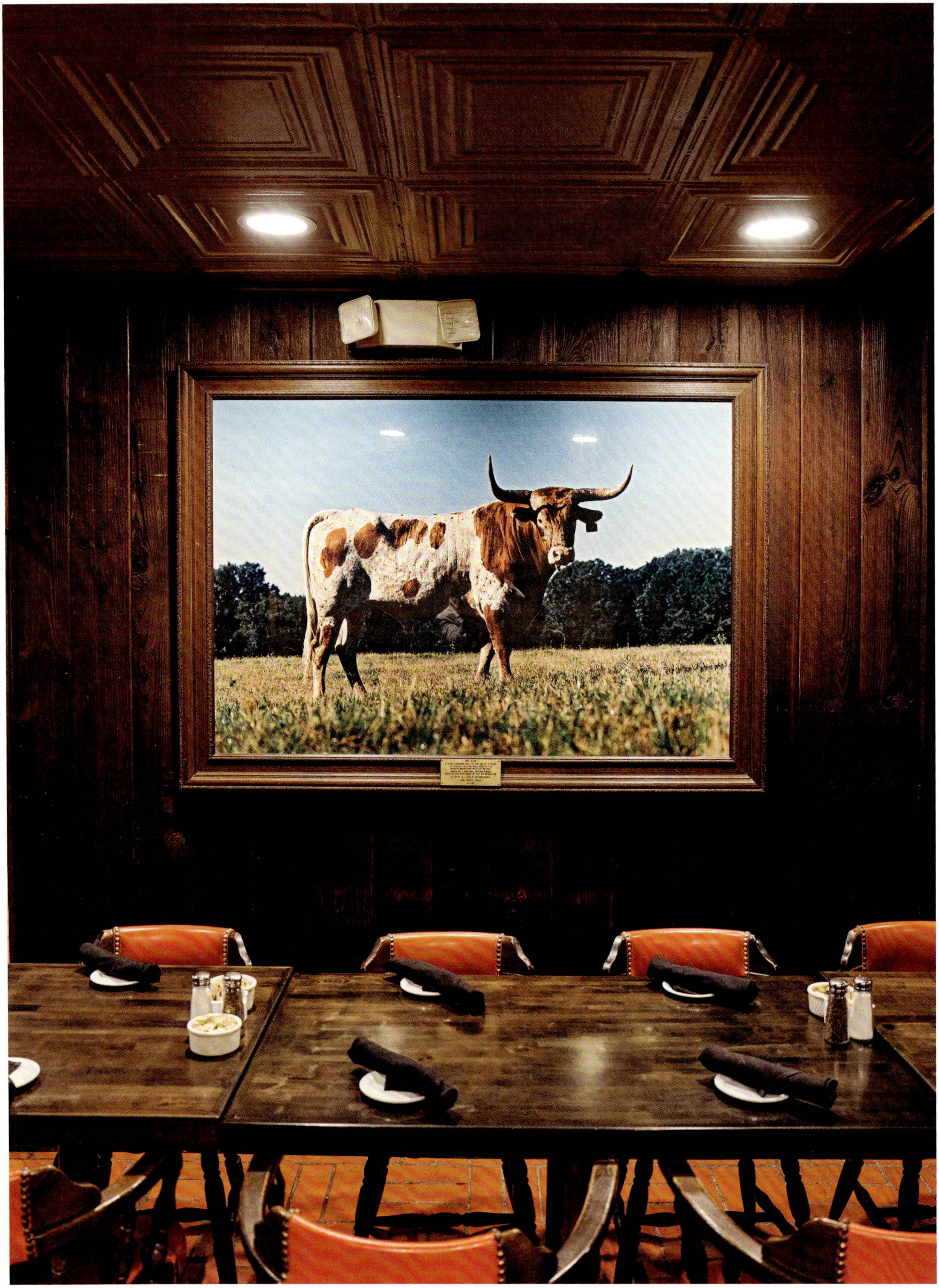

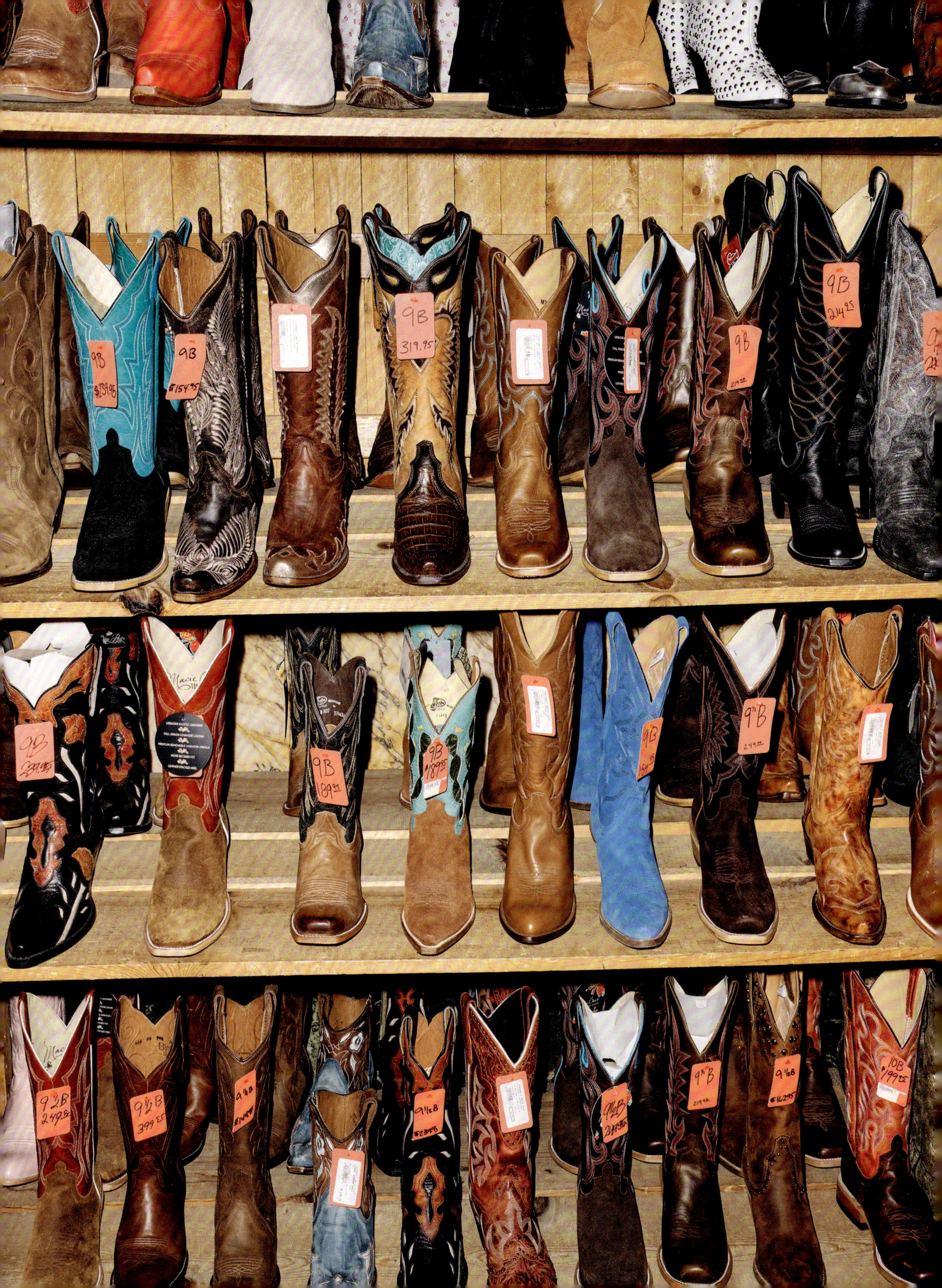

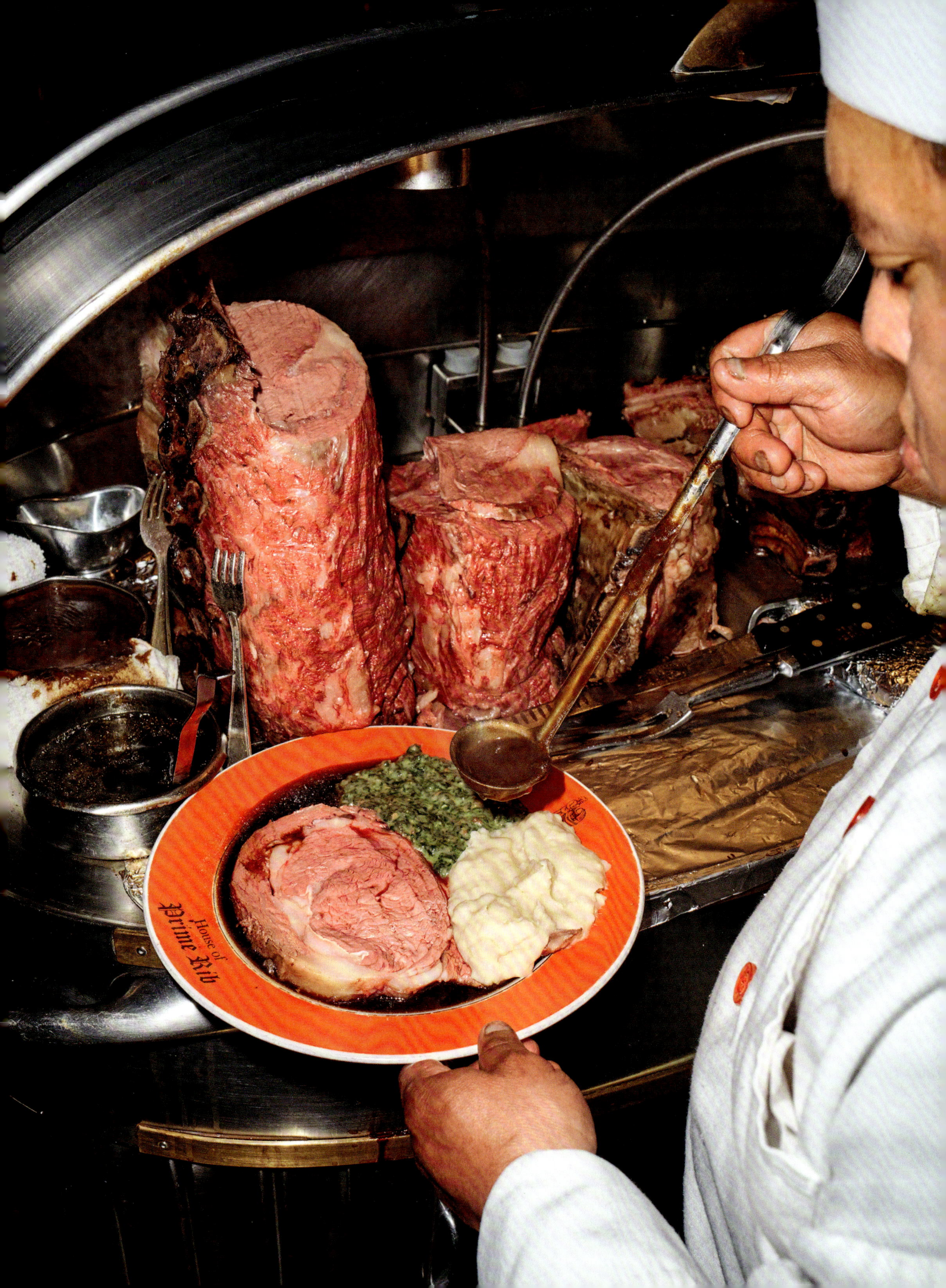
House of
Prime Rib

RECIPES

OTHER MEATY DELIGHTS

POLLO ASADO

Serves 2 to 4

Marinated Chicken
One 3-pound organic chicken, spatchcocked

2 cups chicken broth

6 tablespoons freshly squeezed lime juice (about 3 limes)

6 tablespoons freshly squeezed lemon juice (about 2 lemons)

1 garlic head, cloves peeled and smashed

2 tablespoons fine sea salt

1 tablespoon dried Mexican oregano or marjoram

1 tablespoon fresh thyme

Rub
¼ cup neutral oil

2 tablespoons freshly squeezed lime juice (about 1 lime)

1 tablespoon roughly chopped fresh rosemary

1 tablespoon sweet paprika

1 tablespoon crushed red pepper flakes

1 tablespoon whole black peppercorns

1 tablespoon fine sea salt

1 tablespoon dried Mexican oregano or marjoram

Vinaigrette
6 tablespoons freshly squeezed lemon juice (about 2 lemons)

2 ounces Parmesan cheese, grated

2 dried chiles de árbol, stemmed and seeded

3 garlic cloves, peeled

1 tablespoon freshly cracked black pepper

¾ teaspoon fine sea salt

1 cup neutral oil

For Serving
1 bunch fresh cilantro, tied together with kitchen twine

Corn or flour tortillas

Salsa, ideally spicy

Famously referred to as Chuy Chicken in my household, after chef Chuy Villarreal of Monterrey's CARA DE VACA, this is one of the best dang birds I've ever experienced. The smoke, the rich citrusy sauce, the glorious sight of the thing splayed out before you . . . it is something to devour. The art of cooking chicken is something I am still mastering. You must understand the chicken and respect it. A spatchcock, which your butcher can do for you, makes for even cooking and simple carving. You'll have to marinate the chicken for at least 10 hours. Time is *sabor*.

Marinate the chicken: Remove the chicken from its packaging and pat dry. In a large bowl, add 2 cups water, the chicken broth, lime juice, lemon juice, garlic, salt, oregano, and thyme and mix well until the salt dissolves. Add the chicken and submerge it in the marinade. Cover and refrigerate for 2 to 4 hours.

Make the rub: In a blender or using a mortar and pestle, add the oil, lime juice, rosemary, paprika, red pepper flakes, black peppercorns, salt, and oregano and blend or grind into a paste.

Remove the chicken from the fridge, discard the marinade, and pat the chicken dry. Coat the chicken with the rub, including the underside. Cover and refrigerate for at least 8 hours or up to overnight.

When ready to cook, preheat a smoker to 250°F for indirect cooking. Add the chicken and cook until the thickest part of the thigh or breast reaches an internal temperature of 165°F on an instant-read thermometer. Start testing after 90 minutes.

While the chicken cooks, make the vinaigrette: In a blender, add the lemon juice, Parmesan, chiles, garlic, black pepper, and salt and blend until smooth, then add the oil in a thin stream with the machine running so it emulsifies. Transfer the vinaigrette to a bowl, cover, and set aside.

Prepare a charcoal grill for direct high-heat grilling or preheat a gas grill to high (alternatively, place a cast-iron griddle over medium-high heat). Hang the cilantro bundle over the grill or place it on a low-heat part of the grill until the leaves dry out without burning, 5 to 7 minutes.

Meanwhile, grill the chicken, skin-side down, rotating as needed for even cooking, until the skin crisps and lightly chars, 5 to 7 minutes.

Place the chicken on a serving platter, drizzle with just enough vinaigrette to coat the chicken and the bottom of the platter, sprinkle with the dried cilantro leaves, and serve immediately with tortillas and (spicy) salsa of your choice.

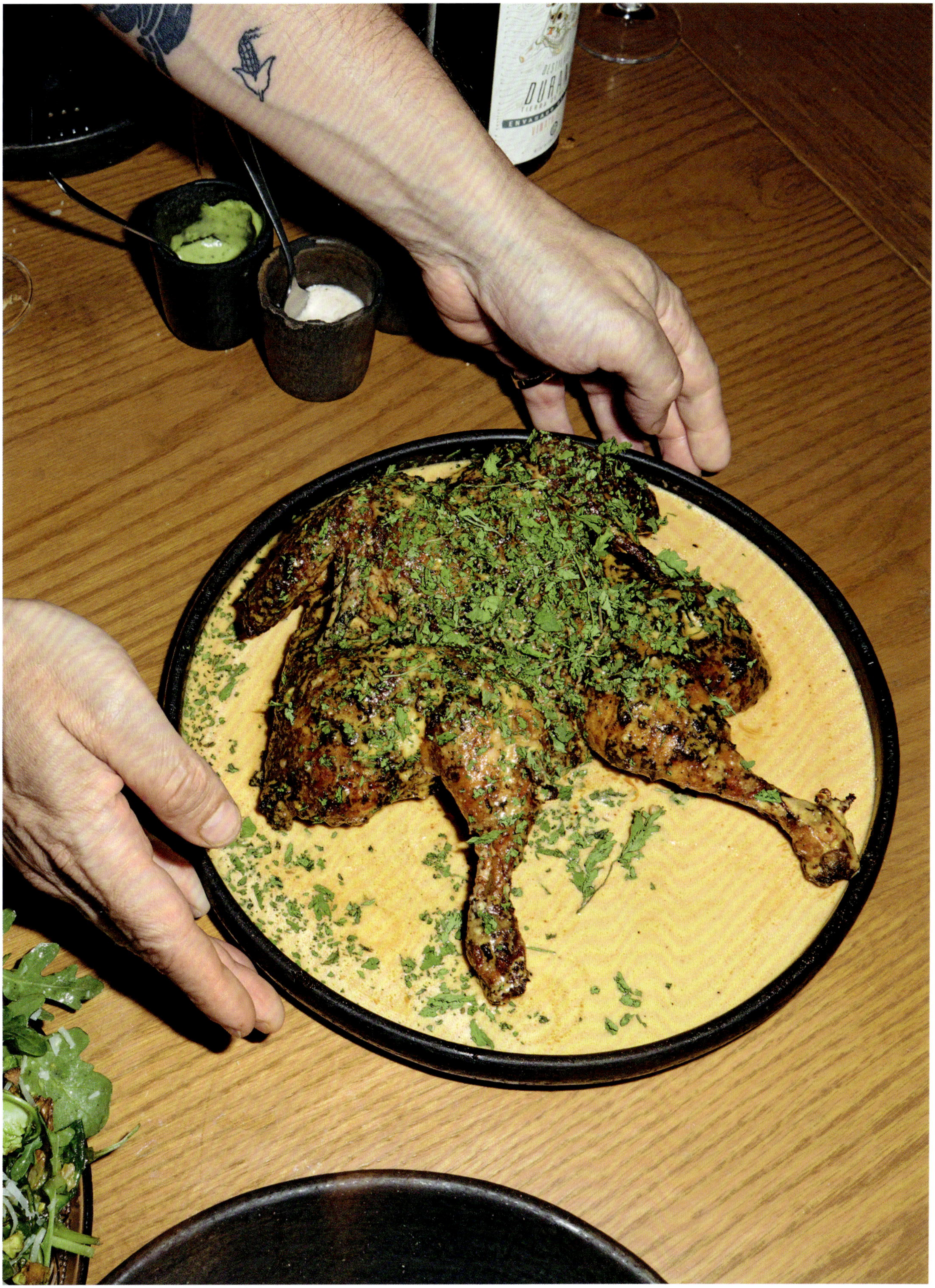

A FINE PORK CHOP

Serves 2 to 4

Brined Pork
1 tablespoon plus 1 teaspoon Diamond Crystal kosher salt, plus more for seasoning
1 tablespoon sugar
One 2-pound pork chop, about 1 inch thick

Mushrooms & Sauce
2 cups trimmed and chopped chanterelle or maitake mushrooms
Kosher salt
1 large shallot, minced
2 garlic cloves, minced
¼ cup vin jaune or dry white wine
1 cup veal stock
1 thyme sprig
2 tablespoons (¼ stick) unsalted butter

It looked like any other pork chop. By which I mean that when I first laid on eyes on it, I instinctively wanted to grab the caramelized, sweet-smelling thing with my hands. BAVETTE'S (page 104) knows how to strike that chord in people. In the case of their pork chop, it's about cooking with a light, wise hand. The sauce in their pork chop isn't a heavy reduction. It eats more like a jus, bright yet so savory. And all the pork really asks of you is your patience: an overnight brine and a proper tempering. Time is flavor.

Brine the pork: In a large bowl, add 6 cups water and stir in the salt and sugar until dissolved. Add the pork chop to the brine, cover, and refrigerate for at least 2 hours or up to overnight.

Remove the pork from the fridge, discard the brine, and pat the pork dry. Salt generously on both sides, and let the pork sit for about 45 minutes to come to room temperature.

Preheat the oven to 400°F. Fit a sheet pan with a roasting rack.

Place a large cast-iron pan over medium-high heat. When the pan is hot, use tongs to sear the pork's fat cap without moving it, until some of the fat is rendered, 2 minutes. Then sear the pork chop until evenly browned, about 3 minutes per side. Remove the pan from the heat and place the pork chop on the roasting rack, reserving the pan drippings. Roast the pork chop for 20 to 25 minutes, until the internal temperature reaches 145°F on an instant-read thermometer.

While the pork is in the oven, make the mushrooms: Drain the excess pork fat from the reserved pan drippings into a heatproof bowl, leaving about a tablespoon of fat in the pan. Place the pan over medium-high heat. When hot, add the mushrooms in an even layer and let them cook undisturbed until nicely browned and seared, about 5 minutes, then flip and repeat on the other side for 2 minutes. If the pan dries out, continue to add the reserved pork fat about 1 tablespoon at a time. Once browned, season with a pinch of salt, stir, then transfer the mushrooms to a plate and set aside.

Make the sauce: In the same pan, add the shallot, garlic, a pinch of salt, and more pork fat, if needed. Cook, stirring often, until fragrant and browned, about 5 minutes. Deglaze the pan with the wine and veal stock and add the thyme. Lower the heat to medium and let the sauce reduce by half, 7 to 10 minutes. Stir in the butter, then remove from the heat. Taste and adjust with salt as needed. Strain through a fine-mesh strainer into a heatproof bowl and discard the solids.

Serve the pork on a platter with the mushrooms and sauce spooned on top.

CHICKEN-FRIED IBÉRICO PORK STEAK

Serves 4

Seeing chicken-fried steak on a menu in the South always brings me back to my younger days touring in the hardcore scene, eating at a Waffle House at Jangus knows what hour of the night for the third or fifth time in the span of a week. The tummy ache would set in after every visit. To distract myself from the cold sweats, I'd start to wonder about the cut and type of steak I had just consumed. Probably not something you'd want to bring home to Momma. So I jacked up the recipe using my new love, which is Ibérico pork. It's still a Southern-style schnitzel, but we're holding the cream-dream gravy because I want you to appreciate the juicy and tender qualities of the noble, acorn-fed Spanish hog that has given us delicacies, like the most exquisite sliced jamón in the world and this.

Lay each steak in between two pieces of plastic wrap and use a meat mallet to pound the steaks to a ¼-inch thickness. Season with a pinch of salt and set aside.

In a wide, shallow bowl, whisk together the buttermilk and eggs. In a separate wide, shallow bowl, mix together the flour, panko, fennel seeds, paprika, garlic powder, cayenne, 1½ teaspoons salt, and the black pepper.

Pour enough oil into a large skillet to reach a depth of ¼ inch and place over medium heat until the temperature reaches 350°F. Fit a sheet pan with a wire rack.

Prepare the steaks by first dipping them in the buttermilk mixture and letting any excess drip off, then the flour mixture (being sure to press the fennel seeds into the steak). Gently place in the hot oil, working in batches to prevent overcrowding. Fry for 2 minutes, flip, and fry the other side, 2 minutes more. When the internal temperature reaches 140°F on an instant-read thermometer, remove from the oil and drain on the wire rack. Repeat with the remaining steaks. Serve with mustard and lemon wedges on the side.

Four 8-ounce Ibérico pork steaks
1½ teaspoons Diamond Crystal kosher salt, plus more for seasoning
1 cup buttermilk
2 eggs
1 cup all-purpose flour
1 cup panko breadcrumbs, finely ground
2 teaspoons whole fennel seeds
½ teaspoon sweet paprika
½ teaspoon garlic powder
½ teaspoon cayenne pepper
¼ teaspoon freshly cracked black pepper
Neutral oil for frying
Dijon mustard for serving
Lemon wedges for serving

Serves 10 to 12

One 48-ounce center cut beef tenderloin (see Notes)

Kosher salt

2 tablespoons shio koji (optional; see headnote, page 138)

Two 16-ounce packages puff pastry

2 tablespoons neutral oil or clarified butter

12 thin slices prosciutto, speck, or Parma ham

1 teaspoon minced fresh thyme

2 tablespoons Dijon mustard

All-purpose flour for rolling

2 eggs, lightly beaten

1 teaspoon flaky sea salt, preferably Maldon

Notes: You want any skinny ends of the tenderloin tied so the thickness is as even as possible.

A lattice cutter is a tool that can be purchased online or from a baking supply store. Do not attempt to cut the pattern by hand if you're not a professional pastry chef as it is a major pain in the ass.

BEEF WELLINGTON

The siblings behind BOROS STRAVA (page 282) made their world-famous beef Wellington for the very first time when they were still living in Prague, near their hometown. Their colleague Didier LeGrand had recently landed in the hospital. No one could have predicted it, but that Czechian tragedy birthed one of the finest dishes ever served in Clark County.

Season the beef liberally with kosher salt and then rub with the shio koji, if using. Wrap the meat up into a log with a double layer of plastic wrap. Place on a sheet pan and chill in the fridge overnight. Remove the puff pastry from the freezer and pop that into the fridge as well. The next day, unwrap the beef and pat dry with a paper towel (we're cooking cold meat here, don't get used to it).

In a large, heavy skillet, heat the oil over medium-high heat and sear the beef until deeply browned, 3 to 4 minutes per side. Remove from the heat and transfer to a plate.

Roll out 18 inches of plastic wrap. Shingle the plastic with prosciutto in two rows of six pieces; it should form a rectangle large enough to roll up the entire tenderloin. Sprinkle the thyme over the prosciutto. Rub the beef all over with the mustard and place the long side of the beef perpendicular to the short ends of the prosciutto. Using the plastic wrap, roll up the beef, tucking in the ends of the prosciutto as you go to completely seal it. Wrap the whole thing up tightly in plastic wrap, tying off the ends, and then chill in the fridge for at least 8 hours or up to 24 hours.

Preheat the oven to 425°F. Flour one sheet pan and line a second with parchment paper. Lightly flour a large clean work surface. Remove the beef from the fridge.

Using a rolling pin, roll out the puff pastry package on the floured surface to ¼-inch thickness, then transfer to the floured sheet pan and place in the fridge. Roll out the second puff pastry. Unwrap the beef and place onto the longer edge of the puff pastry. Roll the beef up, tucking in the sides of the pastry, and then seal the long edge with a brush of beaten egg. Trim any excess and make sure the pastry is sealed tightly, pinching and pressing the dough together so there are no gaps. Set the Wellington seam-side down onto the parchment-lined pan.

Remove the puff pastry from the fridge and, using a lattice cutter (see Notes) and firm pressure, roll the tool lengthwise evenly across the pastry. Gently pull the pastry to "open up" the pattern (use a small paring knife to release the stubborn areas). Brush the Wellington with the egg and then gently lift and lay the lattice over, tucking the pastry over the ends and under the length of the Wellington. Brush the lattice with the egg and generously sprinkle all over with the flaky salt.

Bake until the internal temperature reaches 115°F, 50 to 55 minutes. Let rest on a cutting board for 45 minutes to 1 hour before slicing and serving.

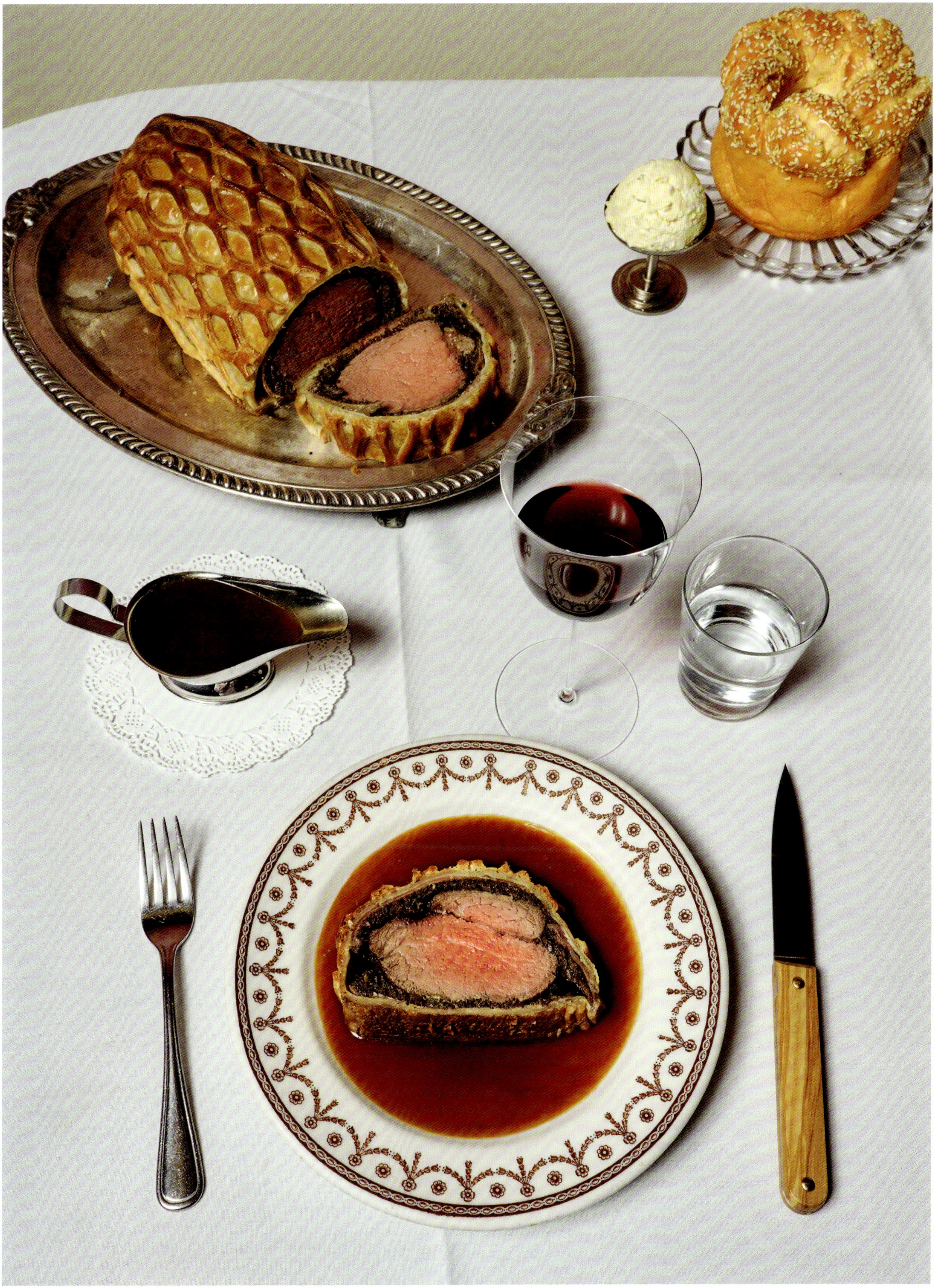

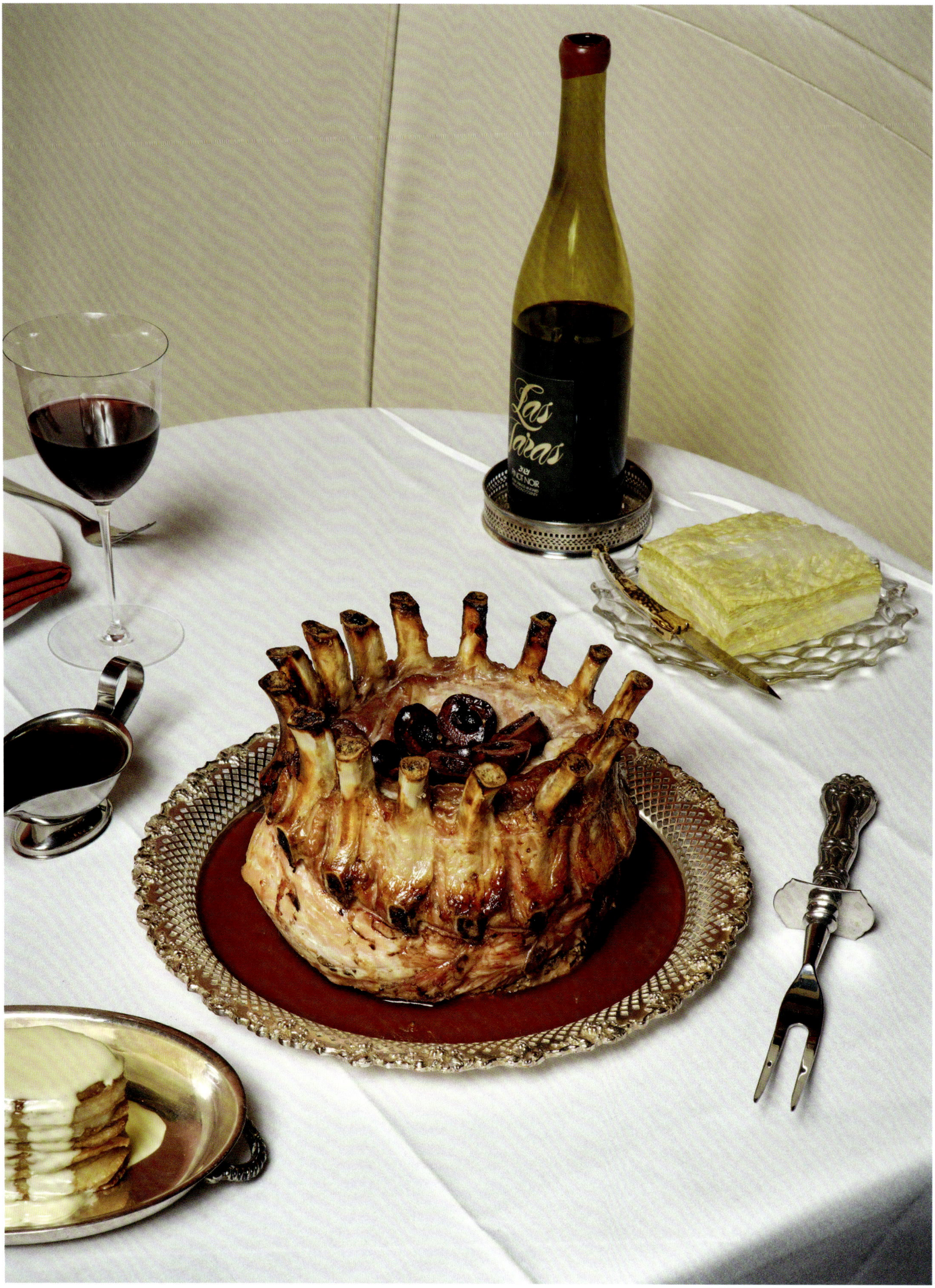
Las

THE CROWN OF PORK

Serves 10 to 12

As we have established, the Czech expats and retired circus performers who own BOROS STRAVA (page 282) are bringing back the royal English classics in a super-regal way. And just like the Boros's Beef Wellington (page 182), their show-stopping Crown of Pork came to life thanks to the suffering of their small and longtime acrobatic partner, Didier LeGrand.

After they moved to Nevada from Europe, Didier sank into a deep depression. One day, Karel Boros decided to do his best to cheer him up. He created a lavish dish of succulent pork loin and stewed fruit, symbols of regal power. The idea being that this could both nourish Didier and remind him of his worth. Soon enough, that little Frenchman would be back to his old antics, strolling into the kitchen at random times during busy services with the Crown of Pork on his head and a saber in his hand to conduct a surprise "inspection" of the premises. At the end of every one of these visits, Didier would pretend to chop off the Boros brothers heads in front of the dishwashers, who would applaud and shower him with sprigs of thyme.

One 16-rib frenched crown roast of pork (see Note)

1 tablespoon Diamond Crystal kosher salt

¼ cup shio koji (see headnote, page 138)

2 cups fresh dark cherries, pitted and halved

Cranberry sauce, red wine sauce, or A.1. sauce for serving (optional)

Place the pork on a sheet pan or a platter and sprinkle all over with the salt. Rub inside and out with the shio koji and let that beast rest overnight, uncovered, in your fridge.

The following day, remove the pork from the fridge and let it sit for at least 1 hour.

Meanwhile, preheat the oven to 275°F. Fit a sheet pan with a wire rack.

Pat the pork dry, place on the rack, and roast until the internal temperature reaches 135°F on an instant-read thermometer, about 2 hours (or longer, possibly up to 4 hours if your roast is larger).

Remove the pork from the oven, tent it with aluminum foil, and let it rest for 30 to 45 minutes.

Crank up the oven to 500°F. Wrap little strips of foil around the ends of the ribs and top the center of the pork with the cherries. Pop the pork into the ripping-hot oven and roast until the fat is crisped and the exterior is nicely browned, 8 to 12 minutes.

Let the pork rest for at least 15 minutes (and up to 30 minutes if you want to serve the meat warm) before slicing. Serve with the sauce spooned over the pork.

Note: Your butcher can french the roast for you and tie the pork together to get 16 ribs.

STEAK HOUSE JUICY LUCY

Makes 2 burgers

12 ounces dry-aged ground chuck
2 slices American cheese
Kosher salt
Neutral oil for cooking
Salted butter, at room temperature
2 fresh thyme sprigs
1 garlic clove, crushed in its skin
2 burger buns
2 slices sweet onion, such as Vidalia
8 thin dill pickle slices

To even *try* to replicate the iconic burgers from BAVETTE'S (page 104), **PETER LUGER** (page 62), and their distinguished peers is risky. But I really wanted to put a burgie in this book. On a visit to Featherblade Craft Butchery in Las Vegas, I got to thinking that maybe I could honor this humble style of burger that I adore and wish I could find at a single steak house.

The Juicy Lucy was born at a dive called Matt's Bar & Grill in Minneapolis. Behind the bar is a well-worn plancha and a guy hammering out burgers nonstop. The elements are quite simple—plain egg bun, pickles, sliced raw onions. The thing that makes the Juicy Lucy a singular American treasure is that the meat is stuffed with American cheese that will burn your lips and mouth like hot magma if you bite into the burger too soon.

After splitting open far too many patties of my own with half-melted cheese and/or insufficiently caramelized surfaces, I phoned a friend who grew up in Minnesota. Even though he trained at The French Laundry and ran the three-Michelin-starred kitchen at Coi in San Francisco, Erik Anderson was quick to identify himself as a card-carrying Juicy Lucy Boy, just as I had hoped. He made it look easy.

Place a round deli container lid, rim facing up, on a digital scale. Weigh out 3 ounces of the beef on the lid. Using gloved hands, shape the meat evenly and gently until it covers the bottom of the lid. Place a slice of American cheese in the center (fold in the corners if necessary so there is a border all around) and add an additional 3 ounces of beef on top of the cheese, then shape until the cheese is evenly covered. Top with a second deli lid and gently squeeze the two lids together to form a patty. Remove the lids and pinch the seam closed all around the patty. Repeat with the remaining beef and cheese slice to make two patties.

Lay the patties on a tray and season to taste with salt. In a medium cast-iron pan over medium-high heat, add a light coating of oil to fill the surface of the pan. When ripping hot, add the patties and press them down gently. (I recommend an 18-ounce chef's press weight.)

Cook with the weight until beautifully charred, 4 to 6 minutes. Remove the weight, flip, and finish cooking unweighted, another 3 to 4 minutes. A minute before the patties are done, add butter to taste to the pan, along with the thyme and garlic. Baste the burgers with the foaming-hot flavored butter for 1 minute. Transfer the burgers to a plate and let them rest for 5 minutes.

Place a griddle over medium-high heat. Spread the split buns with plain salted butter and toast on the griddle until golden and caramelized, about 2 minutes.

To assemble, place a slice of onion on the bottom half of one bun, followed by a burger patty, 4 pickle slices, and the toasted top bun to finish. Repeat with the second patty.

OTHER MEATY DELIGHTS

NORTH
NORTH

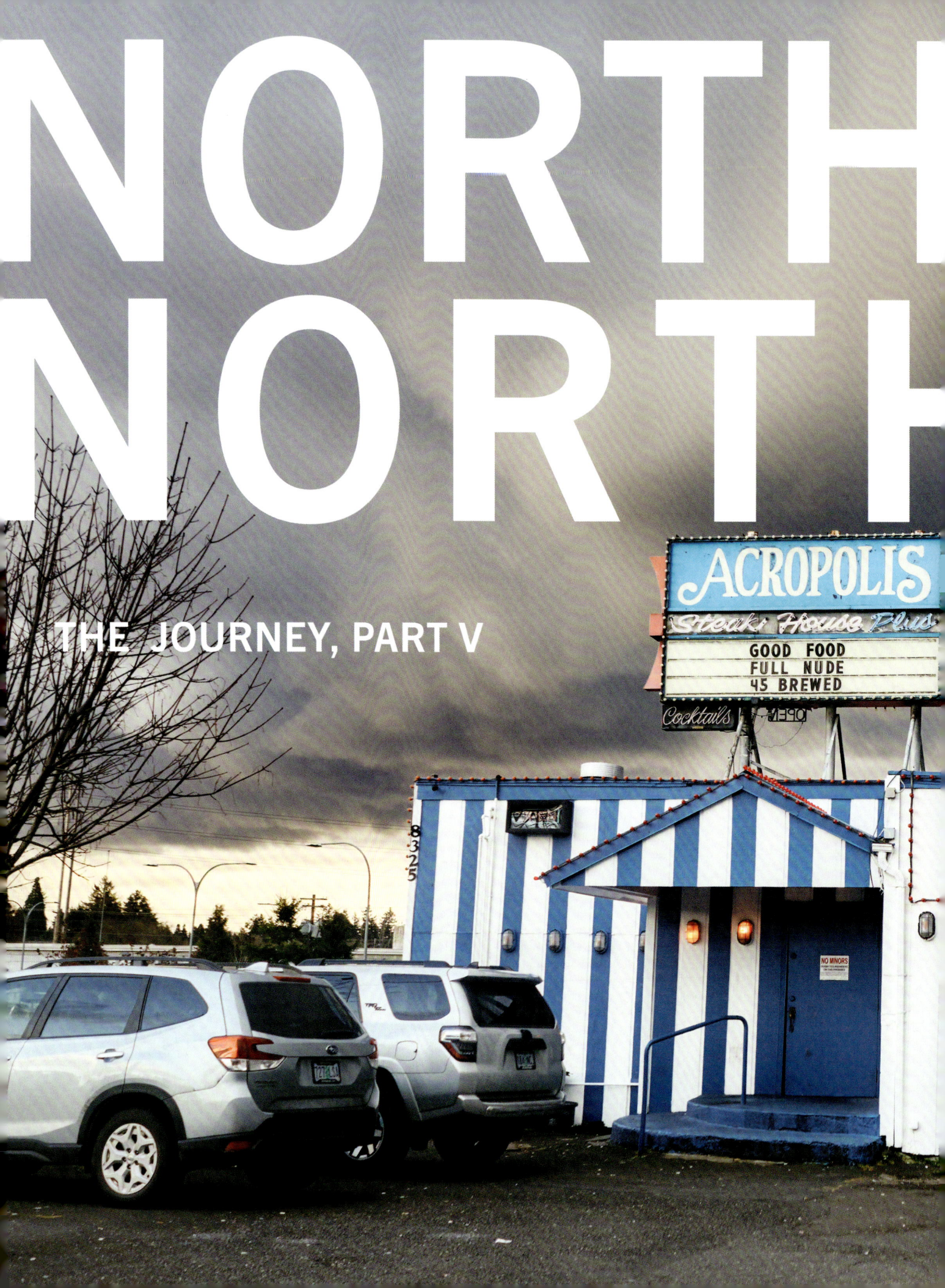

THE JOURNEY, PART V

BY
HWEST

PORTLAND HAS EVERYTHING I NEED: TOP-LEVEL BITES ON EVERY BLOCK AND GORGEOUS NATURE A STONE'S THROW FROM THE CITY. IT HAS BEEN ON MY TOP FOOD BLOG LIST OF GREATS FOR DECADES.

I go there to breathe the pristine mountain air. The boring taboos of other major cities have no place there. There's a law that every bar must serve food—and that food tends to be GREAT. Especially the cowboy steak at a certain beefy strip club.

Visiting PDX for this book was nonnegotiable. You could stop at three steak houses here and get the full sense of the American steak house's range: classic and refined (RingSide), immigrant-owned and idiosyncratic (Acropolis), and community focused (Sayler's). You could, and we did.

After Portland, we traveled to see my brothers from other mothers and sisters from other misters in the Bay Area. I missed the Mariani family so much that we concocted a crazy plan and opened a secret alfresco steak house in the gorge environs of their Sonoma winery, Scribe, along with another of my chosen siblings, Chris Kronner. That night we ate wedge salads lighter than I ever imagined possible, sipped on the complete Scribe collection, and ate aged meat from old cows personally delivered by Cream Co.'s Cliff Pollard.

Sonoma was yet another endurance test, since I had just had a night for the ages in San Francisco along what I like to call the city's unofficial Steak Row. On Van Ness, you can start with an exceptional martini at Harris', letting the calm atmosphere wash over you, because you should probably brace yourself for what's about to happen just a few blocks away when it's time for dinner at the House of Prime Rib.

The Ken French Duo with bassist Scott Chapek. Catch them in the lounge at Harris' on Tuesday and Wednesday nights.

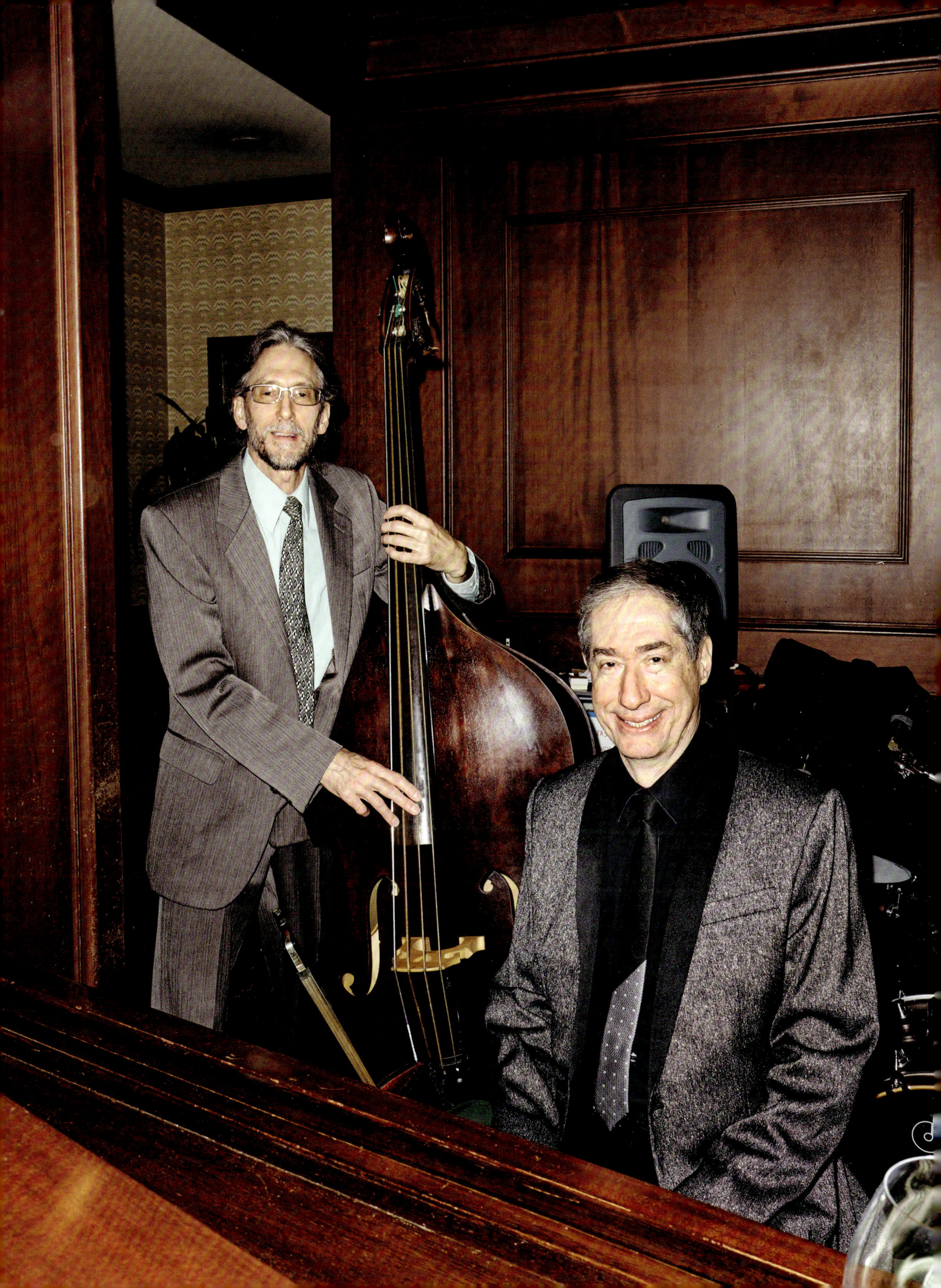

RINGSIDE

BY THE NUMBERS

Opening year: 1944
Founders: Marguerite and Allan Delephine
Address: 2165 West Burnside Street, Portland, Oregon 97210
House specials: Iceberg wedge salad; Onion rings

RingSide is perhaps the most beloved restaurant in Portland. It has been owned and operated by the same family since 1944. That's four generations of Delephines. The onion rings are incredible. The secret house dip that comes with those rings does double duty as the dressing for the fantastic wedge. These are items people line up around the block to eat.

Marguerite and Allan Delephine opened RingSide after they'd moved to Portland. They had left their ranching life in Brownsville, Oregon, in favor of a city education for their kids. The name "RingSide" was inspired by the term for the best seats in the house at a boxing arena; there used to be one nearby. It's easy to miss the inspiration, since there are only subtle nods in the space. But now I get why the bar is sunken. The couple installed the booths, fireplace, everything.

We arrived just in time to watch the bartender fixing the first round of drinks of the night. Toward the back of the bar was a man in a tuxedo vest with his head down. He was wearing black gloves and seemed laser focused on the task before him. I found out that his name is Tyler Ford and that he is the olive stuffer of RingSide. He looked up and kindly gave me two minutes of his time to explain:

> When somebody orders a dirty martini, I ask them if they want regular olives or blue cheese–stuffed olives. When I mention that I stuff them myself, they get so excited. I do it sitting at the end of the bar during pre-shift. It takes me almost exactly the entire time the meeting runs, so that's about half an hour stuffing forty or fifty olives by hand every single day. You can buy them jarred or use a device that you can press into the tub of blue cheese and inject directly into the olive. I have trouble with that thing. With my hands, it's a tactile experience. I can grab a big chunk and mold each piece to get a nice, clean, fully stuffed olive. Not everyone would want to sit and do that over and over for that long, but I like it.

Within ten minutes of the the steaks arriving at the door, the product is cut by hand and sent into the dry-aging room for their twenty-eight days of rest. In the early days, RingSide was among a select few restaurants in town that served "choice steer" meat only (a steer is just a neutered young male). Another choice-grade beef restaurant was Du Pay's Drive-In, which sounds like it was a pretty cool place.

The Delephines have earned a reputation for building a certain kind of work environment. As Tyler finished his soliloquoy, I spied my friend and RingSide sommelier, Kristen Young, across the room with a bottle of Domaine de la Romanée-Conti in her hands, and I talked to her about why it might be that people have said, "RingSide waiters don't retire. They die."

An order of RingSide rings, ketchup, and secret sauce.

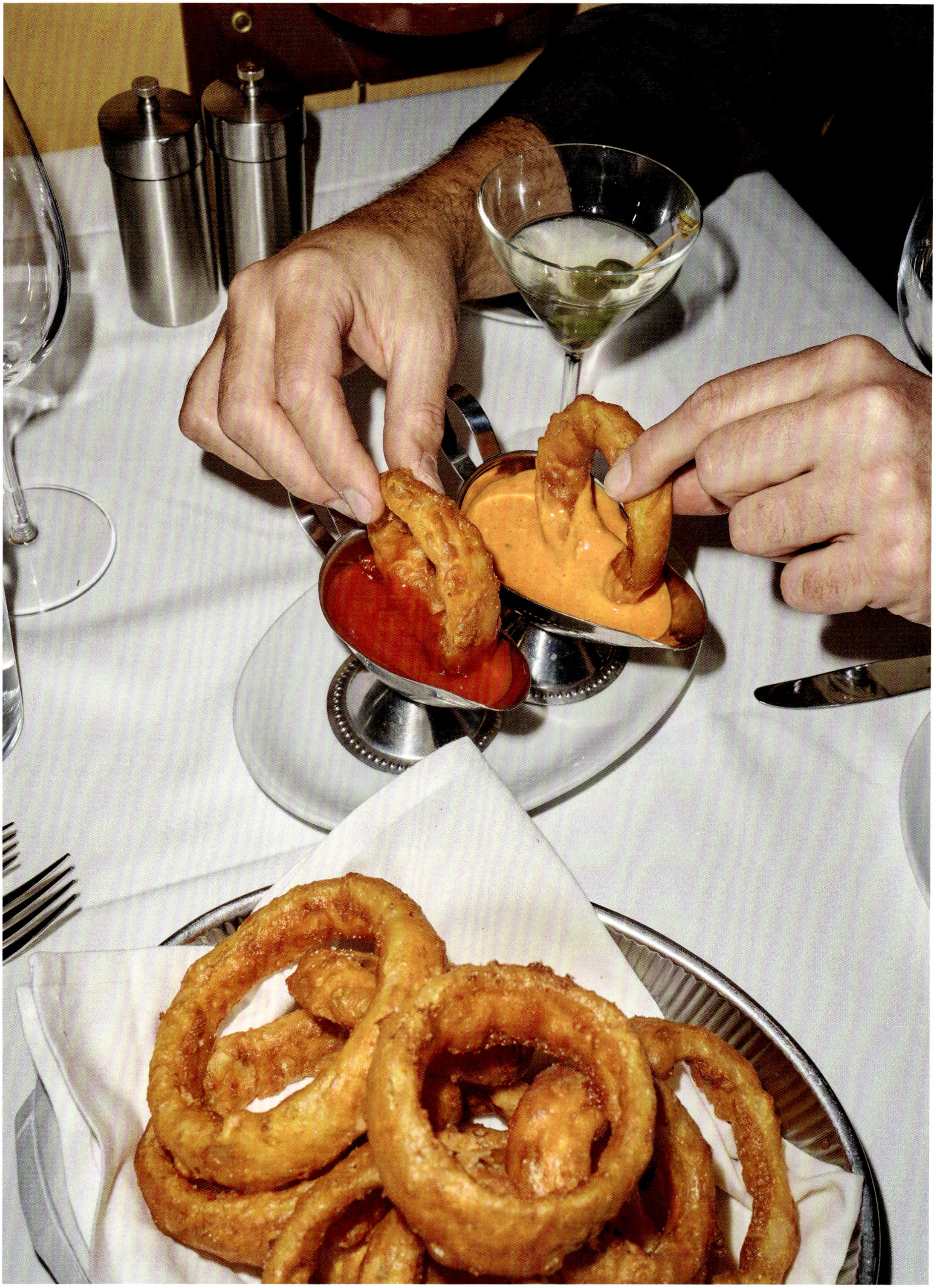

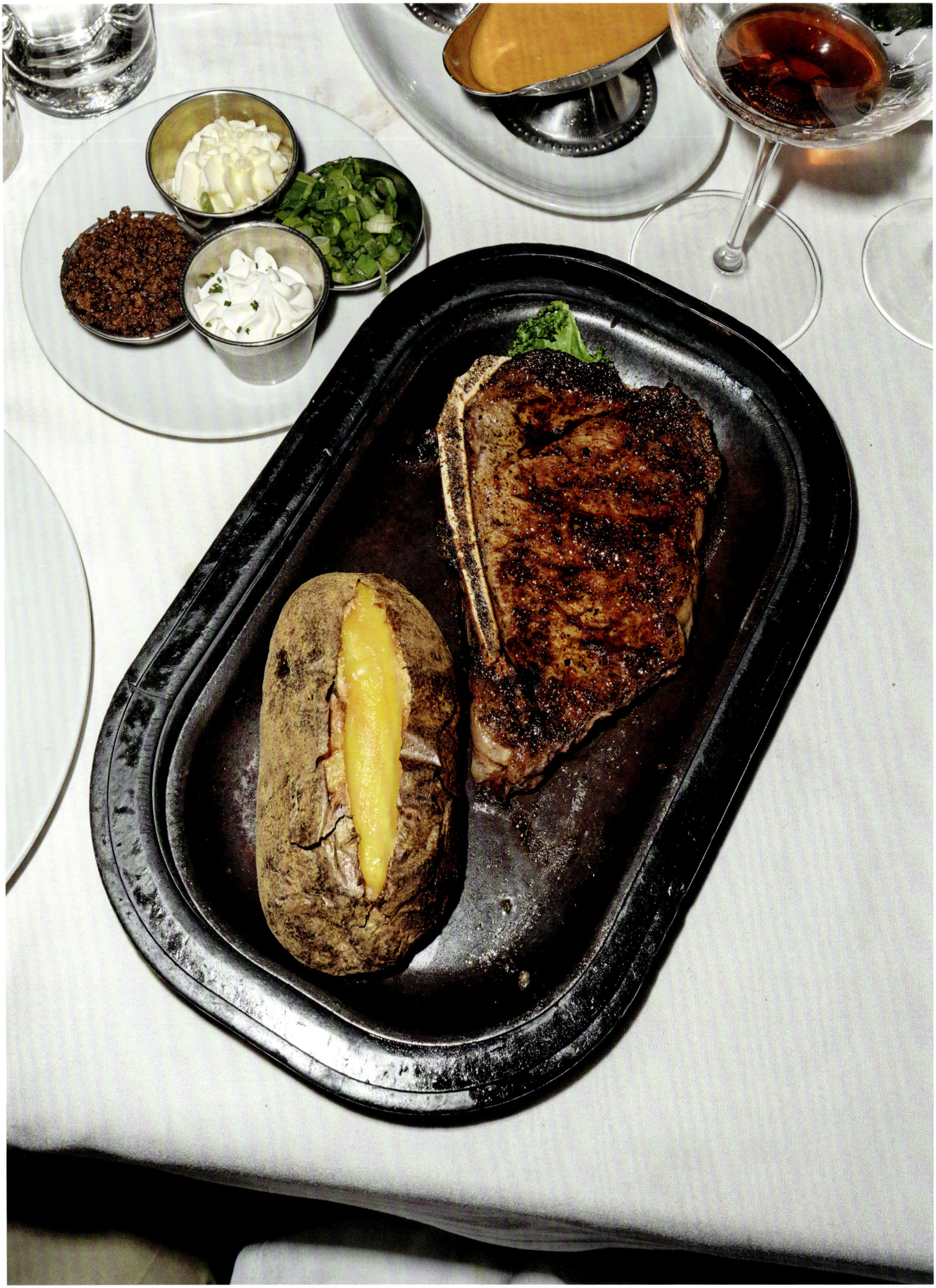

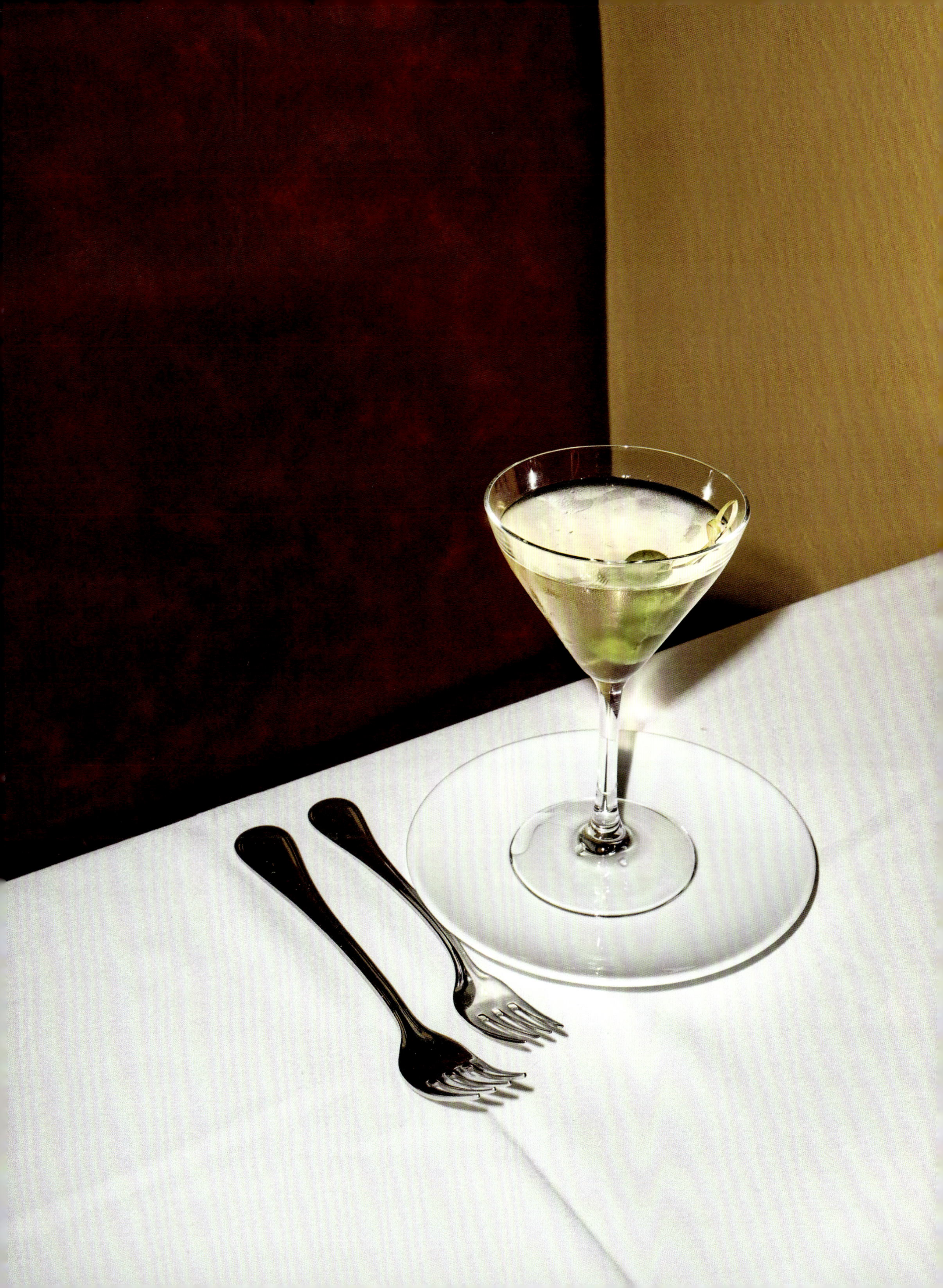

Joseph Phelps Vineyards
1980
Napa Valley
Cabernet Sauvignon
Produced and bottled by Joseph Phelps Vineyards, St. Helena, Ca.

Kristen Young—The Steak House Somm

The first time I ate at RingSide I met Kristen Young, who is a somm with an insane pedigree. In her hands, we drank so well. This time, she reminded me that at the end of that first night, I had mentioned to her that I was thinking about doing a book about steak houses one day.

"I've been at RingSide for five years. It's the holidays right now, December. A fucking madhouse. A lot of people in the restaurant industry, much to their detriment, are adrenaline junkies. Those of us who can admit it to ourselves try to keep in balance. But this is the best challenge—being able to turn tables without shoving anyone out. It requires observational skill: Do the guests have presents with them? How long will they go over? What is plan B if they haven't seen each other in a decade and we don't want to mess with that? RingSide, year-round, is one of those places where we are constantly and mostly pleasantly challenged. We get reservations with notes that say, 'I am meeting my biological sister for the first time. We connected on 23andMe.'

A beloved regular of ours, her husband died ten weeks ago. She sent this beautiful arrangement of flowers with a note: 'Kristen and Geoff, thank you for forty-two years of date night.' For people that occasionally need their love-of-service battery charged, it was extraordinary. I took that whole bouquet downstairs to lineup and told everyone: 'Hey, guys, we are heading into December. What we do matters.'

The regulars really do mean everything. When the bartender rings in stool 98 and the ticket says the guest would like two pieces of sliced tomato, three cheese crumbles, three prawns, and Nantois lemons with her filet, the sous chef who has been here since 1976 knows it's Pam. Being a regular guest is the coolest thing you can be if you want to patronize and show support. They order similar things a lot of the time, which helps us a lot. If you are tending bar and you have four people ordering all kinds of stuff, that takes a little bit of time. So we're grateful when James comes in because he starts with an old-fashioned and gets the same entrée every time. Jimmy, the bartender, does this frozen drink called the Scotch Taco. When I hear that blender start up, I know Jim, a regular, is here because he's been ordering that for twenty-seven years."

ALEXANDER'S CROWN VINEYARD
CABERNET SAUVIGNON
ALEXANDER VALLEY

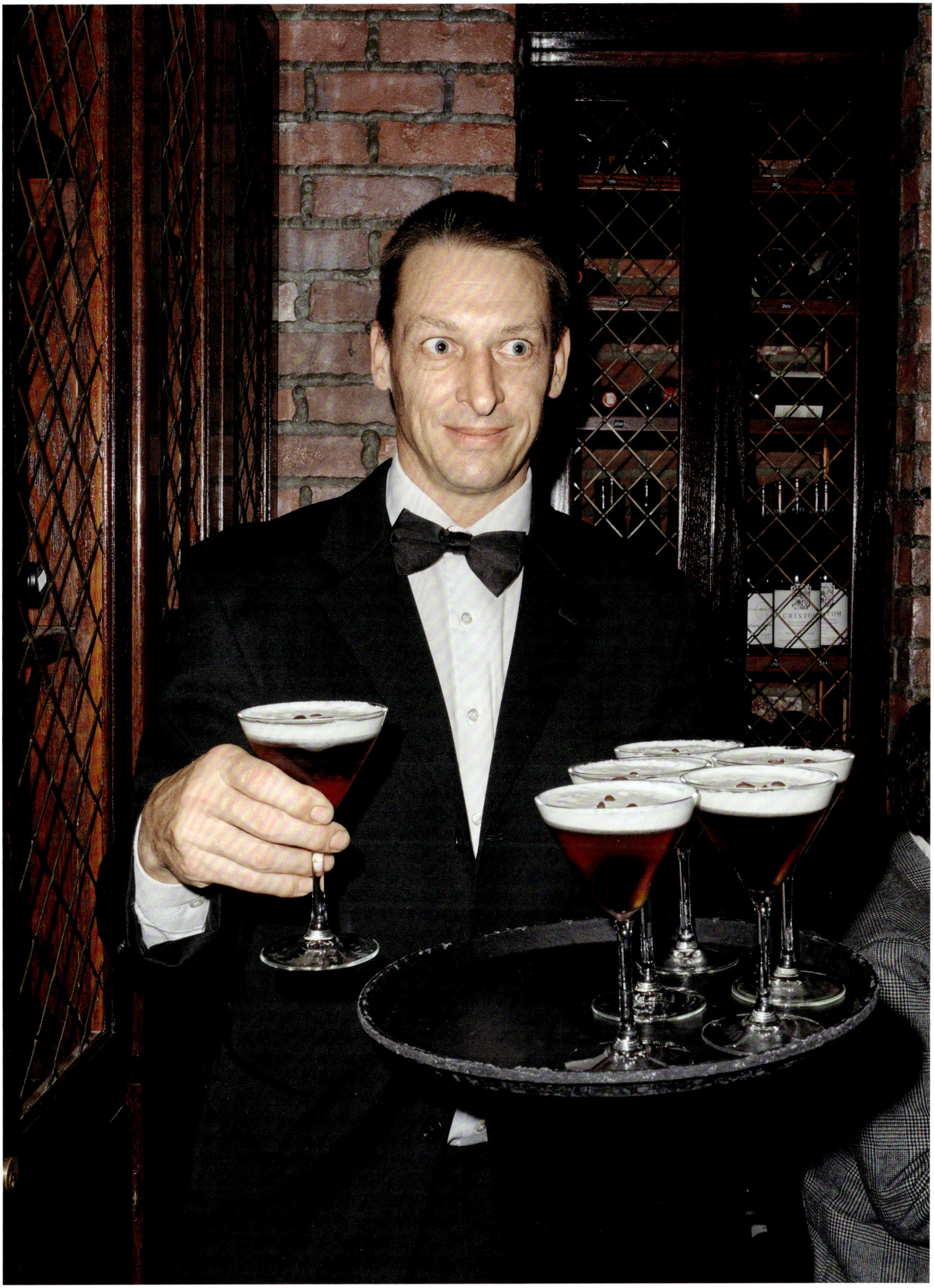

PORTLAND

ACROPOLIS

BY THE NUMBERS

Opening year: 1976
Founder: Haralambos "Bobby" Polizos
Address: 8325 Southeast McLoughlin Boulevard, Portland, Oregon 97202
House special: Steak bites

The next day it starts pissing down over Portland. Before I know it, I'm in a dark room enjoying a lunch of steak bites and secret sauce with a few golden slabs of garlic bread on the side. The fried shrimp are on the way. Jenny, the manager, plunks a pitcher of draft beer onto the table. I notice a statue of a Greek deity nearby. It reminds me that I should also try the gyro. The walls start to shake to the sounds of Slayer. I look up at the stage, the performance begins, and I think to myself, *Isn't this a nice change of pace?*

Our "table" this afternoon is the rack of the Acropolis strip club, where the food, believe it or not, is delicious. That gyro? Fantastic. The chicken fingers are proper. The 8-ounce sirloin steak and fries? It's hard to believe you can still get a tasty, comforting plate of beef in a major American city for ten bucks. It's a cowboy cut that's been butchered nice and thin and cooked properly. I also really like the onion rings, and that's saying something, considering we ate at RingSide the night before.

In Portland, any establishment that serves alcohol must also serve food. It's one of the state's most famous laws, and A-Crop is known for being one of the places that does a lot more than the bare minimum to abide by it. As the story goes, the founder, Haralambos "Bobby" Polizos, spent five years working alone in the kitchen after he opened Acropolis in 1976; none of the cooks he hired met his standards. Once he had the money, he bought a 130-acre ranch in Estacada, where he started raising cattle to supply the kitchen with solidly good beef.

Polizos never planned on going into the adult entertainment industry. He bought the Acropolis location for twenty grand so he could have a second shot at the American dream. His first restaurant, Athens West, had gone out of business. Polizos had opened it with his brother after they arrived in the United States from Greece. The whole thing was such a disappointment that the two of them never spoke again.

At the beginning, Acropolis didn't do very well, either. But Polizos was lucky that he chose to open a small business in one of the most tolerant cities in America. Five or so years into the slog, a friend told Polizos that he might want to follow the example of Mary's Club—the oldest strip club in Portland, where Courtney Love used to dance—and turn his empty dining room into the venue for an all-nude revue. And that's what he did.

Polizos passed away in 2019. His son Andreas, who runs the place now, told us that the restaurant doesn't source much meat from the ranch anymore. The famous salad bar is also gone; it just didn't make sense after COVID. (I'd been looking forward to seeing the sign reminding people not to serve themselves with their hands.)

That afternoon with Andreas, there was beer as we needed it and a nonstop stream of food to try and family members to meet. I'll never forget how Jenny wouldn't let us leave without telling us, with this very real sense of pride, "We're not what most people expect."

We certainly didn't expect to be allowed to take photos. We showed up just to see Acropolis in real life. When we sheepishly introduced ourselves to Andreas, we explained that we could write about it, not show it, no problem. The place being empty, he told us to go right ahead and shoot whatever we wanted—just that if we'd like to take portraits of the performers, we'd have to ask them between songs.

Jenny, who started her career at Acropolis as a dancer and now manages the floor.

STEAK HOUSE

Budweiser
PALLET JACK IPA
BONEYARD
FORT GEORGE
Pabst
NW LAGER
DOMESTICS
Bites
OBLIVION

TRUMER
PILS
BERKELEY, CA
NO
SMOKING OR CONSUMPTION OF MARIJUANA
is allowed in or at a
PUBLIC PLACE
ANY BUSINESS WITH A LIQUOR LICENSE IS CONSIDERED A PUBLIC PLACE

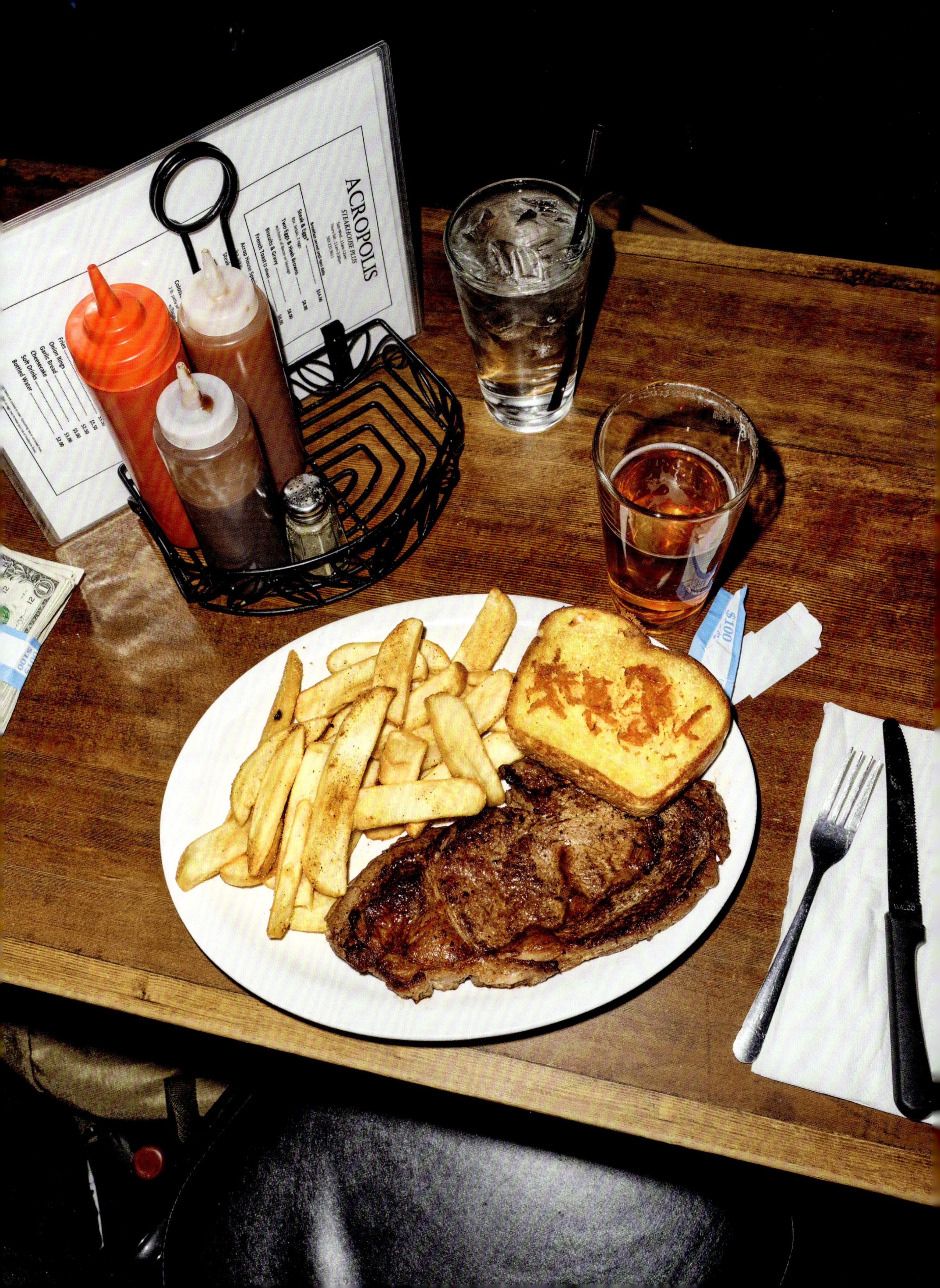

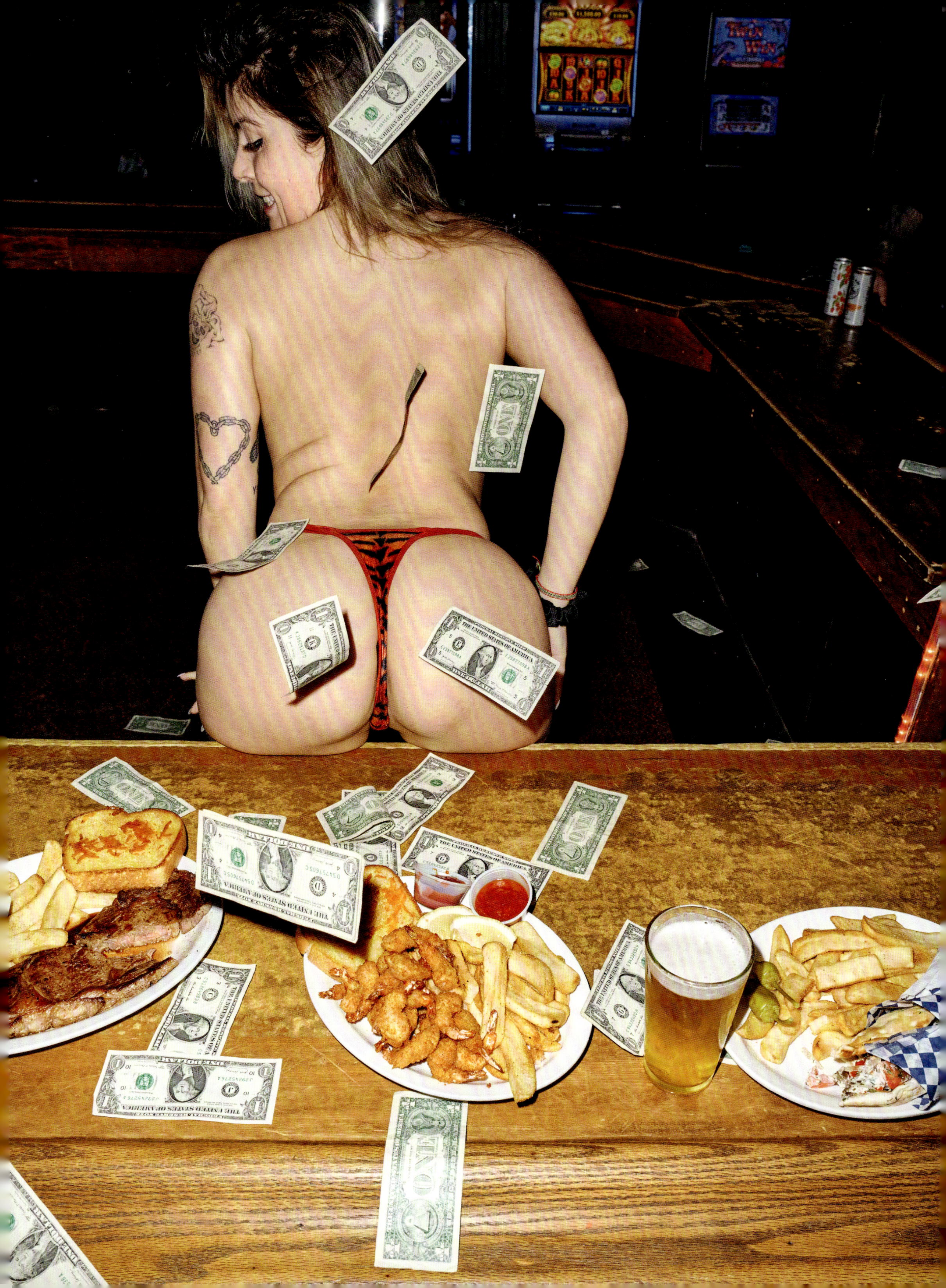
Twin Win

Katrina—The Legend

"For me, what makes it special here is the stage-heaviness of it. We are on for twenty minutes at a time, then off for twenty, then back on for twenty. For the whole shift. I really enjoy that, since I don't like walking around hustling for dances. I mean, we can do lap dances, but it has to be when we're offstage. There is a no-hustle rule here, actually. A lot of that has to do with the food. They don't want the girls walking up to people while they're eating steak. It's more of a relaxed vibe.

People who don't know Portland are surprised by the culture. You'll find a lot of girls wearing sneakers. We do a lot more pole tricks and performance-based work. Even in the strip clubs where girls are allowed to hustle—Lucky Devil, Devils Point, Sassy's, Mary's—they have this kind of dive-y vibe. You don't see as much bleached blond hair and fake boobs. It's more tatted-up, mulleted . . . baddies. I keep it a little more feminine because I have my niche.

But oh man, the shifts are not slow. It's five and a half to seven hours depending on the shift you get. That's another thing that makes Portland strip clubs special: a set number of girls, never too many, which makes your money potential a lot higher. We work damn hard to get those shifts. If anyone hears 'Notorious Thugs' by Biggie or 'Xxplosive' by Dr. Dre, they know it's Katrina onstage.

The thing is, it's not always about the money. There have been times that I have racked out more than $1,000 during a shift but leave work feeling let down. And there are times I have made $200 and go home really fulfilled. It comes down to the customers. I don't know how to describe it, but there's a rudeness you have to deal with sometimes. It's a customer service job, and you're naked. They are showering you with money, and they feel like they're above you or something. It's nice when you meet people on a day shift that are tipping five bucks a dance, the conversation is nice, and the experience is much more enjoyable than just getting showered with money. But I take those days, too; don't get me wrong.

I don't have a dream job yet, but me and my boyfriend would like to get married and open a bar. He's been a bartender for years, and I just started bartending. Maybe I'll have a kid or two in my early thirties. Become a white picket-fencer. That'd be nice."

Specialties of the house.

PORTLAND

SAYLER'S OLD COUNTRY KITCHEN

BY THE NUMBERS

Opening year: 1946
Founders: Art and Dick Sayler
Address: 10519 Southeast Stark Street, Portland, Oregon 97216
House specials: Relish tray; 72-ounce sirloin dinner

When you take a seat at Sayler's, the server hands you the restaurant's famous die-cut menu, which is shaped like the 72-ounce steak you can eat for free if you manage to finish the whole thing in less than an hour. The menu is all about choice: type of cut; size of cut; soup, salad, or coleslaw; fries, baked potato, or pilaf. The sides are included in the meal. Ice cream, too.

I suggest game-planning while you snack on the relish tray and sour cream dip, also complimentary. Order a martini. Usually it's gin for me, but when our server, Morgan Smith, recommended the Peppermintini, I could not resist.

Sayler's opened right after World War II, just as rationing was just coming to an end. The restaurant's founders were wheat farmers from North Dakota who came to Portland with the idea of giving people something they hadn't had much of in a while, and for a fair price.

During our lunch, they sat a party of twelve or so elderly Portlandians at the table next to ours. A younger woman wearing a name tag from the local assisted-living facility helped everybody make up their minds. The guests were there to enjoy the senior dinners, a section that the menu advertises as "lighter complete dinners for those over 62."

Sayler's has made it almost eight decades. These days, under the third generation—brothers Bryan and David—the restaurant continues to put out hundreds of thousands of meals a year, crowning every sirloin, T-bone, and filet with a single onion ring, the way it should be done.

I was tempted (but ultimately too afraid) to accept the 72-ounce steak challenge. These kinds of contests are popular at steak houses across America. I continue to gather research from experts in the field like Morgan so I know what I'm up against when I finally bang on the table and shout, "Bring it on!" Morgan has worked at Sayler's for eighteen years. A ride or die through and through, she says that if she ever left, it wouldn't be to go work at another restaurant.

With the 72-ounce steak challenge, I've seen it all: the people who have done it in three minutes, the people who have done two challenges back-to-back, the people who just get it done methodically and move on, and the people, many people, who just quit. There is a woman who is smaller than I am who did it in two minutes and fifty-three seconds. There's a video of it on YouTube. Look it up—Molly72 is her name. The footage is not for the faint of heart. The popularity of the challenge tends to go in waves. For years, it used to be once a month. Then competitive eating took off and we'd have multiple people trying it in the same week. Now it has dwindled down. Most people just get tired of chewing.

The steak-shaped menu is such a PDX tradition that there's a whole market for vintage copies on eBay.

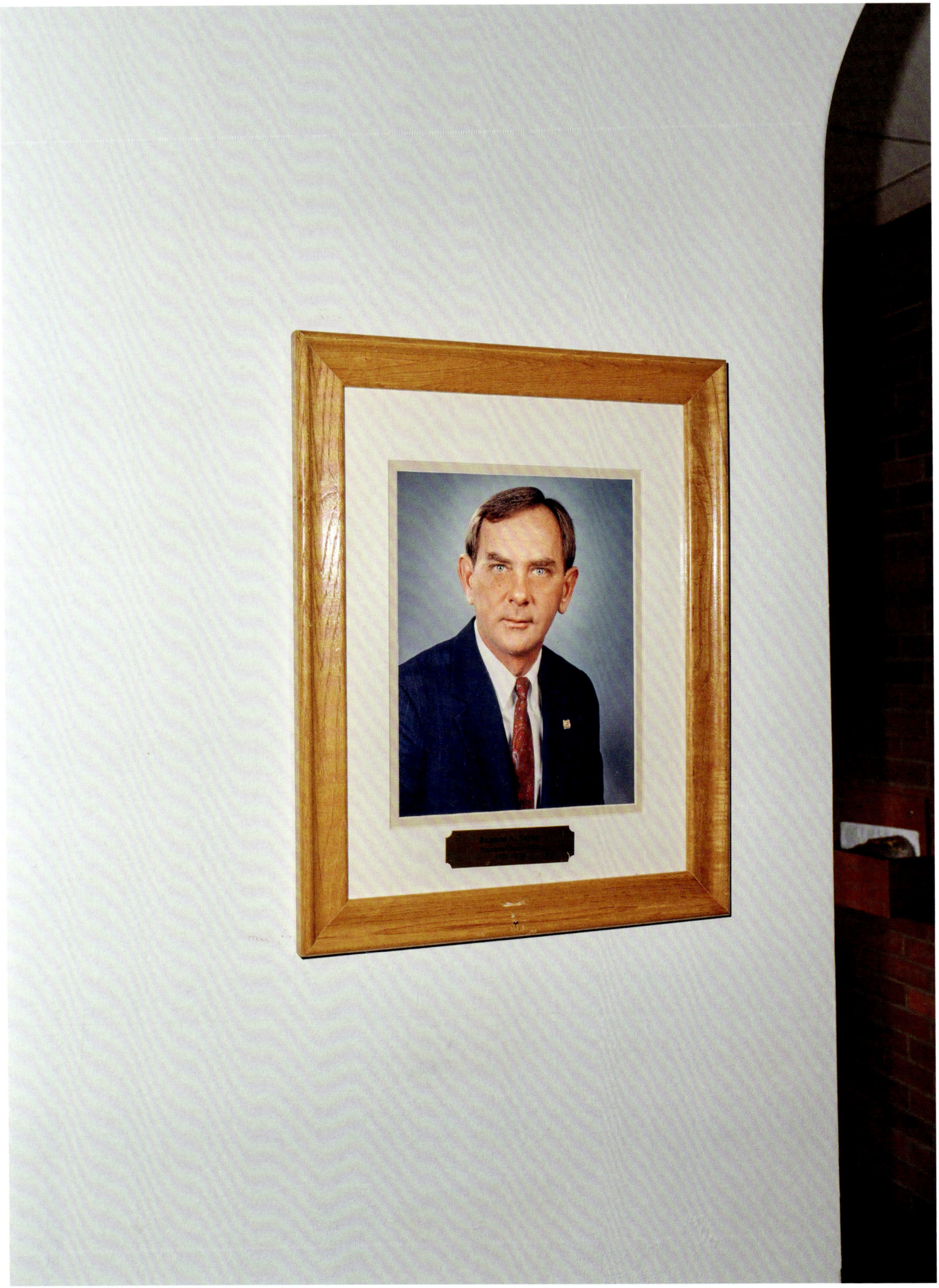

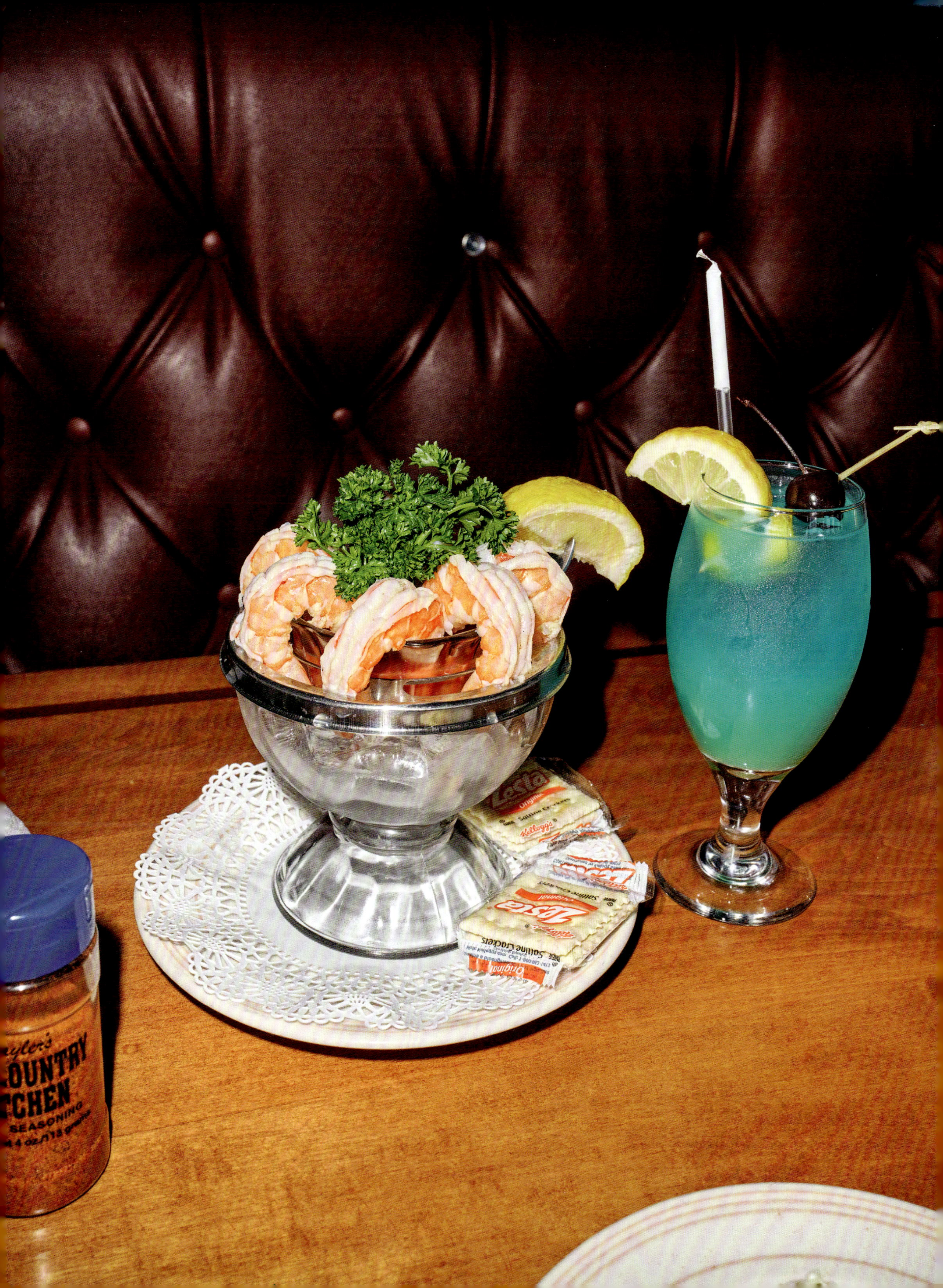
Zesta
Original
Saltine Crackers
Kellogg's
SEASONING

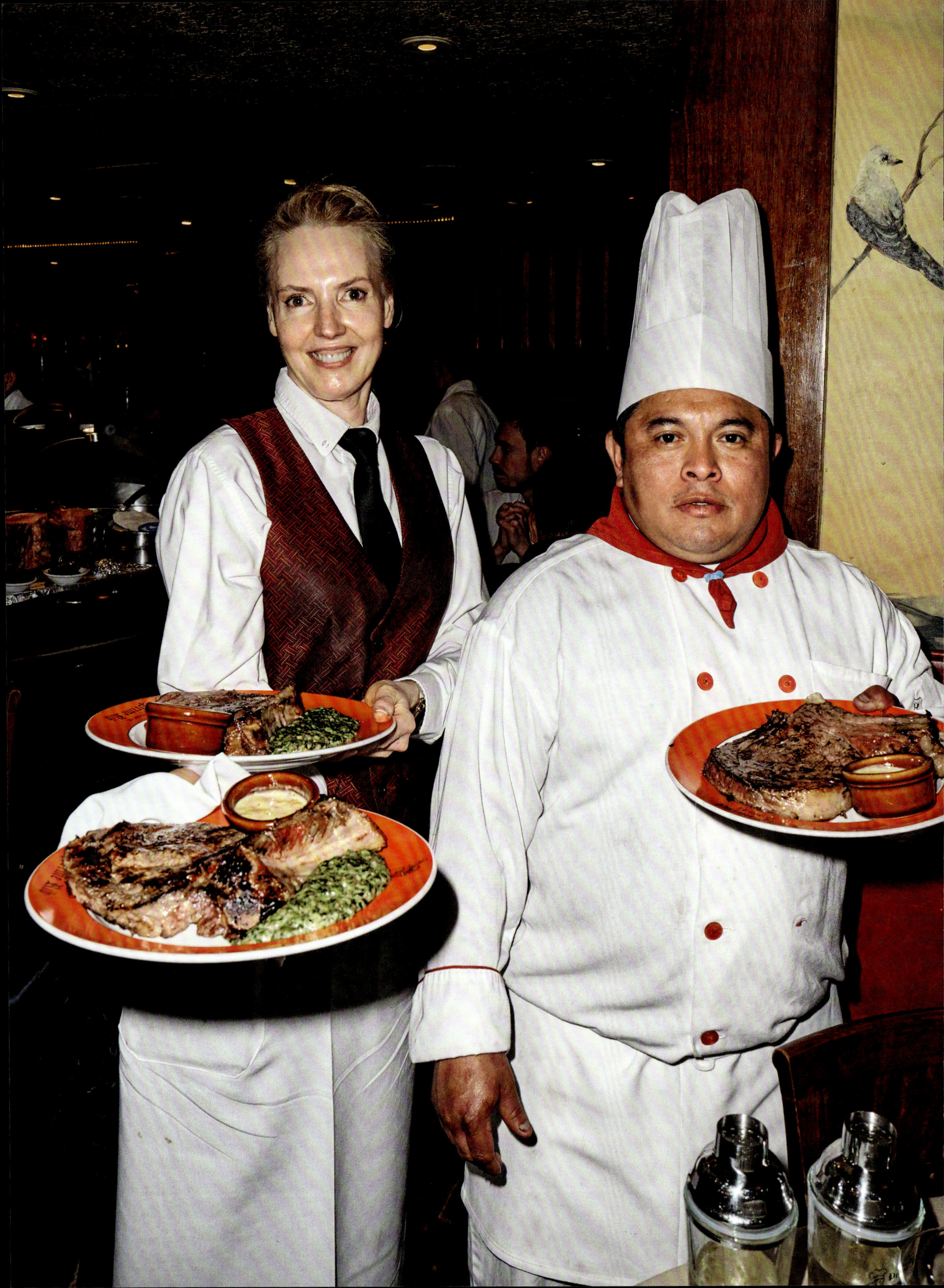

BAY AREA

HOUSE OF PRIME RIB

The best place in America to get your meat sweats on exactly as people did in 1949 is Joe Betz's House of Prime Rib. It's a swirling, psychedelic room pulsing with humanity that will make you feel like you've stepped inside a German Expressionist painting. How do they fit so many people in here? Why are they all going so hard? Are the frescoes melting?

BY THE NUMBERS

Opening year: 1949
Founder: Lou Balaski
Address: 1906 Van Ness Avenue, San Francisco, California 94109
House special: PRIME RIB

The menu is the size of a billboard, with the items written in medieval calligraphy. But you don't need that menu. The only choice to be made is the size and thickness you would like your gifted carver to provide.

Here comes Inessa, our incredible server. She sends the silver salad bowl spinning with her left hand and lifts the right one so high in the air it looks like something out of a cartoon. She starts pouring the secret dressing, and we fall into a trance watching the greens get coated and coated and coated as that cold bowl continues to spin and spin and spin, just like our minds.

Inessa Hearsey—The Natural

"I arrived from Saint Petersburg, Russia, in 1998, when I was twenty-eight. My husband is American. He was a supervisor helping to open casinos in different places and I met him when he was working on one in Russia. My English was just okay. I wanted to improve, so I went to college. I started working at a café in Montecito that was French-Russian, just for fun. My husband was always at work. I didn't want to be alone.

When I applied for HOPR the person [I spoke to] was Gus [Stathis]. He worked here for sixty years. He started as dishwasher and then became general manager, maître d'—his life was this place. He did not make it sound like I was going to get a job. My husband told me that I didn't need to get a job. I told him, 'No.'

I didn't know who Joe Betz was. But I said to him in the interview, 'Take a chance on me. This feels like my place.' It has been twenty years since that day. It is my place. You don't have the Michelin stress. You will never be told to go home in the middle of service because it is not busy. And we are generous. The only thing that is à la carte is the salad. Nobody knows the recipe for the dressing except Joe. It has to ferment for two weeks. It is like a creamy sherry.

Some people think there is a secret menu. I don't know where that came from. It's just a seared King Henry. The one 'secret' that is not a secret is that we will always give you more food if you ask. More creamed spinach? No problem. You just cannot take home the seconds."

Showtime with Inessa and Luis Fernando. That plate she's holding in the front? There's your seared King Henry.

NORTH BY NORTHWEST

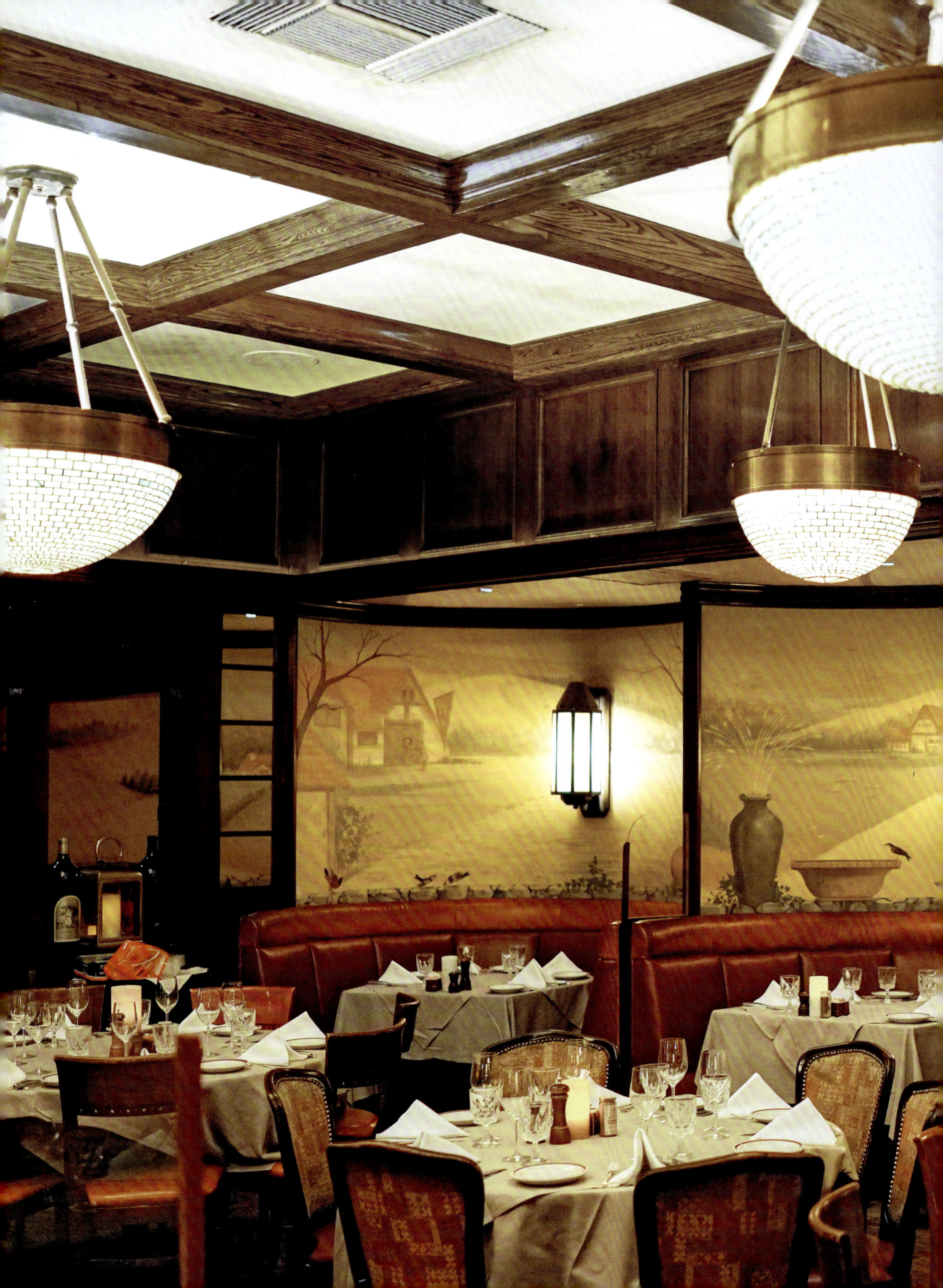

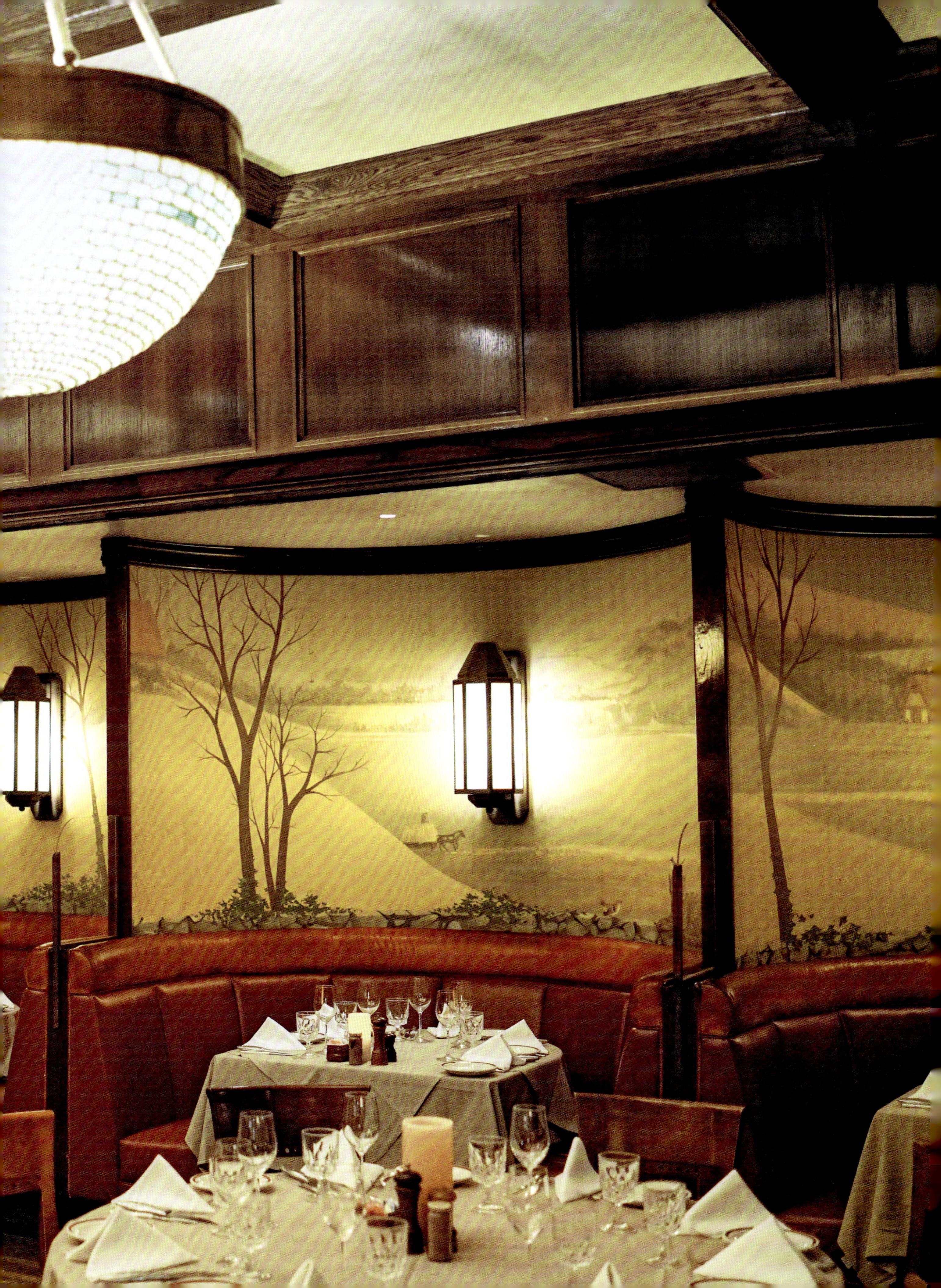

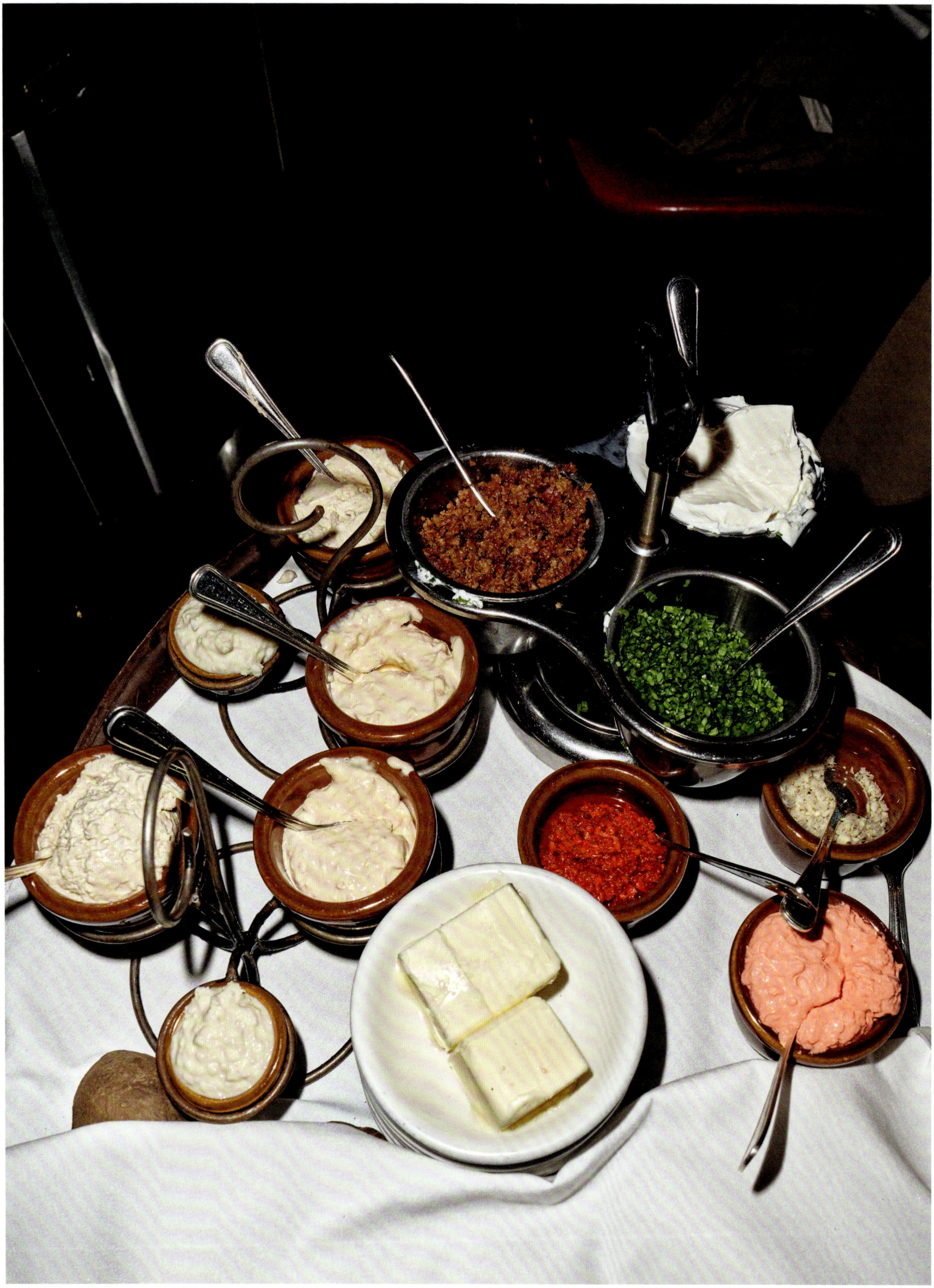

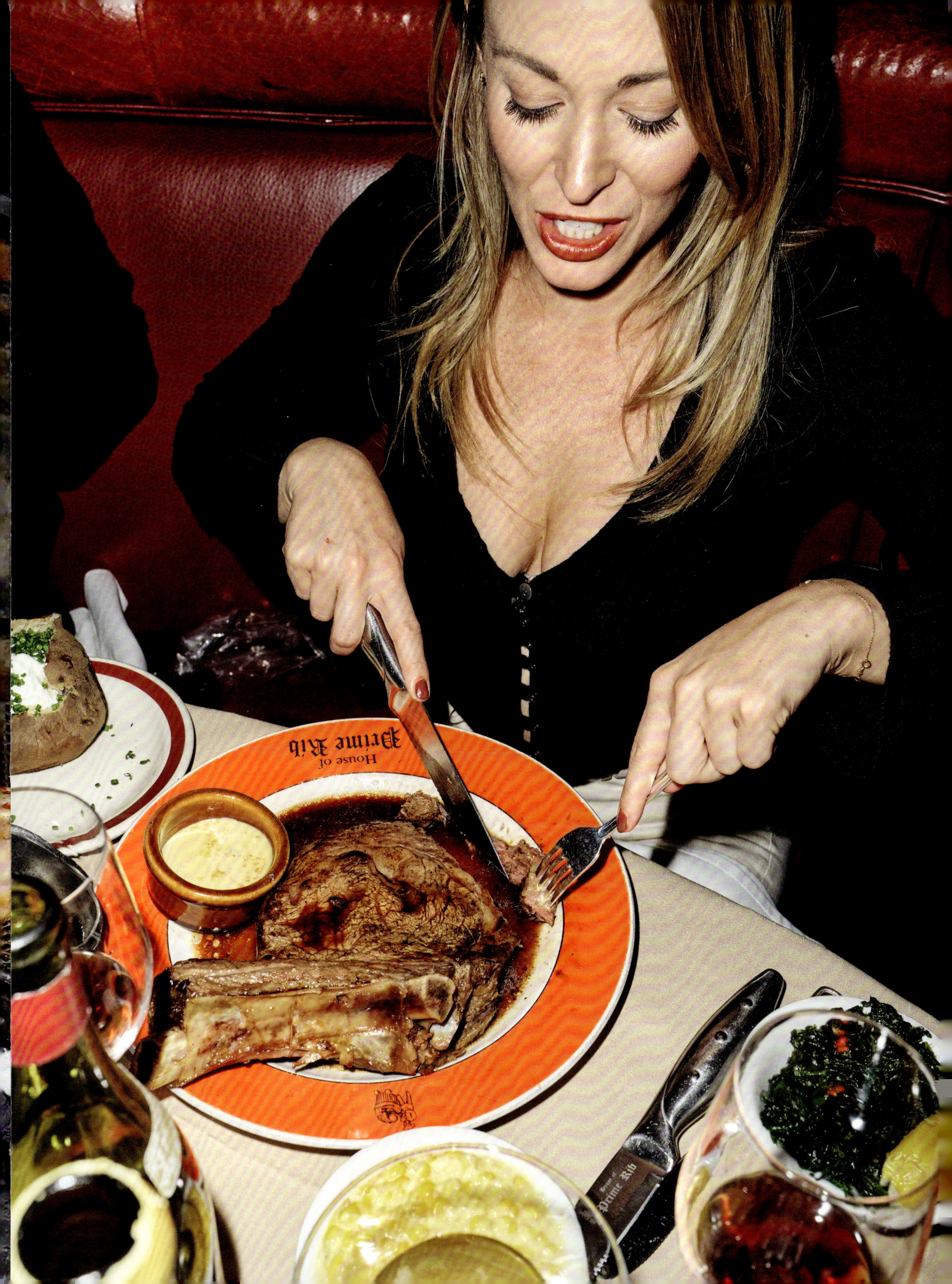
House of
Prime Rib

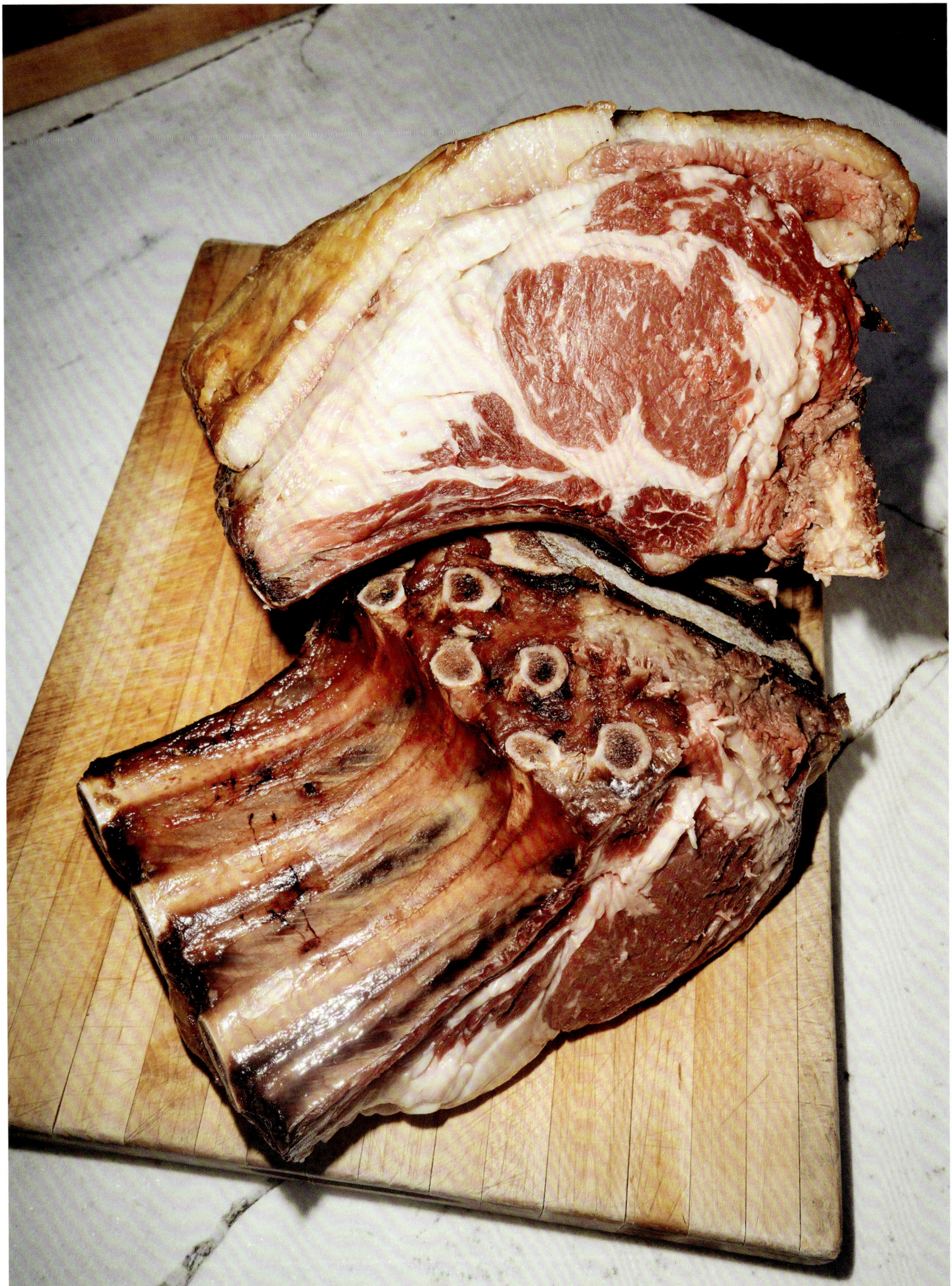

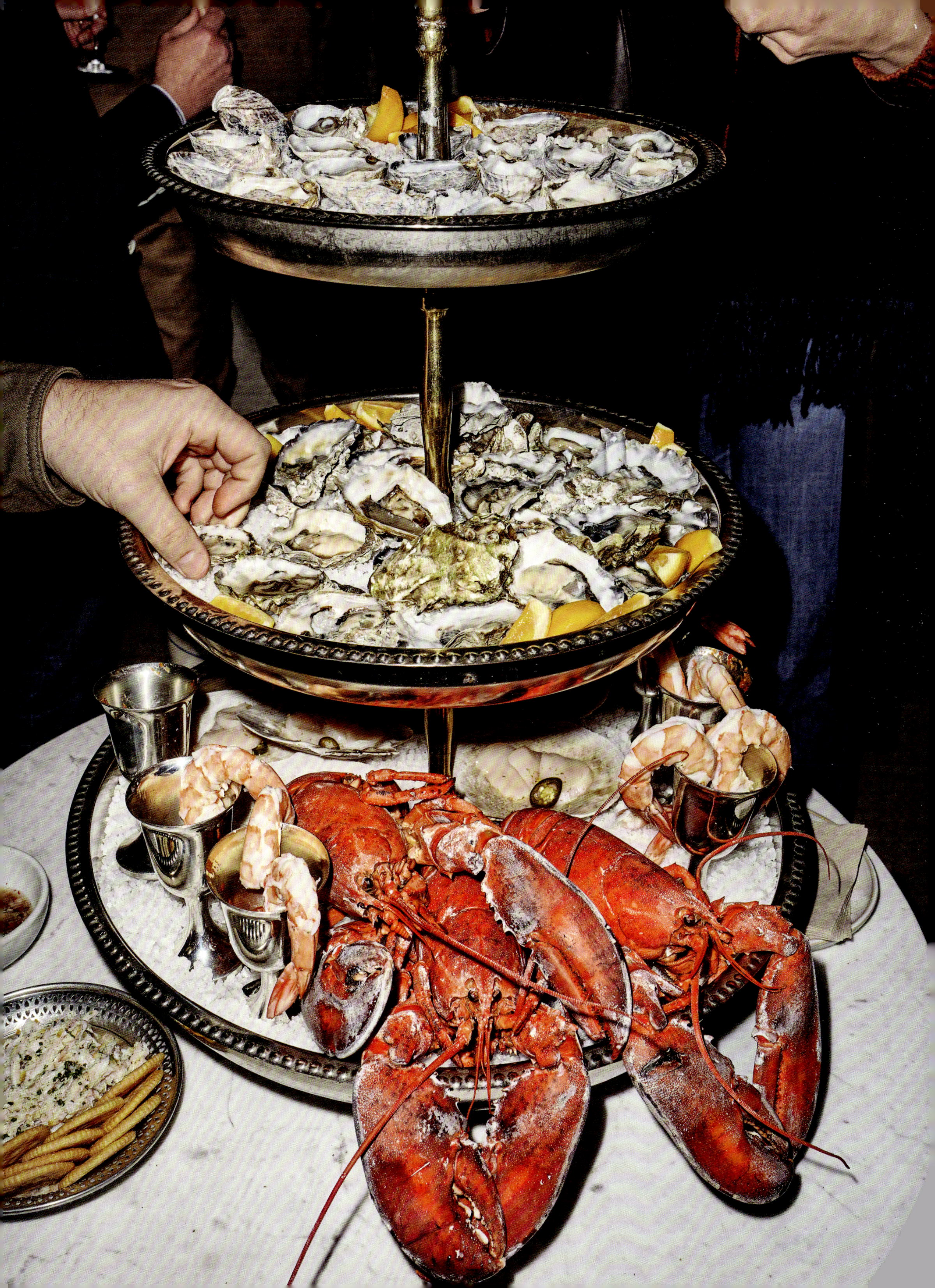

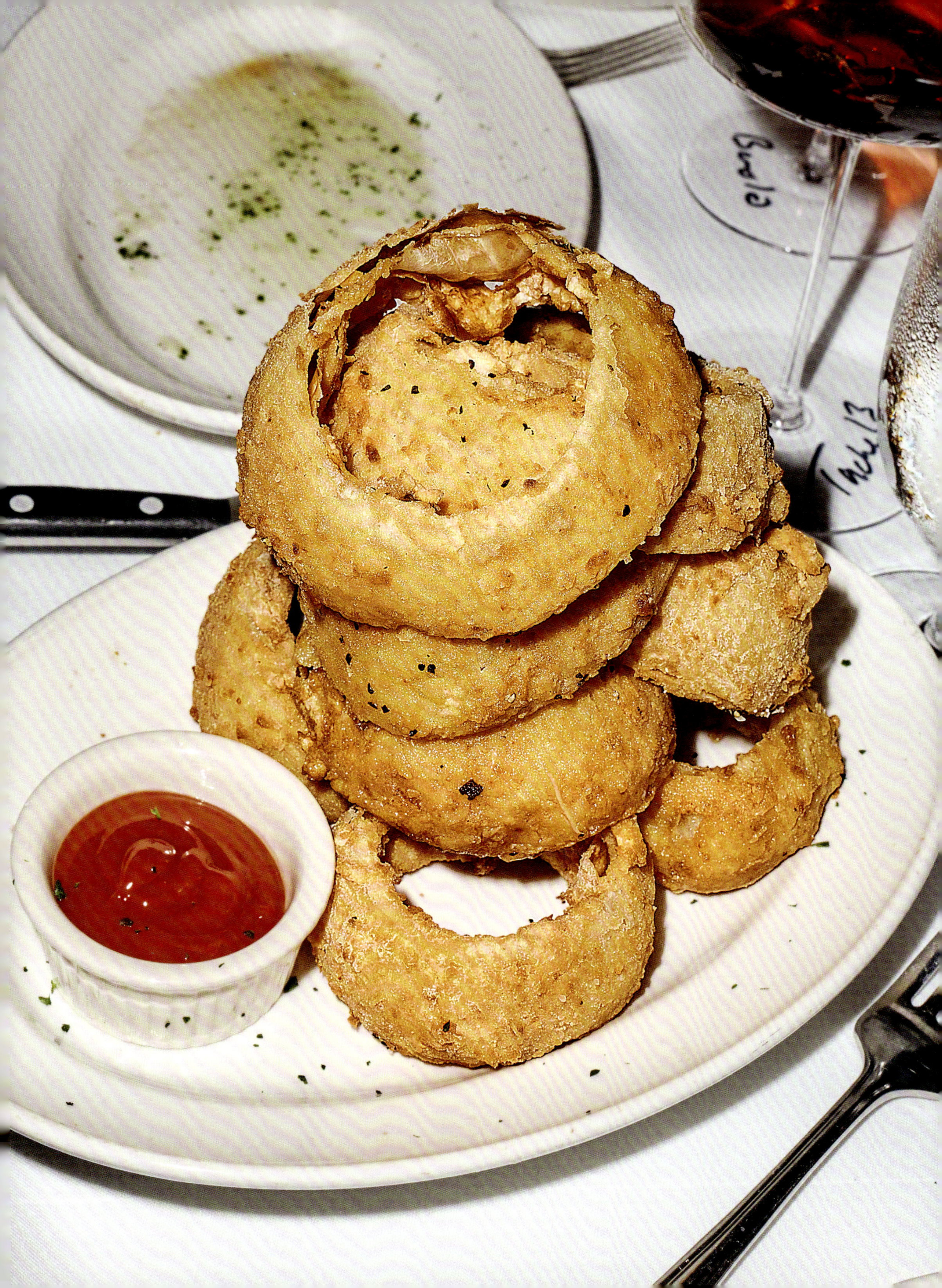
Table 13

RECIPES

SIDES

HASH BROWNS

Serves 6 to 8

4 pounds Yukon gold potatoes, peeled and quartered

1 tablespoon plus 1 teaspoon Diamond Crystal kosher salt

Neutral oil for greasing and frying

1 cup egg whites (about 8 eggs)

2 tablespoons cornstarch

1 teaspoon baking powder

Flaky sea salt, preferably Maldon, for garnish

In my experience, there is no such thing as a so-so hash brown. But there is definitely such a thing as an unforgettable hash brown. When Fermín Nuñez made these for us at ESTE in Austin, he fried them in the same oil as his tortillas. He says he didn't intend for that to happen, but as a member of the Corn Porn Society, I thought it was genius.

Place the peeled potatoes in a large bowl of water to prevent them from browning while you grate them.

Using a food processor with a shredder attachment or the large holes of a box grater, grate all the potatoes. Transfer the shredded potatoes to a separate large bowl, add the kosher salt, then toss with your hands to evenly distribute the salt. Let the shredded potatoes sit for 10 minutes to remove excess moisture (the hash browns will be crispier as a result).

Working in batches, place the shredded potatoes in a cheesecloth or clean kitchen towel over the sink and squeeze out all the excess moisture from the potatoes. (You want the potato shreds to be dry enough that they separate from one another.) Transfer to another large bowl and repeat with the remaining shredded potatoes.

Preheat the oven to 400°F. Line a 9 by 13-inch sheet pan with parchment paper and coat the parchment and the sides of the pan with a thin a thin layer of oil.

In a small bowl, whisk together the egg whites, cornstarch, and baking powder until smooth. Add the slurry to the shredded potatoes and mix to combine. Place the potatoes on the prepared sheet pan and press them down, making sure they're in a flat, even layer. Oil a second sheet of parchment paper and place on top of the potatoes, pressing to adhere, then bake the potatoes until set, 25 to 30 minutes. Let the potatoes cool to room temperature, then refrigerate the pan until the potatoes are firm enough to cut, about 1 hour.

Flip the pan onto a cutting board to remove the sheet of hash browns. If they get stuck, just run your knife around the edge of the sheet pan to loosen it or gently bang on the bottom of the sheet pan. Discard the parchment paper and use a knife to trim the curved edges. Slice the hash brown sheet in half lengthwise, then cut crosswise into eight evenly sized rectangles.

Line a rack with paper towels.

Pour enough oil into a medium pot to reach a depth of 2 inches and place over medium-high heat until the temperature reaches 350°F. Working in batches to prevent overcrowding, add the hash brown rectangles to the hot oil and fry until golden brown, 3 to 5 minutes on each side. Remove the hash browns from the oil and drain on the rack. Immediately sprinkle with flaky salt. Serve warm.

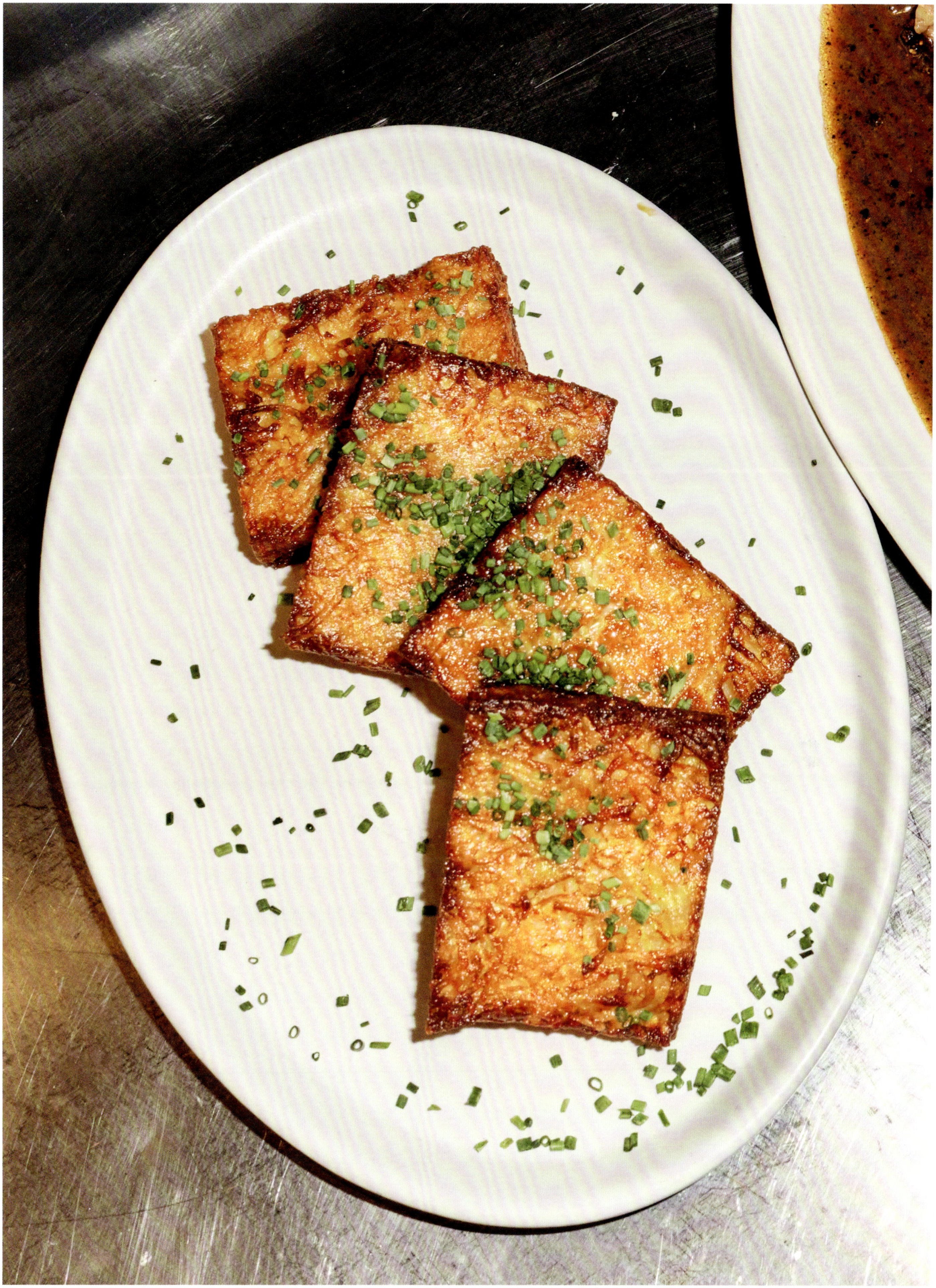

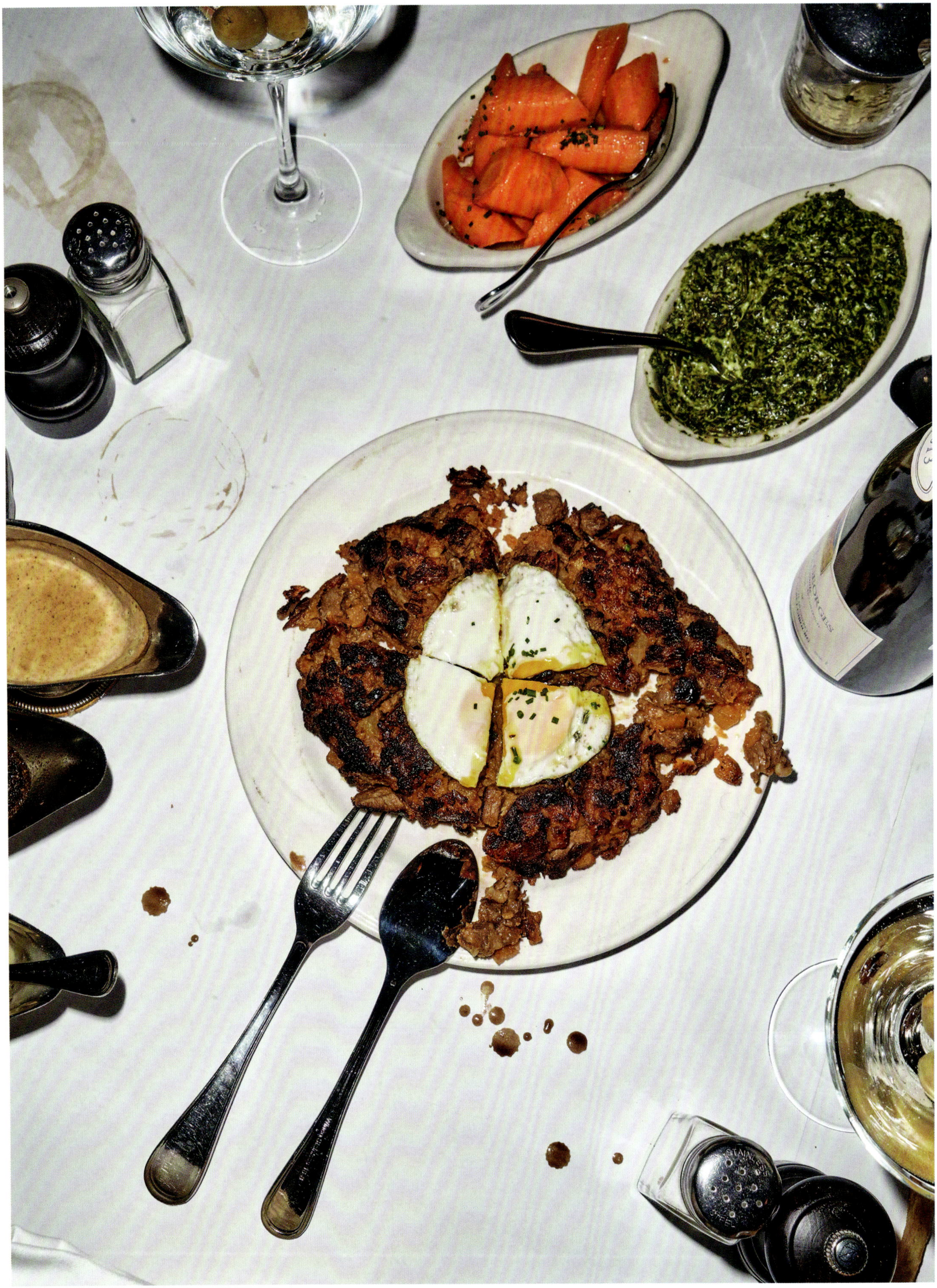

CHOPPED HASH ODE TO KEENS

Serves 2

The prime rib hash at KEENS (page 56) is arguably even more beloved than the mutton. I could never pick between the two—except at lunch, after I've had too much to drink and need a REAL MEAL to kick-start my day. We were hungover enough that we decided to try to replicate it, and hey, it turned out pretty dang amazing. We used prime rib, but it works with any other leftover meat you might have in your fridge. It's especially excellent with pastrami or corned beef.

Preheat the oven to 450°F.

Place the diced potatoes in a small saucepan and cover with cold water. Add the vinegar and a generous pinch of salt. Bring to a boil, lower the heat to maintain a simmer, and cook until the potatoes are tender, 8 to 10 minutes. Drain well and transfer to a medium bowl. Give the potatoes a light mash with a fork, leaving some pieces chunky for texture.

Meanwhile, in a small cast-iron skillet, melt the butter over medium heat. Add the onion, celery, parsley, and rosemary and cook, stirring often, until the onions are translucent, about 5 minutes. Remove from the heat and transfer to the potatoes along with the prime rib, ketchup, and hot sauce. Stir well to combine. Taste and adjust with salt and pepper as needed.

Wipe out the skillet with a paper towel. Add the oil and place the skillet over medium-high heat. Add the hash mixture to the skillet and pack down with a spatula to form a nice compact patty. Don't touch it; when you hear it start to sizzle on the bottom instead of bubble just let that baby brown for 2 to 3 minutes. You can use the spatula to lift it and check the browning process. Once it reaches golden perfection, pop the skillet into the oven and bake until heated all the way through, about 12 minutes.

While the hash is baking, grab a nonstick skillet and cook your eggs how you like them: fried, scrambled, poached. (We're not here to judge; we know egg preferences are personal—but over medium is our personal fave.) Remove the hash from the oven and carefully invert onto a plate. Top with the eggs and chives and enjoy.

1½ cups ½-inch-diced russet potatoes
1 tablespoon distilled white vinegar
Kosher salt
2 tablespoons (¼ stick) unsalted butter
1 cup finely diced yellow onion
1 celery stalk, finely diced
1 tablespoon minced fresh flat-leaf parsley
1 teaspoon minced fresh rosemary
10 ounces cooked prime rib (such as the one on page 140), chopped
3 tablespoons ketchup
1 teaspoon of your favorite hot sauce
Freshly cracked black pepper
1 tablespoon neutral oil
2 eggs
2 tablespoons finely minced fresh chives

CREAMED SPINACH

Serves 4

2 tablespoons (¼ stick) unsalted butter
1 large shallot, minced
1 garlic clove, grated or minced
¾ cup heavy cream
½ teaspoon Diamond Crystal kosher salt
½ teaspoon freshly cracked black pepper
¼ teaspoon freshly grated nutmeg
Grated zest of ½ lemon
¼ cup freshly grated Parmesan cheese
1 pound frozen spinach, thawed and squeezed until very dry
¼ cup crème fraîche or sour cream

I spent so much time on the steak house beat that I now automatically think that something must be wrong whenever I go to a restaurant and they don't pair their greens with like five different types of dairy. What do you mean you don't serve creamed spinach?! I would never deprive my guests of this version. It's homey, it's opulent, and the star ingredient still shines through.

In a medium skillet over medium heat, melt the butter. Add the shallot and cook, stirring often, until soft, about 5 minutes. Add the garlic and cook for 1 minute more, taking care not to brown it. Add the cream, salt, pepper, and nutmeg, bring the mixture to a boil, and then lower the heat to maintain a simmer. Cook until the cream reduces by one-third and is thick enough to coat the back of a spoon, 8 to 10 minutes. Toss in the lemon zest and Parmesan, stirring until the cheese is melted. Stir in the spinach. If it seems watery, continue to cook for a few more minutes to reduce some of the liquid. Finally, stir in the crème fraîche and cook for just 1 minute more, then transfer to a warm serving dish. Serve immediately and enjoy.

HONEY-GLAZED CARROTS

Serves 4

1½ pounds carrots, cut on the bias into 2- to 3-inch chunks
Diamond Crystal kosher salt
¼ cup (½ stick) unsalted butter
¼ cup honey
2 fresh thyme sprigs
2 teaspoons grated orange zest
1 tablespoon chopped fresh flat-leaf parsley

A lotta honey and a lotta butter. That's really all you need to transform the humble carrot. Maybe a little citrus and a little thyme, too.

Place the carrots in a medium saucepan and cover with cold water. Add a generous pinch of salt and bring to a boil over medium-high heat. Cook until the carrots are tender, 8 to 10 minutes.

Drain and add the carrots to a medium nonstick skillet over medium heat. Add the butter, honey, thyme, orange zest, and ¼ teaspoon salt and cook, stirring as the butter melts to coat the carrots. Continue to cook, stirring often, until the sauce is sticky, about 5 minutes. Discard the thyme sprigs and toss the carrots with more salt to taste and the parsley. Transfer to a warm dish and serve immediately.

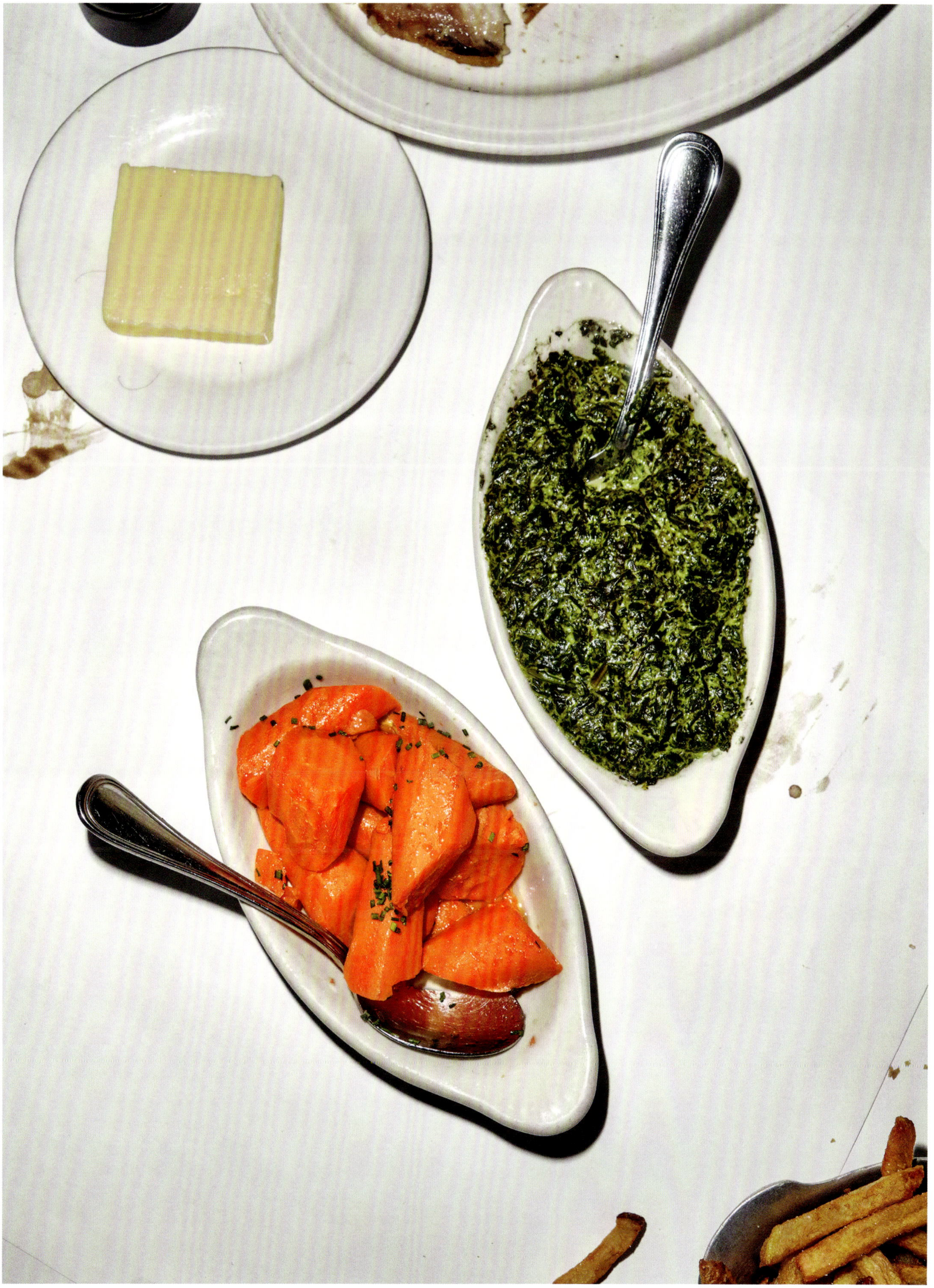

THIN ONION RINGS

You could play ring toss with most of the onion rings we encountered on the road. But I love a shoestring onion ring, à la BERN'S (page 37).

Serves 4

1 large sweet onion, such as Vidalia
1 cup buttermilk
1 cup all-purpose flour
¼ cup fine cornmeal
½ teaspoon sweet paprika
½ teaspoon garlic powder
½ teaspoon cayenne pepper
1 teaspoon Diamond Crystal kosher salt, plus more for seasoning
1 teaspoon freshly cracked black pepper, plus more for seasoning
Neutral oil for frying

Peel and trim the top of the onion. Using a mandoline or really sharp knife, thinly slice the onion crosswise into ¼-inch-thick slices and separate into rings. Add the onion rings to a large bowl and mix with the buttermilk. Let them soak while you prepare the dry ingredients.

In a medium bowl, whisk together the flour, cornmeal, paprika, garlic powder, cayenne, salt, and black pepper and set aside.

Pour enough oil into a large pot to reach a depth of 2 inches and place over medium heat until the temperature reaches 375°F. Line a plate with paper towels.

Dredge the buttermilk-soaked onion rings in the flour mixture, tossing to coat evenly and letting any excess drip off. Working in batches, place the dredged onions in the hot oil, turning occasionally, and fry until golden brown, 1 to 2 minutes. Using a spider or large slotted spoon, transfer the onion rings to the paper towel–lined plate to drain. Repeat with the remaining rings. Season immediately with more salt and black pepper before serving.

THICK ONION RINGS

When I want to eat my raaangs with a fork and a knife, I cook this slamming evocation of the ones at RINGSIDE (page 192). James Beard once said they were "the finest French fried onion rings I have ever eaten in America."

Serves 4

2 large sweet onions, such as Vidalia, sliced crosswise into 1-inch-thick slices and separated into rings
2 teaspoons Diamond Crystal kosher salt, plus more for seasoning
1½ cups all-purpose flour
1 cup rice flour
1 teaspoon baking powder
16 ounces lager-style beer
Neutral oil for frying

Place the onions and ½ teaspoon of the salt in a large bowl of cold water and let them soak while you prepare the batter. In a medium bowl, whisk together 1 cup of the all-purpose flour, the rice flour, baking powder, and remaining 1½ teaspoons salt. Slowly whisk in the beer until smooth and set the batter aside.

Pour enough oil into a large pot to reach a depth of 2 inches and place over medium heat until the temperature reaches 350°F. Line a plate with paper towels.

Drain the onions and pat dry with paper towels. Place the remaining ½ cup all-purpose flour on a large plate and dredge the onions in the flour. Tap off the excess flour and dip each ring into the batter, letting any excess drip off. Working in batches to prevent overcrowding, place the dredged onions in the hot oil, turning occasionally, and fry until golden brown, 1 to 2 minutes. Using a spider or large slotted spoon, transfer the onion rings to the paper towel–lined plate to drain. Season with more salt and serve immediately.

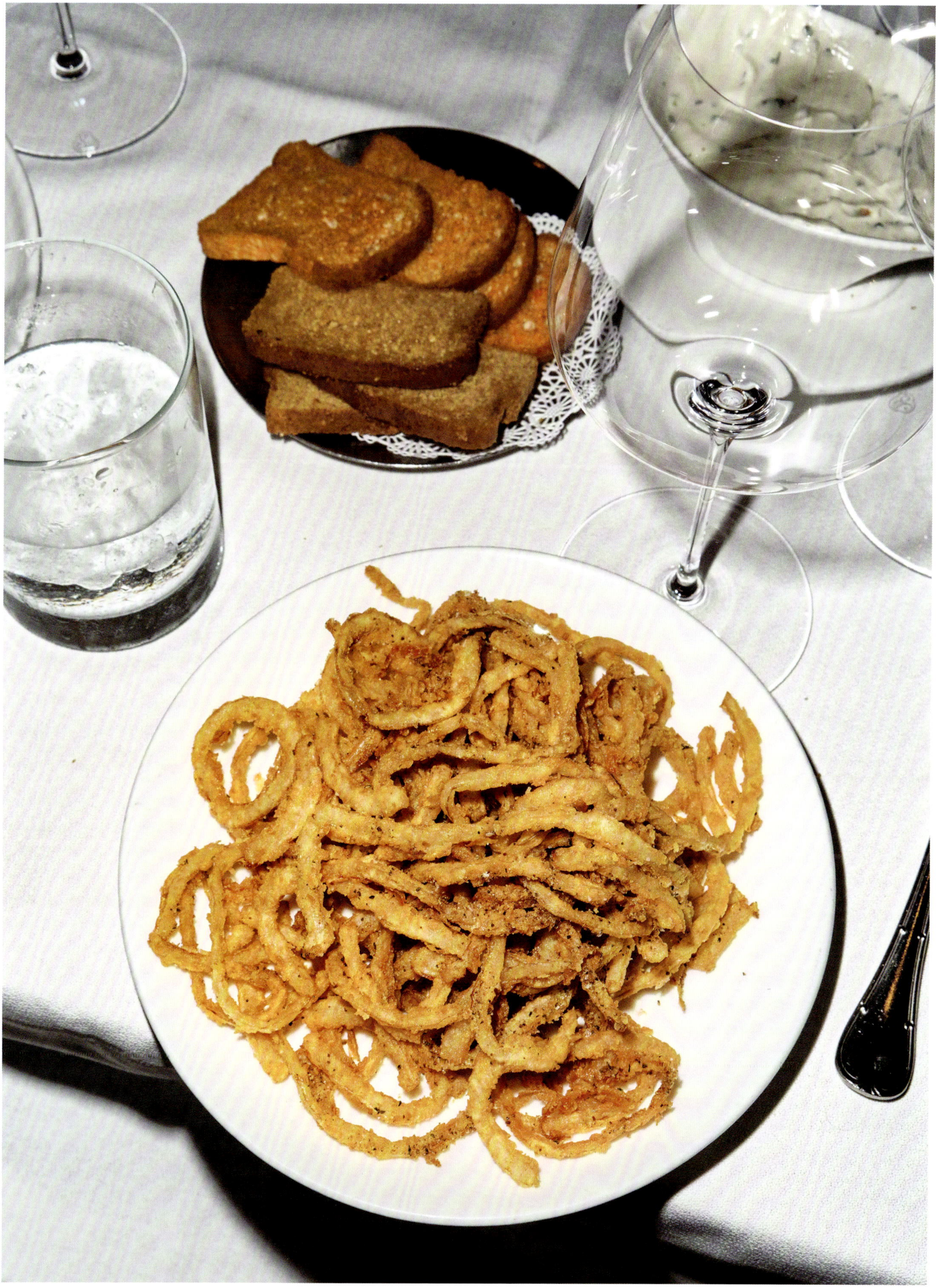

Serves 4

3 pounds Yukon gold potatoes, peeled and quartered

Kosher salt

2 cups (4 sticks) unsalted butter

½ cup heavy cream

Steak Sauce, Rosemary Garlic Butter, and/or Foie Gras Butter for serving (recipes follow)

Chimichurri (page 132) for serving (optional)

MASHED POTATOES & THREE SAUCES

The super-simple technique of passing milled potatoes through a sieve has become a very important tool in my steak house cooking game, because that, my friends, is how you make pommes purée that are Joël Robuchon–level luxurious. The potatoes are amazing on their own with just some salt. But let's be real—we want that sauce. Oh, did you think that tasty dippers were only meant for fries? Nope. Here are three bangers from my friends at JEFFREY'S in Austin to prove it!

Place the potatoes in a large pot and cover with cold water. Add a generous pinch of salt and bring to a boil, then lower the heat so the water maintains a bare simmer. Cook slowly until the potatoes are tender, about 15 minutes. Test the doneness with a knife: if the knife pierces the potatoes easily, they are ready.

Meanwhile, in a medium saucepan over low heat, warm the butter and cream until the butter is melted. Remove from the heat and set aside. Transfer half of the butter mixture to a small bowl and set aside.

Drain the potatoes, reserving the pot, then spread them on a sheet pan to allow steam to escape. To facilitate ricing, process the potatoes with the remaining butter mixture. Over the empty pot and working in batches, fill the ricer with some of the potatoes and butter mixture and press down. Repeat until you've riced all the potatoes and used up all of the butter mixture. Season to taste with salt and the reserved butter mixture a little bit at a time until your preferred potato consistency is reached. Pass the potatoes one final time through a fine-mesh tamis (aka a drum sieve) or strainer to remove any lumps. Take care to keep the potatoes hot during the process by keeping the heat on under the pot to not overwork the starches. Serve with as many of the sauces as you'd like.

Makes 2 cups

1 cup ketchup

¾ cup apple cider vinegar

½ cup Worcestershire sauce

½ cup raisins

¼ cup packed dark brown sugar

2 tablespoons unsulfured molasses

4 anchovy fillets

3 garlic cloves, thinly sliced

CONTINUED

STEAK SAUCE

In a small pot over medium-low heat, combine the ketchup, vinegar, Worcestershire, raisins, brown sugar, molasses, anchovies, and garlic and cook, stirring occasionally, until the mixture is reduced by one-third, about 30 minutes. Let the sauce cool before carefully transferring to a blender. Purée until smooth and pass through a fine-mesh strainer, discarding the solids. The steak sauce will keep in an airtight container in the fridge for up to 1 week.

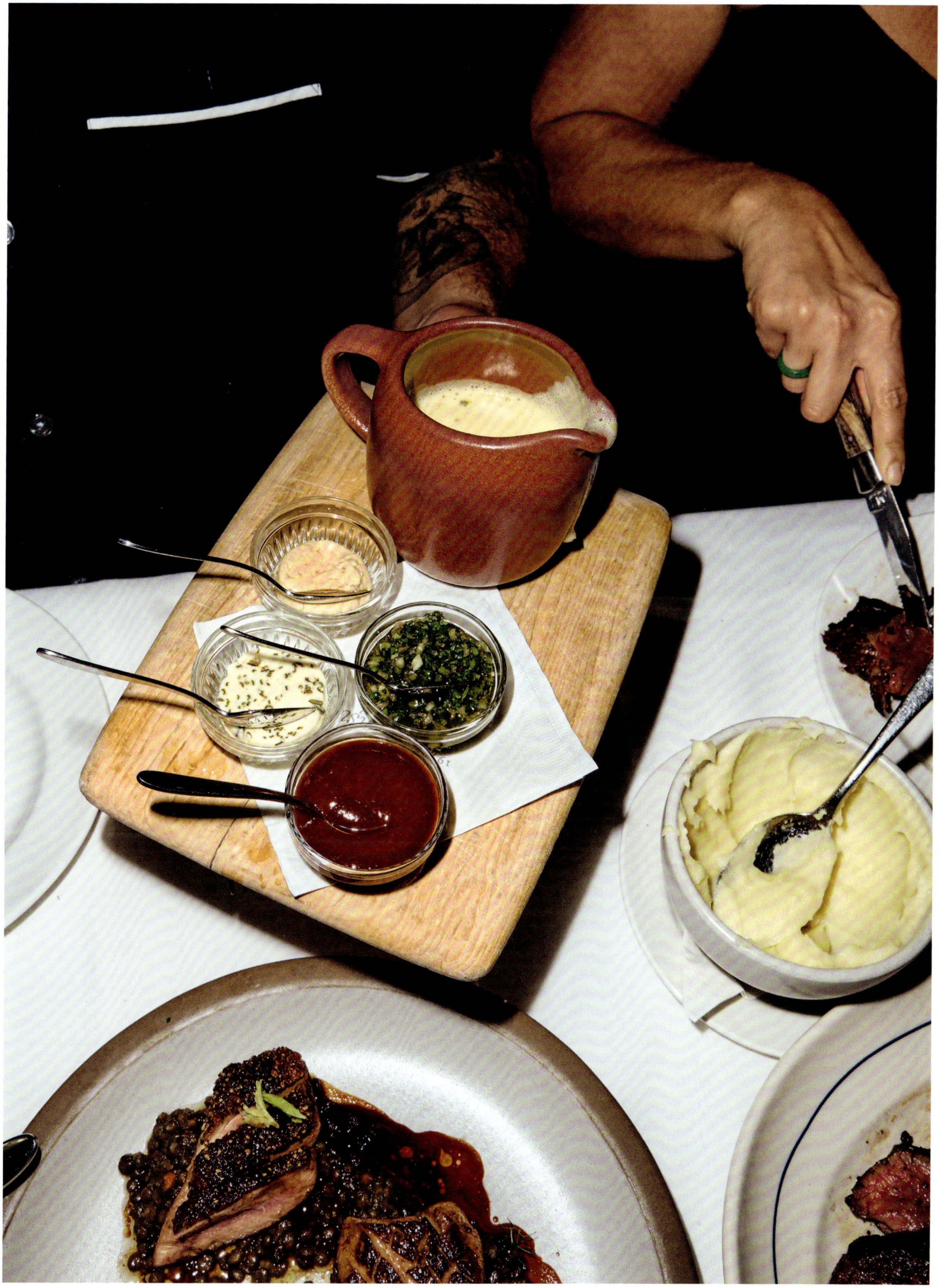

CONTINUED

Makes 1⅓ cups

Neutral oil

1 garlic head, top trimmed to expose the cloves

Kosher salt

2 tablespoons fresh rosemary leaves

1 cup (2 sticks) unsalted butter, at room temperature

ROSEMARY GARLIC BUTTER

Preheat the oven to 350°F.

Drizzle a little oil over the cut side of the garlic and season with a pinch of salt. Wrap the garlic in foil and roast until tender, about 45 minutes. Let cool to room temperature before removing the skins (it should yield about ¼ cup garlic).

Line a plate with paper towels. In a small skillet over medium heat, add a light coating of oil to fill the surface of the pan. Fry the rosemary leaves, stirring occasionally, until crisp and dark green, 2 minutes. Transfer to the paper towel–lined plate and let cool to room temperature.

In the bowl of a stand mixer fitted with the paddle attachment, combine the roasted garlic, fried rosemary, butter, and ¼ cup oil and mix on medium speed until the butter is creamed, about 2 minutes. Serve the butter softened to preference. The butter will keep in an airtight container in the fridge for 1 week.

Makes 2 heaping cups

8 ounces foie gras

2½ teaspoons Diamond Crystal kosher salt

1 teaspoon brandy

¾ teaspoon sugar

½ teaspoon pink curing salt

½ teaspoon freshly ground white pepper

1 cup (2 sticks) unsalted butter, at room temperature

FOIE GRAS BUTTER

Chop the foie gras into cubes and place in a quart container with a lid. Add the kosher salt, brandy, sugar, curing salt, and white pepper and stir. Cover and place in the fridge to cure overnight.

The next day, add the butter to the bowl of a food processor fitted with the blade attachment. With the machine running at medium speed, add the cured foie gras in stages until incorporated and smooth. The butter will keep in an airtight container in the fridge for up to 2 days.

LOBSTER MAC & CHEESE

Serves 4

This is one of the dankadent sides we encountered at LITTLE ALLEY STEAK (page 30) in Atlanta. It's a dish that could be an entire entrée, with its richness and power. Could. The only thing that matters to me is that you try the leftovers of this dish while standing in front of your fridge in the middle of the night: a quick commune with the divine, and then it's back to bed.

Preheat the oven to 350°F.

In a medium skillet over medium-high heat, warm the oil. Add the bell peppers and scallions and cook, stirring often, until tender, about 2 minutes. Add the lobster meat and cook, stirring constantly, until warmed through, 30 seconds. Add the cheese sauce and bring to a simmer, then simmer for an additional 30 seconds. Add the pasta and half of the Gruyère and simmer until the pasta is heated through. Taste and adjust with salt and black pepper as needed.

Transfer the mixture to a 12-inch oven-safe casserole dish and top with the panko and remaining Gruyère. Bake until the cheese is melted and the panko is golden brown, 8 to 10 minutes. Top with the chives and serve.

2 tablespoons neutral oil
½ cup finely diced red bell pepper
2 scallions, sliced
8 ounces lobster meat roughly chopped (about 4 large tails)
2 cups Cheese Sauce (recipe follows)
8 ounces cavatappi pasta, cooked
2 cups shredded Gruyère cheese
Kosher salt and freshly cracked black pepper
1 cup panko breadcrumbs
1 tablespoon chopped fresh chives

CHEESE SAUCE

Makes 2 cups

In a medium saucepan over medium-high heat, add the flour and cook, stirring constantly, until slightly toasted, 1 to 3 minutes. Add the butter and stir until melted, then add the cream and cook, whisking constantly, until thickened, 3 to 4 minutes. Add all the cheeses, the garlic, and onion powder and whisk until smooth. Taste and adjust with salt and pepper as needed. Remove from the heat, transfer to an airtight container, and refrigerate until chilled, about 3 hours (can be made up to 3 days ahead).

1½ tablespoons all-purpose flour
2 tablespoons (¼ stick) unsalted butter
1 cup heavy cream
½ cup shredded white Cheddar cheese
½ cup shredded orange Cheddar cheese
¼ cup shredded Gouda cheese
¼ cup shredded Gruyère cheese
¼ teaspoon garlic powder
¼ teaspoon onion powder
Kosher salt and freshly cracked black pepper

SWEET POTATO CASSEROLE

Serves 4

Sweet Potatoes
1 pound sweet potatoes, peeled and diced
1 cup heavy cream
1 teaspoon ground cinnamon
2 tablespoons (¼ stick) unsalted butter
Kosher salt and freshly cracked black pepper
Chopped toasted pecans for garnish

Meringue
2 cups sugar
1 cup egg whites (about 8 eggs)

We conclude the savory portion of our feast with another naughty number from LITTLE ALLEY STEAK (page 30) that you might want to keep in your back pocket for Thanksgiving.

Make the sweet potatoes: Bring a medium pot of water to a boil. Add the potatoes and boil until tender, about 10 minutes. Drain well, return the potatoes to the pot, and mash until smooth. Add the cream, cinnamon, and butter. Season to taste with salt and pepper. Keep warm.

Make the meringue: In a double boiler, whisk the sugar and egg whites over medium-high heat until thick and with a consistency similar to marshmallow, about 10 minutes. Fill a piping bag with the meringue.

Add the mashed sweet potatoes to an 8-inch oven-safe dish and top with the pecans. Finish by layering the meringue all across the top and toast with a blowtorch (or place under a broiler for 5 minutes) before serving.

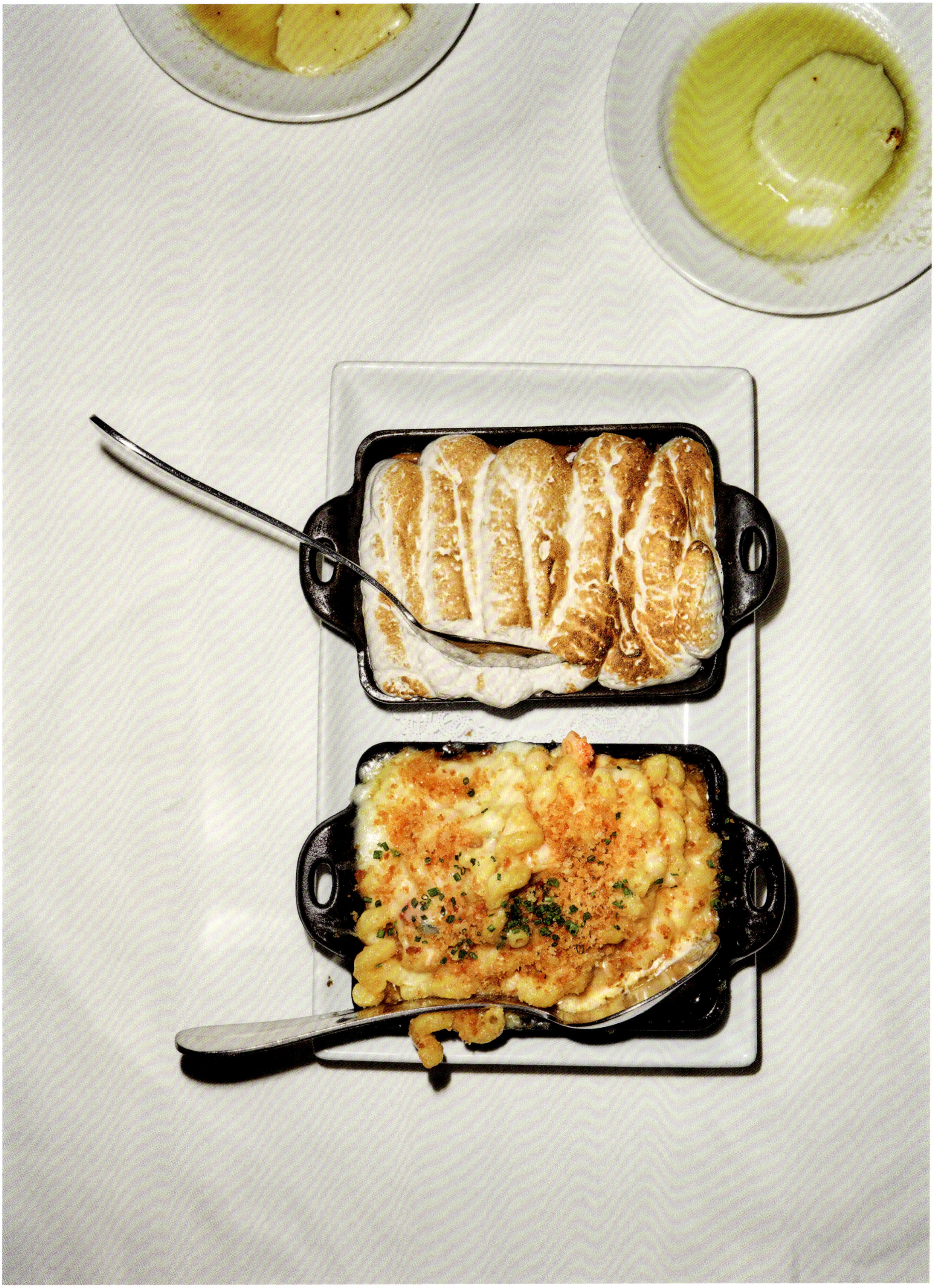

THE JOURNEY, PART VI

LOS AN

NGELES

LOS ANGELES WAS AT ITS BEST IN THE '50S, '60S, AND '70S.

The architecture and the fashion from those decades are still very much present in the city I call home. Big neon signs line the streets of Hollywood. Downtown, classic Mexican restaurants with red leather booths have been serving people for decades upon decades. The old-school dive bar and the classic steak house remain well represented. They're still the ideal places to escape the hustle and either wind down from a wild day or start your engines before heading to someone's over-the-top pool party sponsored by Dingo Dood's Caffeine-Spiked Mochachino.

I was pretty lost when I first moved from Philadelphia to Los Angeles. Granted, this was back in the days when I had to use a Thomas Guide to navigate the city. Luckily, I had a few friends who advised me as I was getting my bearings. There was unanimous agreement on Taylor's Steakhouse. Even the valet and private lot outside Taylor's is a welcome sight, considering the parking situation in Koreatown. Within a few blocks of Taylor's are so many of my favorite meat and steak-adjacent establishments: Soot Bull Jip delivers grand Korean barbecue with real charcoal. If you head toward MacArthur Park, you can sample the best pastrami sandwich in the entire world at Langer's. My order is a pastrami on rye with a side of Russian. I don't do the coleslaw and the Swiss cheese because I don't want to go to hell.

When I asked my good friend Victor Nguyen what the Vietnamese equivalent of an American steak house might be, he replied, "There's no such thing." I got very depressed: a Vietnamese-inspired steak house would serve my dream-come-true cuisine. Victor saw my crestfallen expression and did some quick thinking and asked, "Have you ever had seven courses of beef?" Without speaking, we were in a car driving FAST to Rosemead to go very deep into a beef-centric Vietnamese wonderland. Thien An Bo 7 Mon is just one of many examples.

I've only scratched the surface, but the following restaurants will hopefully inspire you to join me down the rabbit hole. Some of the spots don't exactly fit the definition of a steak house. Luckily, this is my book.

If you would like to reach my management with any feedback, you can easily send them an email at notesforericssteakhousebook@aolinstantmessenger.onlyfans.biz.

At Niku X, they take dry-aging to the extreme. And half the busboys are robots. Pictured here is the flaming tomahawk presentation.

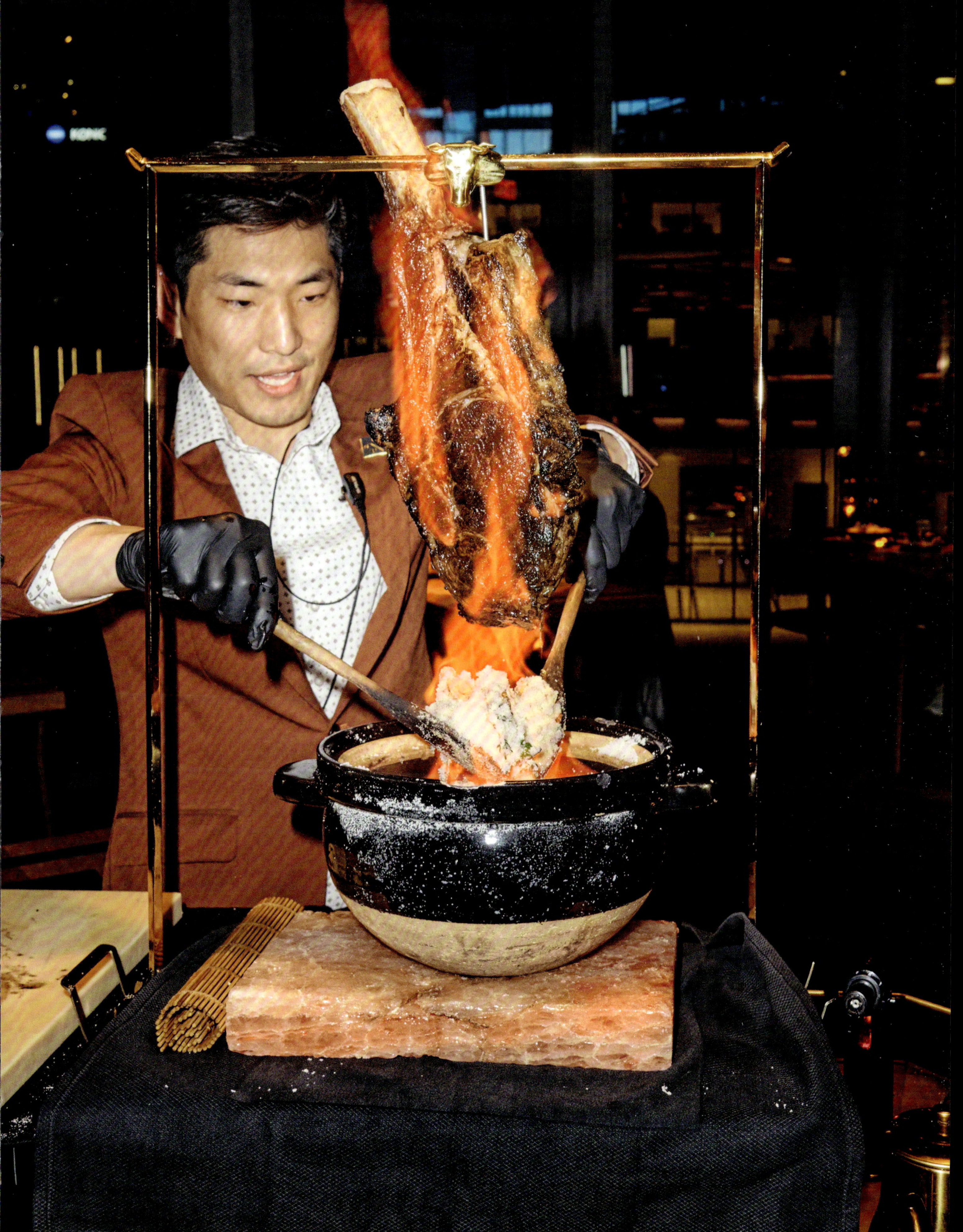

LOS ANGELES

THE MUSSO & FRANK GRILL

BY THE NUMBERS

Opening year: 1919
Founders: Joseph Musso and Frank Toulet
Address: 6667 Hollywood Boulevard, Hollywood, California 90028
House specials: Ground beef steak; The original fettuccine Alfredo

Welcome to Hollywood, the city of glitz and glamour! Stroll along the Walk of Fame, and find the star of your favorite deceased actor. Take a selfie. But if you lean too close to the plaque and happen to graze the surface of the concrete with any part of your skin, please head straight to the local car wash and put in your dollars and stand under the soapy foam for ten minutes, until you are rid of the toxic filth that is already festering on your body.

Sorry, I forgot this was a "food book" for a moment. But it's true; Hollywood ain't what it looks like in the pictures or the Mötley Crüe music videos that I still play on occasion after a trip into that part of Los Angeles. Still, there are gems within the chaos. And one particularly shiny gem is Musso & Frank's.

It's a tough call, but I believe that this is the great American steak house with the greatest dining room of them all. I always have a hard time deciding where to sit: on the casual side with the boxed-in booths and luncheonette-looking bar counter or in the grand dining room next door, where the cocktail bar has a more proper feel to it. No matter where I wind up, I look forward to seeing the streaks of red light flash before my eyes as the servers move through the space with astonishing speed. That brown wooden paneling is the perfect backdrop for the scarlet-tuxedo pop!

The martinis at Musso come with a sidecar. Once in a while I'll swing by, nurse one of those and maybe nibble on the celery stalks with a Roquefort dipper, which are served on a delightful canoe of crushed ice and shredded iceberg. But whenever I'm eating here for real, I get the ground beef steak. It's the hamburger in its purest form. I need only a fork to finish it. And I really appreciate the watercress garnish.

Some nights, I'll head on over to Musso all by my lonesome just to have that splendid chopped steak.

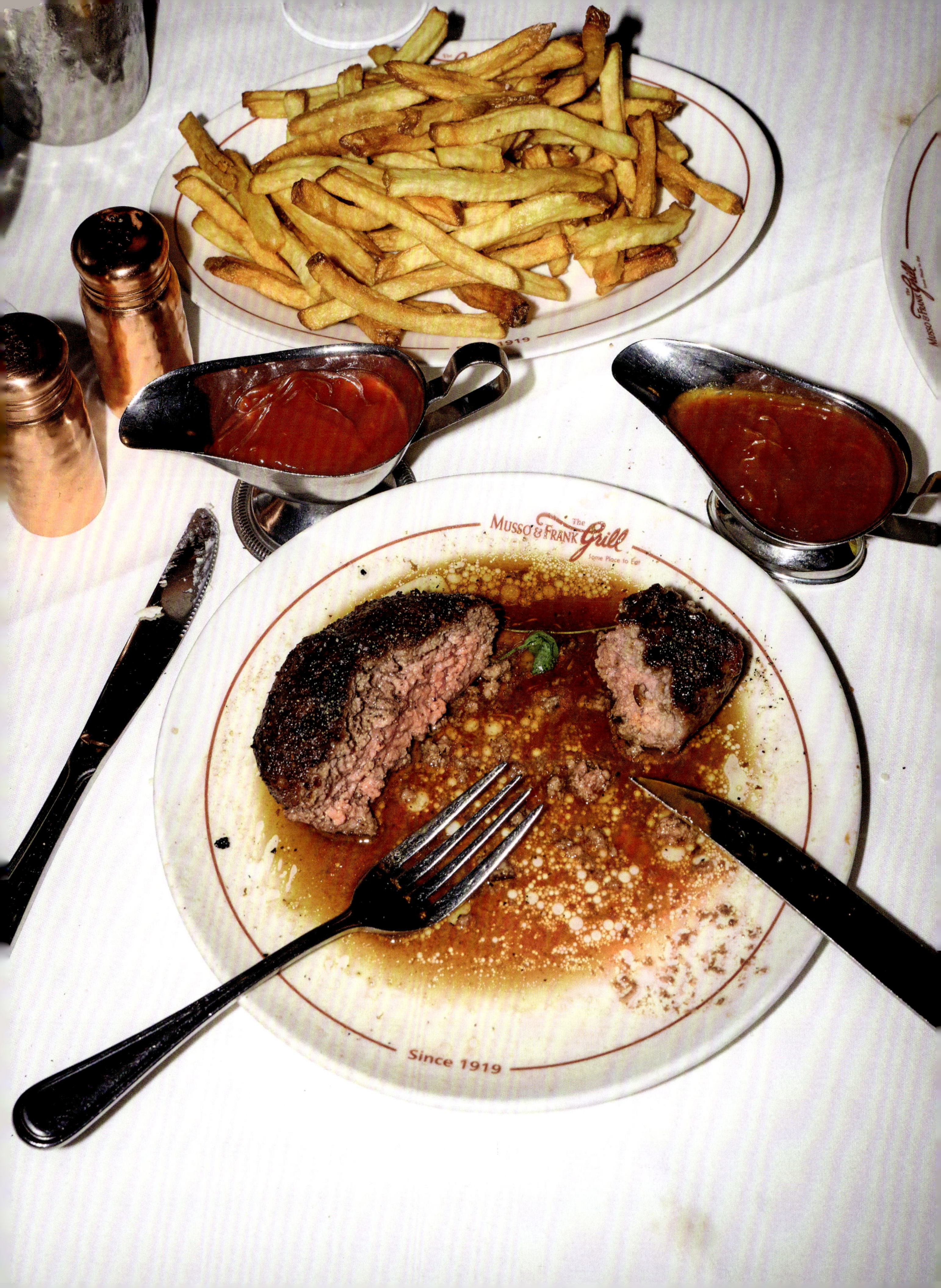
MUSSO & FRANK Grill
Some Place to Eat
Since 1919

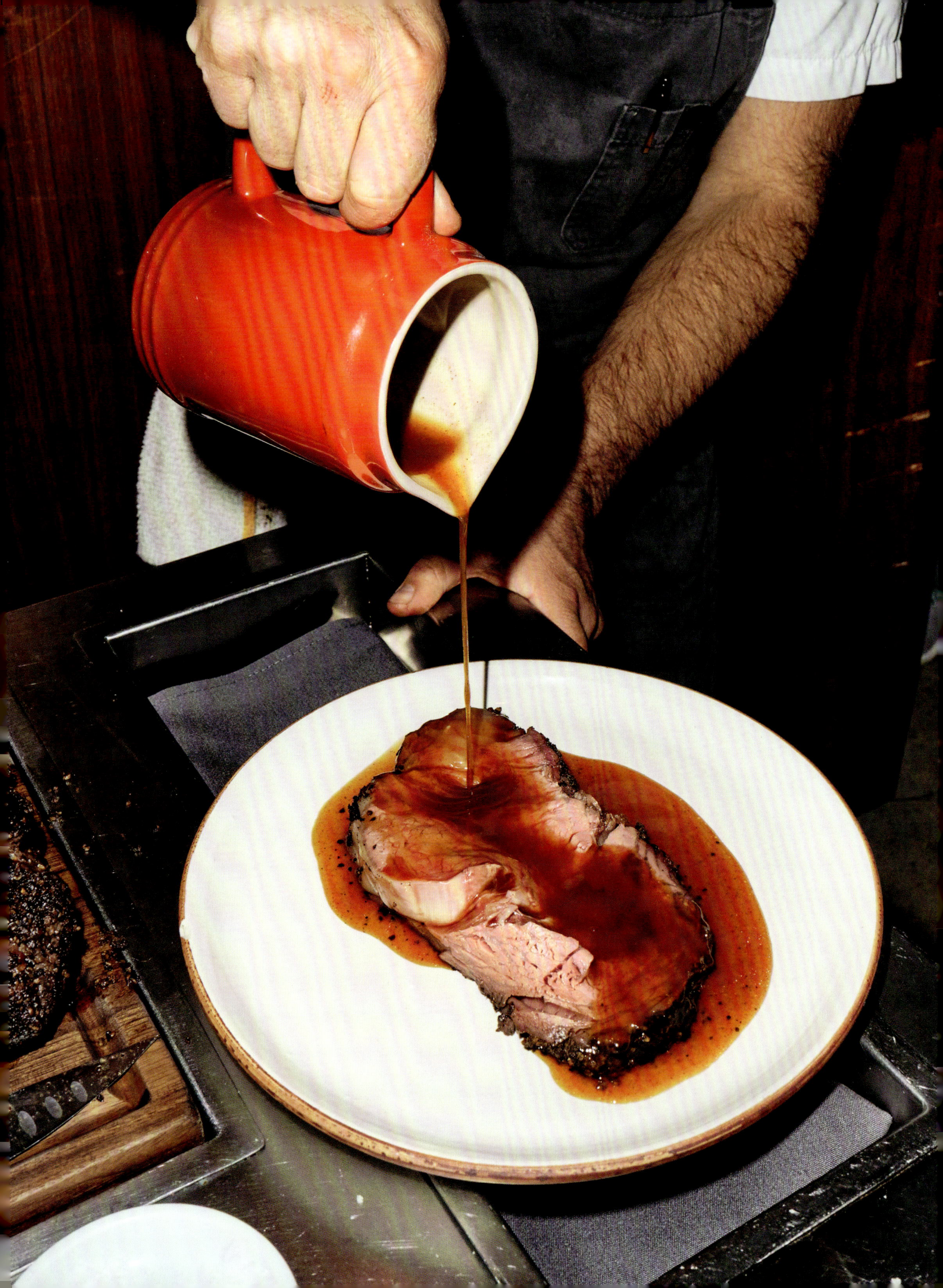

LOS ANGELES

MAJORDOMO

The menu at Majordomo tells a story about LA, which means that it tells a story about America. Before it opened, I remember David Chang describing his vision for the restaurant as a Korean American Cheesecake Factory. Something for everyone. So fun that Angelenos from all over town will happily sit in traffic to eat there. If you ask me, though, it's secretly one of the most exciting steak houses in America.

BY THE NUMBERS

Opening year: 2018
Founder: David Chang
Address: 1725 Naud Street, Los Angeles, California 90012
House specials: House bings; Whole-plate short rib

At Domo, there's bread and butter in the form of bings, the Chinese fried breads used to prepare scallion pancakes, served with all kinds of toppings, dippers, and other accompaniments. Dave's bings are grilled on the plancha. When you tear into these gently charred and ever-so-sweet flatbreads, another influence pokes its head in: the mighty kebab shop. You can order the flatbreads with a variety of dips and sauces, from honey butter and whipped bone marrow to a Mediterranean charred-eggplant-and-pine-nut situation.

At Domo, there's a raw bar—one with kombu in the mignonette; ponzu drizzled over the crudo; yuzu folded into the dipping sauce for the crab claws; and a seafood plateau that is horizontal, not vertical—a box, not a tower—which is a nod to the wooden serving vessels Japanese izakaya use to highlight colorful slices of sashimi.

You find blessed consistency here: slabs of meat, tableside moves, crazy wines, perfect cocktails, and vibrant energy. The sheer force of the place! The bar counter runs the entire length of the giant room. The outdoor patio seats more people than the interior. I don't care what Dave says, he probably took one look inside a space that would feel very awkward empty and decided that a steak house was the best choice. As we have established, everybody likes a steak house.

Chef Jude Parra-Sickels hit us with an assortment of pristine raw fish to start. Everybody kept raving about the tang in the cocktail sauce. They fold sriracha into it. A big part of what makes this food, which is based on classic ideas, so impactful is that they use the kind of California produce that can take your breath away. I'm thinking about that dang salad: stone fruit and tomatoes sliced to the same proportions and tossed together with shiso, sherry vin, and sesame. A total steak house vibe that tastes like switching from black-and-white to color.

Then we were graced with Majordomo's ode to the venerable Lawry's. The prime rib tonight, unlike Lawry's, was seasoned with a shio koji rub for three days and finished low and slow in the smoker, the heart and soul of Domo's vast kitchen. The rib was plated in a pool of textbook beef jus. We kept dipping the jaw-dropping B.S. fries into the horseradish cream sauce (they're named after Dave's friend Bill Simmons). Not a lot of steak houses make their fries in-house. You best believe Domo does theirs from scratch. It's a triple-cook process. They freeze them before frying them the third and final time in beef fat, which gives them the McDonald's-golden-age crispiness that some of us spend our lives chasing—yet rarely find.

Dessert came with a show, starring peach melba and flames high enough to meet my satisfaction. The dish highlighted peak-season peaches and nectarines, which Jude swirled in a pan with rummy syrup that turned to caramel. He poured the mixture over donuts they make from scratch in the style of Krispy Kreme.

Los Angeles's most elusive prime rib: at Domo, they only slice those magnificent slabs on the weekend.

LOS ANGELES

BEEFSTEAK

In 1939, Joseph Mitchell published one of his classic *New Yorker* stories about the beefsteak feasts that started to become popular in the Northeast in the mid-1800s. There were two rules: Black-tie—yes. Napkins and utensils—no. We follow both rules at the annual Beefsteak I've had the great joy of cohosting on the West Coast for the last decade.

You get to dress to the nines, throw on an apron, and spend hours in a converted cathedral downtown eating everything that's put in front of you, only and exclusively with your hands. Then there's ballroom dancing. All proceeds benefit the LA Food Bank.

To keep attendees from tapping out in the old days, people told stories between courses. Bands played. Tables randomly erupted into song. At our Beefsteaks, emcee Billy Harris dresses up in whatever costume I assign to him, like a zentai bodysuit that made him look like roast beef wrapped in kitchen twine. Or a sparkly red Annie dress. Over the years, I've hired my favorite actors from *Tim & Eric* to roam around and create "atmosphere." There's usually at least one circus performer who can swallow a sword. One year, there was a secret sensual culinary performance deep in the catacombs of Vibiana, the jaw-dropping event space where we host Beefsteak!

I bring to the table this cultural curation and the cases of wine, since beer isn't as much of a focus for us as it was in the Tammany Hall times. But the true heroes, who pour their sweat and skill into pulling off a 500-person bacchanalia featuring excellent food, every single year, are the incredible husband-and-wife duo of Amy Knoll Fraser and Neal Fraser. Amy and Neal are LA legends. Neal trained with Wolfgang Puck and Thomas Keller, and these days he and Amy operate Vibiana, and Redbird next door.

Neal believes a true beefsteak should be an uncompromising celebration of flesh, gristle, and tendon—a primal affair where the pigs in a blanket are prepared with Wagyu calves, the blondies are made with beef tallow, and the fish course is a stockpot filled with a coil of whole king salmon with their heads still on—their eyes staring up at you as you make the meat from their bodies disappear.

Once the silver platters start leaving the kitchen and landing on the long tables, it doesn't stop. Amy is a beast with logistics and sees to it that the choreography is totally seamless. Headsets, clipboards, a minute-by-minute run of show—the whole deal.

Thank you from the bottom of my congested heart to Neal and Amy for giving Beefsteak a home, to the attendees who support the cause, and to fellow friends in comedy, like Matt Selman and Cort Cass, for letting me build this tradition with them.

Even the carrots you have to eat with your hands. Taken at Beefsteak 2024.

STEAK HOUSE

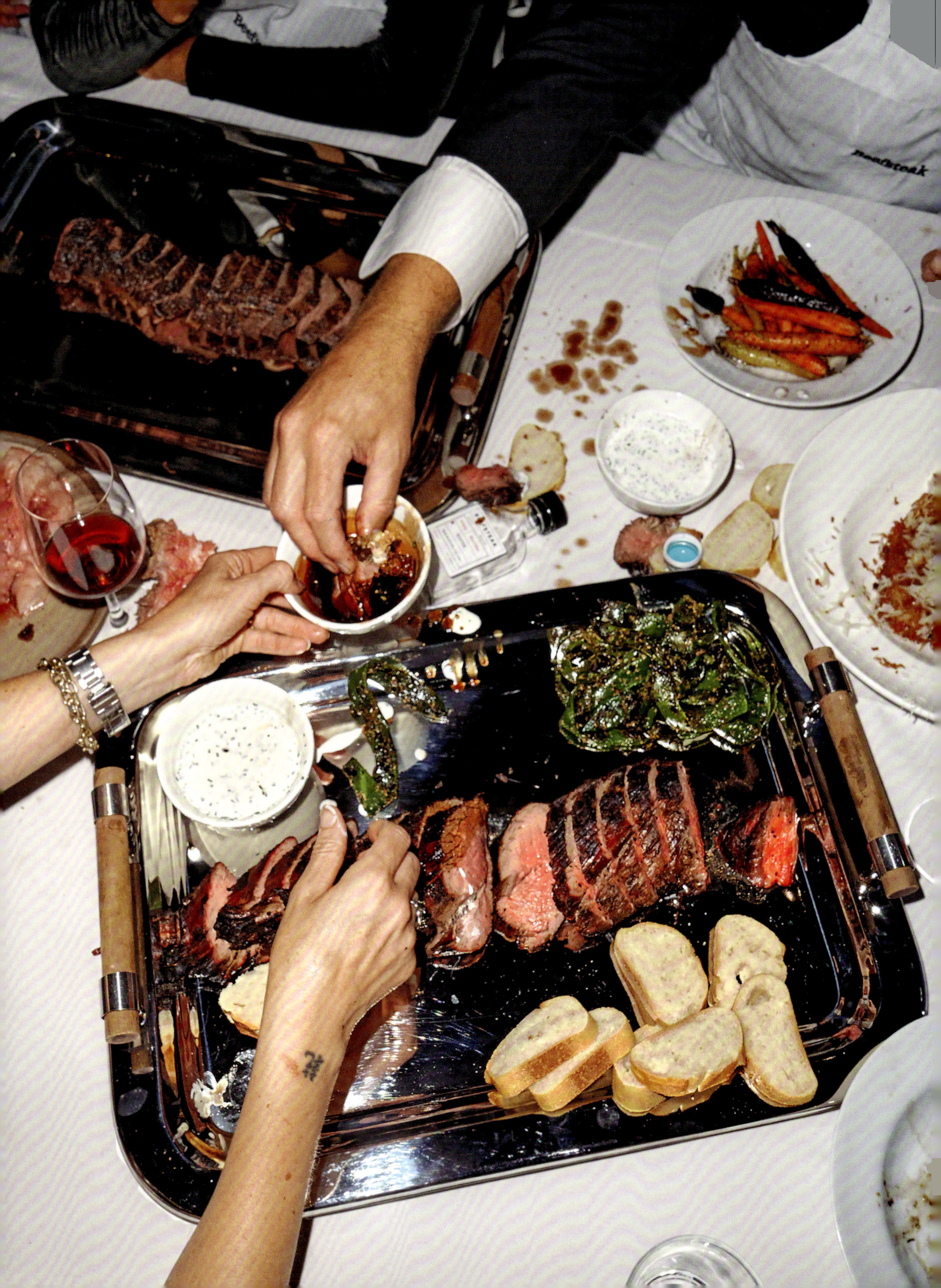

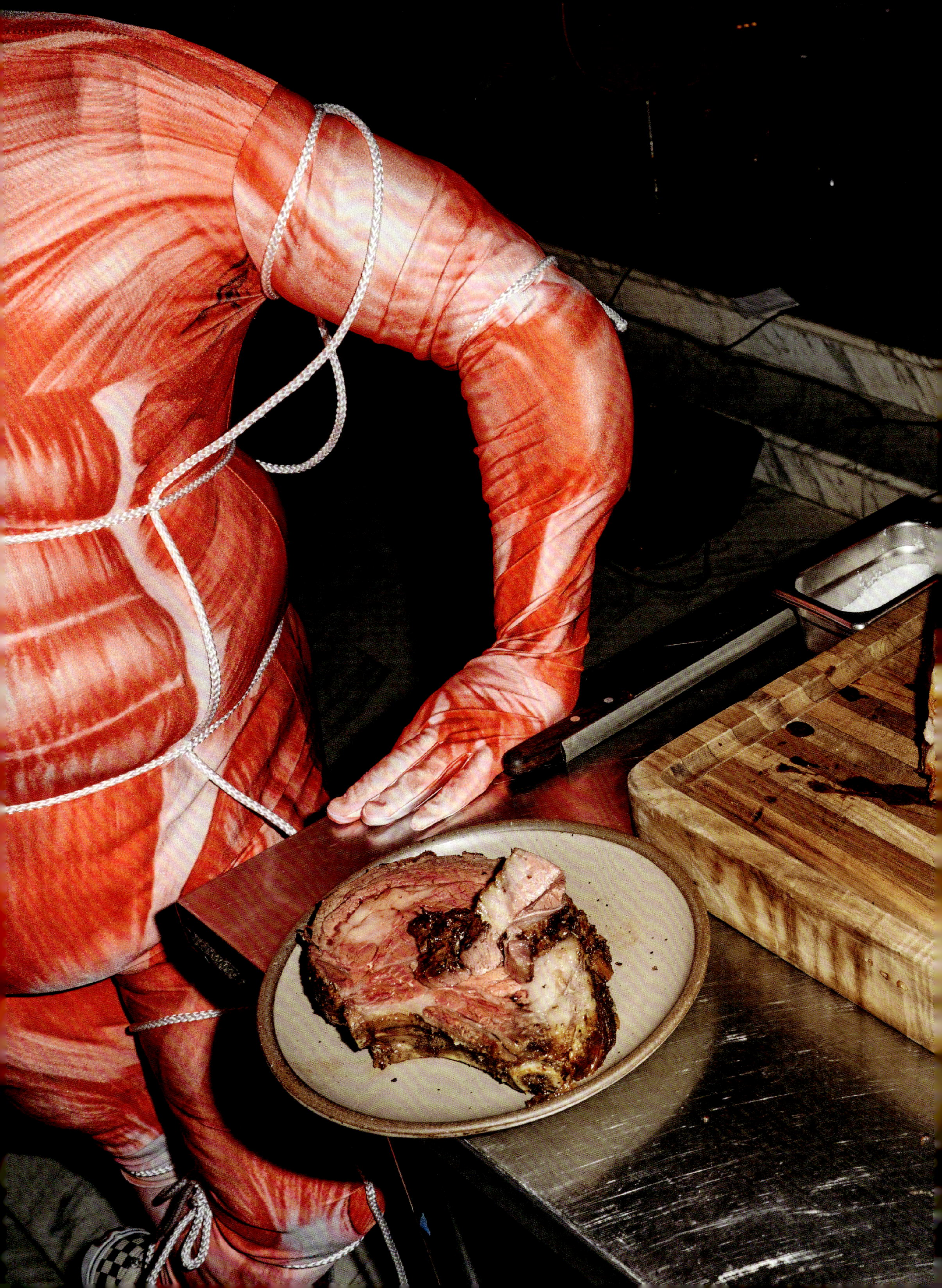

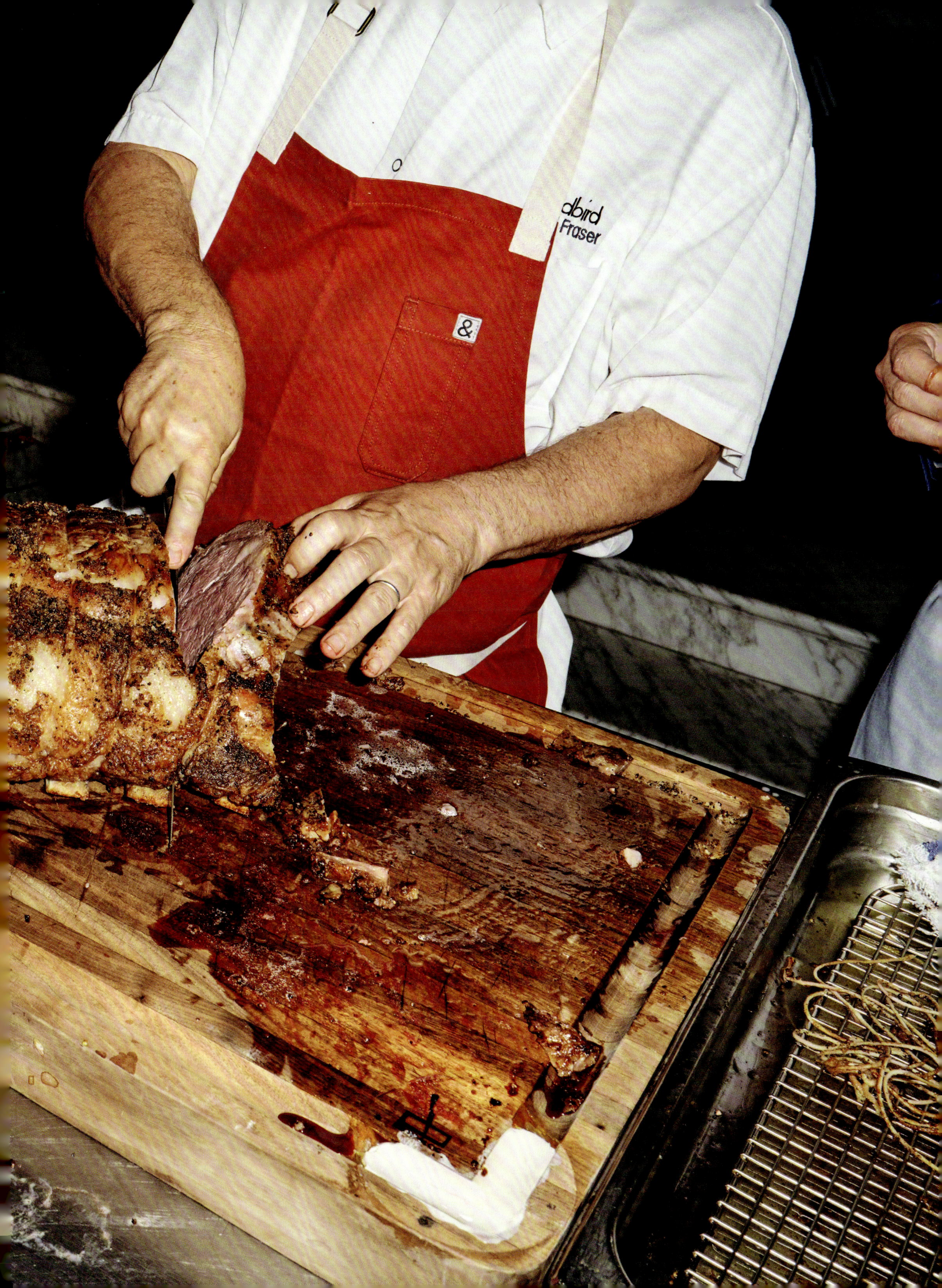
dbird
Fraser

A NIGHT AT TAYLOR'S WITH BOB, TIM, AND JOHN

Within the first year of us moving to Los Angeles, Tim and I had a very, very tiny following. Some fans would reach out from time to time to offer to take us out for a bite. At this point in our careers, a complimentary dinner was an amazing opportunity, so we'd do a light vetting and go eat with generous strangers. One group wanted to take us to Taylor's in Koreatown. We were very excited because many people told us that was the spot to be.

Our hosts turned out to be a very nice couple. It was a good time. They introduced us to their favorite dishes, like the rare cut of coulotte and the onion rings. We were instantly hooked. Similar to Ye Rustic Inn in Los Feliz, Taylor's could exist in almost any city and it would be a gem.

That memory of us jumping at the chance to eat on someone else's dime is what inspired me to choose Taylor's as the place to dine on steak with Tim and two other friends who've looked after us and who need to be in this book—Bob Odenkirk and John Reilly.

That night, I discovered my friends still have a lot to say about Bob Hope. Eventually, we talked about other things as well. Like steak houses. Bob: "They make me smile, but there's a darkness to them, too. My father spent a lot of time in country club bars and steak houses with other salesmen, trying to emulate the Rat Pack." While preparing for a role set in San Francisco during the Gold Rush, John discovered something, "Those prospectors were interested in only three things: steak, cigars, and soliciting prostitutes."

The staff at Taylor's could not have been more attentive, so much so that it inspired the best stories of the night. As it turns out, my friends know what it's like to work in a restaurant.

"Taylor's is decked out with red-vinyl booths, horsey prints on the walls, and a pickle-nose guy at the bar who laughs like Thurston Howell III."
—Jonathan Gold

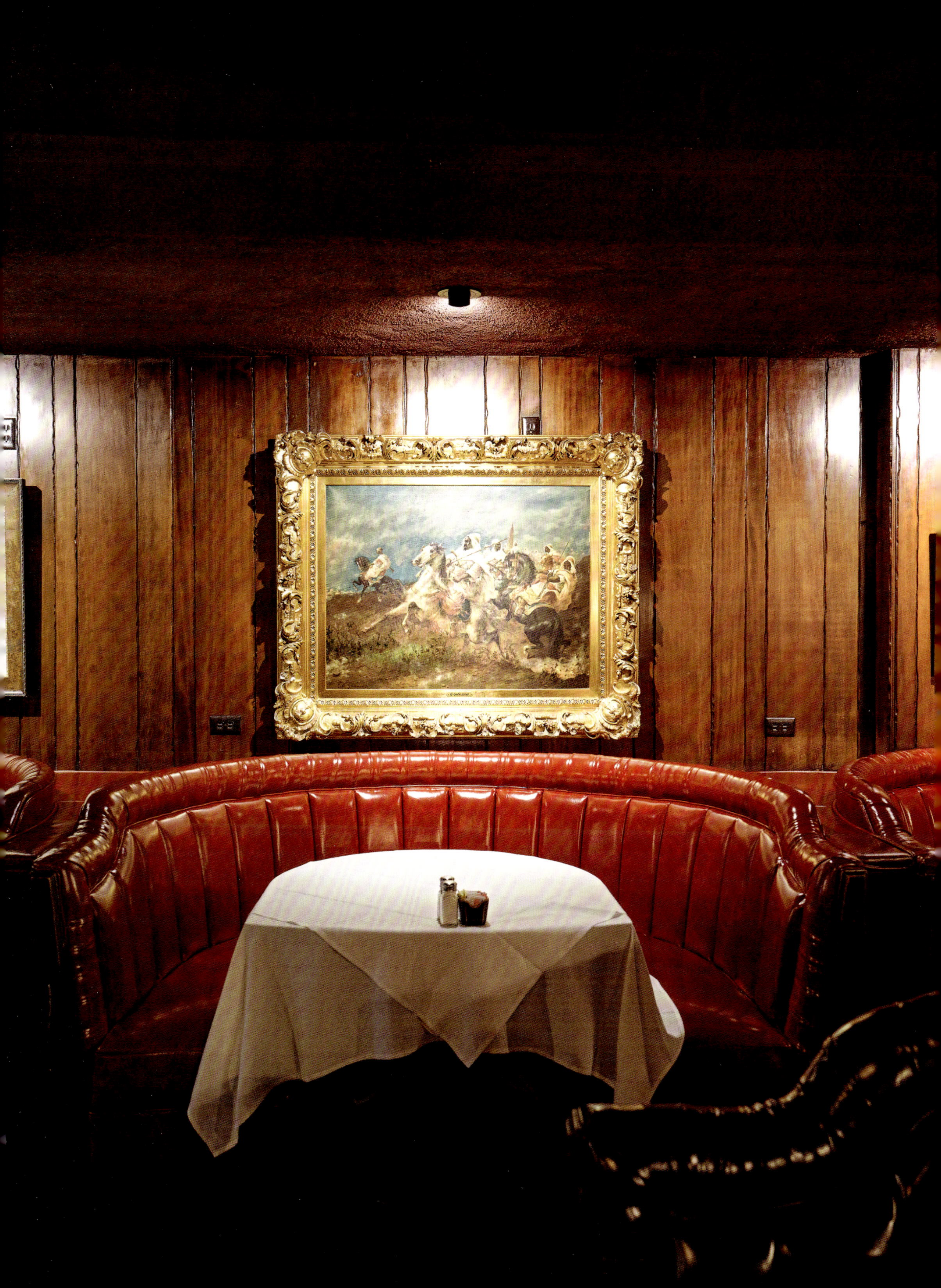

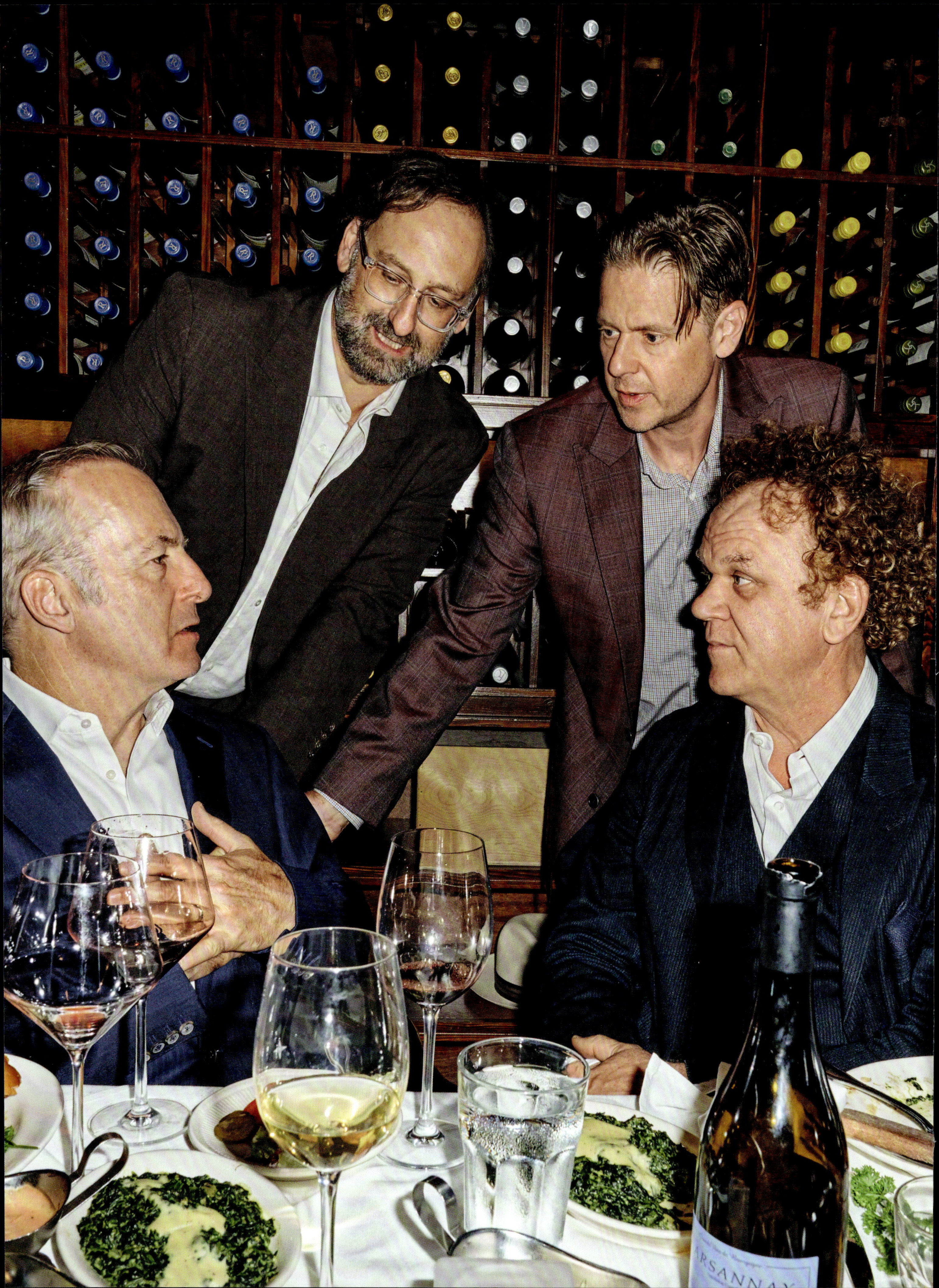

ON WORKING IN RESTAURANTS

John C. Reilly

"I mostly worked as a busboy. I would steal everything I needed for my apartment from the restaurant. In college, I had a five-gallon can of Hershey's syrup that I snatched from a job. I think it lasted me all four years of school. At one point, I was a waiter at the Walnut Room, which was this enormous place on the top floor of the Marshall Field's department store in Chicago with a huge tree in the middle of the dining room. People would make their annual holiday pilgrimage to this big, old-fashioned store, do their shopping, and then have lunch. It was a ritual. I had wanted to be in the Santa show at Marshall Field's, but I didn't make the audition, so they gave me a waiting gig instead. I was not good at it.

You would have eight to ten tables in your section. The way it was supposed to work is they'd seat your tables gradually. What would actually happen is that I'd turn my back for one second to set up at my station and then I'd turn around and *all* ten tables would be full. I remember having to go into the kitchen far too many times to fetch things I forgot. 'Oh yeah, butter! Oh yeah, the food! Of course!' I was really good at the introduction—'Hey, folks, welcome to the Walnut Room'—but it was all downhill from there. The diners would have this look on their faces: *This guy is not on top of it*. I just remember eating lots of pie and chocolate in secret. We used to have to eat while hiding behind our stations because it was forbidden.

I lasted one season. I realized I would be much better suited to doing carpentry or light plumbing. I tried to get handyman jobs. But I did have a brief career as a catering waiter, which was much better for me because it didn't require taking orders and getting them right. All you had to do was ask, 'Who has the fish?' And the only rule was: if you don't have a tuxedo and a bow tie, do not come into work. No other ties were allowed. Well, one morning, while getting ready for work, I realized I had lost my bow tie. I freaked out. All I had was a real bow tie, my father's. I found it in his closet. But I had no idea how to tie a real bow tie, and I had about twenty minutes. Then I remembered that Stan Laurel, in one of the Laurel and Hardy movies, did a whole routine with a bow tie where he'd mistakenly tie it into a napkin on his lap over and over again, until finally, right at the end, he succeeds. I dug out the video from another closet and shoved it into the VCR. I pressed pause when it got to the bow tie section and then slowly, frame by frame, watched him tie the bow tie correctly, and I miraculously pulled it off."

Because he grew up with five ravenous siblings, John still does not share his food at the table. "It was a feeding frenzy."

LOS ANGELES

Tim Heidecker

"I worked at a lot of restaurants. In high school, I was a busboy and dishwasher. During my postcollege years in Philly, I waited tables at a restaurant called Creperie Beau Monde, which I think shut down only recently. I was hired as they were opening. I was part of the first-season cast and stayed for around two years. The owners were great, this gay couple who had come from the art world and were starting this entirely different venture designed to make crepes kind of like a fine-dining experience. I started there as a busboy and moved up to waiter.

Now that I think of it, being a busboy at twenty-two is a little embarrassing. But I loved it—the hang afterwards, sitting at the bar and having a few drinks with my coworkers. It felt very similar to being in theater or show business. You have the backstage, which is the kitchen, where you can tear off the piece of bread as you're picking up food, or eat whatever is left at the end of the night. The performance is out there, on the floor, with all the customers.

I wasn't the best waiter. I was really good personalitywise, being funny and light with the customers and making them feel welcome. But organizationally, I was a complete mess. I would constantly get in the weeds and be confused. The pad where you write your orders, whatever you call that thing: Whenever we got really busy, I could never make heads or tails of it. For me, once it got bad during service, it always seemed to be impossible to come back.

I managed to survive, though. I think it's because the owner had a crush on me. We became very good friends, but originally I think it came from a place of him wanting a little boy toy to look at, which eventually became a joke amongst us.

It was hard for me to leave that place. And while it was very hard work, I got paid in cash, which was cool."

Bob Odenkirk

"I suspected I wouldn't be the most attentive waiter alive, so I wanted a place that wasn't going to ask for too much. I got a job at a spot in Chicago called Ed Debevic's. It's like a faux-'50s hamburger restaurant, with early rock music, the vibe of an old diner. But a bit corporatized.

It was actually pretty great. The people were awesome there. A lot of the waiters and waitresses were happy to be there. It's hard to believe, but they were supportive of each other. I, personally, was just doing the job. I was a runner and thankful to be a runner. I would go to the kitchen, you know, and pick up the food. The cooks would call me names in Spanish. All kinds of horrible things, I'm sure. It would make me laugh so hard. They just killed me.

I was at the restaurant when my first joke made it onto *Saturday Night Live.* It was something I'd written for Dennis Miller, who was the host of Weekend Update at the time: 'The statute of limitations on respecting Bob Hope for his earlier work ran out this week.' I remember the strange moment when I was running food, and it aired. I could see that he had told the joke, but I couldn't hear it. Another weird moment was when I went to New York for a week to help my friend Robert Smigel. I left the *SNL* after-party in the early-morning hours, took a cab to the airport, flew to O'Hare, and went straight to Ed Debevic's.

Ed Debevic's had a thing where you were supposed to be a smart-ass and say things like, 'Sit down, your food's comin'!' Or . . . 'We'll bring it when we feel like it!' The audience—what am I saying? The *patrons* liked it. Except when I was the one doing it, which should have been my first instinct that I should do drama instead of comedy. They did not laugh. Their feelings were hurt. They would get so scared. I would have to apologize. I have the inability sometimes to soften emotions, as a comedian should be able to do."

Taylor's veteran José Mendez, who goes by Tony. His daughter, Isabel, serves as the manager.

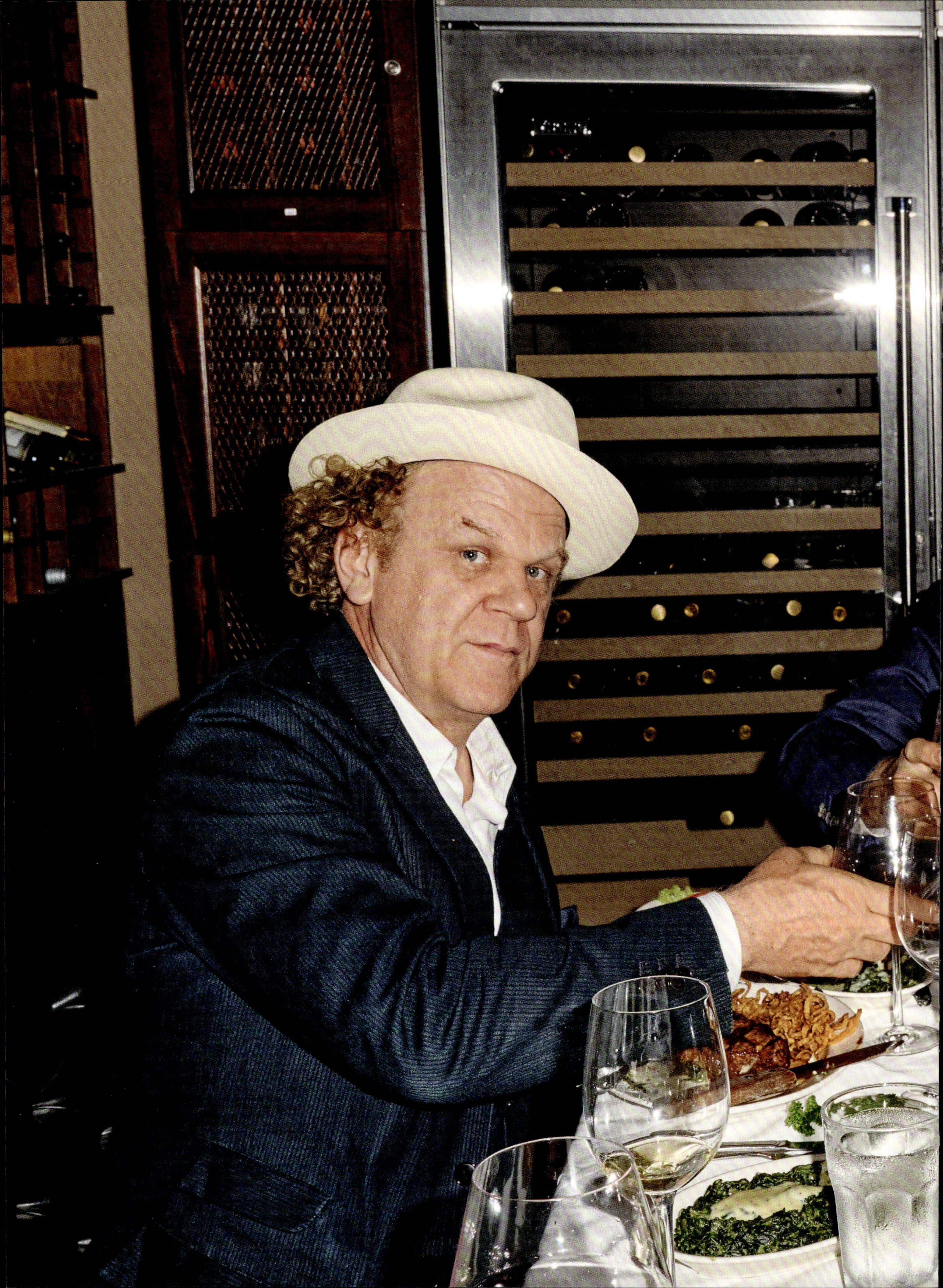

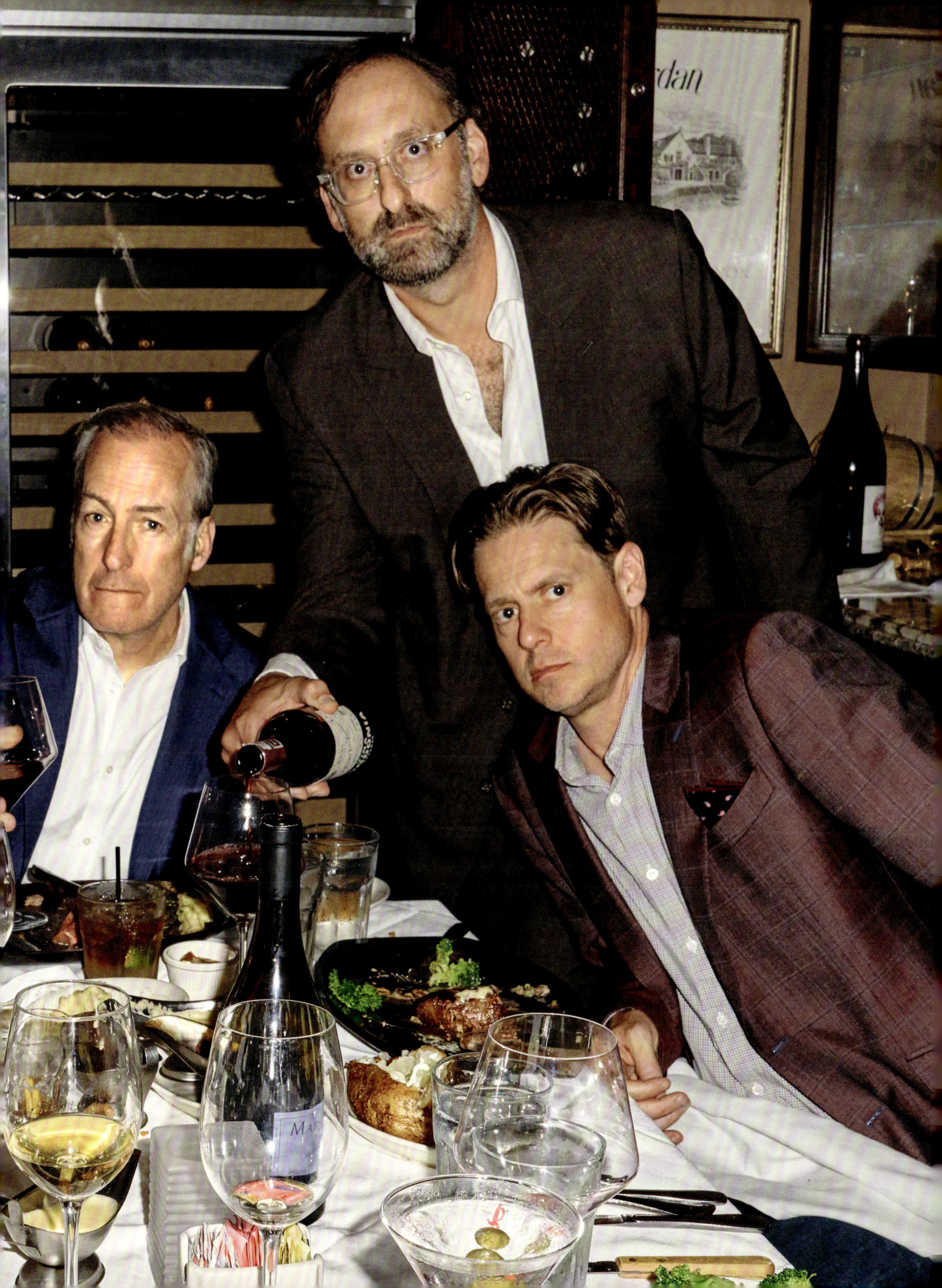

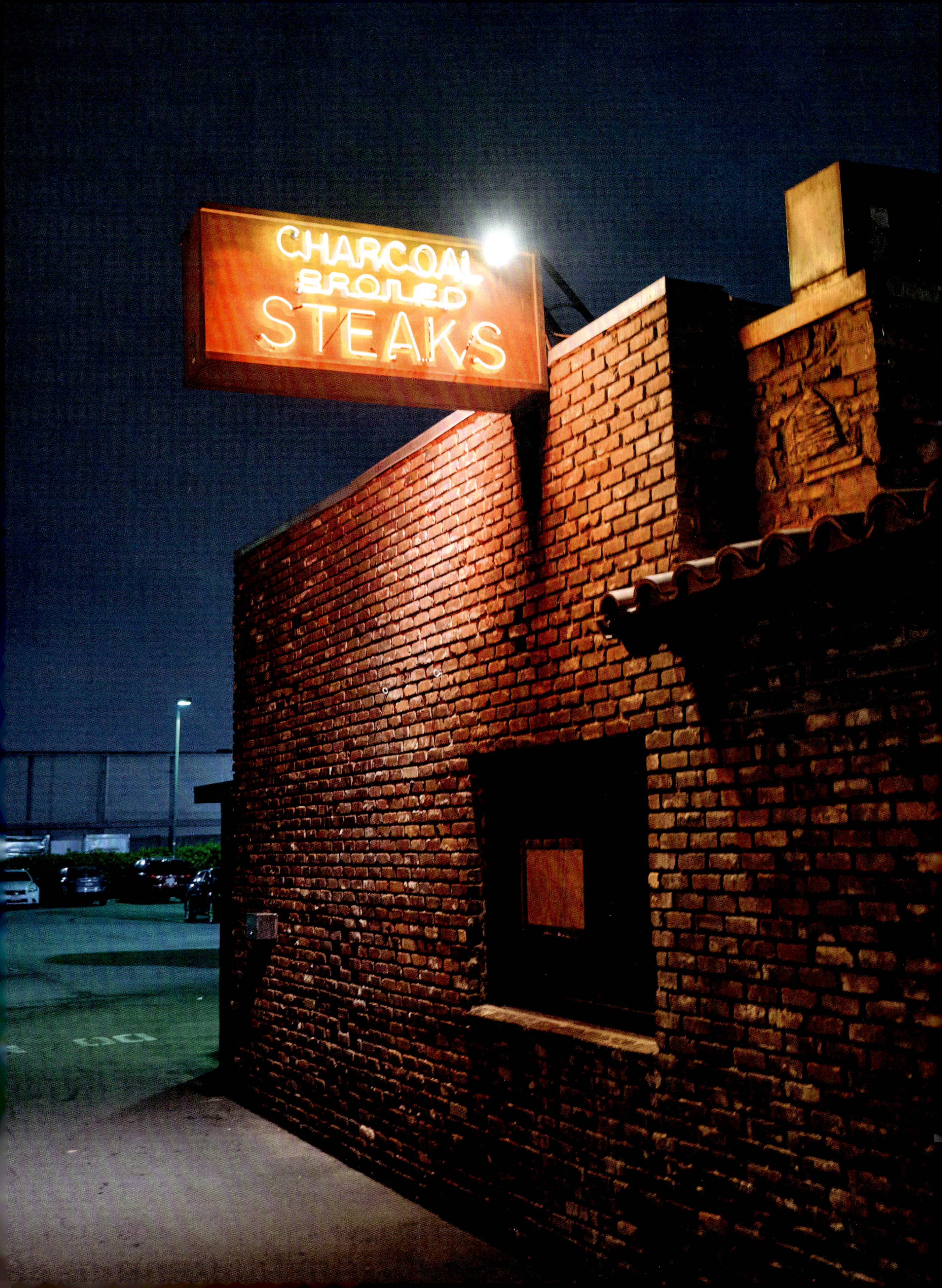
CHARCOAL
BROILED
STEAKS

LOS ANGELES

CLEARMAN'S STEAK 'N STEIN INN

The San Gabriel and San Fernando Valleys are like a living museum to the steak houses that sprang up to cater to all the people who started settling outside Los Angeles after World War II. While there are many options to choose from, I'm most drawn to the steak house that's a little less glitzy—Clearman's. It's a place regulars call "The Stein," and there are many lovely details to appreciate within. There are two that stand out to me because they are ESSENTIAL if you ever wish to make it onto my list of great restaurants:

1. A multicolored fountain in the middle of a circular room with stained glass windows, like a church
2. Tableside baked potato service

The sculpted stone figure standing in the middle of the fountain sets the tone for the evening. She's drinking directly from a jug of wine, an ancient symbol for "This night is going to be breathtaking." In case you don't believe her, look at the cocktail list and tell me you can resist the temptations of an Orange Julius Martini. The garlic cheese bread is an event all its own (see page 48 for my ode to this legend). And then, having a bit of a show for the humble potato is a special thing to witness.

If the Potato Party somehow isn't enough WOW for you, they set your steak on fire at the table, even after it has been cooked to temp by the team in the kitchen.

BY THE NUMBERS

Opening year: 1946
Founder: John Clearman
Address: 9545 East Whittier Boulevard, Pico Rivera, California 90660
House specials: Cheese toast; Red cabbage salad

Beyond that brick wall is maybe the only steak house that will flame your steak with a torch tableside, after it has been cooked.

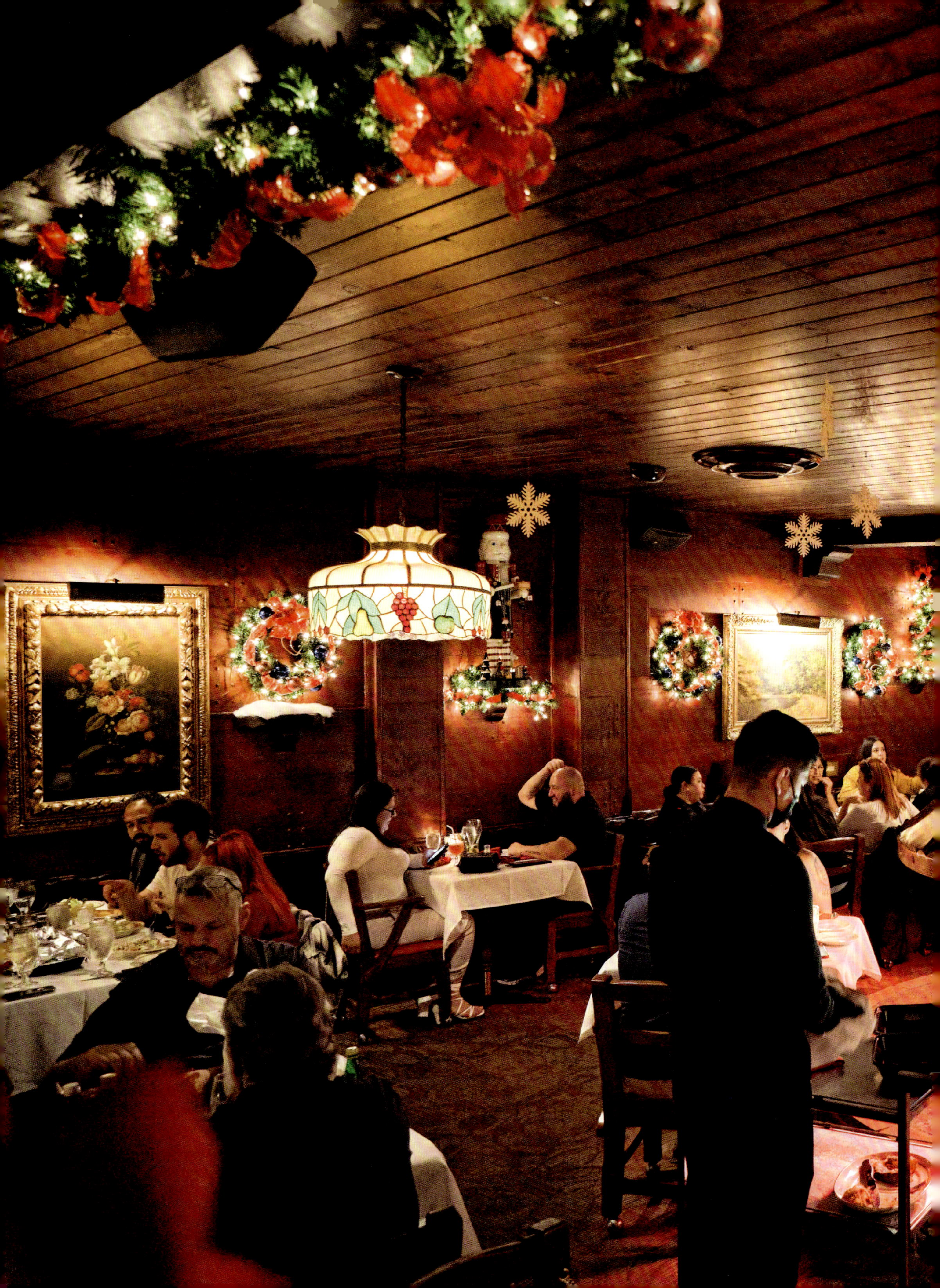

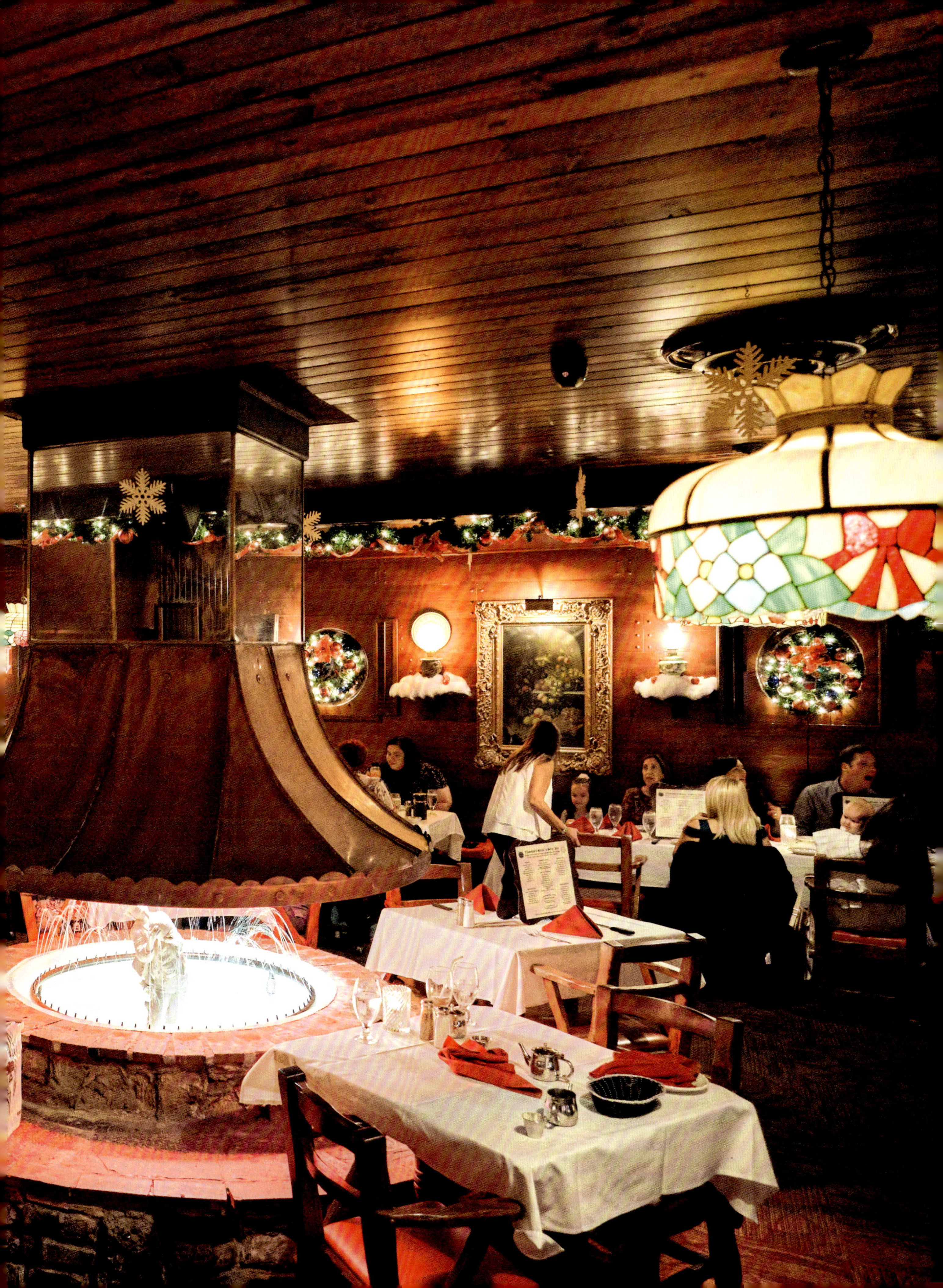

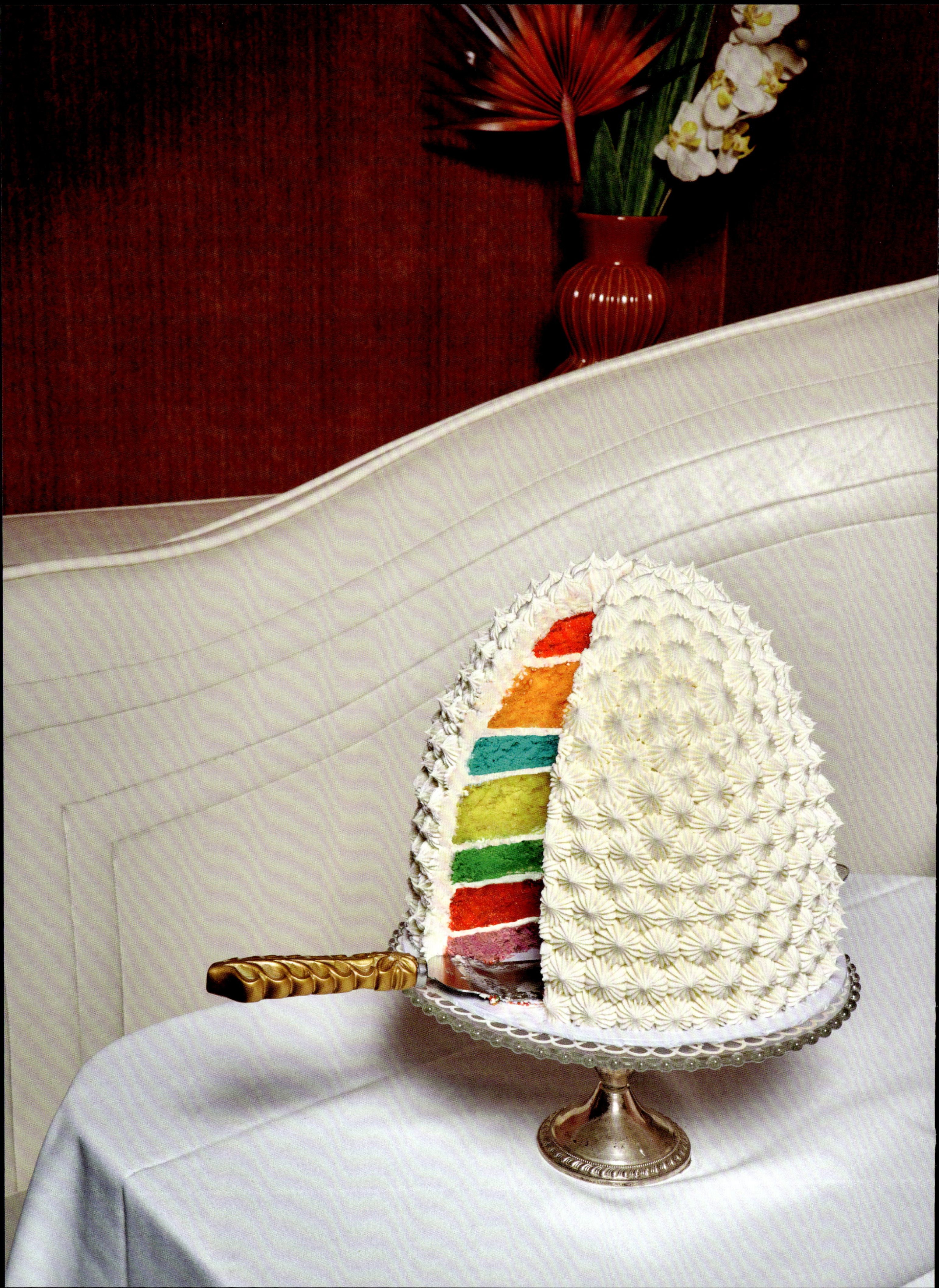

RECIPES

DESSERTS

CHEESECAKE WITH STRAWBERRY SAUCE

Serves 8 to 10

Crust
1½ cups finely ground Biscoff cookies
¼ cup (½ stick) unsalted butter, melted
Pinch of kosher salt

Filling
1¼ cups sugar
2 tablespoons all-purpose flour
½ teaspoon Diamond Crystal kosher salt
Four 8-ounce packages cream cheese, at room temperature
2 teaspoons pure vanilla extract
1 cup sour cream, at room temperature
4 eggs, at room temperature

Strawberry Sauce
3 tablespoons water
1 tablespoon cornstarch
2 cups frozen strawberries
¾ cup sugar
Zest of ½ lemon
Pinch of kosher salt
Fresh raspberries for serving
Whipped cream for serving

Bake your own cheesecake! If the ancient Greeks could figure it out thousands of years ago, then so can you. Incorporating the syrupy zing of a fresh strawberry sauce is an idea we got during the culinary comedown at the HOUSE OF PRIME RIB (page 211) in San Francisco.

Preheat the oven to 350°F. Line the bottom of a 9-inch springform pan with a round of parchment paper.

Make the crust: In a medium bowl, mix together the Biscoff cookie crumbs, butter, and salt until well combined. Press the mixture into the bottom of the prepared springform pan, using the bottom of a measuring cup to press the crumbs down firmly and evenly. Bake until golden brown, about 15 minutes. Remove from the oven and let cool completely on a wire rack.

While the crust bakes, bring a kettle or small pot of water to a boil.

Make the filling: In a small bowl, whisk together the sugar, flour, and salt. In a stand mixer fitted with the whisk attachment or in a large bowl using a hand mixer, add the cream cheese and vanilla and mix on low speed until combined, about 1 minute. With the mixer running, alternate adding ¼ cup of the sour cream, one-quarter of the sugar mixture, then 1 egg, waiting until everything is mostly incorporated before moving onto the next ingredient. Repeat until everything is added, about 5 minutes total. The mixture should be smooth and creamy. Do not overmix as this will create air bubbles.

Wrap aluminum foil around the bottom and up the sides of the springform pan to prevent water seeping in. Pour the filling mixture over the crust and smooth the top with a spatula. Set the pan in a deep roasting pan and carefully pour the hot water into the pan until it reaches halfway up the springform. Immediately place in the oven and bake until the sides have firmed up and the center jiggles slightly, 60 to 70 minutes.

Turn off the oven and leave the door ajar. Let the cheesecake cool completely inside the oven, about 2 hours. (This helps prevent cracks on the surface.)

Meanwhile, make the strawberry sauce: In a small bowl, mix the water with the cornstarch to make a slurry. In a small saucepan over medium-low heat, combine the strawberries, sugar, lemon zest, salt, and the slurry, stirring occasionally. Bring to a boil, lower the heat to maintain a simmer, and cook, stirring occasionally to ensure nothing sticks, until thickened, about 5 minutes. Remove from the heat and let cool. Store in the fridge until ready to use. (The sauce can be made up to 3 days ahead.)

Chill the cheesecake in the fridge for at least 4 hours or up to overnight. Once set, remove the cheesecake from the pan and slice. Serve chilled with the strawberry sauce, raspberries, and whipped cream.

House of
Prime Rib
1906 Van Ness Avenue
San Francisco, CA 94109
(415) 885-4605
www.houseofprimerib.net

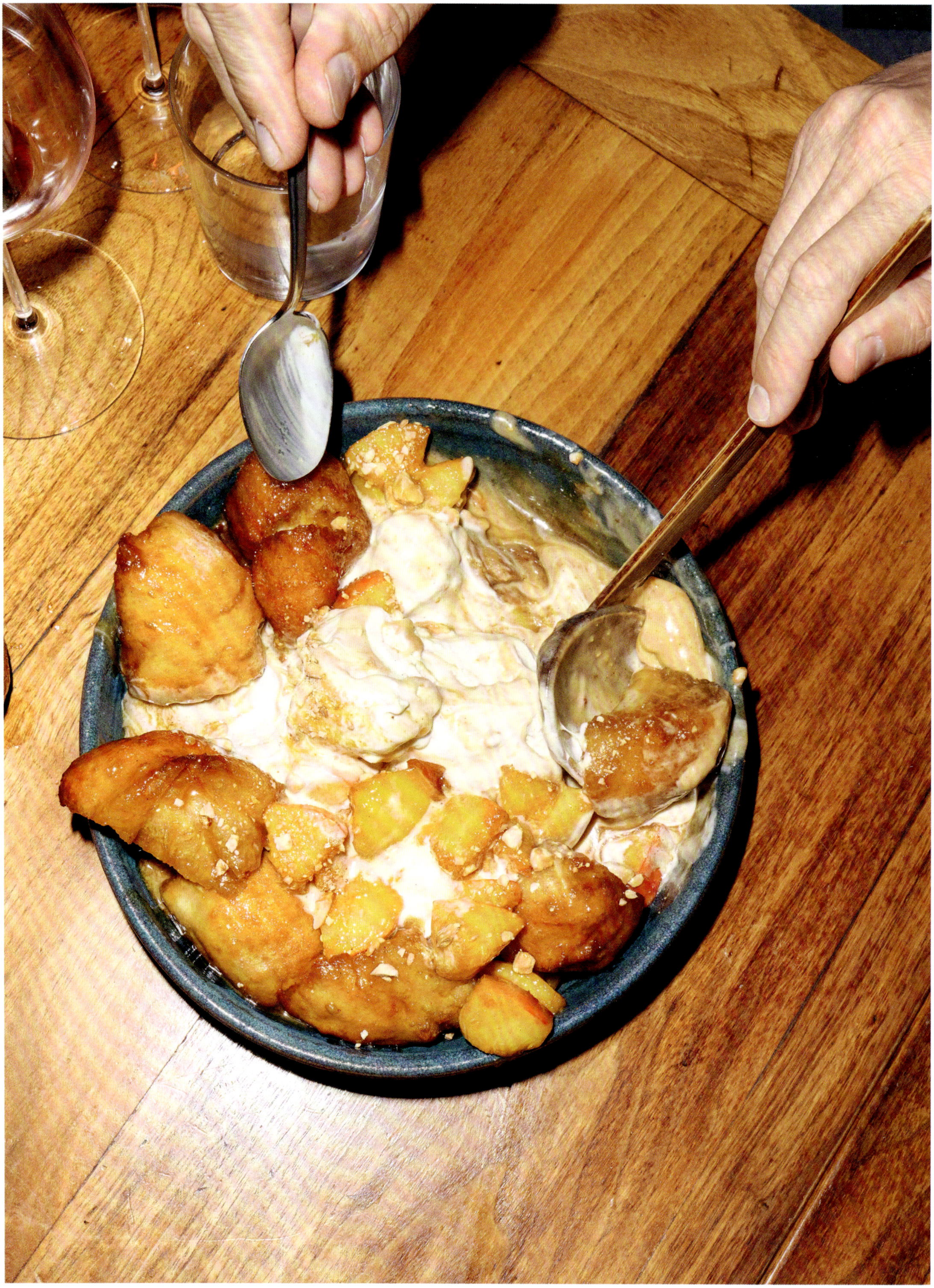

THE MAJOR DONUT

Serves 4

Peaches, donuts, and fire: *that's* **how you end a meal. When chef Jude Parra-Sickels rolls his flambé cart to your table, that means that it's time to experience a peach melba as only DOMO (page 243) could do it. There's gochujang and falernum in the caramel! The gochujang brings subtle Korean heat, while the falernum delivers the warming-spice vibes of a Caribbean rum punch. With chopped-up donuts soaking up all that magnificence, the recipe has a little bit of a baba au rhum vibe to it as well.**

Make the caramel: In a medium saucepan over high heat, combine the brown sugar and water and heat until bubbling. Lower the heat to medium-high, add the butter, and whisk constantly until incorporated. Add the falernum and gochujang and whisk until smooth. Remove from the heat and whisk in the salt. Transfer ½ cup of the caramel to a small skillet and reserve the remaining caramel for another use. (Once full cooled, the caramel will keep in an airtight container at room temperature for up to 1 week.)

Place the skillet over high heat and bring the caramel to a simmer. Add the fruit and lightly stir to coat in the caramel. Return the caramel to a simmer, then move the skillet slightly off the burner and tilt it toward you and away from the flame. Quickly yet carefully add the rum and return the pan to the burner. The alcohol should ignite immediately, but if it does not, tilt the skillet toward the flame so that it does. (If it still does not catch, or you have an electric burner, use a long lighter.) As the flames burn off, lightly sprinkle the cinnamon on the flames to create a "spark" effect. Once the flames subside, add the donuts and quickly stir or toss to coat them with the caramel-fruit mixture.

Put one scoop of vanilla ice cream into each of four serving dishes. Spoon donuts and caramel-fruit mixture over each. Garnish with chopped almonds.

Caramel

1 cup packed dark brown sugar

2 tablespoons water

3 tablespoons unsalted butter

5 tablespoons falernum

2 teaspoons gochujang

Pinch of flaky sea salt, preferably Maldon

2 cups pitted and cubed stone fruit, such as peaches, plums, or cherries

2 ounces Cruzan dark rum

Pinch of ground cinnamon

2 plain yeasted donuts, cut into 8 pieces total

1 pint vanilla ice cream

Marcona almonds, roughly chopped, for garnish

ESPRESSO MARTINI BAKED ALASKA

Serves 6 to 8

Ice Cream Layer
Neutral oil for greasing

2 pints coffee ice cream, softened slightly

1 pint vanilla ice cream, softened slightly

Chocolate Espresso Cake Layer
1 tablespoon neutral oil, plus more for greasing

½ cup all-purpose flour

½ cup granulated sugar

¼ cup unsweetened cocoa powder, sifted

½ teaspoon baking powder

¼ teaspoon baking soda

¼ teaspoon fine sea salt

¼ cup sour cream

1 tablespoon packed dark brown sugar

1 egg

1 teaspoon pure vanilla extract

1 tablespoon instant espresso

¼ cup hot water

1 ounce semisweet chocolate, roughly chopped

Meringue
4 egg whites, at room temperature

¼ teaspoon cream of tartar

Pinch of fine sea salt

¾ cup granulated sugar

½ teaspoon pure vanilla extract

¼ cup vodka (optional)

My coauthor Gabe and I debated whether the espresso martini should be featured. Do we want to risk embarrassing ourselves any more than we already have? We would often have this discussion while sipping espresso martinis. A daydreaming session about THE GRILL (page 72) finally gave us the courage to fuse the essence of the espresso martini into one of the best desserts ever invented. Please enjoy.

Prepare your ice cream layer: Brush an 8-inch bowl with a bit of oil and line it with plastic wrap, making sure the plastic hangs over enough to fold back over the top. Fill the bowl with the ice cream, alternating between 2 scoops of coffee and 1 scoop of vanilla to create a mixed layer, and then use the plastic wrap to help press the ice cream down to fill any gaps to form an even, flat layer. Freeze until very firm, preferably overnight.

Make the cake layer: Preheat the oven to 375°F. Brush an 8-inch round cake pan with oil and line the bottom with a round of parchment paper. In a medium bowl, mix together the flour, granulated sugar, cocoa powder, baking powder, baking soda, and salt.

In a small bowl, mix together the sour cream, brown sugar, egg, the 1 tablespoon oil, and the vanilla until smooth. Gently fold the wet ingredients into the dry ingredients. (It's okay if the batter is thick and isn't completely combined at this stage.) In a small liquid measuring cup, mix together the instant espresso and hot water, then add the chopped chocolate and allow it to melt without stirring. Once the chocolate has melted, gently stir the espresso mixture into the batter until combined.

Pour the batter into the prepared pan and bake until a toothpick inserted into the center comes out clean, 18 to 22 minutes. Remove from the oven and let cool completely in the pan, about 1 hour, then gently unmold the cake. Remove the ice cream layer from the freezer, lift the excess plastic wrap away from the top and place the cake layer on top of the ice cream. Rewrap with plastic wrap and freeze for 1 hour.

Make the meringue: In a stand mixer fitted with the whisk attachment, whip the egg whites on low speed until frothy, 1 to 2 minutes. Add the cream of tartar and salt, increase the speed to high, and add the granulated sugar a little at a time. Continue whisking until stiff peaks form, about 5 minutes total. Gently fold in the vanilla. If using a piping bag, transfer the meringue to the bag.

To assemble: Remove the frozen cake and ice cream from the freezer and invert it onto a heatproof plate so the cake is on the bottom and the ice cream on top. Use the plastic wrap to help dislodge the ice cream from the bowl and peel the plastic off. Working quickly, use a piping bag or a spoon to layer the meringue over the ice cream and cake, covering it completely. If not serving immediately, freeze until ready to toast the meringue.

To serve, in a small saucepan, heat the vodka (if using) and use a long lighter to ignite, then carefully pour over the baked Alaska. Once the flames subside, slice and serve immediately.

ICE CREAM SUNDAE

Serves 4 to 6

There's never been a better time to make an ice cream sundae. You've got easy access to all the nostalgic toppings as well as the finer, more artisanal things in life, like good ice cream, roasted peanuts from South Carolina, and organic olive oil from Sicily. Just open it all up and put it all together. For further inspiration, BAVETTE'S (page 104) in Chicago does a sundae that is a true showstopper. I thank them for reminding me of the magic.

Make sure your bar is fully equipped with an ice cream scoop, bowls or sundae glasses, and spoons. Set out the ice cream with bowls of toppings. Let your guests get creative and build their dream sundaes.

½ gallon Neapolitan ice cream or your favorite ice cream(s)

Toppings
Peanuts or walnuts, roughly chopped
Pretzels, crushed
Kit Kat bars, roughly chopped
Oreo cookies, crushed
M&M's
Mini marshmallows
Chocolate chips
Hot fudge sauce
Caramel sauce
Sprinkles
Whipped cream
Flaky sea salt, preferably Maldon
Maraschino cherries
Good-quality olive oil
Anything else you can dream of

APPLE STRUDEL MIT SCHLAG

Serves 6

Dough

2½ cups all-purpose flour, plus more as needed and more for dusting

¾ cup warm water

1 egg

2 tablespoons neutral oil, plus more for greasing

¼ teaspoon Diamond Crystal kosher salt

Filling

8 Granny Smith apples, peeled, cored, and thinly sliced (preferably sliced in a food processor)

Juice of 1 lemon (about 3 tablespoons)

1 cup granulated sugar

2 tablespoons ground cinnamon

1 cup golden raisins

1 cup rum or orange juice, plus more as needed

1 tablespoon unsalted butter, at room temperature

1 cup breadcrumbs

½ cup (1 stick) unsalted butter, melted

Powdered sugar for dusting

Whipped cream for serving

By the time the battlefield is cleared of the ravaged plates of porterhouse, it means that lunch is coming to a close and it is time for a nap. But I'm not going anywhere until I put down a significant amount of strudel and schlag. The recipe we are sharing for this German-Austrian birthright, however, is not LUGER's (page 62). It's mia mamma's!

As I have told you, my mom is a great cook. Perhaps an even better baker. It's common in Germany to enjoy like five different cakes at birthday parties, which is surprisingly American in concept for typically reserved Germans. The art of a good apple strudel is achieving a balance between sweetness, tartness, and richness. And then, of course, finishing it with what I call Mutti Schlag ("Mom's whipped cream"). When I visit my folks for the holidays, you can often hear me yelling through the halls, "Mutti, wo ist mein Schlag?! Ich brauchen meine mutti Schlag JETZT!" (As Google Translate will show you, my German isn't perfect.)

Make the dough: In a large bowl, combine the flour, water, egg, oil, and salt. Using a wooden spoon, stir until the mixture forms a ball, about 1 minute. Using your hands, knead the dough until smooth and no longer sticky, about 2 minutes. If the dough is very sticky, sprinkle in more flour 1 tablespoon at a time and knead until it no longer sticks.

Grease the outside of the dough with oil, then transfer to a large clean bowl and cover the bowl with plastic wrap. Let rest in a warm environment for 20 minutes. Remove the plastic wrap.

Prepare the filling: In a medium bowl, toss together the apples and lemon juice. In a small bowl, combine the granulated sugar and cinnamon. In a separate small bowl, combine the raisins and rum, adding more rum as needed to cover, and let the raisins soak for 15 minutes. Drain, reserving some of the rummy goodness in the bowl. Add the cinnamon-sugar mixture, raisins, and rummy goodness to the apples and stir until well incorporated. Set the apple mixture aside.

In a small skillet over medium heat, melt the 1 tablespoon butter until foaming. Add the breadcrumbs and toast, stirring constantly, until they are medium brown, 3 to 5 minutes. Transfer to a bowl and let cool.

Preheat the oven to 375°F. Line a sheet pan with parchment paper. Flour a large clean tablecloth set on top of a dining table.

Place the dough on the floured work surface and use a rolling pin to roll the dough into a 12-inch square. While rolling, check that the dough doesn't stick to the surface and can lift easily. Gently lift the dough from the tablecloth and continue to pull the dough toward the edge of the table using the back of your hands. Constantly move your hands, pulling back at the dough, until it stretches as thin as possible without ripping, at least 28 inches by 18 inches.

Brush the dough with some of the melted butter. Spread the toasted breadcrumbs in an even layer over the dough.

Spoon the apple mixture in an even layer over the breadcrumbs, leaving the liquid in the bowl, to create a 1-inch border all around. With a knife, trim any uneven ends so they are straight and tuck the ends of the dough inward. Working from one short horizontal side of the dough, lift the dough and tablecloth together, rolling the long side of the dough up toward the opposite horizontal end until the dough is completely rolled up.

Use the tablecloth to place the dough on the prepared sheet pan seam-side down. Brush the outside with some more melted butter, reserving a bit for later. Bake for 20 minutes. Brush with more butter and rotate the pan. Continue to bake until golden brown, 20 more minutes. Let cool slightly then dust with powdered sugar and top with whipped cream before slicing. Serve warm.

THE JOURNEY, PART VII

LAS V

EGAS

TEMPTATION AWAITS THE MINUTE YOU GET OFF THE PLANE: GO AHEAD, LOSE $500 AT THE SLOTS IN THE AIRPORT TERMINAL IF YOU WANT. IN THIS CITY, ALL IT TAKES IS TEN MINUTES FOR A CAB TO TAKE YOU FROM ANCIENT GREECE TO A GONDOLA RIDE BEFORE DINNER AT PETER LUGER.

Don't try to make any sense of it. You're better off grabbing one of those three-foot-long hurricanes and strolling under the lights. Many moons ago, when we were just kids, Tim and I went to Vegas to direct a pilot for Louie Anderson. The concept: He never gets out of bed. Ever. The shoot was rough. To make matters worse, they put us up at the Excalibur, and I became very ill in the tum from what I believe were the crab legs from the buffet! The sight of that castle haunts me to this day. The pilot never aired and I refuse to visit the Excalibur ever again.

BUT I've kept coming back to this untameably weird monument to instant gratification, which, since 1941, has been big on steaks and the chord they strike in people. That's when El Rancho, the city's first-ever hotel and casino, opened with amenities including The Stage Door Steak House.

You can get any kind of steak house experience in Las Vegas. But seeing as most of the historic spots I read about are gone, I decided to feature two steak houses that feel surprisingly sturdy in a culture that doesn't mind blowing things up at the sight of the first wrinkle to make way for the new.

Then we ventured to the burbs to uncover a true desert gem.

Welcome to the steak house of the circus.

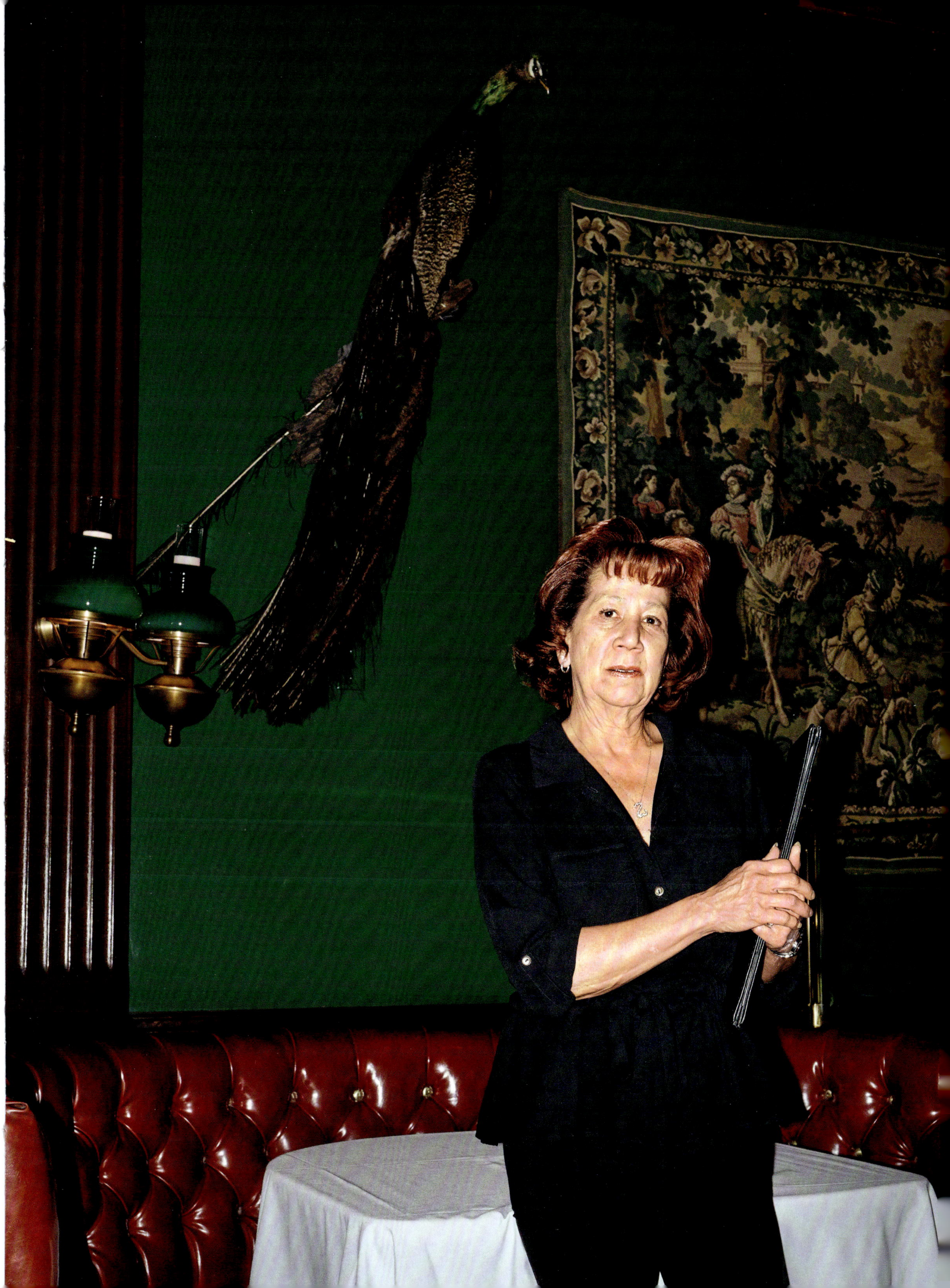

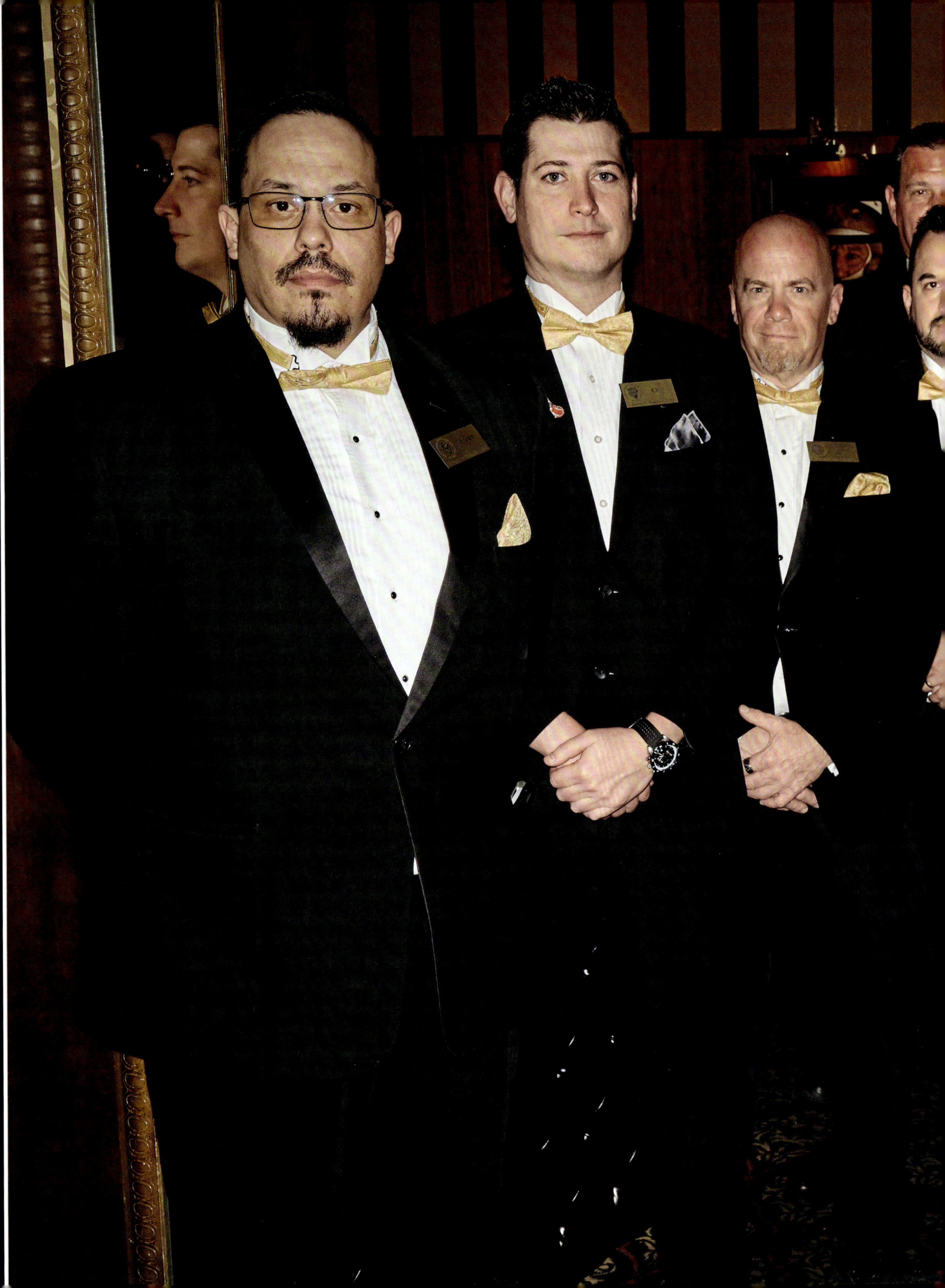

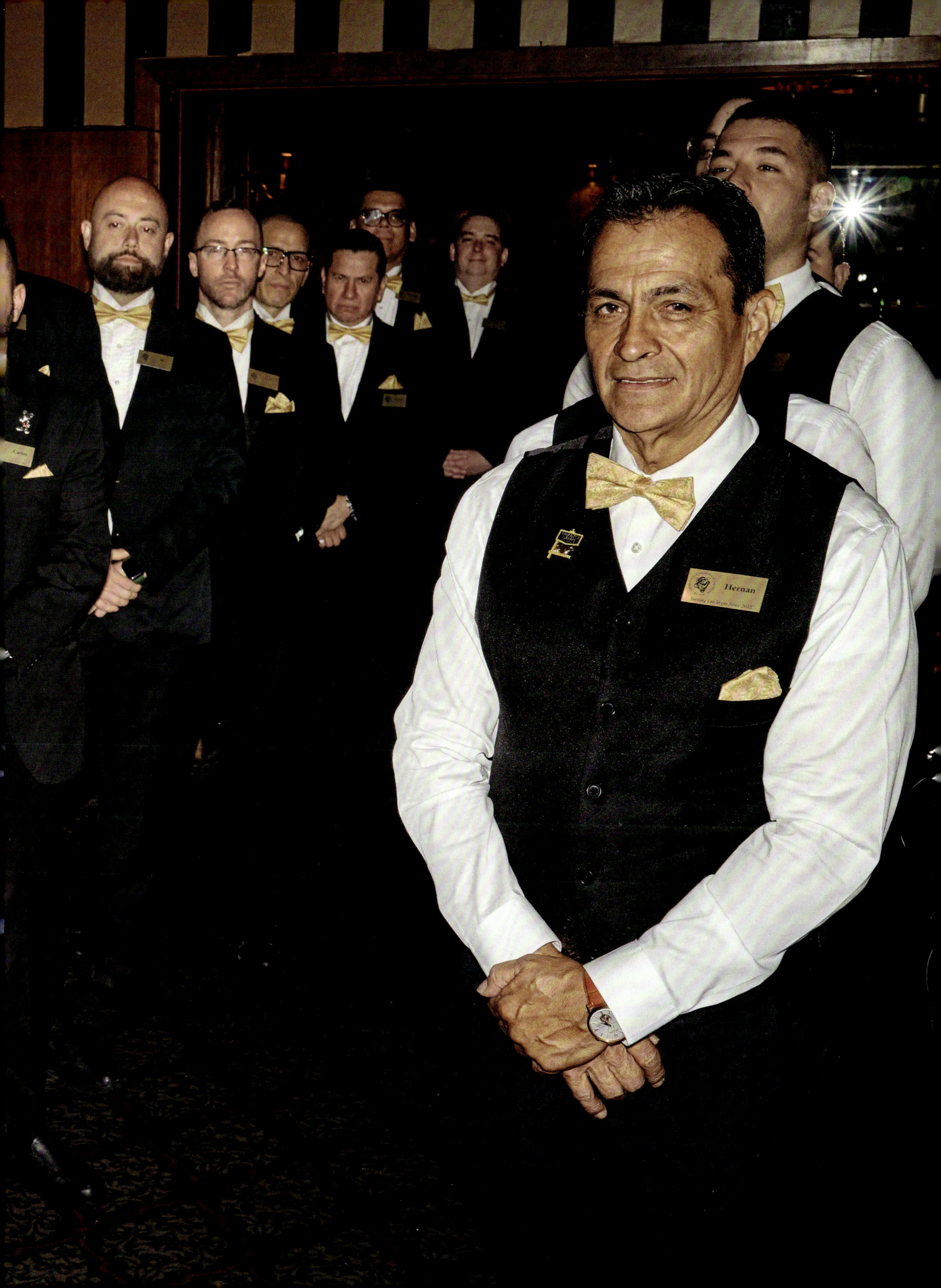
Hernan

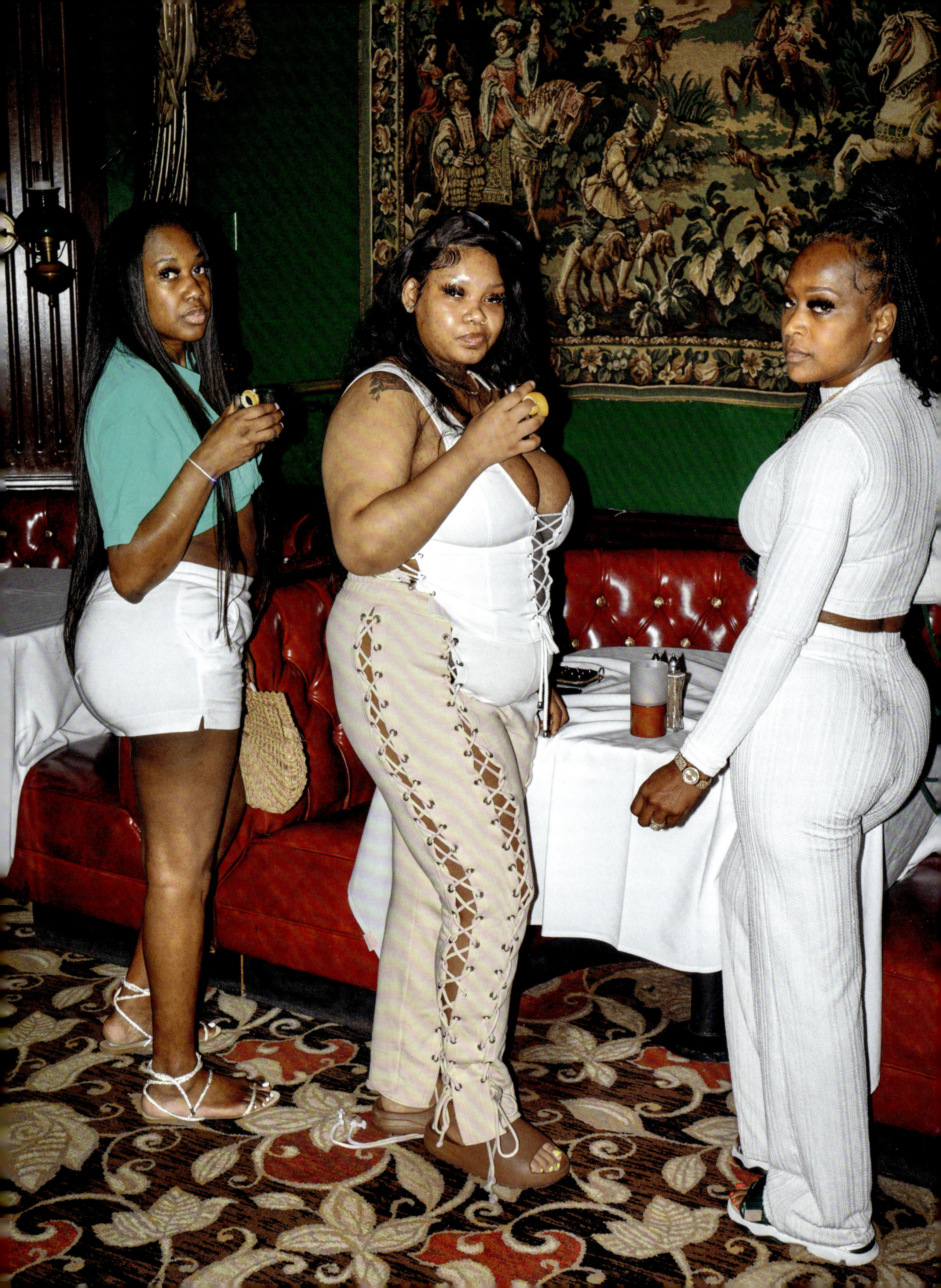

LAS VEGAS

THE STEAK HOUSE AT CIRCUS CIRCUS

I first stumbled upon this secret meat cave many years ago, when I took my friends to see the "magic" that happens inside the casino at twenty minutes past the hour, every hour, every day. Forever and ever. The sad clowns and tired parents waddled back and forth and took their seats at a small open-air theater in the middle of all the chaos. Children won tokens at the Whac-A-Mole, while twenty feet away a poor ole bustard was about to lose his last dime on video poker. This is a quintessential Vegas experience.

After witnessing precisely six minutes of the acrobatic spectacle, we tried to find the exit. Of course, in true casino fashion, we found ourselves doing endless loops. *Wait a minute, is this a steak house? Could be a good recharge moment.* The open grill at THE Steak House is elevated on a platform in the center of the dining room. If you get bored of your date retelling that story about when they met Criss Angel, you can adjust your gaze to the wood-fired grills sizzling many pounds of beef for the hungry patrons.

That first time, there was a sense of "Let's fuel up here 'cause tonight is going to be wild" in the air. It was still there when I went back this time. As we finished off our New York strip and martinis, we were ready for the next adventure . . . as soon as we could find the goddamn exit!

BY THE NUMBERS

Opening year: *1982*
Founders: *William Bennett and Bill Pennington*
Address: *2880 South Las Vegas Boulevard, Las Vegas, Nevada 89109*
House specials: *Black bean soup; Garlic mashed potatoes*

A group of regulars, out for ladies' night. "This is our spot," they told me.

BOROS STRAVA

BY THE NUMBERS

Opening year: 2022
Founders: The Brothers Boros
Address: Directly across the street from the Claim Jumper Steakhouse & Bar
House specials: Beef Wellington; Crown of pork

We made the drive to the suburbs after hearing about an under-the-radar steak house gem with unique Central European flair. It is operated by Rudolph, Radek, and Karel—the Boros triplets from Dobříš, Czechoslovakia. Their mother, Eliska Boros, wrote in an old journal that the first two boys were born five minutes apart and popped right out, but Karel didn't want to leave: "He said, 'No, no.' He stayed inside of me for one full day longer than Rudolph and Radek. That's why he is bad boy."

The Boros brothers followed in their father's footsteps by joining the Dobříš Cirkus, an acrobatic tradition to which Cirque du Soleil owes an enormous debt. They were strong and very flexible, allowing them to twist and tumble and fall from great heights. Their signature routine was the human totem pole. Rudolph and Radek would stand on each other's shoulders, with Karel as the anchor. Rudolph would hold a sword in his mouth, and a French acrobat, Didier LeGrand, would climb the brothers and balance his elegant body on top of the sword. The crowd would go nuts.

During a special performance for the archbishop of Prague, there was a terrible accident at the Cirkus. The Boros brothers started off strong. Radek was shot out of a medieval cannon and executed a triple flip and landed on his feet. The archbishop threw him four gold coins! He was so impressed. The crowd chanted, "Pol! Pol! Pol!" which loosely translates to "totem," or "pole." But Karel was secretly not feeling like himself; the locals suspect it had to do with his distaste for the church. When Didier began his prancing atop the sharp sword, whipping his hair in all its glory, Karel lost his concentration and slipped. Everyone tumbled to the ground. Rudolph and Radek did perfect safety tumbles. But Didier was not so lucky. He flailed and fell directly to the concrete Cirkus floor, breaking his hips. Then the sword that was in Rudolph's mouth punctured Didier's forearm. He was rushed to the Prague General Hospital's Wing of Severe Accidents, where he would eventually have to bid farewell to the entire arm.

The Boros brothers visited Didier in the hospital once a week, bringing homemade goulash and bread dumplings. Karel, who had learned his mother's cooking while growing up, pickled river eel, and Didier really took a liking to that brined, slippery fish. Oftentimes, the brothers would mimic the swimming of an eel to entertain Didier while Karel fed him the savory delights.

One night, for more amusement, they cooked up a majestic beef Wellington and wheeled an old rusty livestock scale into their convalescing friend's room to see if it weighed as much as Didier. This is a Boros family pastime. Rudolph distracted the nurse while Karel lifted the sickly Didier out of his hospital bed and placed him on the old animal scale. The needle went up and down as they all held their breath in anticipation. Success! The brothers cheered and Didier, loopy from the heavy medication, enjoyed the enthusiasm for the game, even though it didn't quite make sense. Karel put Didier back into the bed and tucked him in gently. Radeck grabbed the bedpan and pretended to sauce him like a dish. Didier smiled and drifted off into a lovely slumber.

Didier LeGrand prepares his signature DD-Tini.

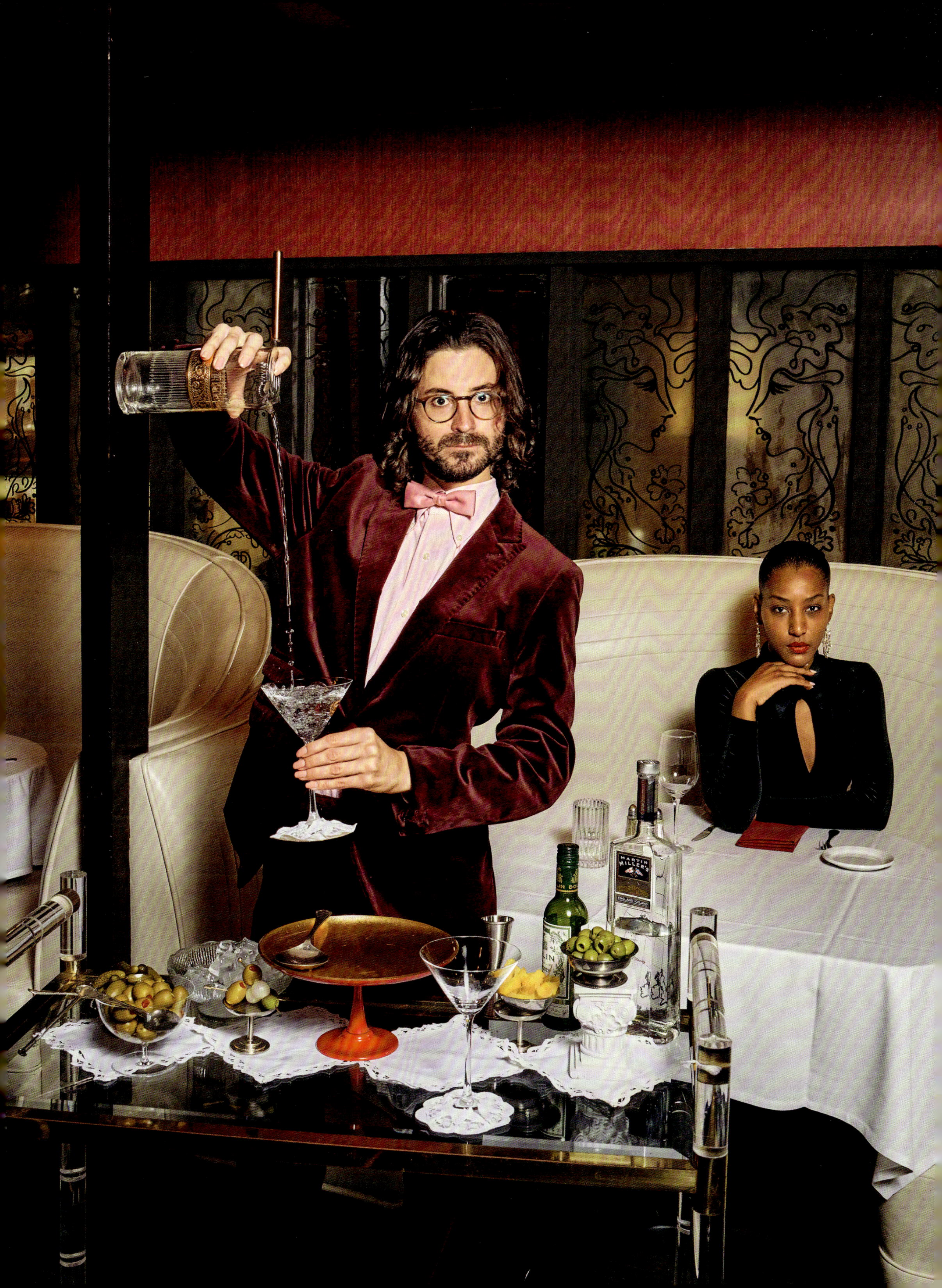
MARTIN MILLER'S
ENGLAND ICELAND

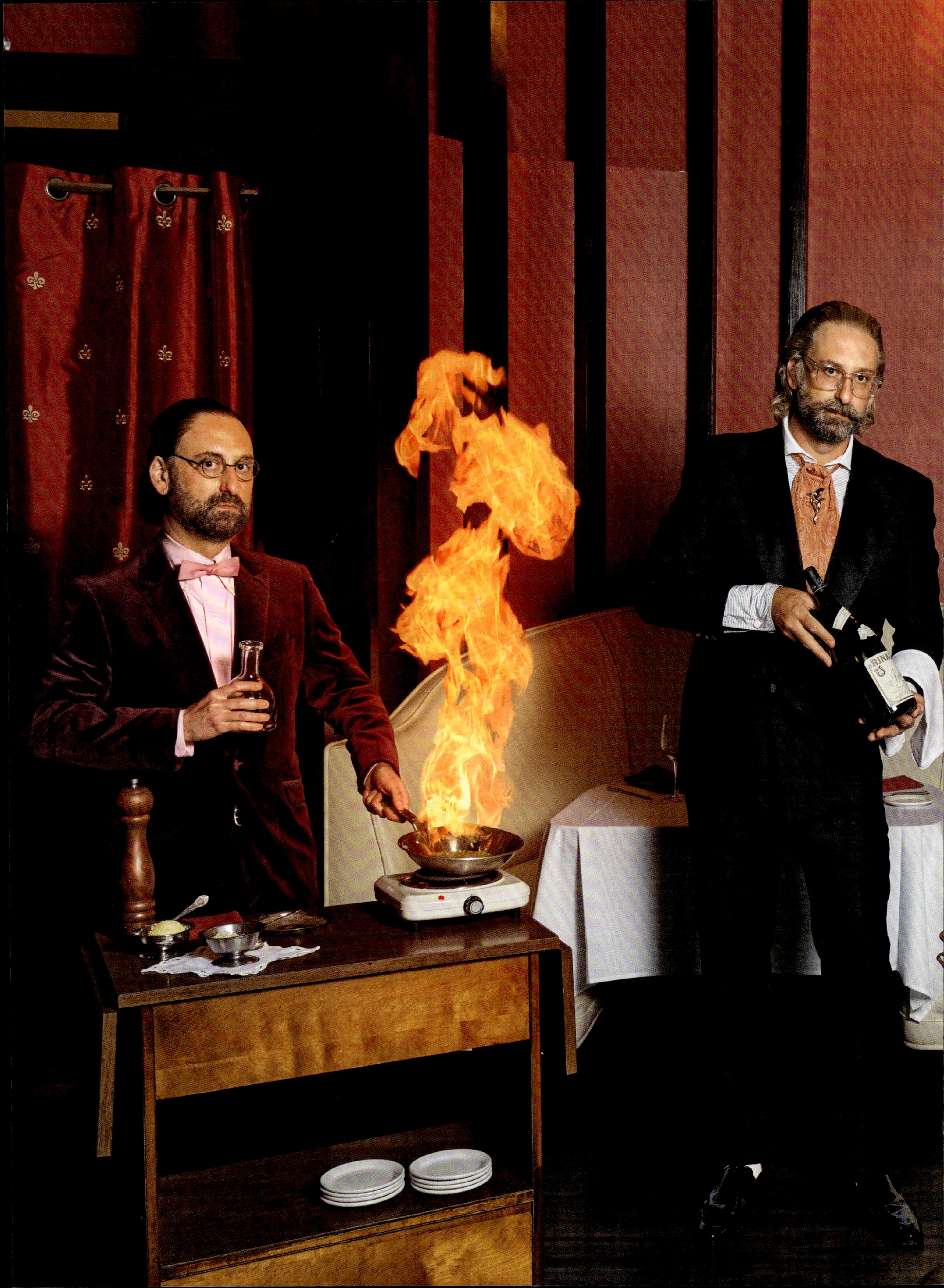

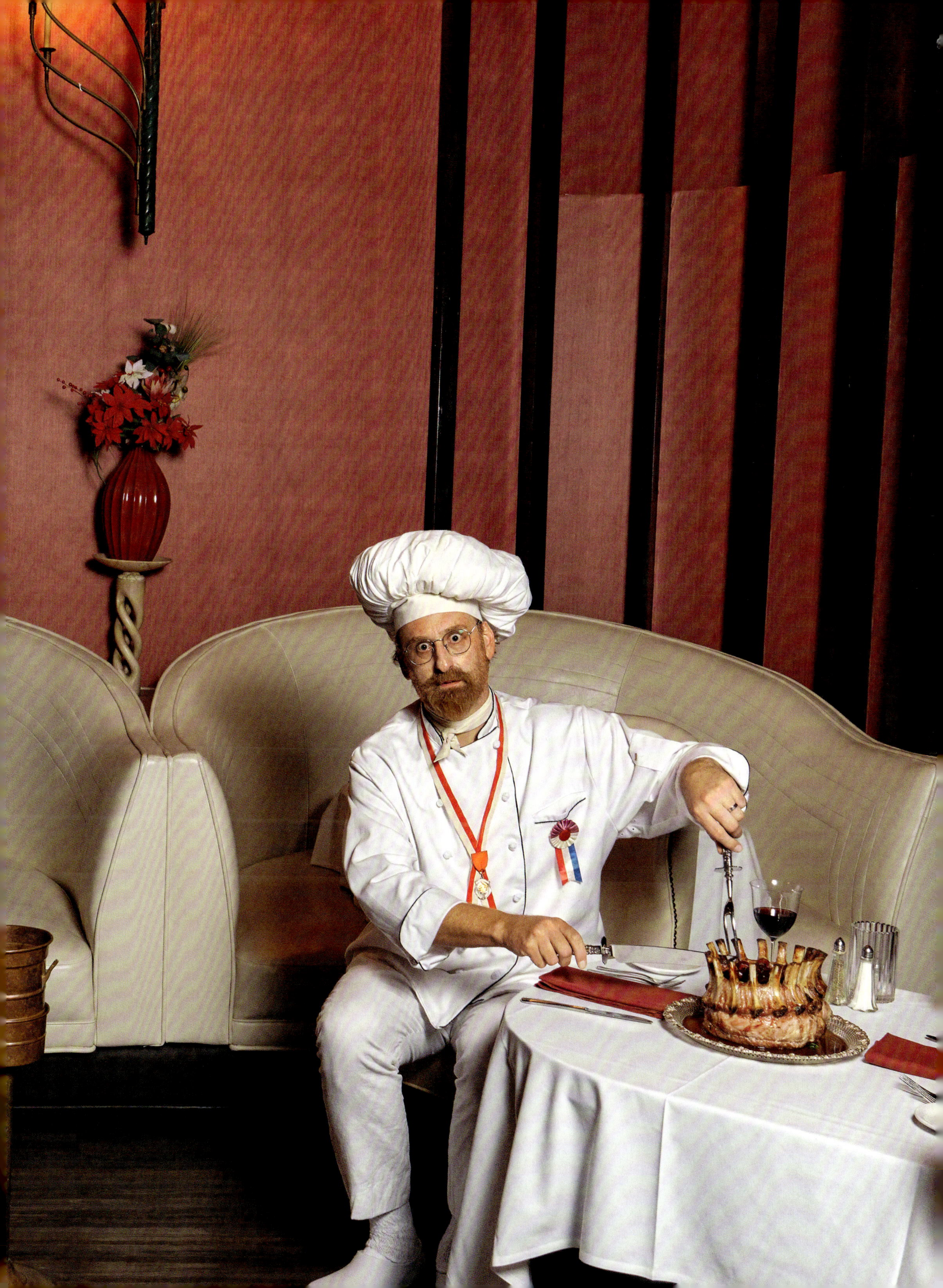

The brothers started a food cart outside the Cirkus to raise money for Didier's new arm. Their showmanship from the Cirkus came in handy while entertaining the long lines of goulash lovers. It was an overnight success and even attracted some international press.

This sensation prompted the Boros brothers and Didier, once his new arm was attached, to move to Las Vegas and open a restaurant. They called it Boros Strava. American tourists enjoyed the Central European ambience but did not have a taste for traditional Czech food. To make matters worse, Didier's prosthetic arm went limp and he had to glue that floppy hand to the bottom of a serving tray for it to look somewhat normal. Karel eventually switched to steak house staples, and the locals started coming in droves.

Two massive kitchen fires led them to relocate to a smaller restaurant in Henderson, outside the city. The brothers blame Didier for the second fire, citing that he could not lift the fire extinguisher with his one good hand. Didier runs the front of house at the new Henderson spot, Karel is the executive chef, Rudolph is the sommelier, and Radek is the manager.

Believe me, I tried, but the brothers refused to give me the recipe for their famous birthday cake. For an equally grand finish, may I suggest my Espresso Martini Baked Alaska? (page 266)

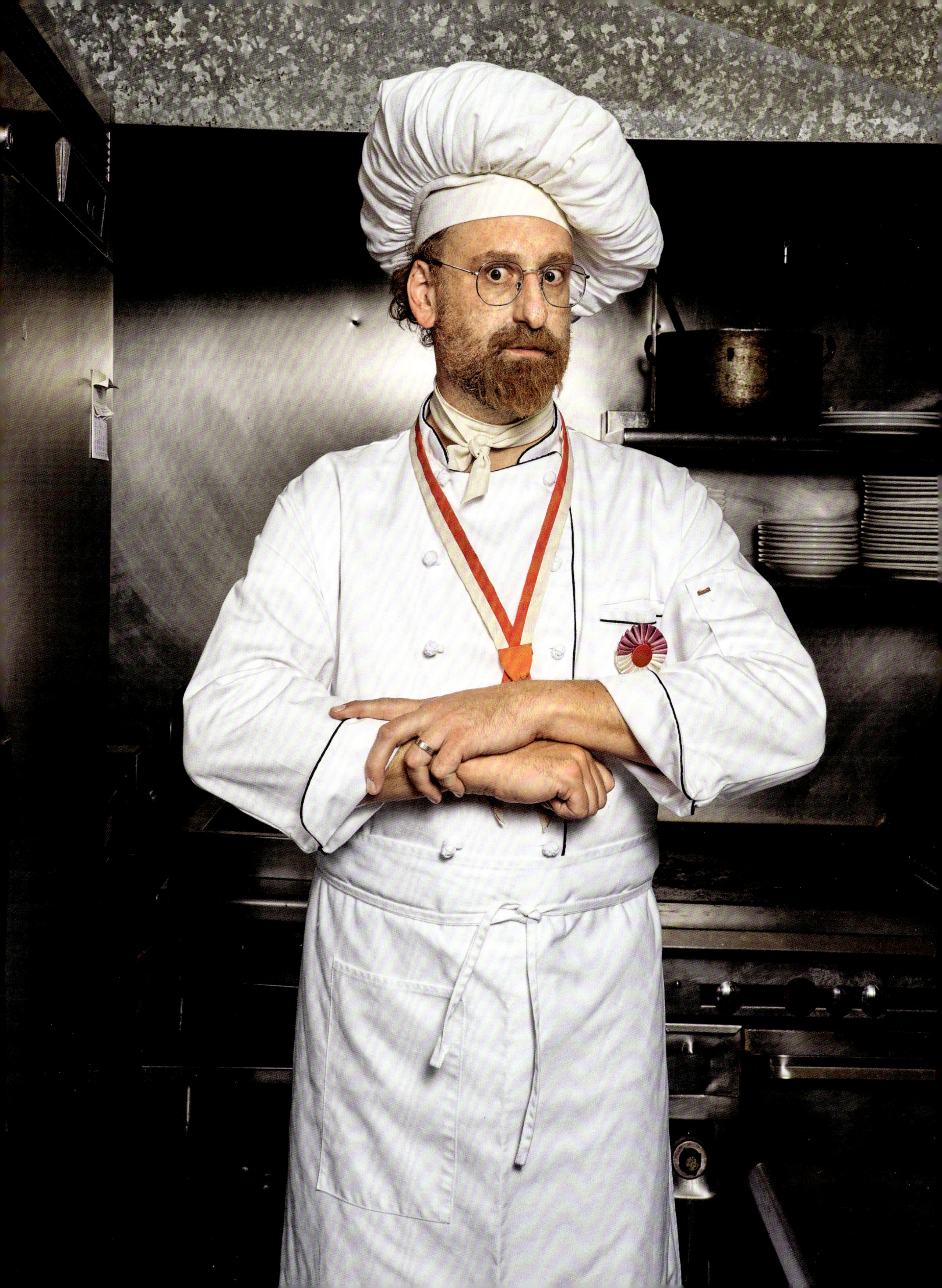

THE JOURNEY, PART VIII

MEX

ICO

MONTERREY IS THE CAPITAL OF THE STATE OF NUEVO LEÓN AND THE PLACE IN MEXICO WHERE PEOPLE EAT MORE BEEF THAN ANYWHERE ELSE IN THE ENTIRE COUNTRY.

Cabrito, or roasted young goat, too. But that's only part of the reason we traveled there. My long-lost sibling Fermín Nuñez, the beautiful person who showed us how to make T-bone au poivre in Austin, invited me to join him in this industrial city that most tourists skip, so I could meet some of his food friends who mean a lot to him. "It's practically America—Texas used to be part of it! Besides, you can see how the people who make it possible for all those steak houses in America to operate do things back home." I thought I knew a thing or two about Mexico, but I was in for an awakening.

Our host, Chuy Villarreal, is part of the current culinary movement that is trying to prove wrong all the stereotypes about Nuevo León's food being one-note. Despite the modernization, everybody still gets the family together to cook meat over a flame once a week. There are Lebanese and Turkish influences here. All that goat? It's because of the Jewish community that sprang up here in the 1500s. There's potential.

I salivate every time I think about the churrasco at his restaurant Cara de Vaca. It's served over steak house fries that have been soaked in stock, with melted cheese on top and what Chuy calls tortillas ribetiadas on the side. The tortillas with the rivets. His mom didn't have a comal at home; she would put the tortillas on the stovetop, and they'd get stiff and crackly. Another revelation was the carne seca, crispy strands of air-cured beef and just one of many jerky styles you can sample in the city. The tradition was introduced to the region by the Tlaxcalan, the indigenous people who settled in the north and had to figure out how to preserve meat in that crazy, arid, ranch-filled HEAT.

After a day and a half we didn't even scratch the surface. I missed out on the menudo as well as a visit to the legendary meat market. But I'll never forget the afternoon when we took a bag of chicharrónes from the famous butcher shop Carnes Ramos back to Fritto Club, Chuy's cool little event space, and sipped some wine. Chuy and his collaborator, Hector, are the first people to import the likes of cult Austrian winemaker Christian Tschida to this part of the country.

We also went to La Nacional, which is Monterrey's answer to Hillstone. I wish the one near my house served tortillas filled with steak tataki, ponzu, avocado, and crispy garlic. I would fly all the way back just to consume their version of a NL culinary birthright, fideo tacos.

The final dinner was at Vernáculo—a spot bringing back ancient local grilling traditions with a dining room that has a big hearth, rustic vibes, and an unforgettable carne asada. I wanted to make a bigger dent, but my secondary mezcal stomach finally refused to process another drink and my body shut down. My host and his friends kept enjoying the sobremesa, perhaps my fave new concept. It means you hang and relax after dinner for as long as you want.

As I tucked myself into bed, I made a list of all the dishes in town I'd need to experience next time. During one last Instagram scroll, I caught a video of Fermín, Chuy, Hector, and their wives dancing their way down the escalator, singing in Spanish.

The mesmerizing hearth at chef Hugo Guajardo's Vernáculo.

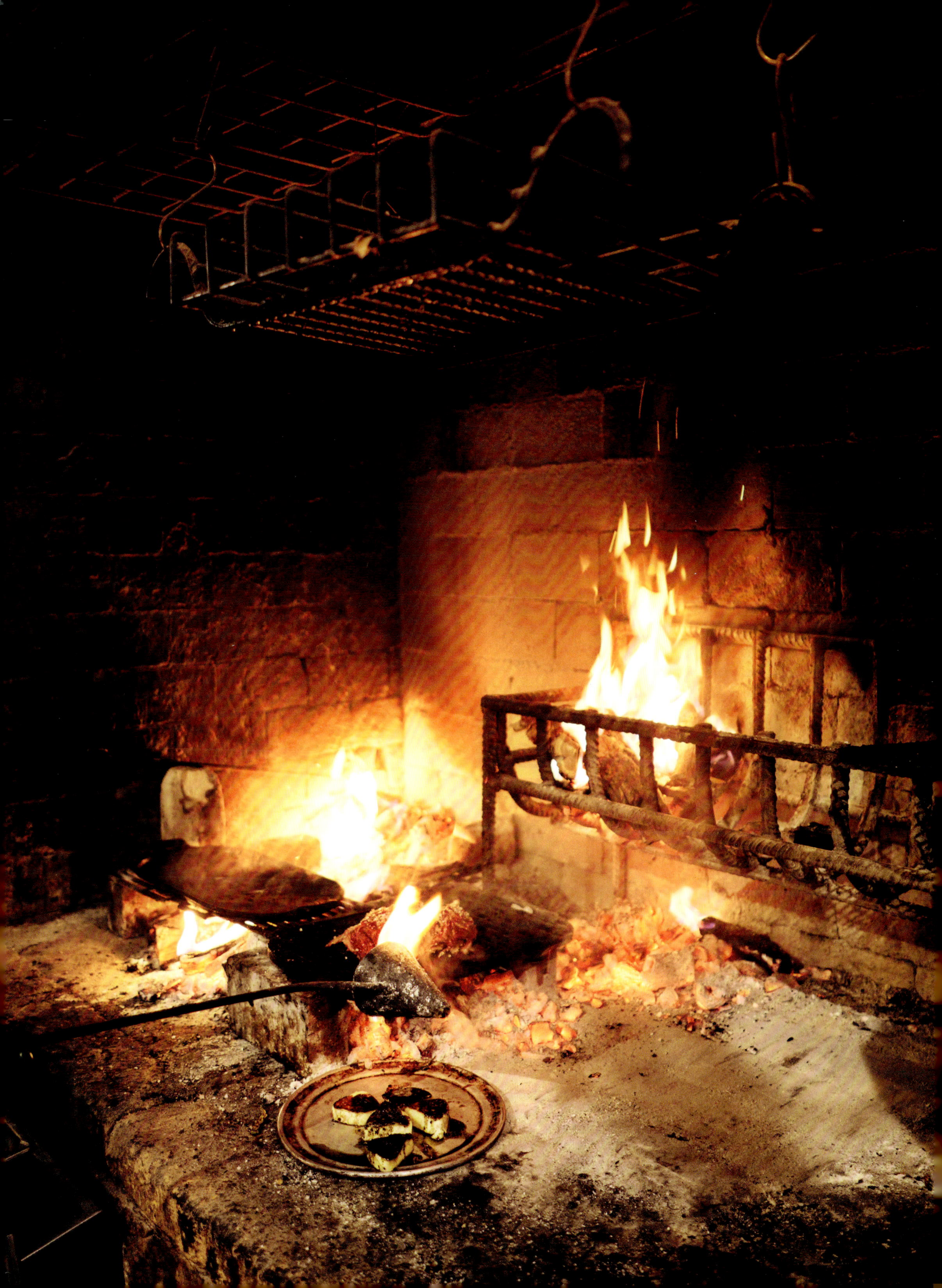

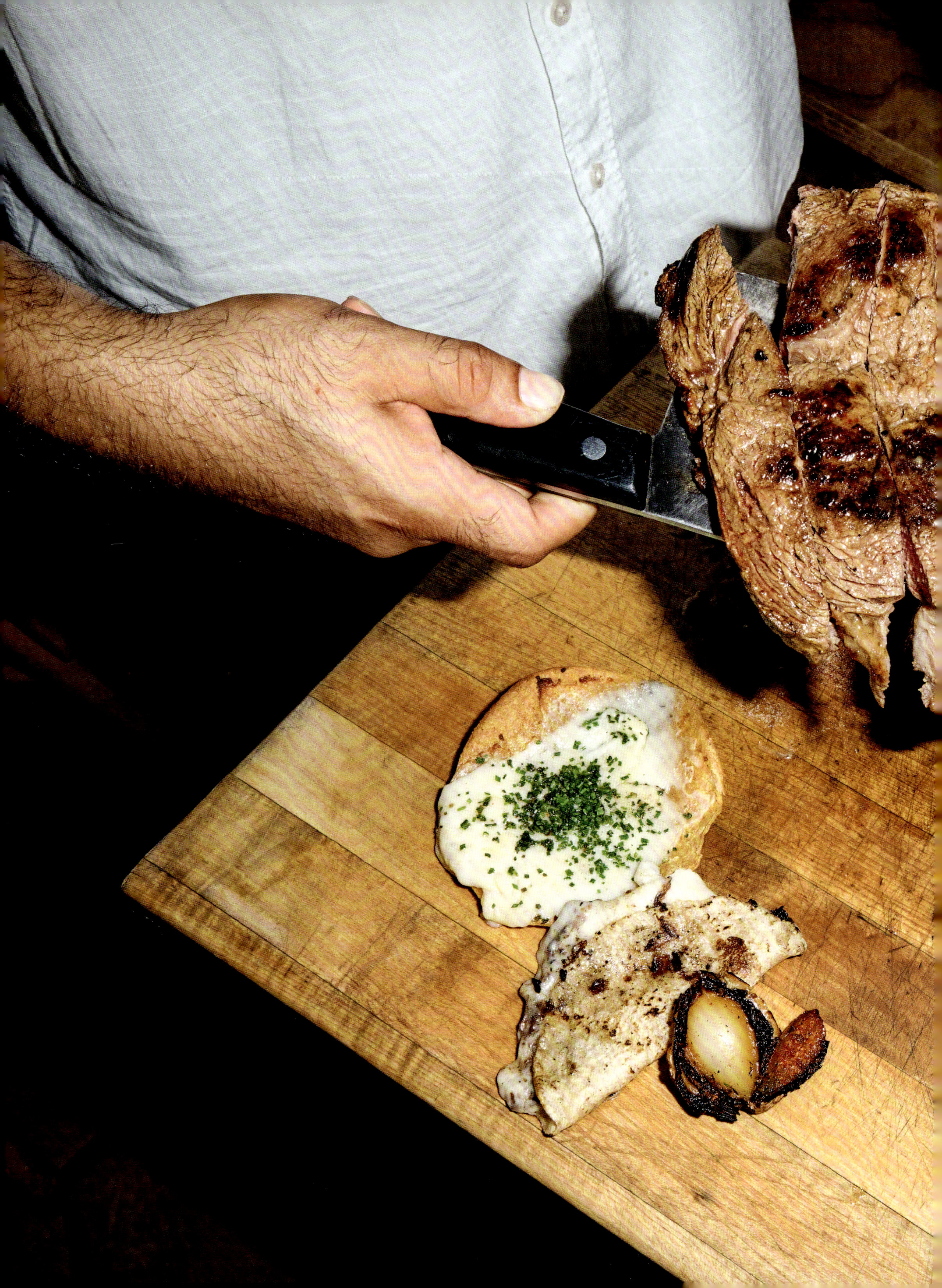

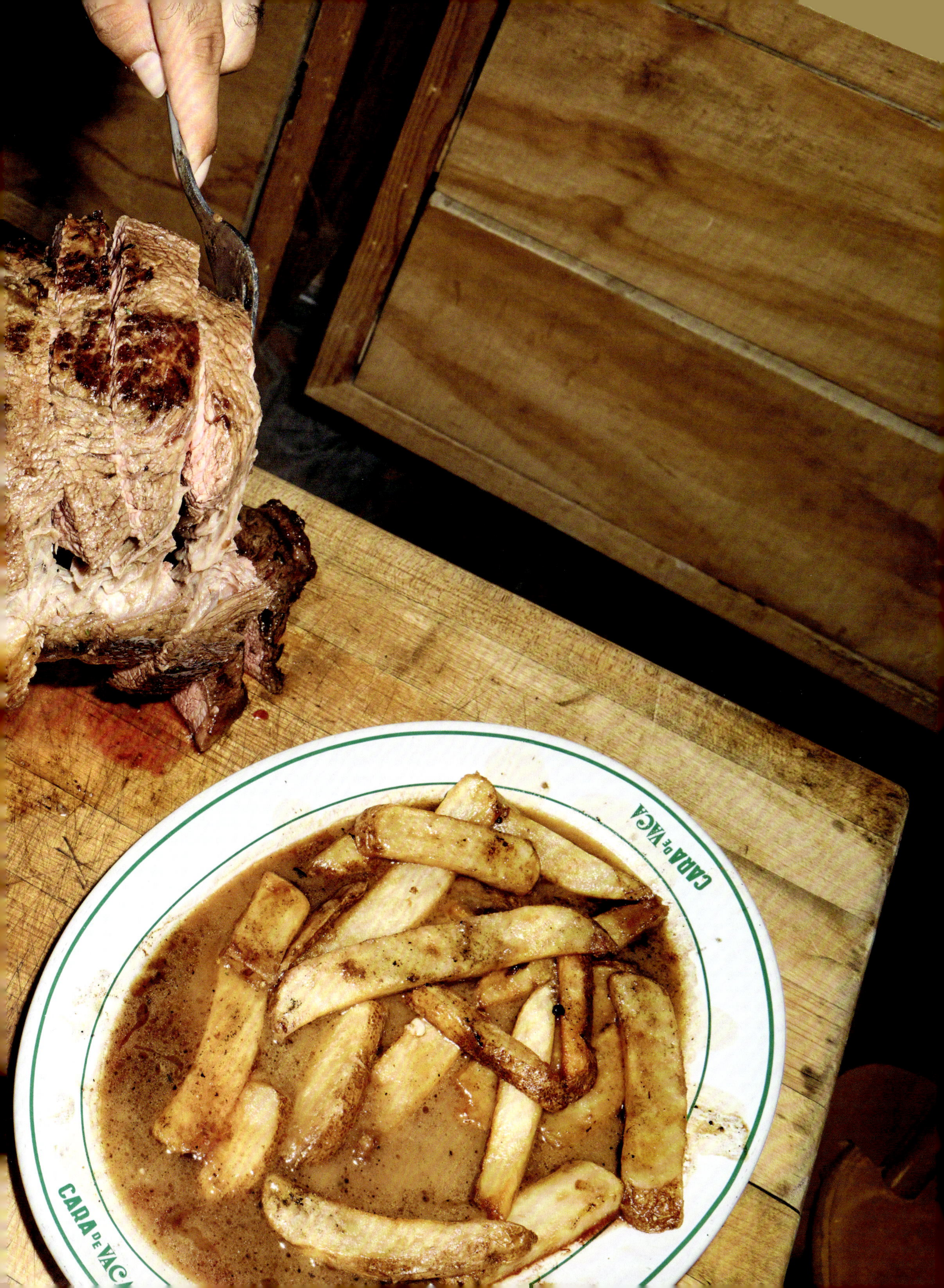
CARA DE VACA

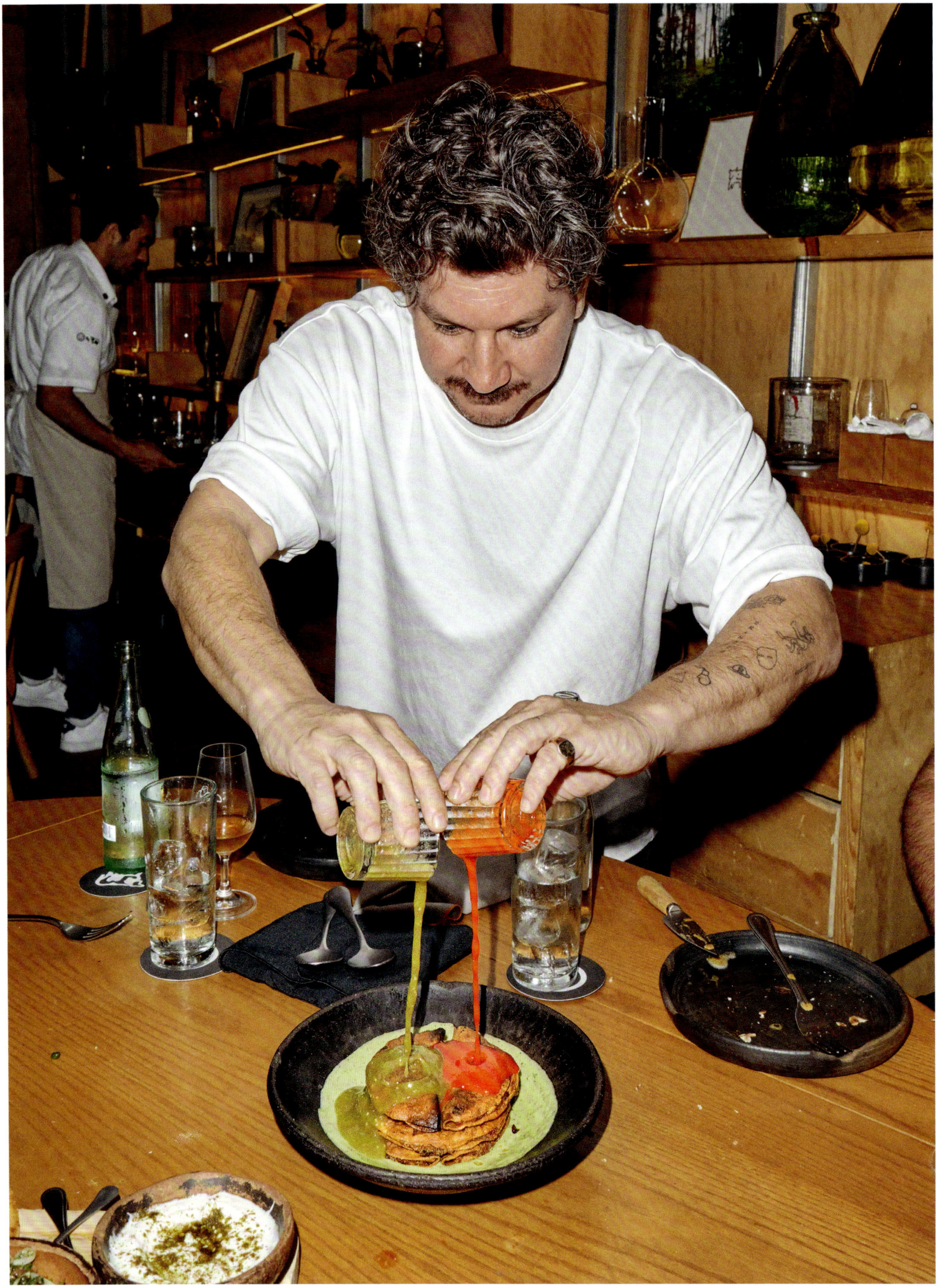

moog
VARIA INSTRU MENTS
Supreme
TSCHIDA
RUŽ MILAN NESTAREC

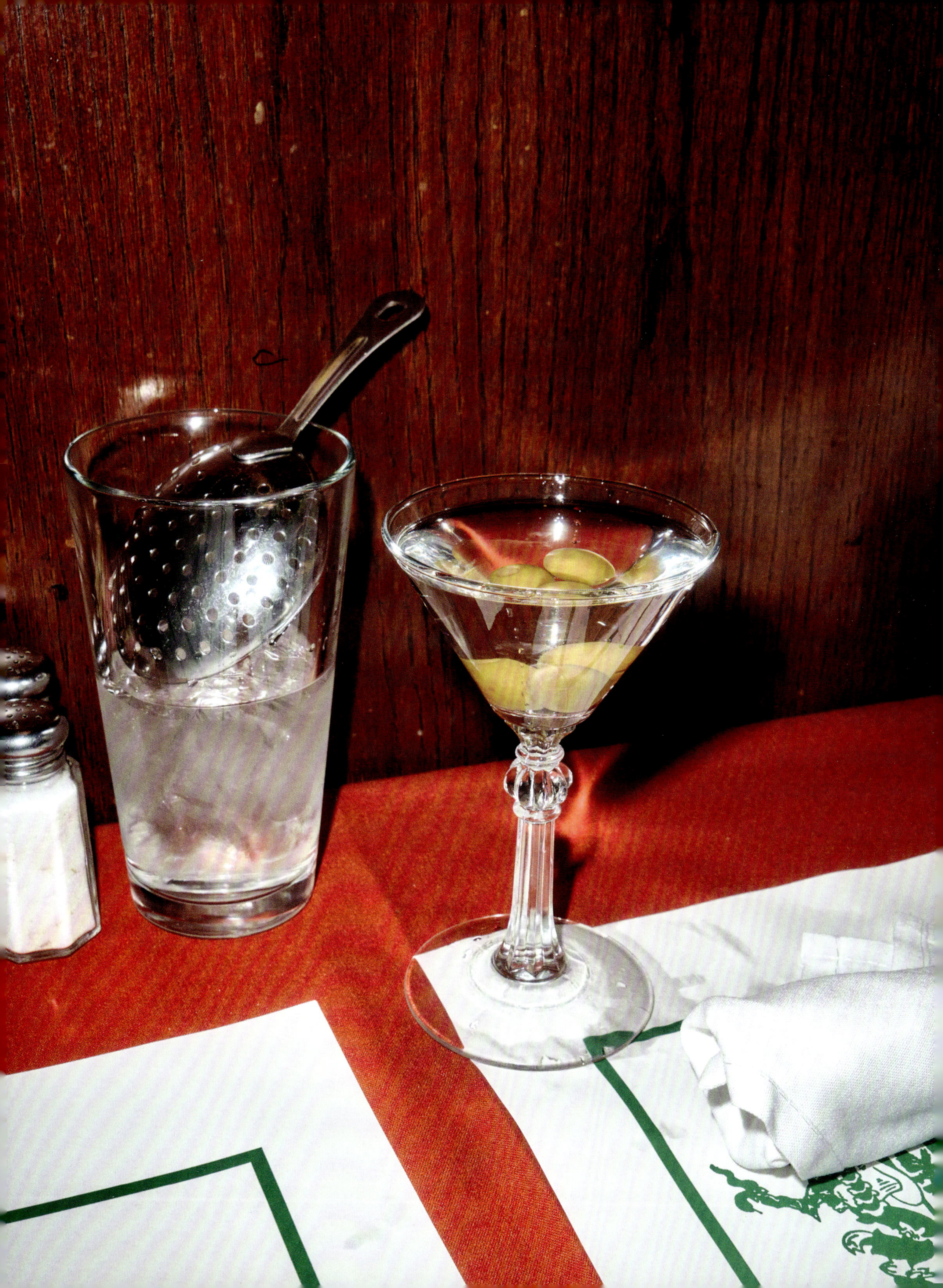

RECIPE

THE MARTINI

AZIZ'S MARTINI: SIMPLE PERFECTION

Serves 1

Martini glass, chilled in the freezer

Dry vermouth of choice (I like Bordiga Extra Dry), chilled in the freezer

Plymouth Gin or Tanqueray No. TEN, chilled in the freezer

Lemon peel

The martini was born in the nineteenth century and is a derivative of the Martinez, which itself is a derivative of the Manhattan. That's about the only thing people seem to agree on concerning the origins of the one and only cocktail highlighted in this book. The recipes for the martini started out on the sweet side, with maraschino liqueur. If you can believe that travesty. By the time the drink was showing up on tables at the Ritz in London, bartenders had thrown out the cherries and sweet vermouth in favor of the dry ideal.

How can two ingredients reach such heights? This isn't the first time in my life when I think it's best to let my friend Aziz Ansari explain. He has this instinctive ability to dive deeply into anything that captures his interest, whether it be the inner workings of a film or the anatomy of a perfect espresso. He doesn't need anyone to notice or care, but inevitably the people around him do. Then they follow along.

A few years ago, Aziz started spending a lot of time in London, by far the world's greatest martini town. Its bars were the places that turned me into a megafan of the drink.

The Connaught is a bit of a hike from where I live. But that stopped bothering me the second I took a sip of the drink you are about to learn how to make.

Ladies and gentlemen: Aziz Ansari.

I never was into martinis. The cocktail is just a glass of cold gin! But one day I happened to go to a party where a former bartender who put in thirty years at the legendary Savoy cocktail bar was making martinis. It was a performance that could not be ignored. He'd spray an ice-cold martini glass with vermouth. Then, he'd cool the gin in a stirring glass filled with ice and do a long pour. As the stream came down from high above, he squeezed a peel of Amalfi lemon to flavor it as it landed in the ice-cold glass. I had to try one. It was fantastic and led me on a martini adventure that eventually landed me at Dukes in London.

When my wife and I went, the bartender rolled up a cart and made our martinis tableside—dry, gin, with a lemon twist. He had ice-cold glasses straight from the freezer at the ready. He first gave a swirl of vermouth. "House made," he noted. After the rinse, he did a high pour of some Plymouth Gin that was also straight from the freezer. The stream of ice-cold gin kept going and going and going. He filled the glass to the BRIM and then dropped in a peel of lemon. "From the Amalfi Coast," he noted. As he served the martinis, he let us know, "Your evening is about to change."

Rinse the ice-cold martini glass with vermouth and pour in gin to the desired level. Drop in a lemon peel. Enjoy and don't drive, please.

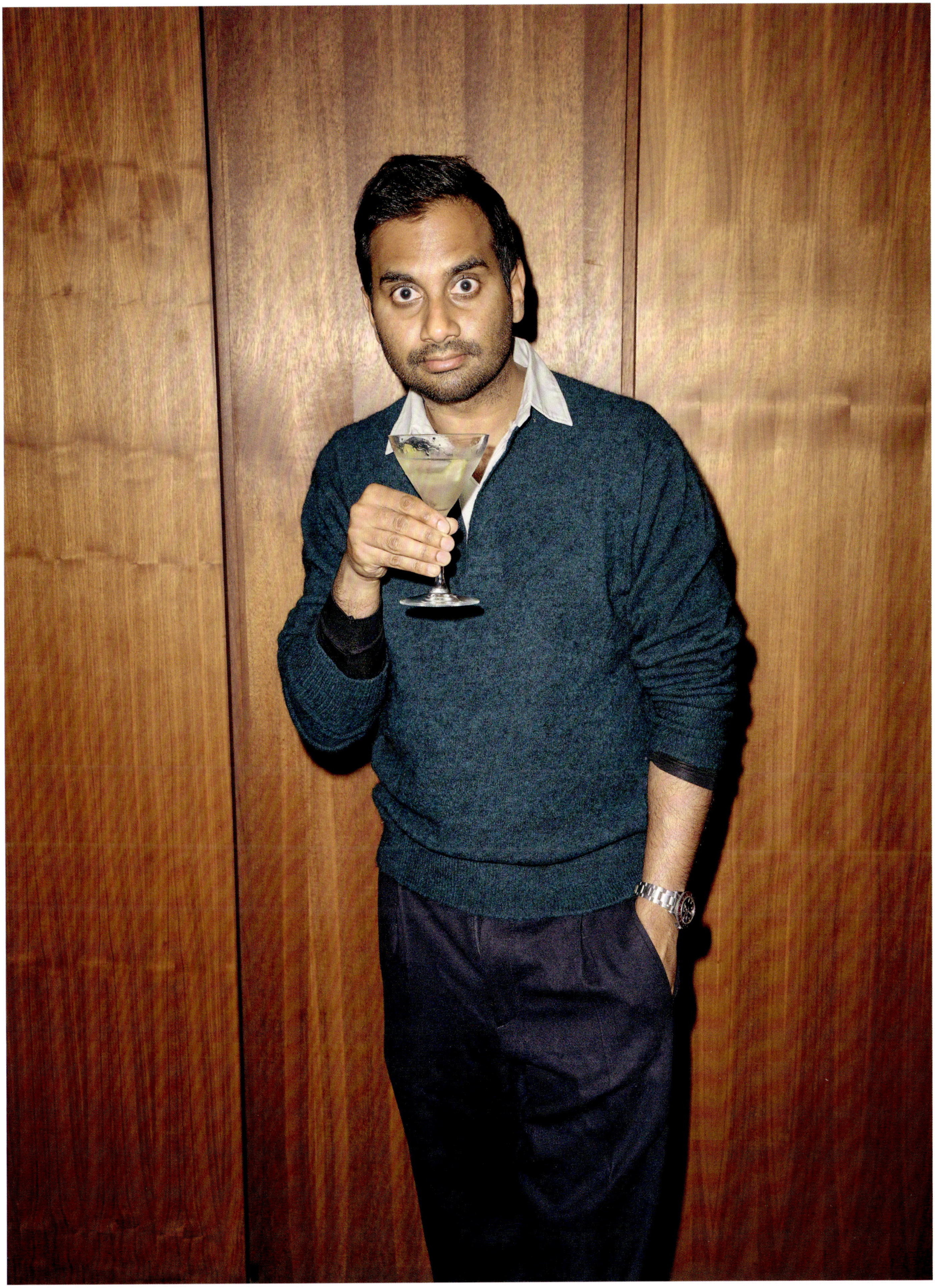

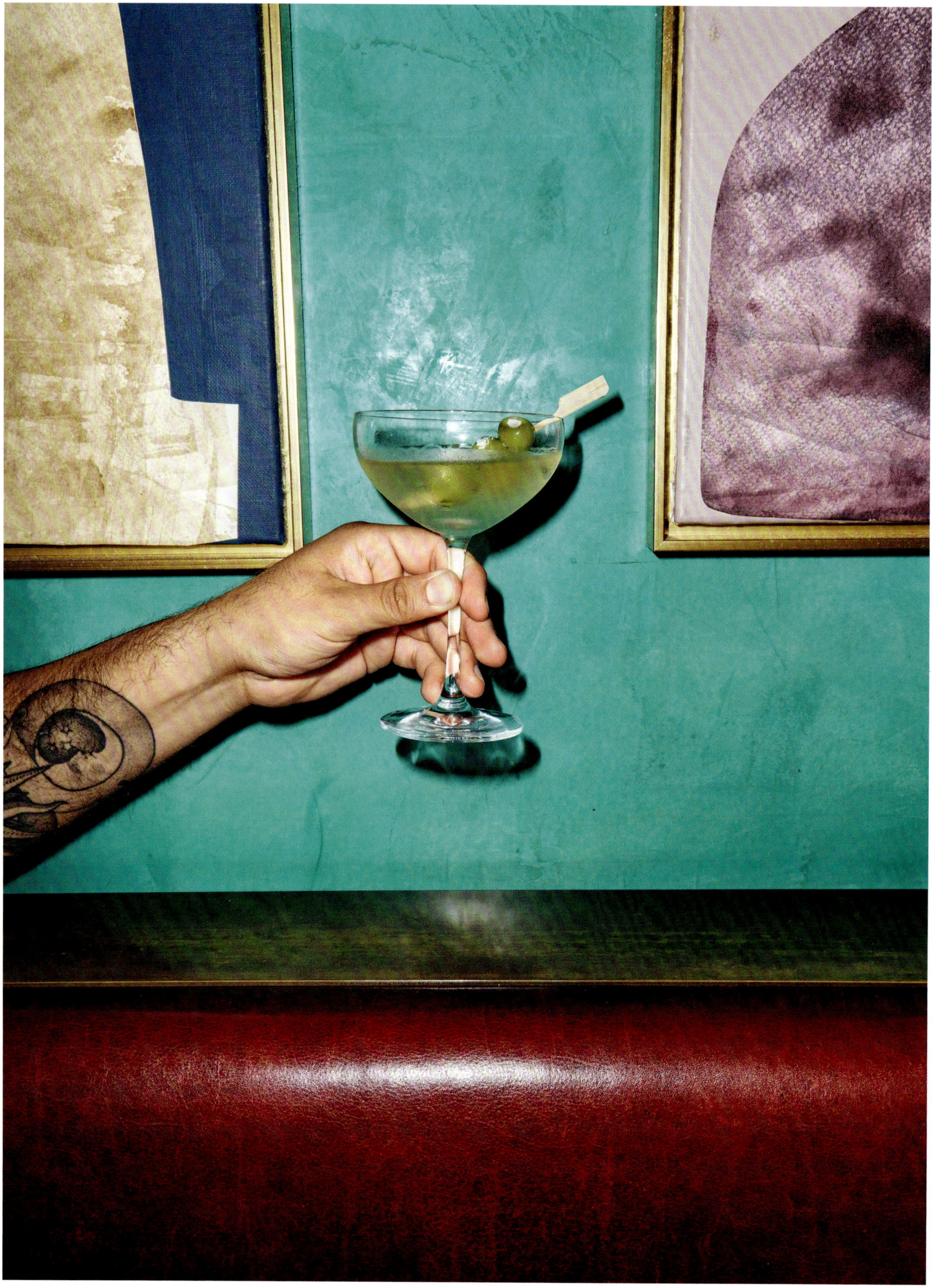

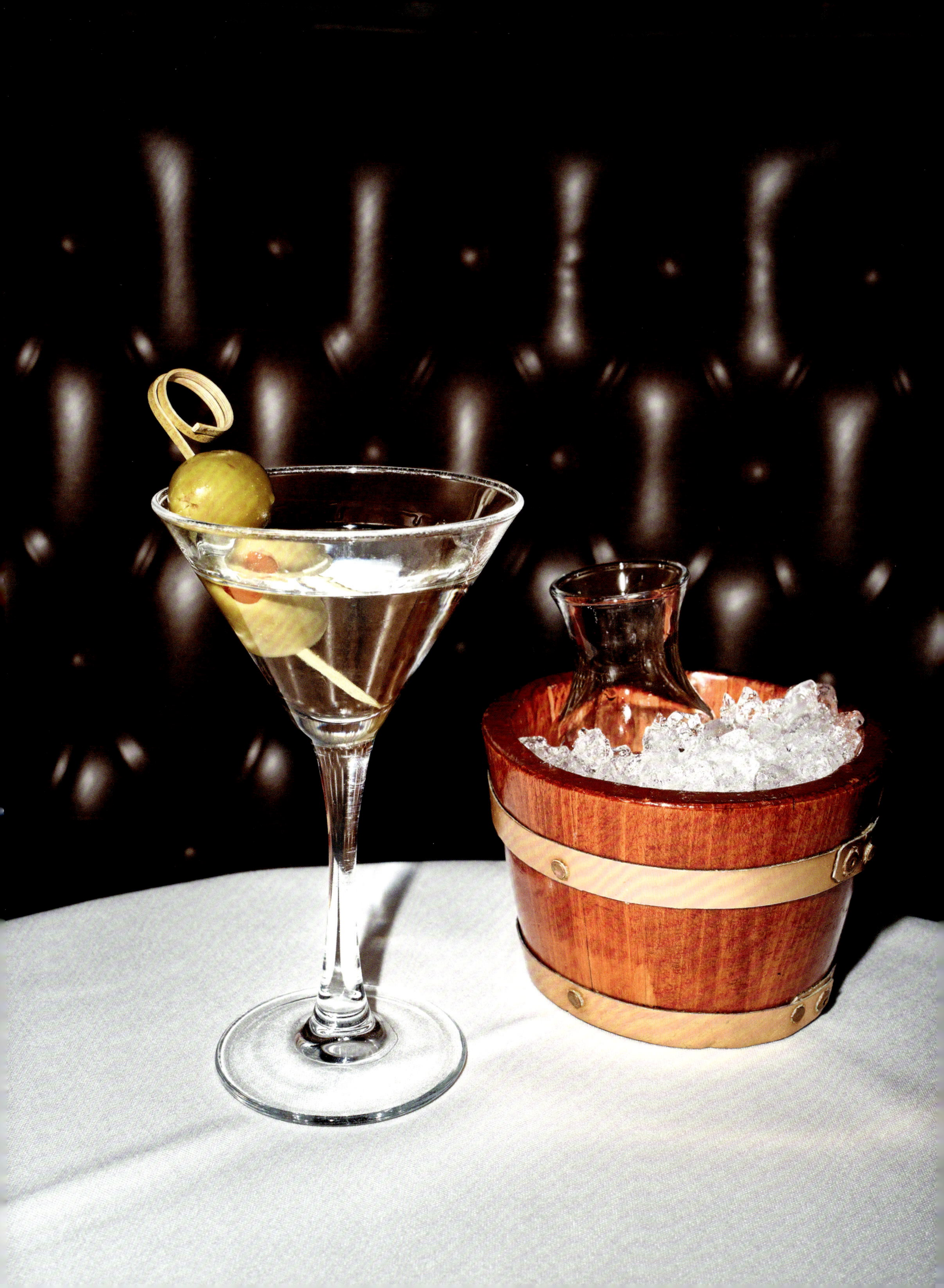

W I

N E

STEAK HOUSE WINE: FOR YOUR HEALTH

I love the way the progression of beverages unfolds during a special meal, starting with a cocktail, gliding smoothly into white wine, and then, if the entrée can stand up to it, finishing with something powerful, juicy, and red. At a steak house, you can skip the white wine on-ramp. That rich meat with its mineral and Maillard-y crust is calling out for tannins and acidity.

I usually like to drink elegant reds with some age from Burgundy or Piedmont, as well as California Cabernet from certain producers (more on that in a second). But I also believe that you should drink whatever the heck you want at a steak house. I'll spot the table of businessmen sipping on an overly ripe, way too young Super Tuscan, chosen because it was the most expensive option, and I'll root for them. Perhaps they will let me have a taste with my bacon-wrapped filet.

I'd say it's a good idea to pop the red as you are taking the first sips of your martini. Let it get some air. Swirl it around in the glass, breathe it in. Give it a taste. Think about what it is doing for you at that particular moment. Then let it sit in the bottle or a decanter. You will be amazed by what happens next. The wine softens, becomes acclimated to the new environment. Hopefully, it arrives at the sweetest of spots right when you need to call it into duty.

The last chapter we get to spend together features some love for four Napa Valley winemakers and a highlight reel of bottles from the journey. The winemakers produce Cabernet, the stereotypical eat-with-steak grape, but in ways that aren't stereotypical at all—each of these characters expresses a one-of-a-kind style. The important thing they all have in common is that they're rugged American iconoclasts who only give a hoot about making the wines they want to make, even when the going gets tough. But look at that. They're still here.

I cheers to them and to you.

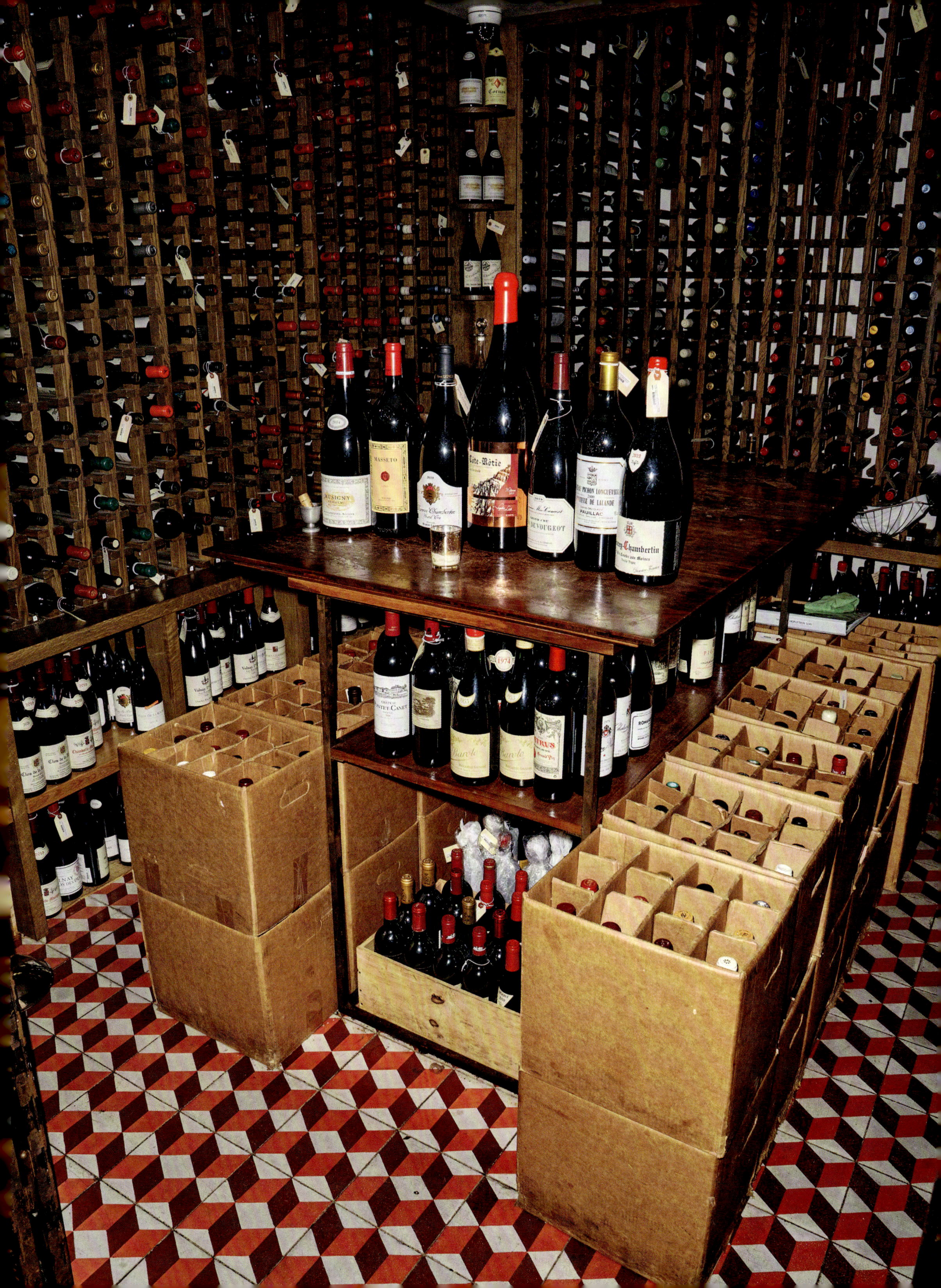
MASSETO
DE VOUGEOT
PAUILLAC
Chambertin

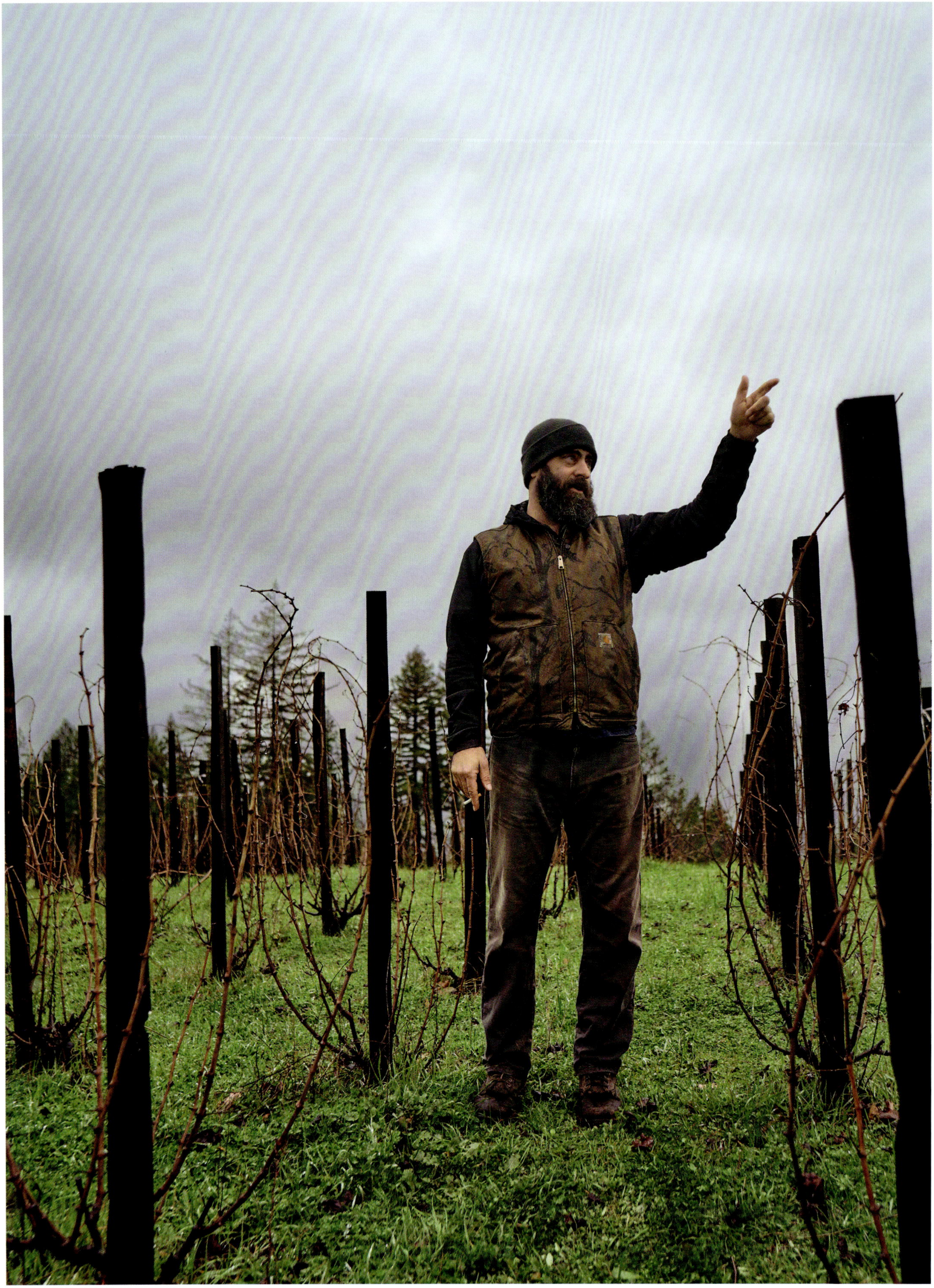

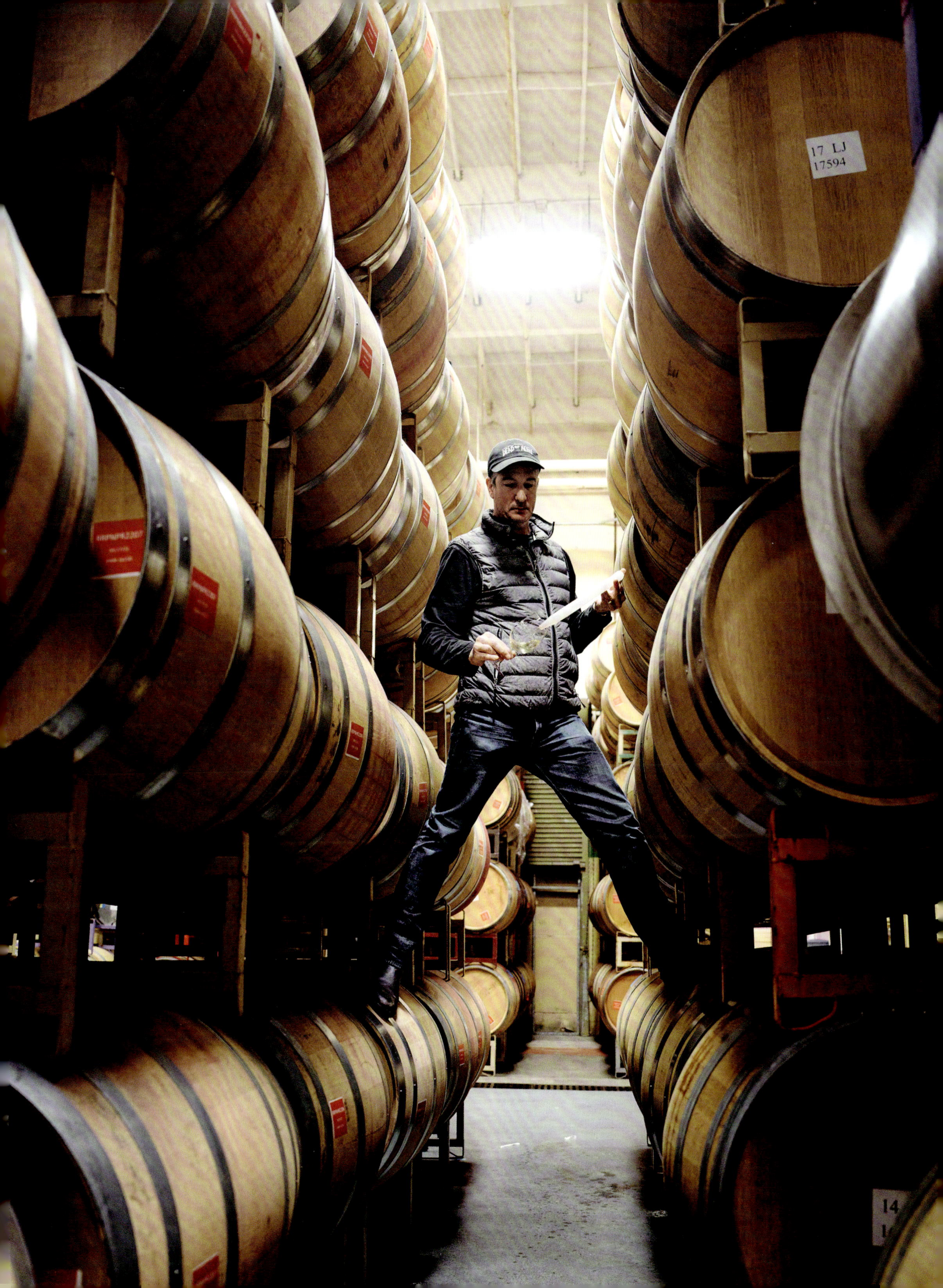
17 LJ
17594

THE WINEMAKERS

Cathy Corison Cathy Corison cares about precision and she has been consistently achieving it with wine since 1987 in St. Helena in Napa County. "It's just farming," she says, which she does organically in the fifty-seven-year-old Kronos Vineyard, her most cherished. She refers to the vines as her "old girls" and picks pea shoots from the cover crops to make salads. She has never added pesticides to these vines. In the cellar, she's as hands-off as in the vineyard, saving the sulfur until it's time to age the wines. She has no doubts about her complete command of the process. She has known certain things like this in her bones since the '80s, when she felt that there was "a wine I had inside of me," she says. She could tell you exactly how that wine was going to look, taste, and feel before a single grape was planted. She also knew exactly where she needed to make it: here on the Valley floor, on Bale loam soil. Looking out onto that tiny plot from the winery's balcony, she mentions that there was a critic who used to live over that way and who once had great influence in this part of the world. He didn't care for her supple style. She doesn't say his name, but I bet it rhymes with Robert Parker, whose rating system in the '70s and '80s prized the overpowering wines that Cathy can't stand. "I have to be careful—you'll always know what I think."

Ketan Mody It's pouring down on Diamond Mountain and Ketan Mody is still working all by himself. Every winemaker will say that the important work happens in the vineyard. This guy went one step further. He built a one-person cabin all the way up here on a crazy incline and lived in it for a few years. Ketan is part of the new school in Napa. He wants to bring things back to the small, trailblazing, bootstrapping ways they were done fifty years ago. All he needs to be happy is a pack of Marlboro Red and a beat-up tractor. And total control. He organizes the vines with plenty of space between them, just like they do in Burgundy and the Mosel. It's insane, considering how expensive land is here. He currently has two very small labels, Beta and Jesud. I tasted them—clear, structured, so proper. You'd think they were made by somebody with an actual winery and not a chain-smoking enigma living on the side of a mountain.

Joel Burt I don't know if I'd be able to write a whole chapter about wines in this book if it weren't for Joel Burt. He's a source of infinite knowledge and friendship and this was something I could sense the minute I met him at that beach party almost a decade ago when he brought a bottle of the pét-nat he'd been making in his garage. It was the beginning of something so super special. We're Las Jaras. Me and him. I think that Joel, after seven vintages, is only now *really* getting into his prime. I feel that deeply. He nails every cuvée and won't compromise on quality. EVER. He's known for having that sort of integrity. It's why our Chardonnay and Pinot Noir, which are made in America, will knock you out. Taste the Alder Springs Chard blind and I bet California won't be your first guess. This is coming from a Burgundy freak. While we're talking Napa, you better believe he can make a '70s-style Cab like it's nobody's business. Owning an independent wine company that wants to do things just like our heroes is not the easiest path. It's the best, though.

Randy Dunn Mr. Randy Dunn, or the Dunnster, as I call him (I would never call him that to his face; I just stand near him with my eyes diverting his powerful gaze), lives in a magical place called Howell Mountain, half an hour of winding roads and dense misty forest away from St. Helena. Randy's hands are large. He uses them to make a restrained, finessed expression of mountain fruit that some people assume doesn't exist in California. These wines are not big, boozy, palate-fatiguing fruit bombs. There's more tannin and spice to them than Cathy's wines. But they're still sumptuous and balanced. This is American wine you can taste blindfolded and still know who makes it.

When we visited Dunn Vineyards, we drank two older vintages and a 2019. The 1987 was as incredible as I expected. But I was completely, absolutely floored by the '19. I thought you had to wait until you were dead to experience Dunn as it should be. This vintage made *Wine Spectator*'s Top 10 of 2023. (Randy once called that magazine a "rag" in the local newspaper.) On our way out, I asked him what kind of food he likes to pair with his wines. He answered with the cutest little grin: "Beef."

THE BANGERS

2001 Corison Napa Valley Cabernet Sauvignon. I wanted to share with the team one of Napa's great winemakers, in the place where the wine was actually made. I'm still a sucker for having a glass while standing on the same fertile soil. This one was definitely an inspiration for our Las Jaras Cabernet. Bright fruit with finesse and medium weight. Cathy Corison has a magical, light, extracted touch, which yields a very elegant wine versus a huge, jammy, tannin-bomb experience. Wines from 2001 are in a great drinking place right now and really nice to pair with Spanish beef!

2000 Henri Bonneau Châteauneuf-du-Pape Réserve des Célestins. Henri Bonneau was one of the important makers in the world, a staple of Châteauneuf-du-Pape and a traditional, hard-headed, and very polarizing figure. Rooted in tradition, he never changed. Long ripening times, long élevage, and slowwww winemaking produce incredibly complex wines here. The year 2000 was a generous vintage that produced big, plump, juicy dark fruit with savory herbs. This was a monster of a wine with all the herbaceous and tertiary hallmarks of the Southern Rhône.

1983 Château Cheval Blanc Saint-Emilion Bordeaux. I don't drink Bordeaux often, but if I'm going to, it might as well be Cheval Blanc! Historic and royal, 1983 was a good vintage for Right-Bank Bordeaux. This bottle was classic Cheval Blanc style, which is big, deep, and jammy yet soft and perfumed with very few sharp edges. Perfectly integrated and ready to drink. Some people would think '83 is far too young for a Bordeaux, as we have experienced many early-1900s examples at Bern's (page 37). But sometimes the wine is in that pocket where it breaks the rules.

2010 Pierre Gonon Saint-Joseph Syrah. The '10 Gonon Saint-Joseph was outstanding as usual. Gonon is on the more natural and wild side of the Northern Rhône spectrum, so the wines are alive, fresh, and expand and contract on the palate more than the average wine from the region. Gonon's wines offer a singular Syrah experience that's both savory and elegant and almost unpredictable and improvisational dance–like. The Northern Rhône can produce such complex and multidimensional wines. And when done correctly, they can be game-changing.

2017 G.B. Burlotto Verduno Barolo. Burlotto is the soft-spoken, quiet king of elegant and red-fruited Barolo. The wines aren't big, tannic, or too oaky. They are singular and very Burgundian. Burlotto always manages to capture the more spiritual side of the Nebbiolo grape. It whispers softly to you yet tells you a very confident long story. It haunts with every sip as the wine breathes.

1983 Domaine Jamet Côte-Brune Côte-Rôtie. Stop everything. Turn off the lights. Light a candle. Grab your finest glass. Polish it and prepare your body and soul for a moment that you will never forget in this lifetime or the next. All of this is to try to describe what happens when Jamet is on! Jean-Paul Jamet is truly one of the top five red wine producers in the world. His Côte-Brune cuvées are treasures, and to experience one with this amount of age on it is transcendental. Syrah personified! The style is more subtle and red fruited than big, peppery, oaky tannin bombs from the Rhône. Côte-Rôtie is the northernmost Appellation d'Origine Contrôlée (AOC) of the Rhône and very rocky and mountainous, so the wines are more cut and mineral. Jamet captures this terroir beautifully no matter what the vintage throws at him. They truly are singular experiences. The silky texture of this wine was so ethereal I wanted to cry. The perfume lingered intensely. Oftentimes you get a bit of menthol. There is magic in these bottles.

2007 Domaine Bizot Vosne-Romanée Vieilles Vignes Pinot Noir. Steven McDonald, master sommelier and wine director at Pappas Bros. (page 155), couldn't help but smirk when he surprised us with this bottle at our epic meal in Houston. He knew he was about to remove our brains, sprinkle some WTF powder on them, and return them to our skulls. And it was a high unlike the others. Jean-Yves Bizot is a professor of viticulture. I mean, literally. And it shows in the wines. Uncompromising farming makes for such unbelievably transparent and pure wines. I recently stayed blocks away from his winery and parcels in Vosne, and it was like being in the nexus of the wine universe. I love it when other winemakers like Henri Jayer share farming and cellar fundamentals that in turn make the entire region and, most importantly, the wines better on the whole! I have never had a bottle from Bizot with this amount of age, and it really helped uncover the dark cherry and Vosne spices that are hidden in that blissful wine.

2016 Chateau Musar Gaston Hochar Grand Cru Red. Red excellence from Lebanon. Ash, forest floor, a bit of volatile acidity, and Brett but at acceptable levels. It's as if Rinaldi and Château Margaux combined forces to make a wine in such a fascinating wine region. And when it's paired with a Sunday roast with popovers and gravy, wow, life is good. Natural winemaking at its finest.

2021 Éric Texier Côtes du Rhône Chat Fou Grenache. I met this incredible man in Beaujolais in 2018 while my friend Sleepy Joe Beddia and I were on a summer wine trip through France. We were heavy into carbonic reds from the region and luckily got a visit with the master. Chat Fou from Éric Texier is always welcome in my glass, no matter where or when. It's light and bouncy and also holds up to a steak. It's a super plump and juicy Rhône blend that's modest and humble yet very seductive and playful. They named it after their crazy cat; I met the cat's daughter, Chat Fou Two! Another affordable selection that will thrill you.

2021 Arianna Occhipinti Terre Siciliane Il Frappato. I have always been a fan of Sicilian red wines, especially the wines made by Occhipinti. I visited Vittoria two times during my early Sicilian adventures and was always amazed by how the wines tasted like the terroir we were in. Driving through this part of Sicily, I saw thousands of those sweet red oranges all over the highways and roads because they had an abundance of the crop and not enough people to pick all the fruit. The area seemed very wild and natural, and that's the expression I get in their wines. They don't hold anything back, but they also are such talented winemakers because they don't overmacerate anything. A delicate hand in the cellar combined with unique soil makes for a captivating wine.

2022 Brutal by Christian Tschida Burgenland, Austria. The wines of Christian Tschida were an early part of my wine journey. They skate the line between natural and traditional but certainly lean more natural, as Tschida has been embraced by that world very warmly. Aside from how he'd align himself, the wines are clean, polished, and seductive yet full of life and energy. This "brutal" cuvée is a wonderful alpine expression of Pinot Noir from Burgenland, Austria. Herbaceous, high toned, lean, and full of acid yet sexy and silky.

2017 Roagna Langhe Rosso Nebbiolo. Roagna is one of my favorite producers in Piemonte. This Langhe Rosso is a modest wine, but the fruit is some of the greatest Nebbiolo out there! It is a blend from young vines of famed Barolo and Barbaresco vineyards and aged for five years before release. Their vineyards are overgrown, and the vines look like small trees. There is tall grass everywhere encompassing the vines. It is truly a gift in a bottle. This particular bottle is always affordable and offers a little snapshot of what's to come with their more expensive cuvées. When I'm not sipping this at a steak house, you know I'm pounding a bottle with my ragooooo!

Domaine Fourrier Gevrey-Chambertin 1er Cru Cherbaudes Vieille Vigne Pinot Noir. Jean-Marie Fourrier cut his teeth in 1988 with Henri Jayer, arguably the greatest Pinot Noir producer of all time. He now employs these same practices with his domaine wines. He has holdings in some of the most prized vineyards on earth. These sites yield elite fruit, so not much intervention is needed. He is very hands-off. They are ethereal yet explosive out of the glass with age, red fruit, earth, and spice. When they are on, nothing can compare. I teared up for this bottle.

1953 Pierre Ponnelle Pommard Pinot Noir. The '53 Pommard was ALIVE. Pommard from this era is massive. The winemaking style back then saw much more wood and longer élevage, causing the wines to go the long haul, even at village level like this bottle. It was such a treat to be time-warped and taste what this bottle had to say. It faded very fast, but there was lots of life in that first glass. Maderized roses, decaying flowers, brown sugar. Boom!

1961 Domaine Leroy La Romanée Grand Cru Pinot Noir. This was a dream-come-true wine, and the reason you go to Tampa to find some of the greatest stored wine on the planet. The Leroy La Romanée was stunning! Profound texture and aromatics. There was an almost herbal-tea-like quality to the wine, and it was so quiet and soft yet persistent and haunting. Delicate cherry and lifted floral and light grand cru spice. This was a once-in-a-lifetime event.

1976 Château d'Yquem Sauternes. We had one of the finest meals on our journey at The Grill (page 72) in NYC and just had a tour of the d'Yquem cellar, so I made the decision to grab a bottle of birth-year wine for myself. And it delivered on such a magnificent level. A blend of Sémillon and Sauvignon in the Bordeaux region. These grapes are left to ripen to a place where they are affected by noble rot—the only cool disease to get, in my opinion! This is some real alchemy that I love to read about. (Next book I want to just focus on ice wine—fascinating!) The Sauternes nose is explosive, with tropical fruit rounded off by subtle honey and spices. Its weight is silky and regal and the palate and finish keep the party going with even more complex dimensions.

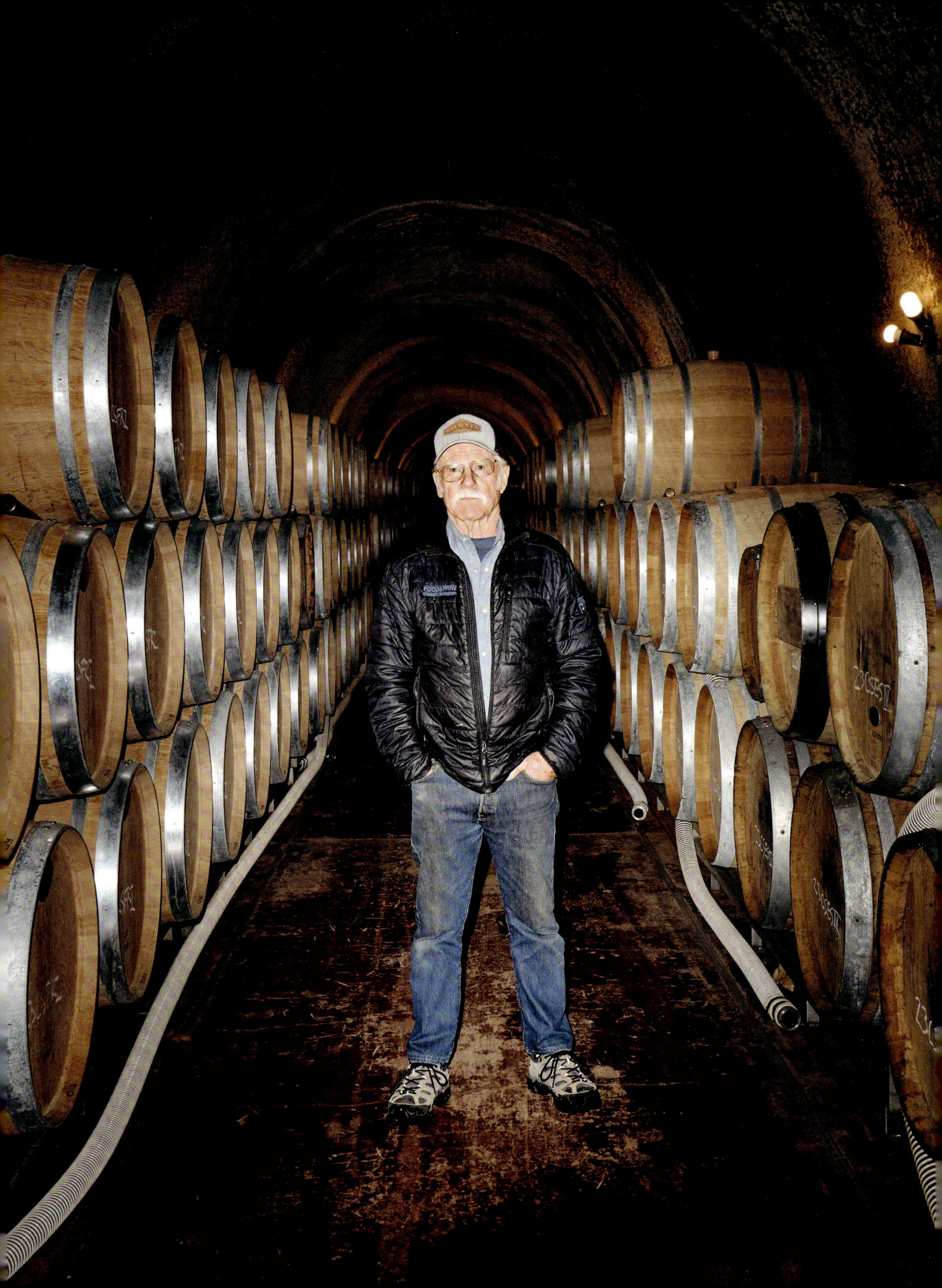

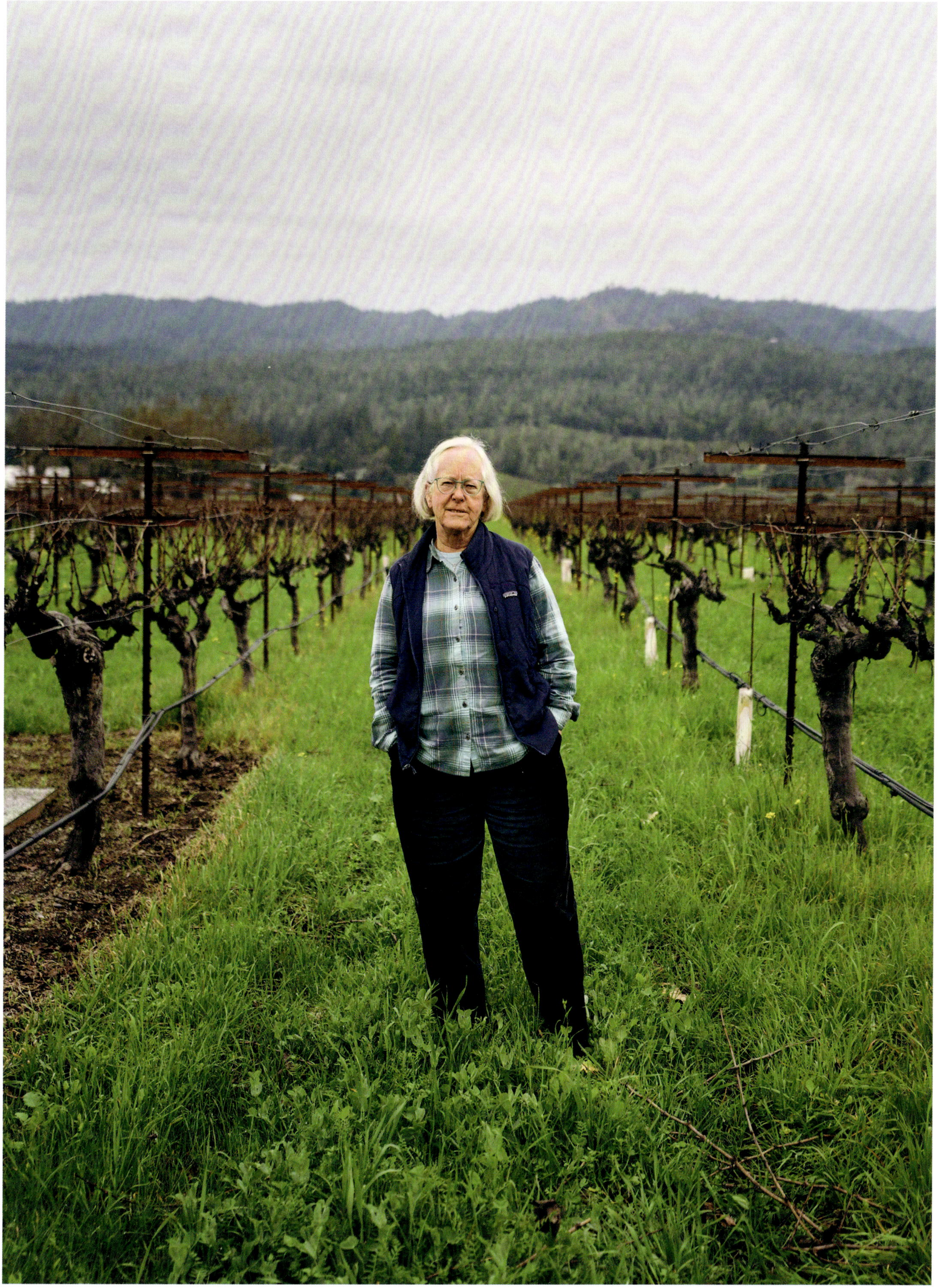

ACKNOWLEDGMENTS

Thank you first and foremost to all the servers, chefs, line cooks, somms, valets, publicists, busboys, winemakers, runners, archivists, interns, butchers, T-Pains, experts, security guards, dishwashers, and owners who made this book possible.

Endless gratitude to Kelly Snowden, Emma Campion, Gabby Ureña Matos, and the entire team at Ten Speed Press for trusting me and bringing this book to life; designer James Casey for being on the money from day one, when he showed up with fifteen perfect visual references; Daniel Greenberg for the incredible support throughout; Emily Stephenson, Jasmyn Crawford, Jesse Pearson, Jenn de la Vega, Sylvie Florman, Emily Ziemski, and Graham Byrne for all the love and care they put into this project behind the scenes, on the recipes, research, readings, and beyond.

I also want to acknowledge the friends who guided us and joined us for many meals: Alex Goose, Jon Castelli, John Cerasulo, Chloe Wise, Joe Beddia, Marguerite Mariscal, Chris Kronner, J. D. Plotnick, Mindy Le Brock, Bryan Hollon, Ben Willett, Brian Tarney, Andrew Mariani, Kat Turner, Magna Howard, and Lily Freedman.

Finally, to the two people who followed me blindly into this life-changing experience . . . here's what I have to say to say about them:

Gabe was a dream come true partner, collaborator, and producer on one of the hardest productions I've ever done—in any field. His natural steadfastness, grace, and humor were integral in getting me to the place where I could find the voice and heart of this book. He rose to the occasion, big time, and he happened to show up in my world just as trustworthiness and enthusiasm were becoming the things I needed most.

I tried getting Marcus, this beast of a photographer, for my first book. Truly, you have no idea how good it felt when I finally snared him for *Steak House* (by lying through my teeth and saying we were only shooting eleven restaurants!). There are no words to explain the monumental contributions that resulted from his unique eye, style, and general Swedish mastery. He's also the reason I picked up my camera again and started shooting. A generous man with all his talents.

ABOUT THE CONTRIBUTORS

Eric Wareheim is a director, actor, and comedian, the author of the *New York Times*–bestselling cookbook *Foodheim*, and the founder of the celebrated independent California wine label Las Jaras. He began his career as one half of the groundbreaking comedy duo Tim & Eric, who have been making TV shows, movies, books, and music for nearly three decades.

Gabe Ulla is a New York–based writer who has collaborated with several noted chefs and contributes to *Town & Country*, *Vanity Fair*, and *WSJ* magazine. He is the co-author of *Estela*, *The Four Horsemen*, *Carbone*, and David Chang's *New York Times*–bestselling memoir, *Eat a Peach*.

Marcus Nilsson trained as a chef in his native Sweden and worked under the likes of Marcus Samuelsson after settling in New York in the '90s. He eventually stepped away from the kitchen and established himself as one of the most influential food photographers of his generation. His cookbook collaborations include *Estela*, *Night + Market*, and *My Mexico City Kitchen*.

INDEX

Page numbers in italics indicate photos.

A

Achatz, Grant, 98
Acropolis, 91, 190, 200, 205
Adams, Taylor, 62
Aioli, Truffle, 140
Alinea, 98
Amber House, 21
Anderson, Erik, 186
Anderson, Louie, 272
Animal, 136
Ansari, Aziz, 298
Apple Strudel mit Schlag, 268–69, *269*
apricots
    Tomato and Stone Fruit Salad, 120, *120*
Arriaga, Jewel, 148
Athens West, 200
Au Poivre Sauce, 133
Azhari, Hicham, 30

B

bacon
    Bacon Roasted Tomato, 121
    Classic Wedge, 112, *113*
    Korean Wedge, 115
    Mariani Wedge, *114*, 115
Baked Alaska, Espresso Martini, 266
Balaski, Lou, 211
Bavette's Bar & Boeuf, 98, 104, 109, 121, 180, 186, 267
Beard, James, 228
Beddia, Joe, 310
beef
    Beef Wellington, 182, *183*
    industry, 124
    from small farms, 124, 127
    Steak House Juicy Lucy, 186, *187*
    See also steaks
Beef 'N Bottle, 11–12, 18, 21, 26, 48, 139
Beefsteak (annual event), 140, 244
Bennett, William, 281
Bern's Steak House, 18, 37, 40, 86, 228, 309
Berson, David, 62
Betz, Joe, 211
Bizot, Jean-Yves, 309–10

Black, Julian, 72
Bonneau, Henri, 309
Boros, Eliska, 282
Boros, Rudolph, Radek, and Karel, 185, 282, 286
Boros Strava, 182, 185, 282, 286
bread
    Garlic Bread, 48
    Sourdough Croutons, 116
Brock, Sean, 49
burgers
    Steak House Juicy Lucy, 186, *187*
Burlotto, G. B., 309
Burt, Joel, 308
butter
    Compound Butter, 139
    De Jonghe Butter, 89
    Foie Gras Butter, *231*, 232
    Rosemary Garlic Butter, *231*, 232

C

Caesar, Classic, 116, *117*
Calamari, Fried, *92*, 93
Camacho, Fernando, 275
Cara de Vaca, 135, 178, 290
Carbone, Mario, 72
Carnes Ramos, 290
Carrots, Honey-Glazed, 226, *227*
Cass, Cort, 244
Castronovo, Frank, 132
Cattlemen's, 172
Chang, David, 243
Chateau Vegas, 276
cheese
    Blue Cheese Dressing, 115
    Cheesecake with Strawberry Sauce, 262, *263*
    Cheese Sauce, 233
    Classic Wedge, 112, *113*
    Creamed Spinach, 226, *227*
    Garbage Salad, 119
    Lobster Mac and Cheese, 233
    Mariani Wedge, *114*, 115
    Port Cheddar Dip, 48
    Relish Tray with Creamy Dip, 50, *51*
    Steak House Juicy Lucy, 186, *187*

cherries
    The Crown of Pork, *184*, 185
    The Major Donut, *264*, 265
Cheval Blanc, Château, 309
chicken
    Pollo Asado, 178, *179*
Chicken-Fried Ibérico Pork Steak, 181
Chimichurri, 132
Chips and Truffle-Ranch Dip, 86, *87*
chocolate
    Espresso Martini Baked Alaska, 266
chuck eye (Delmonico) steak
    Eye of Delmonico with Truffle Aioli, 140
Churrasco con Papas, *134*, 135
Circus Circus, 281
Clearman, John, 257
Clearman's Steak 'n Stein Inn, 48, 257
Cocktail Sauce, 88
Coi, 186
The Continental, 49
Contreras, Sergio Cortes, 275, 276
Corison, Cathy, 308, 309
Coser, Arri and Jair, 170
Cote, 54
Crawfish & Noodles, 146
Cream Co. Meats, 124, 127, 190, 216
Creperie Beau Monde, 252
Croutons, Sourdough, 116
Crudo Sauce, 94

D

De Jonghe Butter, 89
Delephine, Marguerite and Allan, 192
Delmonico's, 15, 54, 140
desserts
    Apple Strudel mit Schlag, 268–69, *269*
    Cheesecake with Strawberry Sauce, 262, *263*
    Espresso Martini Baked Alaska, 266
    Ice Cream Sundae, 267, *267*
    The Major Donut, *264*, 265
Diane Sauce, 138
dips
    Creamy Dip, 50, *51*
    Port Cheddar Dip, 48
    Truffle-Ranch Dip, 86, *87*

Dixie Grill & Grocery, 18, *19*
Doan, Peter, 159
Donohue, Martin, 68
Donohue-Peters, Maureen, 68
Donohue's, 68
donuts
    The Major Donut, *264*, 265
Dotolo, Vinny, 136
dry-aging, 127
Ducasse, Alain, 109
Dukes Bar, 298
Dunn, Randy, 308–9
Dunn Vineyards, 308–9
Durpetti, Michelle, 100
d'Yquem, Château, 311

E
Ed Debevic's, 252–53
El Gauchito, 54
Espresso Martini Baked Alaska, 266
Este, 133, 146, 222

F
Falcinelli, Frank, 132
Featherblade Craft Butchery, 186
Federighi, Alfredo, 100
Fernando, Luis, 11–12, 211
filet mignon
    Steak Bites, *90*, 91
    Surf 'n Turf, 139
Fine, George, 21, 26
Fogo de Chão, 170
Foie Gras Butter, *231*, 232
Ford, Tyler, 192
Fourrier, Jean-Marie, 310
Four Seasons, 72
Fraser, Amy Knoll, 244
Fraser, Neal, 140, 244
The French Laundry, 186

G
Garbage Salad, 119
Garcia's Mexican Food, 146
garlic
    Diane Sauce, 138
    Garlic Bread, 48
    Roasted Garlic, 130
    Rosemary Garlic Butter, *231*, 232
Gene & Georgetti, 93, 98, *99*, 100, 119
gin
    Aziz's Martini, 298, *299*
Gold, Jonathan, 248
Golden Eagle, 276
Golden Steer, 89, 116, 275–76
Gonon, Pierre, 309
The Grill, 72, 266, 311
ground chuck
    Steak House Juicy Lucy, 186, *187*
Grunauer, Aloisius, 62, 64
Guerra, Lisa Massis, 26

H
Hampe, Erik, 100, 109
Harris', 190
Harris, Billy, 244
Hash Browns, 222, *223*
Haynie, Emile, 136
Hearsey, Inessa, 15, 211
Heidecker, Tim, 11, 18, 56, 98, 248, 252, 272
Hendee, Nina and Edd, 164
Henry, Austin, 164, 169
Hernandez, Ralph and Lili, 148
Higgy's, 68
Honey-Glazed Carrots, 226, *227*
House of Prime Rib, 11, 15, 190, 211
House of Steak, 21

I
ice cream
    Espresso Martini Baked Alaska, 266
    Ice Cream Sundae, 267, *267*
    The Major Donut, *264*, 265

J
Jamet, Jean-Paul, 309
Jayer, Henri, 309, 310
Jeffrey's, 46, 130, 146
Jenkins, Bernice, 21
Jenkins, Bonnie, 56
Jon G's Barbecue, 18, 21, 143

K
Keen, Albert, 56
Keens, 50, 54, 56, 225
Keller, Thomas, 244
Kelly, Johnny, 68
Kennedy, John F., 72
Kennedy Onassis, Jackie, 72
Kirkman, Garren and Kelly, 21, 143
Kissinger, Henry, 72
Korean Wedge, 115
Kovac, Fikret, 30
Kronner, Chris, 190, 216
Kronos Vineyard, 308

L
La Nacional, 94, 290
Langer's, 238
Laurel, Stan, 251
Lawry's, 243
Laxer, Bern, 37
LeGrand, Didier, 182, 185, 282, 286
Leroy, Domaine, 310–11
lettuce
    Classic Caesar, 116, *117*
    Classic Wedge, 112, *113*
    Garbage Salad, 119
    Korean Wedge, 115
    Mariani Wedge, *114*, 115
Lippold, Richard, 72
Little Alley Steak, 8, 30, 33, 233, 234
Little Red Barn, 146
lobster
    Lobster Mac and Cheese, 233
    Surf 'n Turf, 139
Love, Courtney, 200
Luger, Peter, 54, 62, 64, 119, 186

M
Mac and Cheese, Lobster, 233
Majordomo, 120, 138, 243, 265
The Major Donut, *264*, 265
Mariani, Andrew, 216
Mariani, Kelly, 112, 216
Mariani Wedge, *114*, 115
Marinara, 93

martinis
    Aziz's Martini, 298, *299*
    Espresso Martini Baked Alaska, 266
Mary's Club, 200, 205
Matt's Bar & Grill, 186
McDonald, Steven, 309
mezcal
    Au Poivre Sauce, 133
Michelotti, Gene, 100
Miller, Dennis, 253
Miller, William S., 15
Mitchell, Joseph, 244
Mody, Ketan, 308
Monkey Bar, *54*
Musar, Chateau, 310
mushrooms
    A Fine Pork Chop, 180
Musso, Joseph, 238
The Musso & Frank Grill, 136, 240

N

New York strip steak
    Chopped Steak au Poivre, 136
    New York Strip with Chimichurri, 132
    Steak Crudo, 94, *95*
Nguyen, Victor, 238
Nuñez, Fermín, 133, 222, 290

O

Occhipinti, Arianna, 310
Odenkirk, Bob, 248, 252–53
Old Homestead Steakhouse, 54
Oliveira, Selma, 170
onions
    Thick Onion Rings, 228
    Thin Onion Rings, 228, *229*
    Tomatoes and Onions, 119

P

Pappas, Chris and Harris, 155
Pappas Bros., 146, 155, 159–60, 309
Parker, Robert, 308
Parker House Rolls, 49
Parra-Sickels, Jude, 138, 243, 265
Parsell, Mike, 78

pasta
    Lobster Mac and Cheese, 233
peaches
    The Major Donut, *264*, 265
    Tomato and Stone Fruit Salad, 120, *120*
Pennington, Bill, 281
Peter Luger, 54, 62, 64, 119, 186
plums
    The Major Donut, *264*, 265
    Tomato and Stone Fruit Salad, 120, *120*
Polizos, Andreas, 200, 205
Polizos, Haralambos "Bobby," 200
Pollard, Clifford, 124, 127, 190, 216
Pollo Asado, 178, *179*
Ponelle, Pierre, 310
Popovers, 46, *47*
pork
    Chicken-Fried Ibérico Pork Steak, 181
    The Crown of Pork, *184*, 185
    A Fine Pork Chop, 180
    See also bacon; prosciutto
Port Cheddar Dip, 48
potatoes
    Chips and Truffle-Ranch Dip, 86, *87*
    Chopped Hash Ode to Keens, *224*, 225
    Churrasco con Papas, *134*, 135
    Hash Browns, 222, *223*
    Mashed Potatoes, 230
prime rib
    Chopped Hash Ode to Keens, *224*, 225
    Classic Prime Rib, 140, *141*
prosciutto
    Beef Wellington, 182, *183*
The Pub, 78
Puck, Wolfgang, 244
puff pastry
    Beef Wellington, 182, *183*

R

radishes
    Garbage Salad, 119
    Mariani Wedge, *114*, 115
raisins
    Apple Strudel mit Schlag, 268–69, *269*
    Steak Sauce, 230, *231*

Redbird, 244
Reichl, Ruth, 12, 64
Reilly, John C., 98, 248, 251
Relish Tray with Creamy Dip, 50
Renaud, Eric, 37, 40
Rib Eye with Roasted Garlic, 130, *131*
RingSide, 88, 112, 190, 192, 197, 228
Roach, Jesse and Mozelle, 172
Roagna, 310
Rolls, Parker House, 49
Rosemary Garlic Butter, *231*, 232

S

salad dressings
    Blue Cheese Dressing, 115
    Caesar Dressing, 116
    Tangy Dressing, 112
    Tofu Sesame Dressing, 115
salads
    Bacon Roasted Tomato, 121
    Classic Caesar, 116, *117*
    Classic Wedge, 112, *113*
    Garbage Salad, 119
    Korean Wedge, 115
    Mariani Wedge, *114*, 115
    Tomato and Stone Fruit Salad, 120, *120*
    Tomatoes and Onions, 119
salami
    Garbage Salad, 119
sauces
    Au Poivre Sauce, 133
    Cheese Sauce, 233
    Chimichurri, 132
    Cocktail Sauce, 88
    Crudo Sauce, 94
    Diane Sauce, 138
    Luger-Style Sauce, 119
    Marinara, 93
    Steak Bites Sauce, 91
    Steak Sauce, 230, *231*
    Strawberry Sauce, 262
    Truffle Aioli, 140
Sayler, Art and Dick, 206
Sayler's Old Country Kitchen, 12, 190, 206

Scribe Winery, 112, 190, 216
Seafood Shanty, 88
Selman, Matt, 244
Shepherd, Chris, 160
Shook, Jon, 136
shrimp
   Garbage Salad, 119
   Shrimp Cocktail, 88
   Shrimp de Jonghe, 89, *89*
Sieben, Nicholas, 40
Simmons, Bill, 243
Smigel, Robert, 253
Smith, Morgan, 12, 206
Sodikoff, Brendan, 100, 109
Soot Bull Jip, 238
Spinach, Creamed, 226, *227*
Stathis, Gus, 211
Steak and Ale, 164
The Steak House at Circus Circus, 281
steak houses
   appeal of, 8, 11
   history of, 15–16
   See also individual steak houses
steaks
   Chopped Steak au Poivre, 136
   Churrasco con Papas, *134*, 135
   Classic Prime Rib, 140, *141*
   Eye of Delmonico with Truffle Aioli, 140
   New York Strip with Chimichurri, 132
   Rib Eye with Roasted Garlic, 130, *131*
   Smoked Tomahawk, 143
   Steak Bites, *90*, 91
   Steak Crudo, 94, *95*
   Steak Diane, 138
   Surf 'n Turf, 139
   T-Bone au Chipotle, 133
   See also individual cuts
Steak Sauce, 230, *231*
Strawberry Sauce, Cheesecake with, 262, *263*
Strudel, Apple, mit Schlag, 268–69, *269*
Sundae, Ice Cream, 267, *267*
Surf 'n Turf, 139
Sweet Potato Casserole, 234, *235*

T
Tam O'Shanter, 140
Taste of Texas, 164, 169
Taylor's Steakhouse, 238, 248
T-bone steak
   T-Bone au Chipotle, 133
Texier, Éric, 310
Thien An Bo 7 Mon, 238
Tofu Sesame Dressing, 115
Tomahawk, Smoked, 143
tomatoes
   Bacon Roasted Tomato, 121
   Classic Wedge, 112, *113*
   Korean Wedge, 115
   Mariani Wedge, *114*, 115
   Marinara, 93
   Tomato and Stone Fruit Salad, 120, *120*
   Tomatoes and Onions, 119
top sirloin steak
   Churrasco con Papas, *134*, 135
Torrisi, Rich, 72
Toulet, Frank, 238
T-Pain, 18, 30, 33
truffles and truffle oil
   Truffle Aioli, 140
   Truffle-Ranch Dip, 86, *87*
Tschida, Christian, 290, 310

V
vegetables
   Relish Tray with Creamy Dip, 50
   See also individual vegetables
vermouth
   Aziz's Martini, 298, *299*
Vernáculo, 290, *291*
Vibiana, 244
Villarreal, Chuy, 135, 178, 290
Villaverde, Johnny Hernandez, 160
vodka
   Espresso Martini Baked Alaska, 266

W
Walnut Room, 251
watercress
   Bacon Roasted Tomato, 121
Wells, Pete, 62, 64
Williams, Jerome, 11–12, 21, 48
wine, 304, 308–11

Y
Ye Rustic Inn, 248
Young, Kristen, 197

Z
zabuton (Denver) steak
   Steak Diane, 138
Zalaznick, Jeff, 72

Ten Speed Press
An imprint of the Crown Publishing Group
A division of Penguin Random House LLC
tenspeed.com
penguinrandomhouse.com

Text copyright © 2025 by Eric Wareheim
Photographs copyright © 2025 by Marcus Nilsson, except as noted below
Photographs copyright © 2025 by Eric Wareheim: pages 16–17, 34–35, 52–53, 79, 80–81, 82 83, 128, 137, 144–45, 162–63, 187, 188–89, 236–37, 241, 256, 258–59, 270–71, 273, 277, 278–79, 280, 288–89, 296, 299, 301, 302–3, 306, 312, 313

Penguin Random House values and supports copyright. Copyright fuels creativity, encourages diverse voices, promotes free speech, and creates a vibrant culture. Thank you for buying an authorized edition of this book and for complying with copyright laws by not reproducing, scanning, or distributing any part of it in any form without permission. You are supporting writers and allowing Penguin Random House to continue to publish books for every reader. Please note that no part of this book may be used or reproduced in any manner for the purpose of training artificial intelligence technologies or systems.

TEN SPEED PRESS and the Ten Speed Press colophon are registered trademarks of Penguin Random House LLC.

Typefaces: OurType's Arnhem Fine Pro and Linotype's Trade Gothic Next

Library of Congress Cataloging-in-Publication Data
Names: Wareheim, Eric, 1976- author. | Ulla, Gabe, author. | Nilsson, Marcus (Photographer), photographer. Title: Steak house : the people, the places, the recipes / by Eric Wareheim and Gabe Ulla ; photography by Marcus Nilsson. Description: First edition. | California ; New York : Ten Speed Press, [2025] | Includes index. Identifiers: LCCN 2024044057 (print) | LCCN 2024044058 (ebook) | ISBN 9781984862297 (hardcover) | ISBN 9781984862303 (ebook) Subjects: LCSH: Cooking, American. | LCGFT: Cookbooks. Classification: LCC TX715 .W25 2025 (print) | LCC TX715 (ebook) | DDC 641.5973—dc23/eng/20241029
LC record available at https://lccn.loc.gov/2024044057
LC ebook record available at https://lccn.loc.gov/2024044058

Hardcover ISBN 978-1-9848-6229-7
Ebook ISBN 978-1-9848-6230-3

Acquiring editor: Kelly Snowden | Project editors: Kelly Snowden and Gabby Ureña Matos
Production editor: Sohayla Farman
Designer: James Casey | Art director: Emma Campion | Production designers: Mari Gill and Faith Hague
Production: Serena Sigona | Prepress color manager: Neil Spitkovsky
Boros Strava recipe developer and food stylist: Kat Turner | Boros Strava hair and makeup: Dominie Till
Boros Strava layer cake: Alana Jones-Mann
Recipe developers and testers: Jasmyn Crawford, Jenn de la Vega, and Emily Stephenson, with guidance from the featured restaurants
Copy editor: Heather Rodino | Proofreaders: Michelle Hubner, Rachel Markowitz, Tess Rossi, and Kate Bolen
Indexer: Ken DellaPenta
Publicist: Jina Stanfill | Marketer: Brianne Sperber

Cover design: Eric Wareheim and James Casey
Cover photographs: Marcus Nilsson
Back cover photograph: Eric Wareheim

Manufactured in China

10 9 8 7 6 5 4 3 2 1

First Edition

The authorized representative in the EU for product safety and compliance is Penguin Random House Ireland, Morrison Chambers, 32 Nassau Street, Dublin D02 YH68, Ireland, https://eu-contact.penguin.ie.